Somali youth now at the Royal Military Academy,
Sandhurst

EDITORIAL NOTE:
THE LOCATION OF THE PHOTOGRAPHS

In this reprint of a 1982 impression all the photographs, apart from the two used as the frontispiece ("A Northern Somali Sultan" and "Somali youth now at the Royal Military Academy, Sandhurst"), have been placed between pages 152 and 153. In the Author's Note, however, the location is wrongly given; the page numbers mentioned there refer only to where the photographs were originally placed in the first edition.

I. M. Lewis

A Pastoral Democracy

A Northern Somali Sultan.

Classics in African Anthropology

Series Editor: Murray Last

for the

International African Institute

LIT

James Currey

with the

IAI

I. M. Lewis

A Pastoral Democracy

A study of pastoralism and politics among the Northern Somali of the Horn of Africa

New introduction by
Said Samatar
and
New afterword by
I. M. Lewis

LIT
James Currey
with the
IAI

First published by Oxford University Press for the
International African Institute 1961.
1999 reprint published by arrangement with the International Africa
Institute by LIT Verlag Münster-Hamburg and
James Currey Publishers

ISBN 978 0 85255 280 3 (James Currey paper)

Transferred to digital printing

James Currey
www.jamescurrey.com
is an imprint of Boydell & Brewer Ltd
PO Box 9, Woodbridge, Suffolk IP12 3DF, UK
and of Boydell & Brewer Inc.
668 Mt Hope Avenue, Rochester, NY 14620, USA
www.boydellandbrewer.com

A catalogue record is available from the British Library

This publication is printed on acid-free paper

PREFACE

The International African Institute's series of 'Classics in African Anthropology' is drawn from two generations of a single, distinct family of texts which, taken all together, dominated the academic analysis of society in mid-20th century Africa. They were the product of two programmes of publication and research - the first, in the 1930s when Bronislaw Malinowski at the London School of Economics was invited by the Institute to train its Research Fellows in his 'new branch of anthropology'[1] prior to their doing field work; the second in the 1950s, when further money for publications from Carnegie and research funding from Ford enabled a new series of publications and a second field research programme to get under way, this time under the overall direction of Daryll Forde at University College London.

The new anthropology that Malinowski offered – 'practical anthropology' he called it – was not concerned with reconstructing the pre-contact social systems and cultures, nor was the Institute under its Constitution, to concern itself with policy or administration.[2] Research was to focus on the contemporary changes that were occurring in African social life, in order especially to understand better 'the factors of social cohesion in original African society, the ways in which these are being affected by the new influences [and the] tendencies towards new groupings and the formation of new social bonds ...'[3] Economic forces were to be given special attention - but more was involved than land, labour and craft production: the family, social organisation, religion, language, as well as nutrition and education, child psychology and music were all explicitly on the agenda. Malinowski's methods were spelt out first in the Institute's journal *Africa* and later as a special memorandum ('Methods of Study of Culture Contact in Africa') which was to be re-published by the Institute again in 1959. Although there were also smaller grants, the Research Fellows of the 1930s could take their time: after 18 months' training, they had a further two and a half (or more) funded years for fieldwork; writing-up came

[1] B.Malinowski, 'Practical anthropology', *Africa*, 2, 1929, p.37.

[2] 'Practical anthropology', pp. 22-38. International Institute of African Languages and Cultures, 'A five-year plan of research', *Africa*, 5.1, 1932, p.2.

[3] 'A five-year plan of research', p.1.

later. Meanwhile the Institute set in motion a broad programme of publication.

The bias towards social change and development was intrinsic in the way the Institute was first conceived and then established in 1926. The original concern, of both missionaries and administrators, was with formulating and implementing new methods of education in Africa, with its emphasis in primary schools on the vernacular being used in class and in textbooks. 'The child should learn', the new Institute's Council argued, 'to love and respect the mental heritage of his own people, and the natural and necessary expression of this heritage is the language. We are of the opinion that no education which leads to the alienation of the child from his ancestral environment can be right, nor can it achieve the most important aim of education, which consists in developing the powers and character of the pupil.'[4] In order to make this programme more than mere rhetoric, not only was a standard orthography required for use by printers throughout the continent to accommodate all the different languages, but locally relevant texts, in English and the various vernaculars, were needed too. For this purpose the International Institute of African Languages and Cultures was set up with the linguist Dr Diedrich Westermann as the first Director. Hence, after the Journal, the Institute's very first publication, in 1931, was Thomas Mofolo's novel, *Chaka*, translated into English from Sotho. Subsequently an annual prize was awarded to the best work in a vernacular by an African (over 200 manuscripts were submitted in the first four years). The Institute's work, then, was initially linguistic, and this remained a primary function. But for its anthropological research and publishing the Institute's Council in 1931 appointed a well-connected 'missionary statesman' (or bureaucrat), Dr J.H.Oldham, as Administrative Director to look after the whole programme and the Institute's much expanded finances; for several years Oldham had been advocating grass-roots research as the key to finding solutions to problems in Kenya, and he had been centrally involved in the formation of the Institute.[5] The Institute's interest in a new 'practical anthropology' therefore arose out of, and remained linked to, this concern with development and the use of local culture as a medium of education and with the locality as a context for change.

---

[4] Quoted in E.W.Smith, 'The story of the Institute: a survey of seven years', *Africa*, 7, 1934, 1-27.

[5] George Bennett, 'Paramountcy to partnership: J.H.Oldham and Africa', *Africa*, 30, 1960, 356-361.

These concerns remain pertinent today, and thus the processes which these 'Classics in African Anthropology' describe and analyse are still relevant. Indeed, we have chosen for the series those studies which were especially innovatory in their day; ahead of their time then, they continue to read well now. They are also studies of unusual depth - in the 1930s, the product of 4-5 years' research, in the 1950s of 2-3 years'. Such concentrated fieldwork is a rarity today.

The Institute, though administered from London, was markedly international: its funding came from European and African (colonial) governments, mission organisations (both Catholic and Protestant) and, especially for its research programme, from the Rockefeller Foundation; publications were funded by Carnegie. Its Director (and Editor of *Africa*) was German, and its Research Fellows tended not to be British: in the first four years (1932-1935) only one of the fourteen Research Fellows was British as was one out of the nine recipients of field research grants.[6] Even in 1944 there were said to be only about eight trained anthropologists in Britain (and all of these were over 35 years old).[7] Though the initial post-war task was completing the *Ethnographic Survey* (it used a common format to summarise, region by region, the existing anthropological data in French and English), when a new programme of publishing and anthropological field research was started - in part from funds provided under Britain's Welfare and Development Act - many of the new anthropologists were not from Britain, and several of the manuscripts the IAI published in its monograph series originated abroad. Indeed, though the framework was that of a 'British' social anthropology, of the six scholars funded in the first year of the new Ford research programme (1955) only one was British.

Malinowski's 'new branch of anthropology', and its later transformation in the monographs of the 1950s and 1960s, therefore drew on a wide range of talent. Furthermore, men and women (of the seventeen Research Fellows appointed in the 1930s, eight were women) came to anthropology with their initial training in very different disciplines and often with experience of work outside the academy;

---

6 International Institute of African Languages and Cultures, *Report presented to the Rockefeller Foundation on the work of the Institute July 1, 1931 - June 30, 1939* (London 1939), appendix A.

7 The point was made by Meyer Fortes in questions following a lecture by Daryll Forde, 'Social Development in Africa and the work of the International African Institute', November 1944, p.11.

three anthropologists were themselves African - Z.K.Matthews, Jomo Kenyatta and N.A.Fadipe. Thus despite their family resemblance through a common programme and a shared method, these 'Classics in African Anthropology' are nonetheless quite diverse: indeed the method of fieldwork ensured that it was the subject matter that shaped the final publication, and the fine-grain texture of the research data makes each monograph an entrée into its own, distinct world.

The works published by the Institute over the last sixty years make a long and varied list. For this series we are not including Institute classics already reprinted and available under other imprints; nor are we re-issuing monographs researched under the Institute's auspices and written in French, German or Dutch. What we offer the reader here is a series of significant yet often neglected texts which modern experts in each particular field have found to have stood the test of time well. We believe that, now easily accessible again, these books will prove once more to be of real value - not just to the specialist but also to the descendants (and compatriots) of those who first gave the fieldworker the insights and understanding we all now share.

Murray Last

INTRODUCTION

Arguably English ranks as the supplest and richest among modern languages. Its triumphant emergence as the world's virtual lingua franca is no doubt mainly due to the imperialistic conquest of the globe by its native speakers, the Anglo-Saxons, over the last pair of centuries. But it may also be due to English's proven virtuosity in handling the most complex and subtly shaded of concepts in technical and artistic expression. Still, despite its victorious ascendancy in our time, English falls far short of adequate in expressing the range and reach of Somali notions of curse and cursing.

In general 'curse' may be said to yield two meanings in English usage: one is that of the biblical curse as an invocation of mystical evil. An example of this occurs in the Old Testament when the Amalekites, determined to impede the progress of the Hebrews to the promised land, hired the maledictor prophet Baalam to annihilate the Children of Israel with a curse. In modern usage the biblical curse as evil has been secularised to denote almost any kind of thing or state considered to be harmful. Thus we speak of the 'curse of capitalism', or the 'curse of crime'. The second meaning of 'curse' existing in English idiom relates to the whole gamut of obscenities. Thus the hillbilly miners and jack-of-all traders that I did time with in automobile factories in the Appalachian mountains of southeastern Indiana and Kentucky were a cantankerous lot who could 'cuss' for the better part of a morning without ever repeating themselves once. By contrast, the concept of curse occupies a vast dimension in the life of Somalis, a circumstance signified by the half dozen, to be conservative, words used in order to designate distinct shades of mystical maledictions, such as:

1. *na'alad* (*la'ana* in Arabic) Allah's darling form of invoking evil against mischief-makers in the community of faith

2. *habaar* usually used by parents against unruly offspring

3. *asmo* used by *wadaads*, or holy men, against rival parties

4. *yu'asho* used by persons of clairvoyant abilities to 'disable' an enemy

5. *kuhaan* (*guhaan* or *haanfiil*) used by poets who are believed to possess a 'hotline', as it were, with the Deity against blatant offenders, and

6. *inkaar*, at once the most common and versatile, is available as an instrument of affliction to all undeservedly 'wronged' beings from the inanimate to innocent humans maligned unjustly by the envious for their exemplary moral uprightness.

Inkaar is the type of curse that forms the subject of this piece; and it is Lewis's *inkaar* for the undeserved, often envious, blows he has taken with dignity over the years from an assortment of unworthy sources. (More of this shortly.) From its eventful publication in 1961 to its present reprinting, *A Pastoral Democracy* has continued to stir great interest from two distinct quarters – academics on the one hand, and Somalis of both nationalist and intellectualist interests on the other.

As regards the academic community, the work took the world of African studies by storm, as it still does, with scholars rightly hailing it as a masterpiece on the order of Evans-Pritchard's *The Nuer*. Lewis's is in fact a magisterially ground-breaking piece of seminal research that amounts to a definitive study of northern Somali pastoralism, which is to say a definitive study of the entire 'Somali thing', as one observer put it, since the character foibles, habits and institutional vagaries that Lewis observed first and then registered apply, with minor exceptions, to the entire Somali peninsula.

What are these institutional vagaries and 'national character' foibles that, taken together, make up the Somali polity, whose exploration forms the central contribution of the work? Although Lewis dissects the whole anatomy of the Somali way of life (with particular emphasis on the organic relationship between ecology and clan organisation, the structure of pastoralism and the patterns of grazing, clanship and the social contract, authority and sanctions, the social roots of such matters as spirit possession, ecstasy, the centripetal and centrifugal force of genealogy), the central idea that animates the book throughout turns on a thoroughgoing exposition of our peculiar lineage segmentary system, the humpty-dumpty of Somali social relations. Although lineage segmentation as a primary principle in state formation was first formulated by the fourteenth century North African philosopher of history, Ibn Khaldun, in his concept of *'assabiya*, the modern study of this principle in social relations has been largely the achievement of

British social anthropologists, from A. R. Radcliffe-Brown, to the late E. P. (Evans-Pritchard), to the living I. M. Lewis.

Stripped of the scientific razzle-dazzle with which it is often presented, segmentation may be expressed in the Arab Bedouin saying: my uterine brother and I against my half-brother, my brother and me against my father, my father's household against my uncle's household, our two households (my uncle's and mine) against the rest of the immediate kin, the immediate kin against non-immediate members of my clan, my clan against other clans and, finally, my nation and me against the world! In lineage segmentation one, literally, does not have a permanent enemy or a permanent friend, only a permanent context. Depending on a given context, a man – or group of men, or a state, for that matter – may be your friend or foe. Everything is fluid and ever-changing. (This incidentally explains why opposition Somalis to Siad Barre's regime did not hesitate to cross over to Ethiopia, the putative quntessential foe of the Somalis.) Segmentation, in other words, is a social system that results in, and enshrines, structural precariousness as a norm. The social relations in the community are so arranged – or so arrange themselves, unplanned – as to institutionalise instability as the standard in human relations.

The second great contribution of the book relates to such matters as its brief but competent reconstruction of Somalia's colonial history, the rise of modern nationalism and party politics right up to independence, Somalia's foreign relations in terms of the young nation's tragic nascent territorial disputes with its African neighbours of Kenya and Ethiopia, two states containing large minorities of unintegrated Somalis. Here I would underscore how, although he is writing in the heyday of 'functionalism' in anthropology and in a colonial setting, Lewis incorporated the local colonial superstructure within his analysis of Somali politics and dealt also with socio-political change. This may be news to critics of functionalist anthropology in this period who often seem poorly informed.

As social anthropology rounds out its first century of development as a field of scientific inquiry, the span of nearly forty years since the first publication of *A Pastoral Democracy* has done little to diminish Lewis's productive energies and the vast output of scholary works on Somali history and politics in particular, and in especialised examination of formal and informal religion (his latest work is entitled, tellingly, 'Religion in Context') in general, as well as his forays into the evolution and aims of social anthropology, all testify to the giant footprints he has left in the field. For more of Lewis since this work appeared nearly four decades ago, the reader would do well to browse (the pastoral metaphor makes a good fit here) his revealing 'Afterword' below.

What about the segmentary lineage politics in Somali nationalism that so exercised Lewis's attention forty years back? Well – *Sadaqadaan ka dhargi doono, sansaankeedaan ka gartaa*, 'The charity meal from which the poor shall have their fill can easily be divined from its preparation'. It has now become evident that Lewis has had good reason to worry about the future wellbeing of his 'Somalis' (all anthropologists have, in a manner of speaking, their different 'peoples') from the preparation of their half-baked nationalism. Which leads to the question of Somali responses to the publication and subsequent life of the book. While recognising the importance of the work, Somali observers (among whom I am afraid I numbered one) displayed a mixture of admiration and hostility: admiration for the manifest triumph of the work and for the gentleness with which Lewis has handled our 'national warts', and hostility for the 'lineage segmentary' nightmare that he has rightly identified as constituting the heart of our political institutions. Lewis, who was trained as a natural scientist first and then as a social scientist, turned his scientific precision of method and rigour of analysis augmented by his proficient command of spoken Somali to the study of 'us Somalis'. The scientist turned anthropologist viewed us through his field glasses and saw through us, slicing through layers of acquired artificialities right to our unaccoutred core, in the process uncovering some dark truths that made us uncomfortable. In the euphoric independence days of the early 1960s, we opted for 'denial', in respect to the 'call of kinship' dissected uncomfortably in *A Pastoral Democracy*, a call that was to prove incompatible to the centralised nation-state we were buoyantly at work constructing. Unwittingly, Lewis made those Somalis who think at all feel naked; for though he did not say so, unmistakably implied in his sage tones is the thesis that any attempt to force a centralised government on so manifestly a 'centrifugal polity' of schismatic clans would result in reaping the whirlwind. Still, the Somali grudging respect for the work remained intact, to judge by Prime Minister Abd ar-Razak H. Hussein's sentiment when he introduced the author of *A Pastoral Democracy* to his cabinet as 'that chap who writes about us. We don't always like what he says, but the important thing is that he writes about us!' The ambivalent attitude toward Lewis has extended to General Mohammed

Siad Barre's regime. Indeed given Lewis's role as thorn-in-the-flesh critic of Mr. Barre's regime, it is perhaps surprising – as he recalls in his 'Afterword' – that he was tolerated for so long by the mercurial dictator. This may well be explained by Lewis's well-known sympathy (and proven support) for the Somali nationalist cause – a circumstance that no doubt enabled him to get away with a great deal.

With respect to Somali intellectuals, Lewis has been the object of criticism by some Marxist (neo-Marxist?) Somali academics (which was of course taken up by their expatriate associates) for his analysis of clan and lineage politics and the links between 'tradition' and 'modernity'. For example, my namesake, the Somali political economist, A. I. Samatar, has been contending, rather polemically, that the political use (and abuse) of clanship is a modern innovation linked to class stratification and the growth of petit bourgeois urban politics. He even goes on to claim that kinship relationships (*tol*) are to be distinguished conceptually as well as linguistically from this debased form of clan politics which he attributes to the Somalised Arabic term *qabila*. This is a bizarre interpretation for someone like A. I. Samatar who commands a robust proficiency in both Arabic and Somali. Lewis's analyses in this work, springing from first-hand research on clan and kin mobilisation in urban and rural Somalia, demonstrates conclusively that Samatar's construction of a dichotomy between *tol* and *qabil* is false. The longing to paint a rosy picture of 'traditional kinship', in the light of our depressing recent political mishaps, and to distance it from modern cut-throat, clan conflict is understandable, but in fact against the evidence. This shows, incidentally, that being a Somali with a greater linguistic accessibility to Somali culture than an expatriate does not ipso facto substitute for detailed, meticulous documentation, based on first-hand empirical research. The anthropologist's claim to legitimacy – 'I was there and saw this, and heard that' – still has a lot going for it.

Meanwhile, I. M. Lewis's *inkaar* struck with a vengeance in the spring of 1991 when the whole sham edifice of a centralised state came crashing down about our ears and disintegrated before the eyes of a horrified world into its component clusters of antagonistic lineages. And maybe this is to the good, for a global trend of scepticism about the whole idea of the nation-state as presently constituted is at work, even in Europe where it was fatefully born. One final remark: *A Pastoral Democracy* remains a stunning achievement, but by reason of its arcane subject and scientific style, it does not make easy reading and therefore is not for the uninitiated; only a labour of love will sustain those who would try to get through. But the enduring reader will not have tried in vain.

Said S. Samatar
Rutgers University, Newark, N. J.

AUTHOR'S NOTE FOR THE 1999 REPRINT

The reader should note that the related Cushitic people, referred to here as 'Galla', no longer accept this term and refer to themselves as 'Oromo'. Usage of the ethnic term 'Oromo' has greatly expanded since the 1980s with nationalist currents in Ethiopia and the Horn of Africa.

There is an error on page 22, line 26. Instead of 'To the same group belong the Ellay of Baidoa. . . ', the sentence should read: 'To the same group belong *some of* the Ellay of Baidoa. . . '.

The identity of the men in the photographs is as follows:

frontispiece: 'A Northern Somali Sultan' is the late Suldaan Abdillaahi, Sultan of the 'Iidagalle clan.

facing page 226: 'Somali Sheikh' is the late Sheikh Mahammad Sirad, then Chief Qadi of the Somaliland Protectorate.

facing page 227: 'Somali youth now at the Royal Military Academy, Sandhurst', is the late Hassan Qa'id who in 1961 led the first military coup in Somalia.

facing page 243: 'Somali District Commissioner speaking with lineage elders' is the late Sheikh Ahmad Sheikh Musa, son of Sheikh Musa of the Dandaraawiya *tariiqa*.

To the memory of Muuse Galal,
one of the founders of
Somali studies

'A fierce and turbulent race of Republicans'

BURTON

Contents

List of Maps

List of Figures

Preface to the 1982 Edition

THIS book was written primarily as an analysis of the social and political institutions of a nomadic Muslim people: the northern Somali. As the comparative references in the text and in the concluding discussion (Chapter 10) indicate, I had also a number of wider theoretical objectives in mind. Above all, I wanted to emphasize how the institutions I described were not static and self-contained. Somali society was, on the contrary, involved in a process of change that could only be understood by taking into account many external factors, including the overarching political framework created by colonial administration. I was also strongly attracted by the heady currents of Somali nationalism and hence sought to explore how modern Somali political movements related to the traditional social order.[1]

Frequent subsequent visits to Somalia since independence in 1960 have enabled me to pursue this "macro" political perspective both before and after the "revolution" introduced by the military coup of October 1969. This has involved charting the transformation of an African nation into a state, a process not uncommon in precolonial Africa where nation-states and multiethnic political units were common types of political unit. Its rarity today highlights how the colonial partition of the continent has given currency to the pluralist form of state in postcolonial Africa, producing new states which have yet to become new nations.[2]

My experience thus does not confirm the charge, frequently made, that because of its colonial circumstances anthropological research in this period was unable to deal with the issue of change or to incorporate the administrative superstructure

[1] One of my earliest publications after my initial fieldwork (1955–1957) is in fact on this subject: "Modern Political Movements in Somaliland," *Africa*, 1958, pp. 244–261, 344–364 (reprinted in C. Turnbull, *Africa and Change*, 1973).

[2] See e.g. I. M. Lewis, *A Modern History of Somalia: Nation and State in the Horn of Africa*, 1980.

within its analysis.[3] I saw no other way of making any sense of the institutions I had come to study. And, as I have explained elsewhere,[4] it so happened that I was also fortunate to be carrying out fieldwork in a Protectorate where the dominant concerns of the expatriate authorities were to avoid offending the local population and to prepare it for self-determination. Here there was a significant contrast between the generally pro-Somali policy of the Colonial Office (although difficulties developed later in relation to Kenya) and the pro-Ethiopian policy of the British Foreign Office.

On a more abstract level, by treating Somali political institutions historically, as evolving forces, I also wanted to demonstrate that a flexible version of what is now generally known in the social sciences as "structural functionalism" can indeed not only come to terms with social change but can also help to elucidate its direction and content.[5] It seems self-evident to me that the ultimate test of the authenticity of an anthropological analysis of a society at a particular point in time lies in its compatibility, or otherwise, with what happens when the society changes. If the situation at time B makes no sense in terms of that described by an anthropologist at time A, then there is something seriously wrong.

Thus, as far as the argument of this book is concerned, it is reassuring that the institutions that it described in 1955–1957 still continue to play a major (though not the only) role in contemporary politics in what is now (following the military coup in October 1969) the Somali Democratic Republic. With other factors (including endemic *internal* conflict) this resilience in a modern state of segmentary lineage organization demonstrates that this social formation has a much wider range of evolutionary and ecological specification than that proposed for it by Marshall Sahlins.[6]

[3] See e.g. A. Kuper, *Anthropologists and Anthropology; the British School, 1912–1972*, 1973, p. 147; R. Blackburn (ed.) *Ideology in Social Science: Readings in Critical Social Theory*, 1972; T. Asad (ed.) *Anthropology and the Colonial Encounter*, 1973. For more accurate information, see the collection edited by P. Loizos, "Anthropological Research in British Colonies," *Anthropological Forum*, vol. iv, no. 2, 1977.

[4] "Confessions of a 'government' anthropologist" in *Anthropological Forum*, vol. iv, 1977, pp. 226–238.

[5] See I. M. Lewis, "Introduction" to *History and Social Anthropology*, 1968, pp. ix–xxviii.

[6] M. Sahlins, "The Segmentary Lineage: An Organisation of Predatory Expansion," *American Anthropologist*, 63, 1961, 322–345. (See Lewis, "Problems in

As would be expected, changes in lineage organization occur among the southern cultivating Somali where they are associated with the development of agriculture, the presence of other ethnic groups, and the expansion and intensification of political organization. My own exploratory work here has been carried much further by Dr Virginia Luling,[7] whose analysis of the economic foundations—with slaves to cultivate and client pastoralists to manage livestock—of the nineteenth-century Geledi Sultanate south of Mogadishu is currently in press.[8] The Geledi are only one, not necessarily the most typical, of the cultivating southern Somali. There are still no other intensive studies by social anthropologists of any other southern Somali communities.

Northern Somali kinship and marriage has made a significant contribution to anthropological theories on the relationship between kinship structure and marriage. Gluckman has argued[9] that a strong emphasis on patrilineal descent is associated with stable marriage and high marriage payments from the groom's family to the bride's. Since northern Somali lineages are as strongly patrilineal as any of those discussed by Gluckman and combined with high marriage payments and *unstable* marriage, his theory requires modification. A wider survey of the variables involved suggests that what is perhaps ultimately at issue here is the position of the bride as a jural person—separate from her sexual and reproductive attributes.[10] A more realistic, if perhaps not altogether surprising hypothesis, is that the fragility of marriage is at least partly dependent on the extent to which wives retain strong ties after marriage with their own natal kinsfolk, or achieve by other means significant extramarital independence.[11]

the Comparative Study of Unilineal Descent," in M. Banton (ed.) *The Relevance of Models for Social Anthropology*, 1965.)

[7] "From Nomadism to Cultivation: The Expansion of Political Solidarity in Southern Somalia," in Douglas & Kaberry (eds.) *Man in Africa*, 1968; "Conformity and Contrast in Somali Islam," in Lewis (ed.) *Islam in Tropical Africa*, 1980.

[8] V. Luling, *A Southern Somali Sultanate: The Geledi* (in press).

[9] M. Gluckman, "Kinship and Marriage among the Lozi of N. Rhodesia and the Zulu of Natal," in A. R. Radcliffe-Browne and D. Forde (eds.) *African Systems of Kinship and Marriage*, 1950.

[10] I. M. Lewis, *Marriage and the Family in Northern Somaliland* (East African Studies No. 15), 1962; see also, Lewis, "Problems in the Comparative Study of Unilineal Descent" in Banton (ed.) *The Relevance of Models for Social Anthropology*, 1965.

[11] For a recent discussion, see E. L. Peters, "Aspects of Bedouin Bridewealth Among Camel Herders in Cyrenaica," in J. Comaroff, *The Meaning of Marriage Payments*, 1980.

To an extent that I appreciate better now than when this book was first published, an important indicator here is the involvement, especially in urban contexts, of Somali women in the spirit possession cult known locally as *saar* (see below, pp).[12]

Somali patriliny and marriage are thus of considerable theoretical interest outside their local ethnographic setting. Although it has so far attracted less attention among anthropologists, this, I believe, applies with even greater force to the Somali nomads' form of political contract *(heer)*, an institution which provides important factual data for theory in political science and international law. It is at least refreshing to confront the various hypothetical theories of social contract with a concrete case where this institution is systematically employed, within a kinship ambience, in the formation and definition of political units, to an extent which, so far as I know, is unparalleled elsewhere.

The social institutions analyzed in this book have also found a wider context of discussion in the growing literature on pastoral nomadism[13] and the problems of drought relief. This leads ultimately to the question of the continuing viability of this precarious mode of production. In countries where the pastoral economy is a marginal activity the issue is not in the national context an acute one. But where in a country such as the Somali Republic the majority of the population depend on livestock for their subsistence, and provide in the offtake from their herds the major national export product,[14] the problem assumes a different dimension. Following the terrible drought of 1974, although the government of the Somali Democratic Republic had shown

[12] It was the intriguing character of this Somali data which eventually provoked my comparative study, *Ecstatic Religion*, 1971.

[13] See e.g. G. Dahl and A. Hjort, *Having Herds*, 1976; T. Monod, *Pastoralism in Tropical Africa*, 1975; *Pastoral Production and Society*, 1979; P. Salzman (ed.) *When Nomads Settle*, 1980.

[14] For the effects of this external trade on the internal pastoral economy and social structure, see Lewis, "Lineage Continuity and Modern Commerce in N. Somaliland," in Bohannan and Dalton, *Markets in Africa*, 1962. A paper on fieldwork in 1971 and 1973, the fullest analysis of these trends—involving increasing privatization of water and pasture and monopolistic and entrepreneurial livestock export—is provided by Abdi Gaileh Mirreh, *Die sozialökonomischen Verhältnisse der nomadischen Bevölkerung im Norden der Demokratischen Republik Somalia*, Berlin, 1978. See also, J. Swift, "The Development of Livestock Trading in Nomad Pastoral Economy: The Somali Case," in *Pastoral Production and Society*, 1979; D. R. Aronson, "Kinsmen and Comrades: Towards a Class Analysis of the Somali Pastoral Sector," *Nomadic Peoples*, November 1980.

great initiative in creating large farming settlements in the riverine areas of the south and fishing cooperatives along the coast, there was little to suggest that these projects could be extended to embrace the majority of the rural population. Indeed, the huge influx of over a million refugees, mainly women and children and old people fleeing from the war in the Ogaden (Western Somalia/Eastern Ethiopia), housed in over thirty refugee camps in 1980 has imposed an even greater burden on the country's fragile economy. This has paradoxically increased the importance of its livestock exports and of the remittances sent home by those Somali migrants who work in the neighboring Gulf States.

Drought and war have brought Somali issues to the attention of the world, and the dramatic transfer of Russian patronage from Somalia to Ethiopia has naturally enhanced Somalia's strategic appeal for the West. A more positive development, receiving less publicity, is the astonishing growth of Somali studies as an area specialization. In 1964,[15] I described this subject as so highly specialized that it could hardly be expected to attract widespread interest. It was thus with a mixture of bewilderment and delight that I participated in the inaugural International Congress of Somali Studies held in Mogadishu in July 1980.[16] From the point of view of social and cultural anthropology, the most interesting developments here are to be found in the work of Somali scholars—mainly linguists, historians, and political scientists—some of which is now beginning to be published in English.[17]

The majority of these scholars, either teachers at the National

[15] See "Recent Progress in Somali Studies," *Journal of Semitic Studies*, 9, 1964, pp. 122–134. For more recent surveys of the literature, see Lewis, *Peoples of the Horn of Africa*, 1969, pp. x–xiv and 185–188; and Lewis, "The Cushitic-Speaking Peoples: A Jigsaw Puzzle for Social Anthropologists," *L'Uomo*, 1979.

[16] The success of this remarkable venture owed much to the energy and enthusiasm of the Somali authorities and of Drs Lee Cassanelli and Charles Geshekter, who, jointly with Dr Hussein M. Adam of the Somali National University, organized the congress.

[17] See e.g. M. K. Salad, *Somalia: A Bibliographical Survey*, 1977; A. A. Hersi, *The Arab Factor in Somali History* (in press); S. S. Samatar, *Poetry in Somali Politics: The Case of Sayyid Mahammad 'Abdille Hassan* (in press). Another view of Somali culture in English is offered by the Somali novelist Nuruddin Farah, whose works include *From a Crooked Rib*, 1970; *A Naked Needle*, 1976, and *Sweet and Sour Milk*, 1979. The most substantial Somali anthropological contribution to date is A. G. Mirreh, *Die sozialökonomischen Verhältnisse der nomadischen Bevölkerung im Norden der Demokratischen Republik Somalia*, 1978.

University, researchers at the Somali National Academy of Culture,[18] or those holding university posts outside Somalia have, naturally, been trained—at least in their postgraduate work—overseas. An outstanding exception is the self-taught Somali historian, Sheikh Jaama' 'Umar 'Ise, whose definitive collection and annotation of the poetry of the national hero, Sayyid Mahammad 'Abdille Hassan, is a brilliant achievement. I am delighted to be able to claim some inadvertent part in Sheikh Jaama's formation as an oral historian. When we first met in the barren pastures of Las Anod district in 1956, Sheikh Jaama' was an itinerant man of religion who viewed my anthropological activities with deep suspicion. But, after scrutinizing me carefully for several months and making further inquiries about my research, he came to the conclusion (as he confided to me many years later) that I was a harmless student of his culture. He also decided that if foreigners like myself, possessing only a limited command of his language, had the audacity to collect and study his countrymen's traditions, it was difficult to see why this work could not be carried out at least as competently by Somali nationals. So he decided to become an oral historian and began his monumental collection of the traditional history and poetry of Sayyid Mahammad. He has been kind enough to tell me that he did pick up a few useful tips from what he observed of my methods. Many of Sheikh Jaama's publications are in Arabic, but since the adoption in 1972 of written Somali (in Roman characters) they are now appearing in his mother tongue.[19]

It is impossible to foresee the long-term effects of what has been called the "Somali miracle" of instant literacy.[20] But its immediate consequences are striking. Nationals and foreigners literate in Somali now have access to a vast and constantly grow-

[18] The Academy falls within the Ministry of Higher Education and includes leading Somali linguists, poets, and playwrights on its staff. In linguistic research, Dr Yasin Isman Kenadid has played a major role, producing a dictionary of the Somali language in 1976. Another distinguished linguist, Shire Jaama', was formerly head of the Academy.

[19] See *Taariikhdii Daraawiishta (History of the Dervishes)*, Mogadishu, 1976; *Diiwaanka Gabayada Sayid Maxamad Abdulle Xassan, (Collection of the Poetry of Sayyid Mahammad)* Mogadishu, 1974.

[20] See O. O. Mohamad, *From Written Somali to a Rural Development Campaign*, Mogadishu, 1975; B. W. Andrzejewski, "The Modernisation of the Somali Language," *Horn of Africa*, 1978, pp. 39–45; H. M. Adam and C. L. Geshekter, *The Revolutionary Development of the Somali Language*, 1980. See also D. Laitin, *Politics, Language and Thought: The Somali Experience*, 1977.

ing volume of poetry, plays, and prose material written by Somali authors.[21] On a broader front, what is even more impressive is the widespread use of written Somali in town and countryside as a means of communication between people who possess no formal schooling. Command of the oral tradition has always rested primarily in the hands of the illiterate clan elders. Now through literacy, this is shared on a more equal footing with those trained in the literate Western tradition, whose knowledge of their native Somali culture is correspondingly less extensive. All sorts of intriguing opportunities are raised here for those interested in exploring the effects of literacy on culture.[22]

As biographers of culture, it is obvious that social anthropologists are perpetually indebted to the peoples whose institutions and beliefs they live by publicizing,[23] for whom they act, as Malinowski put it, as "impresarios." In exceptional cases, such as the present, when the people concerned become an independent nation-state, the anthropologist may find that his works attract intense political interest. This is a challenging situation in which to attempt to honor the debt which, I believe, the anthropological enterprise inevitably entails.

London, 1981 I.M.L.

[21] The pioneering work here, written long before the adoption of the new script by one of its main inventors and advocates, the well-known poet and folklorist Muuse Galal, who died in December, 1980, is *Hikmad Soomaali* (Somali wisdom), a collection of traditional folktales and stories. This study, with the Somali written in an earlier version of the present Latin script, inspired other local scholars, particularly Shire Jama Ahmad, who also published a collection of oral literature in 1965 and in the following year edited a journal mainly containing oral literary works. For a detailed account of these developments and of subsequent work, see B. W. Andrzejewski, "The Rise of Written Somali Literature," *African Research and Documentation*, 1975, pp. 7–14; and "Five Years of Written Somali: A Report on Progress and Projects," *Bulletin of African Studies: Notes and News* (supplement to *Africa*) 1977. See also J. W. Johnson, *Heellooy Heelleellooy: The Development of the Genre Heello in Modern Somali Poetry*, 1974.

[22] See e.g. J. Goody, *The Domestication of the Savage Mind*, 1978.

[23] See Lewis, *The Anthropologist's Muse*, 1973.

Preface

THIS book[1] is based primarily on field research carried out in Somaliland between September 1955 and June 1957 under the auspices of the Colonial Social Science Research Council and financed from Colonial Development and Welfare funds. I am grateful to the Council and to Sir Theodore Pike, Governor of the Somaliland Protectorate during my stay, who through the good offices of my friend Dr J. H. M. Beattie readily accepted my research scheme and gave me every support and encouragement. I owe a similar debt to the Protectorate Administration as a whole and should like to thank especially Mr P. Carrel, Mr J. G. S. Drysdale, Mr Abdulrahim Abby Farrah, Mr E. H. Jones, and Mr M. Wilson. To Mr J. M. Watson, then Director of Natural Resources, I owe a special debt for generous friendship and hospitality at all times.

During the twenty months which my wife and I spent in Somaliland I had the opportunity of visiting all the principal northern Somali clans and also of making a brief visit to Somalia. I shall not readily forget the kindness and hospitality which I received on that occasion from Somali Provincial and District Commissioners, from the Somali Government, and from the Italian Trusteeship Administration.

In northern Somaliland most of my time was divided between the nomadic Ḍulbahante of the east and the Jibriil Abokor cultivators of the west, a concentration of interest which will be seen in the present book. Here I must thank particularly Sheikh Mahammad Sirad, Sheikh Isman Sheikh Umar, Sheikh Ali Sheikh Ibrahim, Sheikh Mahammad Warsamme, Sheikh Ahmad Sheikh Muse, Sheikh Abdarahman Sheikh Nur, Mr Muse Galal, Mr Ahmad Adan, Mr Abdalla Haji Muse, Mr Yusuf Maygag, Mr Umar Sheikh Ibrahim, Mr Adan Isaq; and those with whom I was most closely associated, Mr Shirre Ilmi,

[1] I take the opportunity of pointing out here that my *Peoples of the Horn of Africa* (Ethnographic Survey of Africa: North Eastern Africa, Part I) International African Institute, London, 1955, was written from a survey of the literature on the Somali before I went to Somaliland and when indeed I had little prospect of going there. To some extent the terminology and findings of that book differ from those recorded here.

Mr Ahmad Hassan, Mr Jama Dere, Mr Awil Adan, and Mr Yusuf Adan. For his interest and friendship I should also like to record my gratitude to Mr Michael Mariano.

In putting my findings together in the present book I have leant heavily upon others for support and encouragement. Professor E. E. Evans-Pritchard has read the manuscript in its entirety and it would be difficult for me to express adequately my continuing debt to him. With Professor J. C. Mitchell I have discussed most aspects of the book while writing it and his interest and comments have been invaluable. Mr R. Brown has also kindly read the text and helped to clarify some of its obscurities. Mr Osman A. Hassan has again read the text and his continuing interest and authoritative criticism have been a constant stimulus. I must also thank Dr G. Benardelli and Dr M. Pirone of the Italian Trusteeship Administration of Somalia for their unfailing enthusiasm and help. To Professor R. B. Serjeant I am again particularly grateful for his interest and encouragement. Finally I owe a unique debt to Mr B. W. Andrzejewski who taught me my first words of Somali and has since been my main guide on linguistic matters.

For generous grants towards the cost of publication I thank the University College of Rhodesia and Nyasaland and the International African Institute. I am especially grateful to the Institute's Director, Professor Daryll Forde, for his support and interest, and also to Miss Barbara Pym who has given much time to seeing this book through the press.

I take the opportunity here of explaining the orthography followed in the book. In recording Somali and Arabic words alike long vowels are represented by doubling, as e.g. *aa*, *oo*, etc; the Cushitic and Arabic aspirate *h* by *ḥ*; and the Somali post-alveolar plosive *d* by *ḍ*. Other Arabic letters are transliterated according to standard usage. Place-names, however, have not been transcribed according to this system but usually left in the form in which they appear on local maps.

Finally, it is necessary to refer briefly to the major constitutional changes which have taken place since the completion of the manuscript in May 1959. In February 1960 the British Protectorate held its second general election for a reconstituted legislative council with thirty-three elected members, three ex-officio members[1], and a Speaker appointed by the Governor.

[1] The Chief Secretary, Attorney-General, and Financial Secretary.

Twenty seats were won by the Somaliland National League[1]; twelve by the United Somali Party, a new organization drawing much of its support from the Dir and Daarood clans of the Protectorate; and one by the National United Front. The Somali Youth League, the government party of Somalia, gained no seat. The new Executive Council consisted of the Governor, Chief Secretary, Attorney-General, Financial Secretary, and four other Ministers (2 S.N.L., 2 U.S.P.) appointed from the elected members of the legislative council with responsibility for Local Government, Natural Resources, Communications and Works, and Social Services.

Following a motion of 6 April 1960 in the Protectorate Legislative Council calling for independence and union with Somalia by 1 July, 1960, the date set for that territory's independence, the British Government agreed to hasten the Protectorate's advance to full autonomy. Events moved with unprecedented speed, the replacement of expatriate by Somali staff was greatly accelerated, and on 26 June 1960 the Protectorate became an independent state. With the attainment of independence the Anglo-Egyptian Agreement of 1954, reasserting Ethiopian sovereignty over the Haud and granting the Government of British Somaliland certain special facilities in the area, lapsed. The grazing rights of Somali pastoralists from the north of the Republic in the Haud are, however, still protected by the unpopular Anglo-Ethiopean Treaty of 1897.[2]

On 1 July 1960 Somalia was proclaimed independent and merged with the ex-Protectorate as a unitary state with a single National Assembly and government at Mogadishu.[3] In the new Somali Republic what was formerly the Somaliland Protectorate is now divided into an Eastern and a Western region, the former based on Burao, and the latter on Hargeisa, the old capital.

Glasgow University, January, 1961 I.M.L.

[1] This party had boycotted the earlier elections held in March 1959, see below, p. 281.

[2] Protectorate Somali have never acknowledged Ethiopia's right to this area which they consider was ceded by Britain in defiance of earlier Anglo-Somali treaties of protection. See below, p. 19.

[3] On the formation of the Somali Republic in July 1960, the two existing legislatures combined to form the National Assembly. A coalition S.Y.L., S.N.L., and U.S.P. government was formed on 22 July 1960.

I

Introduction

I

THIS book is a study in the pastoral habits and political institutions of the northern Somali of the Horn of Africa. Like many pastoral nomads who range far and wide with their herds of camels and flocks, the Somali have no indigenous centralized government. And this lack of formal government and of instituted authority is strongly reflected in their extreme independence and individualism. Few writers have failed to notice the formidable pride of the Somali nomad, his extraordinary sense of superiority as an individual, and his firm conviction that he is sole master of his actions and subject to no authority except that of God. If they have perceived it, however, they have for the most part been baffled by the shifting character of the nomad's political allegiance and puzzled by the fact that the political and jural unit with which he acts on one occasion he opposes on another.[1]

Few societies can so conspicuously lack those judicial, administrative, and political procedures which lie at the heart of the western conception of government. The traditional northern Somali political system has no chiefs to run it and no formal judiciary to control it. Men are divided amongst political units without any administrative hierarchy of officials and with no instituted positions of leadership to direct their affairs. Yet, although they thus lack to a remarkable degree all the machinery of centralized government, they are not without government or political institutions.

In the first place the key to Somali politics lies in kinship. All northern Somali political units are based on kinship and are composed of men who trace descent through males to a common male ancestor from whom they take their corporate name. Political affiliation is thus determined by agnatic descent and political divisions correspond to differences in agnatic origin.

[1] Richard Burton's *First Footsteps in East Africa*, 1856, remains the best general description of northern Somali society.

It is of the first importance to appreciate that a Somali genealogy is not a mere family tree recording the historical descent and connections of a particular individual or group. Whatever its historical significance, in the sphere of politics its importance lies in the fact that it represents the social divisions of people into corporate political groups. By reference to his ancestors, a man's relations with others are defined, and his position in Somali society as a whole determined. Thus an understanding of the political relations between groups requires a knowledge of their genealogical relationships. As Somali themselves put it, what a person's address is in Europe, his genealogy is in Somaliland. By virtue of his genealogy of birth, each individual has an exact place in society and within a very wide range of agnatic kinship it is possible for each person to trace his precise connection with everyone else. Somali political philosophy is thus an evaluation of agnatic connection. At the same time, the range of agnatic relationship recognized on one occasion need not be the same as that on another, so that the corporate kinship group in which an individual has political status varies with the context. Thus political and legal affiliation is elastic and fluctuates generally within the range of agnatic connection defined in the genealogies.

The barren terrain in which nomadic pastoralism is the prevailing economy does little to foster, and indeed actively militates against the formation of stable territorial groups. In general there are no political units whose membership reflects territorial allegiances and the strength of common residential ties, save in a few especially favoured areas, is negligible. Since the term 'tribe' is generally taken to connote a stable political and jural group whose members are united in respect of common attachment to territory as such, it is inappropriate to speak of Somali 'tribes'. It is in any case not necessary to speak of tribes in northern Somali society since in principle every pastoral political unit is described exactly in terms of agnatic descent. All political units are first and foremost lineages, and the segmented lineage structure which the genealogies represent has no regular counterpart in a tribal structure on the ground.

In conformity with this shifting system of movement and lack of absolute ties to locality, lineages are not based primarily on land-holding, and possession of land has no mystical or ritual value. Political ascendency is not conferred by or symbolized in mystical ties to the earth but derives from superior fighting potential. In Somali lineage politics the assumption that might is right has overwhelming authority and personal rights, rights in livestock, and rights of access to grazing and water, even if they are not always obtained by force, can only be defended against usurpation by force of arms. Political status is thus maintained by feud and war, and self-help—the resort of groups to the test of superior military power—is the ultimate arbiter in political relations. With this political philosophy it is not surprising that fighting in northern Somaliland is a political institution of every-day life.

I have said that in the first place the key to the understanding of the political constitution of Somali society lies in kinship. The second basic principle and one that is complementary to kinship is a form of social contract. All lineages which act corporately do so first because of their agnatic basis, and secondly through an explicit treaty defining the terms of their collective unity. In a formal sense, contract operates structurally as at once a unifying and dividing principle within the various spheres of extended agnation. Genealogies represent generally the widest range of possible political unity by dividing and uniting groups of kinsmen according to the ancestors from whom they stem. Contract galvanises the diffuse and manifold bonds of kinship at any point and through any ancestor, giving rise to opposed political units.

I do not claim that Somali political contract (*ḥeer*) corresponds in all respects to any one of the many doctrines of the Social Contract of the political philosophers. But I do hold that it includes essentially contractual elements having closest affinities with those political theories which saw the origins of political union in an egalitarian social contract.

From what has been said it will be clear that the northern pastoral Somali belong to that class of egalitarian societies, with little social stratification and no centralized government, which were first identified in Africa in the works of Evans-Pritchard on the Nuer of the Sudan[1] and of Fortes on the Tallensi of the Northern Territories of the Gold Coast.[2] These uncentralized societies stand at one extreme on a scale of tribal political organizations whose other limit is defined by tribal states with organized

[1] E. E. Evans-Pritchard, *The Nuer*, Clarendon Press, Oxford, 1940.

[2] M. Fortes, *The Dynamics of Clanship among the Tallensi*, Oxford University Press, 1945. See also, M. Fortes and E. E. Evans-Pritchard (Eds.) *African Political Systems*, O.U.P. 1940.

government and at least something of a formal hierarchy of offices of state.

II.

Although all Somali political units are lineages or alliances of lineages and share the same properties as kinship groups, tracing descent through named ancestors to a founder, they are diversified in other respects. I propose to speak of clan-family, clan, sub-clan, primary lineage, and dia-paying group as divisions of decreasing size and to some extent of different characteristics. I discuss these distinguishing attributes first before describing the geographical positions of the six Somali clan-families and their various cultural and economic features.

The clan-family is, generally speaking, the upper limit of clanship,[1] but most clan-families are so vast (the Daarood number over a million) and so widely scattered that they cannot act corporately as political units. Nevertheless, when there is enmity between them, members of one clan-family have a strong identity of purpose against those of another. Thus clan-family allegiance strongly colours the relations between individuals. In towns where members of rival clan-families are concentrated, there is often friction and sometimes fighting between them. And in modern party politics clan-family allegiance plays an extremely important part. It is thus not surprising that the members of a particular clan-family should show such pride in their membership of it and conserve and cherish the genealogies which record their affiliation. The length of genealogy tends to vary with the size of the clan-family so that it is not possible to state a definite genealogical span which is characteristic of this unit. However, many people of the Daarood clan-family count not less than thirty named generations to their common ancestor.

Unlike its larger homologue, the clan, whose members often count about twenty generations to their founder, frequently acts as a corporate political unit. The clan differs also from other lineage units tending to have some territorial exclusiveness. While it does not occupy a specific area rigidly defined by natural boundaries, its fairly regular seasonal movements establish some degree of localization within a very general tract of territory. But it cannot be said that the clan is always a clear-cut geographical

[1] This expression is used throughout this book to refer to corporate agnatic identity at all levels of political cleavage.

unit. Nor do its members derive their strong sense of corporate identity from any feeling of territorial unity, but from their common agnatic descent. Within a clan the general area in which its members are concentrated is for the purposes of grazing in principle open to the stock of all those of its constituent lineage segments.

The clan generally marks the upper limit of corporate political action. But although it is often led by a clan-head, commonly styled 'Sultan', it has no centralized internal administration or government.

Moreover, some clans which are as firmly integrated as those with Sultans, have no formal clan-head to lead them. Again, in some of the larger clans, such as the Ḍulbahante (with a strength of about 100,000), the immediate lineage sub-divisions which I call 'sub-clans' are each led by a Sultan.

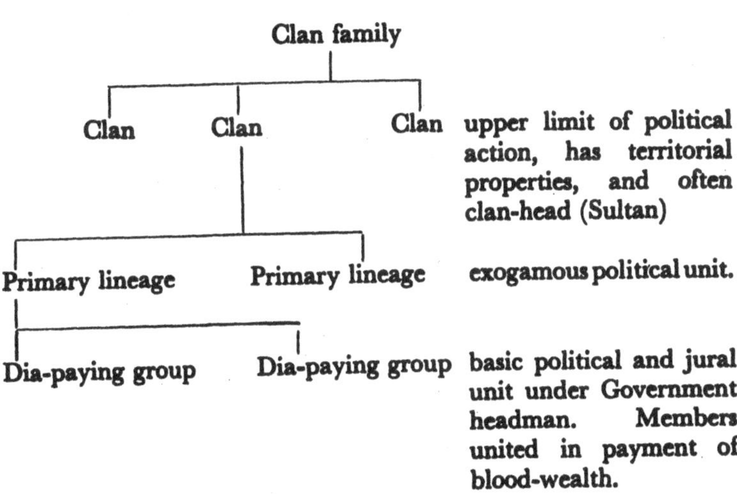

As I have indicated, some clans, especially the larger ones, contain segments immediately below the level of the clan, which from their size and distinctiveness may conveniently be distinguished as sub-clans. But the most distinct descent group within the clan is usually what I refer to here as a 'primary lineage'. Within his clan this is the lineage of which a person normally describes himself as a member. Marriage is usually outside the primary lineage and only in rare cases within it. Because it is so strongly integrated in agnation, although it has no formally installed leader, its members feel little need to supplement their already strong agnatic ties by subsidiary links through marriage. While primary lineages are thus often linked externally through marriage, stock-theft and feud tend to be endemic between them, although, to some extent these activities are characteristic of the relations between lineages at all levels of segmentation. To the founding ancestor of his primary lineage a person may count between six and ten generations.

At the base of this system of lineage political divisions stands the dia-paying group. This is a corporate group of a few small lineages reckoning descent through from four to eight generations to the common founder and having a membership of from a few hundred to a few thousand men. In 1958 there were over three hundred and sixty such dia-paying groups[1] in the British Protectorate alone. The title 'dia-paying group', employed by the Administrations, is retained here for convenience although it suggests a greater exclusiveness and inflexibility than the group actually possesses. For in fact, while membership of a dia-paying group does not prevent wider lineage alliances and corporate political unity at a higher level of segmentation, dia-paying groups are the most stable political units in a shifting system of agnatic attachment. It is as a member of a specific dia-paying group that a man most frequently acts.

Contract most often defines peoples' relations at the level of segmentation represented by the dia-paying group. So that in this group, which is in effect the basic political and jural unit of pastoral society, contract and clanship meet to give it its specific character. For in terms of their common treaty, the members of a dia-paying group are pledged to support each other in collective political and jural responsibility, and in particular, in the payment and receipt of compensation in respect of actions committed by or against their group. Amongst its members more than in any other unit there is law and order. For, although traditionally there is no official leader, it is the responsibility of the elders to see that the terms of the treaty which unites them are honoured. Not surprisingly, these characteristics have been recognized by the Administrations in the appointment of dia-paying group headmen (Akils; some of whom are now styled 'Local Authorities' in the British Protectorate) with responsibility for the affairs of their group. But as far as the members of

[1] So called from the Arabic *diya*, bloodwit; the Somali expression is *mag*.

a dia-paying group are themselves concerned, these official headmen exercise representative rather than authoritative functions.

In the segmentary Somali lineage system these five divisions (clan-family, clan, sub-clan, primary lineage, and dia-paying group) are those which it is most useful to distinguish. It will be appreciated, however, that as with other segmentary lineage systems an essential feature of the Somali system is the relativity of its political divisions. So that while these particular divisions of society are the foci of political action this does not mean that corporate political units cannot exist at other levels of segmentation. For in principle every ancestor in the genealogies is a point of potential division, and of unity. It is only within this very wide system of manifold political groupings by descent, that the dia-paying group has a certain autonomy as the minimum jural and political unit. For it is the dia-paying group which represents the range of contractually defined agnation which most commonly determines the political and jural status of the individual.

III.

Of the six clan-families into which the Somali as a whole are divided, four—the Dir, Isaaq, Hawiye and Daarood[1]—are mainly and most characteristically pastoral nomads, and two—the Digil and Rahanwiin—settled in southern Somalia are largely agricultural. It is the pastoral life and political institutions of the first group as represented in northern Somaliland that this book describes.

The pastoralists make up the bulk of the total Somali population. Of an estimated total of two-and-half to three million Somali, the Dir, Isaaq, Hawiye, and Daarood collectively comprise well over two million, and, while all are originally of northern provenance, are today widely distributed throughout Somaliland[2]. The Dir who with the Isaaq number some half

[1] I have treated the Isaaq here as a separate clan-family because to some extent they act as such and because they so regard themselves. By other Somali, however, they are grouped with the Dir. I include with the Hawiye a small group of closely related clans which are sometimes classified separately as 'Pre-Hawiye'.

[2] I use 'Somaliland' here to denote all the Somali territories. The French *Côte des Somalis* has a population of about 28,000 Somali (with some 26,000 'Afar). The British Somaliland Protectorate contains some 640,000 Somali, and Harar Province of Ethiopia probably about 500,000. The Somali population of Somalia is variously estimated between a million and a quarter and two million. Since it is possible that the larger estimate is exaggerated, the lower figure of a million and a quarter has been adopted throughout this book. Finally, there are some 80,000 Somali (about half Daarood and half Hawiye) in the Northern Province of Kenya.

million, live mainly in French Somaliland, Harar Province of Ethiopia, and the north-west and central parts of the British Protectorate. Smaller Dir groups are found also in Somalia, especially in Merca District and between Brava and the Juba River. But it is the Daarood who are the largest Somali clan-family with a population exceeding a million. They inhabit the British Protectorate to the east of the Isaaq, northern and southern Somalia, parts of Harar Province and south-eastern Ethiopia, and the Northern Province of Kenya. Finally, the Hawiye number about half a million, and are mainly concentrated in Somalia to the south of the northern Daarood and between them and the Digil and Rahanwiin of southern Somalia; but smaller groups occur beyond the Digil and Rahanwiin and extend across the Juba River into the Northern Province of Kenya.

Despite their numbers and dispersion over a vast area, the four pastoral clan-families have a fairly uniform culture. Such differences as occur are most marked where alien institutions and customs have been adopted from neighbouring non-Somali peoples. There are also dialectal differences. To some extent the northern Dir ('Iise and Gadabuursi) seem to share peculiarities in vocabulary and pronunciation with the northern Hawiye of Somalia. In the north again, particularly among the Daarood of northern Somalia, the pronounced Cushitic post-alveolar plosive *ḍ* of the Isaaq and Dir tends to be modified to *r*.[1] This feature occurs also in the dialect of the northern Hawiye. But despite these and other regional variations—for linguistic differences do not correspond exactly to clan-family divisions—northern Isaaq is intelligible to all but some of the southern Hawiye.

The widest differences in culture and social organization amongst these four clan-families seem to occur with those Daarood and Hawiye clans who are situated across the Juba River, in southern Somalia, and in the Northern Province of Kenya. Here during their conquest of the region from the Galla in the late nineteenth century, the Hawiye and Daarood adopted a military age-grade organization[2] which has now, however, almost completely disappeared. But these southerly groups still

[1] The various dialectal differences in Somali are discussed by M. M. Moreno in his *Il Somalo della Somalia*, Rome, 1955.

[2] See C. Zoli, *Oltre Giuba*, Rome, 1927, pp. 189–93; E. Cerulli, 'Tradizioni storiche e monumenti della Migiurtinia'; 1931, pp. 155–7.

appear to retain distinguishing features in their social organization. Thus in distinction to their northern kinsmen they appear to have a heterogeneous lineage structure which permits the full genealogical identification of strangers and clients within the lineages of their hosts.

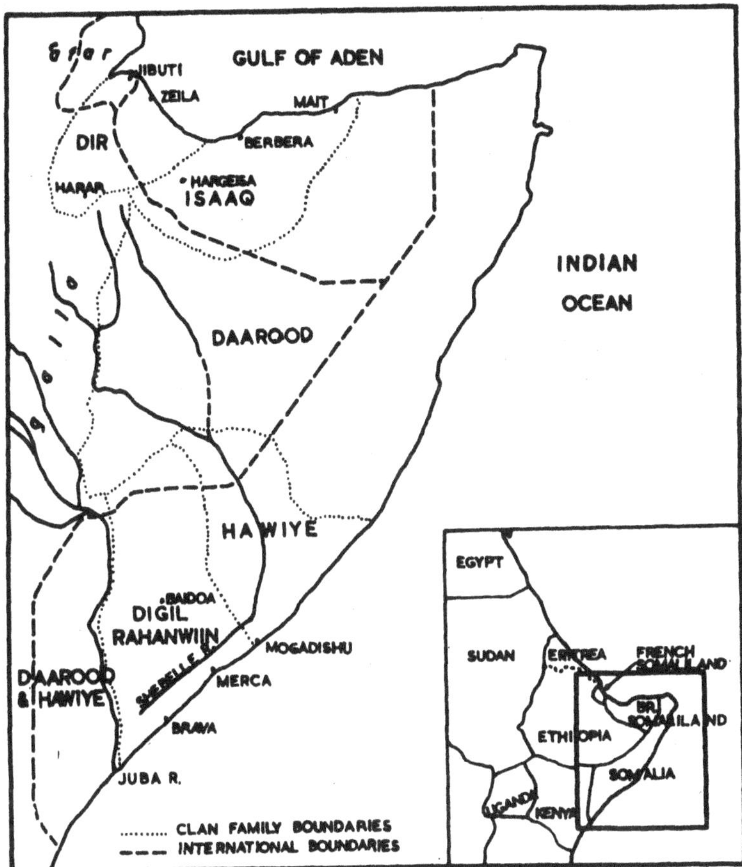

Map 1. Distribution of Somali clan-families and contiguous peoples.

Again, even on the other side of the Juba River in Somalia, the more southerly of the central Daarood and Hawiye clans differ in some respects from their kinsmen further north. Their environment is more suitable to cattle than camel-husbandry and cattle are far more common than in the north. Sorghum too is cultivated in small pockets over a fairly wide area, while in the extreme north grain is only grown in quantity in the north-west of the British Protectorate and Harar Province of Ethiopia.

My analysis, therefore, which is based on a detailed examination of a limited number of groups as they live today in French and British Somaliland, Harar Province of Ethiopia, and the contiguous regions of northern Somalia, applies to the northern pastoral Somali as a whole but cannot be assumed to be fully applicable to the more southerly of the Daarood and Hawiye clans. The clans most frequently referred to are listed in the following table with estimates of their strength and of the numbers of their dia-paying groups.

Clan	Population	No. of dia-paying groups
'Iise (British Protected)	55,000	57
Gadabuursi ,,	45,000	37
Habar Awal Sa'ad Muuse	100,000	50
Habar Awal 'Iise Muuse	30,000	14
Arab[1]	20,000	10
'Iidagalle	40,000	19
Habar Yuunis	130,000	66
Habar Tol Ja'lo Maḥammad Abokor	60,000	31
Habar Tol Ja'lo Muuse Abokor, and 'Umar	40,000	19
Ḍulbahante	100,000	48
Warsangeli	20,000	10
Total (British Protected)	640,000	361

While the Somali are generally classified as, and undoubtedly share physical and linguistic affinities with the South Eastern Cushites (or Hamites)[2] —the 'Afar, Saho, Galla, and Beja, they display marked differences in social and political structure. Thus the 'Afar (known to Somali as *Ood 'Ali*), who occupy similar

[1] The Arab are a Somali clan known officially as 'Arap' to distinguish them from 'Arab, an Arabian, which expatriate officials often have difficulty in pronouncing.

[2] Italian physical anthropologists have usually described the Somali as 'Ethiopic' although Sergi (1897) preferred the name 'Camites'. See N. Puccioni, *Le popolazioni indigene della Somalia Italiana*, Bologna, 1937, pp. 60–2.

country on the northwest frontier of Somaliland and whom Somali raid and despise and rarely marry, have a different territorial and apparently more formal system of government. Although Somali recognize a certain affinity with these neighbours in French Somaliland those 'Afar institutions (such as the true levirate) which differ from their own excite ridicule. Similarly, while Somali again recognize some degree of relationship with the Galla tribes (whom they know as *Gaalla*, or less commonly, *Gaallaawi*)[1] who border them to the west and south, and whom they also raid and scorn, they do not share their age-set system. This, as has been said, was, however, to some extent adopted by the Daarood to the south of the Juba River and historically at least distinguishes them from their northern clansmen.

In addition to their strikingly Hamitic physical features, Somali also exhibit traces of Arabian blood, and, in southern Somalia amongst the Digil and Rahanwiin clan-families, physical evidence of their contact with the pre-Hamitic Bantu and negroid peoples whom they and the Galla before them conquered in this region. But it is their Arabian ancestry which traditionally is their greatest pride. Ultimately all Somali genealogies go back to Arabian origins, to the Prophet's lineage of Quraysh and those of his companions. Yet they do not think of themselves as Arabs, or except in religion, as culturally Arabian. Indeed paradoxical though it may appear, in many ways Somali despise Arabs, especially those whom they meet in Somaliland as immigrant traders and merchants. Nevertheless, it is their proud pretensions to noble Arabian origins which unite all the Somali clans and lineages into one vast genealogical system. In this genealogy, which is shown below, every clan-family has a place and with the exception of the Daarood all are linked agnatically.

It will be apparent that the division between the northern pastoral and southern cultivating clan-families is represented in the genealogy. Thus with the exception of the matrilaterally related Daarood, the pastoral clan-families trace descent agnatically from an ancestor called Samaale who is generally regarded as the source of the name 'Somali' (properly *Soomaali*), while the Digil and Rahanwiin trace their origins to an ancestor called

[1] Although it has been suggested that the name '*Gaalla*' is derived from the Somali *gaal* (pl. *gaalo*) 'pagan' or 'infidel', and refers to the fact that Somali adopted Islam before the Galla, the two words *gaalo* and *Gaalla* are linguistically distinct.

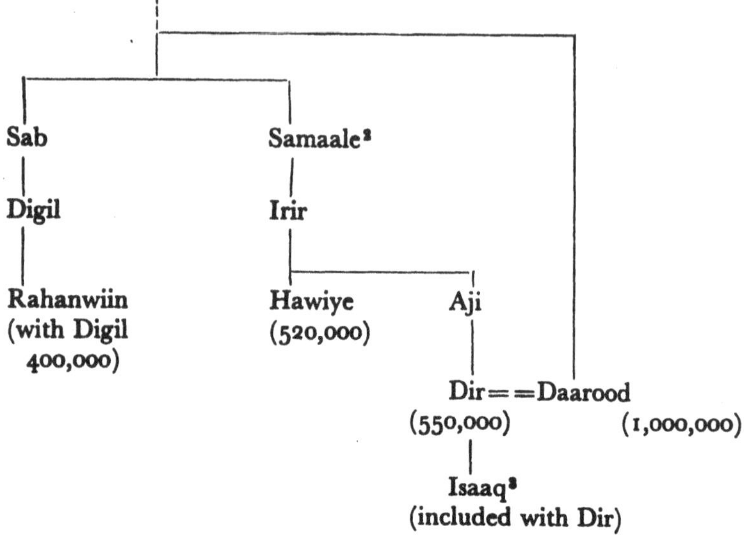

Sab. Since, however, the Samaale pastoralists are numerically, and socially dominant, and indeed regard themselves as a pastoral aristocracy, it seems that the ethnic name Somali has been extended to the Sab in much the same way as the various inhabitants of the British Isles are known to foreigners as 'English'. Various popular etymologies are offered. A widely held derivation of the name is from *soo* and *maal*, 'go and milk', referring to Somali pastoralism. Another very acceptable etymology is from the Arabic 'wealthy' (*dhawamaal*) again referring to Somali riches in livestock.[4]

[1] 'Aqiil, one of the sons of Abuu Ṭaalib, was a cousin of the Prophet, and the brother of 'Ali who married Maḥammad's daughter Faatima. Abuu Ṭaalib himself died at Mecca in A.D. 620.

[2] In his *Bughyat al-amaal fii taariikh as-Soomaal*, pp. 279–81, published in Mogadishu in 1955, Shariif 'Aydaruus Shariif 'Ali records a tradition that the eponym Samaale came from the Yemen in the ninth century to settle in Somaliland and founded the Somali people.

[3] While this is the genealogical position ascribed to the Isaaq by others, they themselves trace descent directly from 'Ali Abuu Ṭaalib (not from 'Aqiil) independently of the genealogy shown.

[4] A less common derivation, with little appeal to Somali, recorded by Burton *First Footsteps in East Africa*, Memorial edition, 1894, vol. i, p. 72, is from the Arabic *samala* 'thrust out', it being stated in some traditions that the ancestor 'Samaale' who migrated to Somaliland from Arabia had 'struck out' his brother's eye. This of course is a very fanciful etymology.

As has been said, it is the northern pastoral clan-families who are the subject of this book and not the Digil and Rahanwiin Sab, although it is necessary to include the latter in the discussion of modern political movements in Chapter IX. But to set this book in its proper perspective (and to avoid confusion) it is essential to say something here of this primary cleavage in the Somali nation. The Digil and Rahanwiin agricultural tribes are settled in southern Somalia, mainly between the Shebelle and Juba Rivers where they grow millets, durra, Indian corn, and a variety of other subsidiary crops and fruits. They have generally fewer camels than the pastoralists and more cattle.

But the division between the two groups of clan-families is not merely an economic one. Linguistically the speech of the Sab differs from that of the northern pastoralists by about as much as French does from Italian. The gulf in language is thus much wider than that between any of the northern pastoral dialects. The distinction has also a strong historical component, for, as I shall presently show, the Sab are a conglomerate people, an amalgam of many different Somali groups with Galla and negroid elements. And where they differ from the northern pastoral clan-families their distinctive culture and social institutions reflect these mixed origins. Their conquest political structure if not that of a tribal state is certainly more formalized and more hierarchical than the political system of the northern nomads. In some cases, Sab political units consist of people of various, and often diverse, origin and provenance, federated together by affiliation to a politically dominant lineage in which land rights are specifically vested. In other cases, Sab tribes—for here there are territorially defined jural and political communities—do not appear to base their political relations upon kinship but upon what Maine called local contiguity. It is impossible to characterize their political organization completely however, since, despite the comprehensive study of Sab customary law made by the distinguished Italian jurist Massimo Colucci[1], no detailed analysis of their political structure has yet been published.

These distinctive features of Sab society, their largely sedentary

[1] M. Colucci, *Principi di diritto consuetudinario della Somalia Italiana meridionale*, 1924. The best general description of any one Sab tribe is U. Ferrandi's study of the Gassar Gudde (*Lugh, Emporio commerciale sul Giuba*, Rome, 1903). For a tentative summary of Sab political structure see Lewis, *The Somali Lineage System and the Total Genealogy*, 1957.

economy, and their hierarchical political system and respect for authority all provide a convenient focus for the hostility and disparagement which the pastoralists display towards them. Whereas hostility and rivalry are endemic amongst the four pastoral clan-families, the division between these and the Sab is more sharply defined and of a different order. This antagonism is not, however, manifest in concerted political action in the traditional structure of Somali society. For both groups are far too large, too widely scattered, and too unwieldy to oppose each other as united polities. But the degree to which the Sab resent the pastoralists' scorn and assumption of complacent ascendency is strongly expressed in party politics as I shall show in a later chapter.

It is essential to distinguish here the Midgaan, Tumaal, and Yibir bondsmen of northern Somaliland who, though known collectively by the same name as that of the common ancestor of the Digil and Rahanwiin, are quite distinct from them. Not only have these traditional bondsmen no connexion with the Digil and Rahanwiin tribes but they also stand outside the cleavage between the latter and the pastoral clan-families. To avoid confusion I refer to these bondsmen as *sab* in distinction to the Digil and Rahanwiin as Sab. The *sab* are today few in numbers and there are estimated to be no more than twelve and a half thousand in Somalia and the British Protectorate.[1] The Midgaans (c. 9,000) are the most numerous, with the Tumaal (c. 2,250) next, and the Yibir (c. 1,300) who are now rarely encountered, last. But these are only very approximate estimates. The three groups are distinguished from noble Somali, with whom they appear to share much the same physical features, by their practice of specialist crafts such as metal-working and leather working, shoe-making, hunting and hairdressing—all activities which noble Somali pastoralists scorn. They are segmented into small lineages on the Somali pattern, and widely scattered throughout northern Somaliland where they are attached in servile status to families and lineages of the four Somali clan-families. And in their distinctiveness and exclusion from full participation in Somali social relations the *sab* have many of the features of an endogamous caste.

[1] Estimates for their numbers in other Somali territories are not available. See K. Goldsmith and I. Lewis, 'A Preliminary Investigation of the Blood Groups of the "Sab" Bondsmen of Northern Somaliland', *Man*, vol. LVIII, December, 1958, pp. 188–190.

IV.

The preceding section outlined the distribution and distinguishing features of the six Somali clan-families and, more particularly, those with which this book deals. In this and a following section I summarize what is known of their history.

I begin by tracing the slender and often broken thread of instituted government which foreign intervention established in a few urban centres and which with many interruptions persisted from about the tenth century through centuries of nomadic life and lineage politics. For in northern Somaliland, formal government has always been tenuous in the extreme, existing precariously on the fringes of the wider and more pervasive field of lineage rivalries over which, until the advent of European administration at the end of the nineteenth century, no firm central authority ever held continuous jurisdiction.

The earliest mention of a Somali clan is of the Hawiye whom the Arab geographer Ibn Sa'iid (1214-87) describes in virtually their present situation, near Merca, in southern Somalia. The name *Soomaali* itself does not occur until the fifteenth century when it is recorded in an Ethiopic hymn celebrating the victories of the Abyssinian King Negus Yeshaaq (1414-29)[1] over the Muslim and partly Somali state of Adal (Awdal) based on Zeila'. Shihaab ad-Diin, the Arabian historian of the following century, who in his *Futuuḥ al-Ḥabasha* ('History of the Conquest of Abyssinia') written apparently between 1540 and 1560 records the recovery of the petty Muslim states and their remarkable, if short-lived, conquest of most of Ethiopia, has occasion to mention Somali frequently.[2] For the Muslim armies which under the leadership of Imaam Aḥmad ibn Ibraahiim al-Ghaazi ('the left-handed')[3] devastated Abyssinia between 1527 and 1543 were heavily dependent upon Somali recruits. Daarood groups which are now strong clans or congeries of clans such as the Geri, the Marrehaan and Harti,[4] played a prominent part as did also the Habar Magaadle (Isaaq)[5]. From time to time the Hawiye who

[1] See, I. Guidi, 'Le canzioni ge'ez—amarina in onore di Re Abissino' 1889, Cerulli, 'La Somalia nelle cronache etiopiche,' 1929.

[2] Edited and translated by R. Basset. Paris, 1897–1909.

[3] In Somali, Aḥmad Guray, and known to the Abyssinians as Aḥmad Granhe.

[4] The Harti today embrace a large number of Daarood clans, see below p. 145.

[5] For the Habar Magaadle division of the Isaaq (who are not mentioned as Isaaq in the *Futuuḥ*) see the genealogy below, p. 157.

lay further to the south lent their support, but there is apparently no mention of the 'Iise or Gadabuursi or for that matter of the other main Isaaq division, the Habar Tol Ja'lo. Somali leaders (styled *Garaad*) such as Mattan of the Geri, and Aḥmad Guray, a namesake of the Imaam were among his strongest and most able generals.

Imaam Aḥmad's headquarters were at Harar where he had wrested control of the Muslim state of Adal from the hereditary Sultan Abuu Bakr ibn Maḥammad replacing him by his brother 'Umar Diin, but little is known of his origins.[1] According to one legend he was the bastard son of a Coptic priest and Muslim harlot. But for the Somali, and other Muslims of the small states and sultanates of the Horn of Africa at this period, he was the saviour who led them to victory sweeping all before him, laying waste the Christian towns, sacking their churches, and killing those who refused to abjure their faith to the glory of Allah. In relation to the heterogeneous and fragmented character of his followers, their endless internecine struggles, and the strength of Abyssinian resistance his success was remarkable.

Although the *Futuuḥ* often records the strengths of his armies and the numbers of Somali cavalry and infantry—many armed with bows and arrows—who joined the Imaam, it is impossible to deduce the size of Somali clans at this period. It is clear, however, as I have indicated, that what are today strong clans or groups of clans were then small lineages. And the impression is given of a much smaller Somali population than that of today.

The *Futuuḥ* is of more value, however, in depicting Somali clan politics in the sixteenth century as of essentially the same character as they are now. When not participating in the holy war (*jihaad*) the Somali are described as dangerous, and savage brigands, ambushing travellers, and harrying the main trade-routes which lay through their territory. But in the campaigns against Abyssinia they are constantly praised for their bravery and daring and for their devotion to the cause of Islam. Yet, even under the Imaam's banner they were often troublesome and difficult to manage. Frequently quarrels and struggles between Somali lineages took a similar course to that which they follow today. Moreover, in settling disputes, as now, superior strength was decisive and blood-compensation could only be exacted by

[1] See the *Futuuḥ* passim and *Encyclopaedia of Islam* vol. ii, article 'Harar', pp. 263–4.

the threat of force. Thus on one occasion, the Habar Magaadle refused to pay tax to the Imaam and attacked some of his followers. The Imaam sent an army which ravaged their country, but they in return harried the other Somali who had joined him. Geri followers of the Imaam complained, and a punitive expedition was sent which penetrated far into Habar Magaadle territory laying waste their towns and settlements. Only then did they make peace with the Imaam and acknowledge his suzerainty.

At the time of Imaam Aḥmad's campaigns the capital of the Muslim Sultanate of Adal was Harar. Originally, however, Adal was based on the port of Zeila', whose foundation by immigrant Arabs dates from the tenth century, and was no more than an emirate in the larger Muslim state of Ifaat which lay in the plateau region of eastern Shoa in what is now Ethiopia. Early in the fifteenth century the capital was moved to Dakar, further from the threat of Abyssinian attacks, and Adal then became the principal centre for the struggle of the Muslim communities against the expanding Abyssinian kingdom. Only at the beginning of the sixteenth century were the military headquarters of the sultanate moved to Harar from which base the Imaam launched his attacks. With Zeila' as principal port, through which cannons were imported from Arabia for the Imaam's armies, and trading in slaves, ivory and other commodities with Abyssinia and the Arabian Peninsula, Adal reached the summit of her prosperity in the fourteenth century. After the Imaam's short-lived conquest in the sixteenth century, Abyssinia gradually recovered, making good her losses with Portuguese aid, and both Adal and Zeila' declined fairly rapidly[1]. And in the following century with Berbera, the other principal northern port, Zeila' became a dependency of the Shariifs of Mukha. Thus almost from its foundation until this time the political history of Zeila' is one of intermittent conflict with Christian Abyssinia. As a bulwark against the Christian hinterland the ancient city was one of the main northern seats of Muslim Somali power and an important centre in the long series of wars against the Abyssinians.

While Zeila' was the northern hub of Muslim and Arab influence, Mogadishu occupied a similar position in the south.

[1] The most easily accessible and most comprehensive account of the relations between these small Muslim states and the expanding Abyssinian kingdom is J. S. Trimingham's *Islam in Ethiopia*, Oxford, 1952.

Founded by Arab and Persian immigrants about the beginning of the tenth century, from a loose federation, a sultanate with a local dynasty arose three centuries later. But as a commercial centre for the export trade from the hinterland, Mogadishu appears to have reached her greatest prosperity only in the fourteenth and fifteenth centuries. In the seventeenth century the port's importance waned and Mogadishu became a hegemony of small townships. Shortly afterwards, during the struggle between Oman and the Portuguese, Mogadishu was briefly occupied by the forces of the Imaam of Oman and remained afterwards loosely under his suzerainty. But when the Muscat state was divided early in the nineteenth century Mogadishu was allotted to the Sultan of Zanzibar. Then the town was occupied by Sultan Barghash b. Sa'iid (died 1888) who appointed a Governor (*waalii*) to rule it for him. In 1892, however, the Sultan leased the town to Italy and the other southern coastal centres attached to Zanzibar were purchased by the Italian Government in 1905.[1]

Prior to European colonization, Zeila' and Mogadishu were the two main centres with some degree of centralized government and some, though irregular, tradition of authority more formalized than the egalitarian structure of Somali pastoral politics. Loosely associated with them in their hostility towards Abyssinia, were lesser coastal centres such as Berbera, and Mait in the north, and Brava and Merca in the south. Less is known of the many ruined Muslim towns which are widely scattered in northern Somaliland, centres such as 'Amuud, Aw Barre, and Abbaasa in the north-west, but they seem to have been contemporary with Zeila' and Mogadishu at least in the mediaeval period. Their relations with the more important and better known coastal Sultanates must remain a matter for conjecture until they have been fully excavated by archaeologists.[2]

Harar as we have seen, was the last important centre of the crumbling Adal state after the decline of Zeila'. It marked the north-west boundary of Somali interest and Somali have played a less significant part in the city's history than in that of Zeila' or

[1] For a fuller account see Cerulli's article 'Makdishu' in the *Encyclopaedia of Islam*, vol. iii, pp. 165–6; C. Guillain, *Documents sur l'histoire, la géographie et le commerce de l'Afrique Orientale*, Paris, 1856, vol. i, pp. 524, 908; Trimingham, 1952, p. 68, and 214–5.

[2] See A. T. Curle, *Antiquity*, September, 1937, pp. 315–27; G. Matthew, *Antiquity*, 1953, pp. 212-18.

Mogadishu.[1] Nevertheless, and with good reason, Harar is still regarded by Somali as much as Zeila' or Mogadishu as a traditional seat of their Muslim culture. Even today under Ethiopian rule, the city enjoys a reputation throughout Somaliland as a centre of Muslim scholarship and learning. And for the Somali these were the three principal poles of the faith, the focal points of Arabian settlement and Muslim civilization.

After the Shariifs of Mukha and the Imaams of Oman had acquired control of the northern and southern coastal settlements in the seventeenth century penetration by foreign powers lapsed for nearly two centuries. But, in the era of Egyptian aggrandisement under Ismaa'iil Pasha, the northern Somali coast from Zeila' to Cape Guardafui came under Egyptian jurisdiction in 1874. Although they did not remain long in possession of northern Somaliland, they improved the coastal ports, constructed piers and lighthouses, and they did much to encourage and promote Islam. Mosques were built and saints' shrines such as that of Sheikh Yuusuf Mamma (Geri, Abba Yuunis) at Berbera (1881) erected. The Egyptians appear also to have made some contribution to indirect rule for they utilized a system of lineage-group representation through appointed headmen (Akils) which has since formed the basis of rudimentary local government amongst the pastoralists in all the Somali territories. Their brief occupation terminated when, at the time of the revolt in the Sudan, defeated in her efforts to extend her dominion over Ethiopia and threatened by unrest at home, Egypt abandoned her possessions to France and Britain.

Glowing accounts of the potential resources of the Somali coast had been published by Burton and other early European travellers. But possessing Aden since 1839, the British Government became interested in this region mainly apparently for its strategic importance. And having acquired control of Egypt in 1882, treaties of protection were signed with the Gadabuursi (1884) and the Habar Awal (1884 and 1886), and the boundaries between the British and Italian spheres were settled by an agreement of 1894 and with Ethiopia in 1897. The 1897 treaty with Ethiopia is of particular significance because it recognized Ethiopian sovereignty over most of the Haud in northern Somaliland at a time when events in the Sudan made Britain

[1] On the history of Harar see E. Cerulli, *Studi Etiopici I. La Lingua e la storia di Harar*, Rome, 1936, and Trimingham loc.cit.

anxious to secure the friendship of Ethiopia. But it was only in 1954 that the territory, which is an important grazing area of many of the Protectorate clans, was actually placed under Ethiopian jurisdiction. Somali have never recognized the treaty which they regard as a flagrant breach of faith on the part of Britain, and the recent transfer to Ethiopian administration has stimulated anti-Ethiopian and nationalist aspirations.

France had entered this barren arena as early as 1839 and obtained the port of Obock in what is now French Somaliland by treaty in 1859. Lagarde, to whom much of the credit for the present extent of French dominion is due, signed a treaty of protection with the 'Iise in 1885 and the frontiers between the new British Protectorate and what was to become the *Côte des Somalis* were established by treaty in 1888. After Lagarde had left, in 1894 France obtained from Ethiopia the concession to build the railway between Jibuti and Addis Ababa which is the *Côte's* main source of revenue and which allowed Jibuti gradually to eclipse Zeila', the traditional outlet for the trade-routes from Harar.[1] As Ethiopia's main sea-port, Jibuti prospered and Zeila' declined. What was left from earlier times of the distinctive amalgam of Arab, 'Afar, and Somali culture known as Seylaawiya gradually disappeared. Many of Zeila's former urban population—the Reer Seyla'—settled in Ethiopia and others moved to Jibuti. Thus the tenuous thread of urban Zeila' culture which had survived from the tenth century was severed and the British Protectorate lost a cosmopolitan and flourishing port which might have been as important as Mogadishu is to Somalia.

At first as a Dependency of India, the Protectorate was administered by the Resident in Aden. Administration was limited mainly to the three ports of Zeila', Bulhar, and Berbera, of which only Berbera is now important. At this time local officials had at their disposal little over a hundred Native Infantry from the Aden garrison and a combined force of about a hundred Somali police and Camel Corps. The interior was hardly administered at all and expeditions undertaken against Somali clans, only when they attacked caravans, looted government property or threatened rebellion. Thus in 1886 and 1890 forces were sent against the 'Iise, in 1893 against the 'Iidagalle, and in 1895

[1] For a concise summary of the history of the *Côte des Somalis*, see H. Deschamps et al. *L'Union française, Côte des Somalis—Réunion—Inde*, Paris, 1948, pp. 39–51. On the struggle between the Imperial Powers for control in the Somali area generally, see L. Woolf, *Empire and Commerce in Africa*, London, 1920, pp. 156 ff., 208–28.

against the Jibriil Abokor (Habar Awal) of Hargeisa. Three years later government was transferred to the Foreign Office who in turn ceded control to the Colonial Office in 1905.

Italy had in 1889 signed treaties of protection with the Majeerteen (Daarood) and, as we have seen, obtained Mogadishu and the other southern ports in 1905. In 1897 the left bank of the Juba River was occupied as far as Lugh, which was then regularly harried by Ethiopian raiding parties. Part of the Juba basin was added in 1908 by treaty with Ethiopia, and in 1925 the province of Jubaland was ceded with the port of Kismayu by Britain.

When France collapsed in 1940 a neutral Vichy regime was established in the *Côte*, and in the same year when the British Protectorate was invaded by Italian forces based on Ethiopia, the British Administration withdrew to Aden. But British forces returned to the Protectorate in 1941, the Italians were forced to withdraw, and a British Military Administration was set up. Shortly after, the East African campaign closed, and Italian Somaliland and Eritrea came under British military administration. For several years much of Harar Province of Ethiopia remained under British control, although the administration of the Ogaden was returned in 1948, until in 1954 there were only two British Civil Affairs Officers in the Haud. By the terms of the Anglo-Ethiopian agreement of 1954 mentioned above, these were withdrawn and replaced by a British Liaison staff. Under British Military administration from 1941, Somalia was visited in 1948 by a 'Four Power' commission, and in November 1949 the United Nations General Assembly agreed to return Italy as administering authority of a United Nations Trusteeship with a ten years mandate to independence (1950-1960).

V

The preceding pages briefly outlined the history of foreign intervention in Somaliland, and the irregular transmission of the principles of centralized authority first established in the Muslim sultanates founded by Arab and Persian immigrants. Within this sphere of action, which only touched the majority of the Somali peripherally, the population was growing and was moving generally towards the south. This Somali migration, certainly at some points stimulated by Arabian settlement and the spread of Islam, started in the north and led to the Somali conquest of southern Somalia and of its pre-Somali populations. It is this internal phase of Somali history which is of greatest significance in understanding the historical basis of the segmentary lineage system. Here our information is less well documented, consisting as it does for the most part of local clan traditions evaluated in the light of Arabic inscriptions, early records, travellers' accounts, and material stored in Government archives. This subject has been most fully explored by Dr. Cerulli and the late Massimo Colucci[1]. Their account which incorporates material from the history of the coastal towns accords so well with all that is definitely established that its general accuracy can be in little doubt.

In the south, between the Shebelle and Juba rivers and to some extent north of the Shebelle, there appear to have been three major movements of population. For before the incursions of the Hamitic Galla and Somali, this region was occupied by a mixed population—the Zengi of mediaeval Arab geographers—who seem to have comprised two distinct elements. Sedentary agricultural tribes, settled in the inter-riverine area and akin to the North-Eastern Coastal Bantu formed one component. And residues of this Bantu, and Swahili-speaking population, supplemented by slaves from further south freed by the suppression of the Slave Trade at the end of the nineteenth century, survive today in the Shidle, Kaboole, Reer 'Iise, Makanni, and Shabeele peoples, on the Shebelle River, and on the Juba River in the WaGosha and Gobweyn. To the same group belong the Elaay of Baidoa in the hinterland, and the Tunni Torre of Brava District. The other section of the pre-Hamitic population consisted of Bushmanlike hunters and gatherers, and along the rivers of fishermen, of whom contemporary representatives are the WaRibi, and WaBooni or Booni of Jubaland and southern Somalia, and the Eyle of Bur Hacaba. If they ever lived further north none of these groups survive today in northern Somaliland.[2]

Although it is not yet known how long they had been established, in mediaeval times the Galla were north of the Zengi

[1] The principal sources are cited in Lewis, *Peoples of the Horn of Africa, Somali, Afar, Saho*, 1955, p. 45. To these should be added Basset's edition and translation of the *Futuuḥ al-Ḥabasha*. Cerulli's historical articles are collected in E. Cerulli, *Somalia: Scritti vari editi ed inediti I.* Rome, 1957. See also my article 'The Somali Conquest of the Horn of Africa'. *Journal of African History*, I, 2, 1960.

[2] For fuller details on these tribes see Lewis, 1955 and 1957.

block, and north beyond them again, the Muslim Somali massing along the shores of the Gulf of Aden. Probably several centuries earlier, but certainly by the sixteenth century, the Galla, driven southwards by pressure from the Somali to their north, were expanding into the riverine regions and displacing the earlier negroid and Bantu populations. The majority of these they drove southwards towards the Tana River, and into Kenya and Ethiopia leaving only the residual groups found today along the rivers. To some extent this Somali expansion and Galla withdrawal coincided with Imaam Aḥmad's invasion of Abyssinia. It may be that the latter's campaigns were at least in part occasioned by these movements and corresponded to a sudden influx of Arabian settlers in the north. Certainly prior to their retreat to the south and south-west pushing before them the bulk of the Zengi tribes, the Galla occupied central Somalia to the north of the Shebelle River, and part of north-eastern Ethiopia including the Haud now occupied by the Ogaadeen Somali. To their north, the Somali were established and expanding apparently under the stimulus of increased migration from Arabia. It was from such settlement at an early period that the Muslim sultanates such as Adal based on Zeila' grew up.

The position in the north in early times is less certain. From local traditions of battles between Somali and Galla in northern Somaliland it seems probable that the latter formerly occupied the region. This appears to be fairly definitely established for areas in the north-west of what is today the British Protectorate where some place-names are still Galla, and where there are remnants of Galla tribes such as the Akisho whom we shall meet with in later chapters.[1] It seems also that the Galla occupied at least parts of north-eastern Somaliland; but whether the Somali are simply Arabized Galla, or whether they are a separate Cushitic group who reached Somaliland after the Galla, remains undetermined.

More circumstantial are the traditions which record the arrival from Arabia of the patriarchs Sheikh Isaaq and Sheikh Daarood, founders of the corresponding clan-families.[2] The Daarood are regarded as older than the Isaaq; and Sheikh Daarood is supposed to have crossed from Arabia about the tenth

[1] See Lewis 'The Galla in Northern Somaliland', *Rassegna di Studi Etiopici*, xv. 1959, pp. 21–38.

[2] For the situation of their tombs, see below, p. 131.

or eleventh century, and Sheikh Isaaq to have followed some two centuries later. Whether or not these traditions are historically valid, they have great social importance since they provide a charter for the existance of the clan-families descended from the two sheikhs. And whatever their origins, the expansion of their descendants led to the dispersal of the Dir who traditionally preceded them in northern Somaliland. The latter were driven south where the Biimaal of Merca are their strongest representatives; and to the north-west where their largest groups today are the 'Iise and Gadabuursi. By the twelfth century, the Dir and Daarood Somali were pressing upon their southern Galla neighbours and the great sequence of movements which ultimately disestablished the latter in Somaliland was under way. The main lines of Somali penetration were either down the system of wells along the Indian Ocean Coast, or from the north-west down the valley of the Shebelle River and its tributaries.

From the folk traditions analysed by Cerulli it appears that by the thirteenth century Somali from the north had penetrated southwards to the extent that the coastal area between the present ports of Itala and Merca was occupied by the Hawiye Somali, while further south and towards the interior lay the Somali Jidu tribe (Digil-Sab), and finally to the west the Galla. About this time the Ajuraan (derived from the marriage of an immigrant Arabian with a woman of the Hawye) were expanding and pushing the Galla westwards towards Bur Hacaba in the interriverine region in the fifteenth century. The Ajuraan consolidated their position under a hereditary dynasty, and dominating the lower reaches of the Shebelle were linked commercially with the port of Mogadishu. In the seventeenth century their defeat at the hands of the Hawiye and the collapse of their dynasty, contributed to the decline of Mogadishu. Other Somali clans now continued to pour into this region, but in the early part of the century the zone south of Bur Hacaba and between the rivers was still occupied by the Galla. Not long after, however, the Galla were finally driven across the Juba River by the expanding Rahanwiin. The Somali advance continued; and by 1909 the Daarood had reached the Tana River where in the interests of the other inhabitants of Kenya their advance was arrested by the establishment of fixed grazing areas.

This marked the end of the great series of migrations which, over a space of some nine hundred years, had brought the Somali from their northern deserts into the more fertile regions of central and southern Somalia and finally into the Northern Province of Kenya. These movements had great social repercussions. Through contact with the Galla and the absorption of the few Galla who remained behind and through the influence of the earlier Bantu communities, the Digil and Rahanwiin tribes emerged with their distinctive characteristics. From the Bantu they adopted cultivation, and from the Galla temporarily copied their system of military age-grades. In much the same way the trans-Juban Daarood briefly adopted the Galla age-set system and like the Rahanwiin later relinquished it. But to what extent these southern pastoral Somali bear the marks of their contact with the Galla will not be clear until their social organization has been thoroughly investigated.

At every stage the migrations illustrate the Somali concept of political authority as stemming from numerical supremacy alone. Although at various times, small groups and lineages, the spearheads of the greater clan migrations, accepted the protection of their numerically superior Galla hosts, as soon as they had mustered sufficient strength they overthrew their protectors and made them their subjects. In every case where by force of numbers and arms they could, the Somali conquered. They were never content to accept the authority of a Galla minority which they could successfully challenge. This is the procedure characteristic of the northern pastoralists. But when they had adopted cultivation and settled as sedentary communities on the land a new pattern emerged. Thus amongst the agricultural Sab small lineages of Somali origin have achieved a position of political supremacy through their ties to the land as founding settlers.

In conclusion it is important to emphasize that although the northern Somali have been colonized they have never really been conquered. Despite innumerable punitive expeditions, and the final extinction of the rebellion led by Sheikh Maḥammad 'Abdille Ḥassan which, lasting from 1900–1920, was until recently the main event in the modern history of northern Somaliland, the northern pastoralists have never been decisively subjugated. Only in the northern province of Kenya has a poll tax been imposed. By the establishment of international frontiers the great movements of the clans have to some extent been arrested, but the pastoralists' inordinate pride and contempt for other nations remains unchallenged.

VI.

To throw the argument of later pages into relief I conclude this chapter with a few general remarks. I have already pointed out that most writers have correctly appraised Somali individualism and their lack of stable government. They have often, however, misrepresented the northern pastoralists' devotion to Islam. Somali are in fact devout and even fervid Muslims, and, as Sunnis, follow almost exclusively the Shafi'ite school of Muslim Law. The stranger who lives amongst them cannot avoid being impressed by their possessive attitude towards and close identification with Islam. And while Somali are well aware that they are only one among the many communities of Islam, through their fervent attachment to Islam their faith becomes a vehicle for the expression of their remarkable pride as a people. Indeed, certain purely religious Muslim practices become so firmly integrated in Somali life that they are often described, at least by the less sophisticated, as 'Somali' custom rather than as Islamic practice. Of course here they are right, for in a very real sense Islam is the mainspring of Somali culture. Thus in a religious context the Muslim profession of the faith has almost the force of an initiation rite into their society.

In contrast to the power of religion, magic, witchcraft, and sorcery play minor roles in the society of the northern pastoralists and to a large extent appear to be of Arabian origin rather than traditional Somali practise. It may therefore be, that where tensions are resolved as freely by fighting as they are in Somaliland, there is little need of witchcraft. In a later chapter I argue that this is to some extent the case, for where sorcery or witchcraft occur it is usually between people who, for one reason or another, are prevented from fighting.

For although they allow, and on occasions stress, the mystical powers of sheikhs and saints through Islam, the pastoralists are highly pragmatic in their assumptions, living as they do from day to day and with no assurance that conditions obtaining in one year or season will hold in the next. Life itself is precarious in the extreme. Accordingly the sociologist who constantly looks for the roots of this or that custom in some non-Islamic system of supernatural belief is likely to be disappointed. In enquiring, for example, why a certain plant was supposed to have curative powers, which clearly did not depend on any Muslim sanction,

I was usually told that it had been tried and found to be efficacious. In eminently practical reasoning of this kind, the Somali pastoralist excels to a greater degree, I believe, than many other African peoples. Thus when I enquired why sexual relations were abstained from on the eve of a battle or raiding expedition, I was told that sexual intercourse was exhausting, and that tired men who were not fully alert could hardly be expected to give a good account of themselves.

I have already referred to the fact that ultimately unsettled disputes are left to the test of military strength. The pastoralists, indeed, regard fighting, whatever its circumstances, as essentially the proper pursuit of men. And war and feud occur constantly. To enumerate the number of engagements which occurred even in my twenty months in Somaliland would be difficult. Thus I frequently sought some relief from the general banter of which I was a ready target by accusing the pastoralists with whom I lived as being no better than bandits and robbers. And while such remarks were received with some show of resentment people seemed at heart flattered. For as it was often put to me, can women hold-up trade-trucks or loot and kill? But although they esteem fighting so highly, the pastoralists have no standing military organization or system of regiments. Armies and raiding parties are always *ad hoc* formations, and while feuds often last for years, and sometimes generations, they are generally waged in guerilla campaigns. Pitched battles are rare. Spears are the traditional weapons of aggression and are still to some extent employed although they have largely been replaced by rifles. One convenient source of these are the arms and ammunition with which the Ethiopian Government periodically presents its subjects and which find their way into other Somali territories where their unauthorized possession is illegal. Moreover, today, in addition to the use of burden camels and ponies—the traditional means of transport—motor vehicles are frequently employed in battle, not least those which private individuals obtain from the auction of surplus Government equipment.

Not all men however are warriors. Pastoral society is traditionally divided into two classes: men of religion (sg. *wadaad*) and warriors (*waranleh* lit. 'spear-bearers'). And although there is now and has long been a greater occupational stratification, these divisions retain their validity. However else he gains a livelihood any one who practises as a religious expert is a *wadaad*: all others are *waranleh*. *Wadaads*, by definition if not always in practice, are excluded from direct participation in fighting. Ideally their task is to reconcile rivalries and to mediate in disputes between warriors to whom their functions are complimentary.

Faced with this pattern of life the Administrations at first found little purchase and attempted little beyond extending communications between the ports and the interior, striving to keep these open to traffic, and generally maintaining a modicum of law and order. In this period the rebellion of Sheikh Maḥammad 'Abdille (1900–1920) greatly disorganized government, especially in the British Protectorate between the years 1910 and 1914 when the Government ill-advisedly withdrew to the coast and abandoned the interior to the Dervishes, and to universal pillage, disorder, and eventually to famine.

Since the last war, the scope of government in all the territories has greatly expanded, particularly in the fields of social services, education, agricultural and pastoral betterment, and the development of water resources. Modern economic developments have made their greatest impact in French Somaliland where half the population is concentrated in the commercial town and port of Jibuti. None of the northern towns in other territories are so heavily industrialized and in the north Jibuti is outstanding in this respect. In southern Somalia, a small-scale industrial revolution is in progress in the centuries-old coastal trade centres. British Somaliland and Harar Province of Ethiopia however—at least as far as Somali are concerned—have been relatively little affected.

But in comparison with the early days, despite an immense increase in administrative staff, Government still rests lightly upon the pastoralists. And although modern administration is in conflict with the traditional procedure where might is always right and self-help is the ultimate sanction, yet it has become firmly integrated in the pastoralists' social system. For a new balance has been struck between traditional segmentary principles and bureaucratic government. While the pastoralist may complain of Government's tardiness to attend to the demands to which his sectional interests give rise, to build a road from one place to another, to dig wells and build water storage tanks in particular areas, yet he still makes the utmost use of the administrative machine to his own advantage. Government in fact has become a *tertium quid* in the system of relations between rival parties. Thus although Somali repeat the proverb 'he who is weak has found the European as his protector',[1] in their own segmentary interests they seek to play off against each other different sections of the Administration and different members of its personnel. In Districts where several rival clans or lineage-groups are present, Somali constantly complain of unjust representation in all spheres in which the Administration exercises authority. Complaints range from such matters as the allocation of trading licenses to recruitment in all departments of Government, particularly in the police, and armed forces. To a certain extent they are successful for anyone who has worked with Somali will appreciate how difficult it is to stand entirely aloof from the interplay of their sectional rivalries.

From our point of view, the most important way in which bureaucratic administration influences the pastoralist is through mediation between rival political units. That centralized government in any dispute is now a third power to be reckoned with, is evinced in many situations. Thus when testifying to the truth of a statement before a panel of arbitrators it has become customary to refer to the presence of the local District Officer's court as an added sanction and guarantee of good faith. Or again, when an attack has been planned by one clan or lineage-group, information is sometimes deliberately allowed to leak through to Government but the date of attack is set forward a few days. The forces of law and order then tend to arrive after the assailant has struck and just as the outraged group is preparing its reprisal. Moreover, when two lineages are at war and through Government intervention a man of one is shot by a policeman or by a member of the Rural Constabulary (Illalos)[2] his death is added to the score of his rivals. Both the police and Illalo force attached directly to District Officers are in all mixed Districts recruited from component clans roughly in proportion to their strengths.

From what has been said it will readily be appreciated that it is no easy matter to administer a people who traditionally recognize no instituted authority, where every adult male[3] has a say in council, and where decisions tend always to be made on an *ad hoc* basis. The principle that might is right is applied critically even to the Administrations in their attempts to maintain law and

[1] *Ninki faralahaa frenji baa loo helay.*
[2] From *ilaali* (v.) to watch over or guard.
[3] With the general exception of the *sab* bondsmen.

order and to control clan and lineage-group strife. Thus during the bitter clan fighting of 1956, I was told that if the Government could not maintain peace it should leave Somali to settle their disputes in the traditional manner.

To conclude this introduction it may be of some value to record a few reflections on Somali character. Different writers have offered often conflicting characterizations of the Somali and I can only describe the pastoralists as I found them. No one, however, is likely to dispute that the Somali are a sophisticated and extremely complex people; and if this is not already plain it will be seen clearly from later pages.

It will also be evident that where every man has a direct say in traditional government all are politicians, and, as such, the pastoralists excel in guile and strategy. Above all else, in their harsh environment they display great talents as politicians, poets, and essentially pragmatists, with however a deep trust in the power of God and His Prophet. With all their pride they have a keen sense of humour and their own acute sense of dignity does not prevent their enjoyment of those situations where others are reduced to ridicule. Moreover, paradoxical though it may appear in relation to his own egalitarian system, the Somali pastoralist is keenly sensitive to differences in others, especially among Government officials. With Europeans he displays a snobbish regard for status and rank.

Although normally aloof, and always preoccupied with the care of his livestock in the struggle to survive, always austere, brusque to the point of dourness, and quick to take offence and easy to rile, the Somali nomad places a high value upon hospitality for the honour which generosity brings him. However impoverished and burdened with the care of his stock, the pastoralist treats the stranger who seeks his protection with great kindness. But the highly segmentary and exclusive character of the Somali political system makes it impossible, or at least extremely difficult, for one who is not a kinsman to be trusted. Suspicion operates structurally. It is easy to see, moreover, how well this prominent feature of Somali character accords with the continuous strife and shifting hostilities which divide groups and which usually relate, at least in some degree, to the intense competition which prevails over access to pasture and water in their arid environment.

2

Ecology and Clan

It is impossible to reach any understanding of Somali political relations without having some knowledge of the country and of the climatic conditions which limit their economy and patterns of territorial dispersion. Accordingly, I begin this analysis of political organization with an account of the main ecological and climatic factors to which the grazing movements of the northern pastoralists have to conform. And in a later chapter I discuss the modifications wrought in the pastoral territorial organization by settlement in towns and trade villages and by the adoption of cultivation.

As a whole the environment is not promising. Northern Somaliland is for the most part a semi-desert area of low rainfall and scrub bush. The annual precipitation in many places is less than four inches, although on high gound it is generally more, and in some parts attains as much as twenty inches. The distribution of rain is thus uneven and for the major part of the country cultivation, under the present conditions, is impossible. It is only the richer soils of the highlands in the west of the British Protectorate and Harar Province of Ethiopia which, with their relatively abundant rainfall, allow sorghum to be grown in quantity. In these favoured regions mixed farming is practised and, as will be shown in Chapter IV, here there is some development of a sense of attachment to territory. But this is not found elsewhere. For the barrenness of the greater part of the country has led the majority of the northern Somali to live as nomadic pastoralists, rearing sheep, goats and camels, and less commonly, cattle. Cattle husbandry is really only important in the cultivating regions where it is associated with agriculture. And it is the husbandry of camels, sheep and goats, which characterizes the northern Somali economy.

The monotony of the seemingly endless wastes of bare plain which make up much of northern Somaliland is broken in many places by massive and magnificent mountain ranges, particularly those which sweep from the northern escarpment to the coast. But whatever the country's appeal to the stranger, for the pastoralist it is home, the country which he knows and understands how best to exploit in the management of his stock. While he regrets the scarcity of rain, and in the dry seasons may complain of his lot, in the wet, when green pasture is abundant, the Somali nomad is exultant in his praise of his herds, land, and way of life. Seamen and others who have often worked for years overseas, and travelled in many parts of the world, return to invest their savings in larger flocks of sheep and goats, and larger herds of camels, and readily resume the harsh rhythm of the pastoral life.

According to their capacity to endure arid conditions, the livestock of the northern pastoralists are divided into two herding units. Camels (collectively, *geel*) which can go without water for over twenty days in dry grazing, have greater powers of endurance and mobility than sheep and goats (collectively, *aḍi*), which, in the same conditions, need water every few days.[1] When fresh green grazing is available watering is not required for either, so that the separation between the two stock units is least accentuated in the rainy seasons and most marked in the dry. Sheep and goats move with the nuclear family and nomadic hut (*aqal*) with a man, his wife, and young children, and sufficient burden camels for their transport. Apart from the beasts of burden required by the nuclear family and an odd milch camel, camels are in the care of boys and unmarried men. The nuclear family moves with close relatives of the husband in nomadic hamlets containing usually between two and four families. With a married woman are her un-married daughters and infant sons still too young to be out with the camels, and from time to time her husband. The latter shares his time amongst his various wives, and is often absent on expeditions to towns, or on clan affairs, or busy seeing to the needs of his camels, especially in the dry seasons when he helps with their watering. The family lives mainly on the milk and meat of the flocks herded with it, although this diet is supplemented by rice, grain, sugar and tea etc., obtained by trade, and wild berries and fruits.

The grazing camels (*geel ḥer*) are herded in camel-camps containing the stock of a few close agnates, and the youths who look after them live mainly on camel's milk. They have no hut to sleep in, and usually no means of cooking.

[1] Sheep are of the black-head, fat-tailed Persian variety and extremely hardy. Camels are one-humped dromedaries of which there are several local breeds.

The duties involved in these two types of husbandry and the grazing patterns of the two units will presently be discussed in some detail. But it is necessary first to describe the ecology of the country and the annual cycle of the seasons.

II

Northern Somaliland is divided into three main topographical zones which Somali call Guban, Ogo and Haud. The Guban (from *gub* to burn) is the region, of desiccated and largely desert, coastal plains, backed by the barren northern escarpment of the main maritime range. The only rains of importance here are the scattered showers which fall in the comparatively cool months of October to March. Sometimes these are sufficiently heavy and extensive to produce a good covering of green vegetation over wide areas and to attract a general movement of man and stock to the pastures along the coast. Yet over most of this dry zone the annual rainfall is rarely more than four inches, but permanent water is plentiful immediately below the sandy topsoil. For the maritime hills are scarred with innumerable valleys carrying the northern run-off from the central highlands. Shallow wells in the Guban are known as 'sand-wells'[1] and water is so easily obtained and so abundant, that specific rights of use are seldom maintained.

The next zone is the Ogo highlands which lie behind the Guban and extend southwards from the top of the maritime escarpment approximately as far as the southerly limits of the main permanent water-points in the British Protectorate. The southern boundary of the Ogo is thus roughly defined by a line running from Jigjiga in the west, along latitude 9.30° to Odweina, then east-south-east to Bihen.[2] From as high as 6,000 ft. at the edge of the escarpment the Ogo falls to about 3,000 ft. in the south. Rainfall varies roughly with altitude from three to twenty inches in the north-west, where sorghum is cultivated.

The Ogo highlands are fairly well watered; but wells often in dry river beds have generally to be sunk to a greater depth than in the Guban. Two types of well are distinguished. From the shorter 'mud wells' (*'eel ḍoobeed*) water is raised in a bucket, part

[1] *'Eel 'iideed*, or *'eel 'ammuudeed*.

[2] Although Ogo is the name employed in the west and that generally used by Europeans, the zone is usually known in the east as *Al* (or with the article, *Asha*) meaning high ground.

of the inner tube of a motor tyre, or other vessel, tied to a rope. Here the mouths of the wells are lined with interlaced branches and sometimes extend to a considerable depth to keep them open and to prevent them from collapsing. The wood at the lip of the wells is heavily scarred from the friction of the drawing ropes. From the deeper and wider-mouthed wells (*'eel wadaameed*) water is brought up in skin-buckets (*wadaan*) tossed from man to man in a human chain. This is the most exhausting of the work at the wells and men chant work-songs as they sling the spilling containers to each other. In relation to the labour initially expended in their excavation, maintenance, and in the raising of the water, these deep wells are the property of clans and lineage-groups. And to the shallower 'mud-wells' smaller lineage-groups similarly maintain exclusive rights. Where, however, water is particularly abundant, as for example in the deep wells of the Nugal Valley of the eastern highlands, exclusive rights are commonly not asserted and men and stock of different and even rival lineages and clans sometimes frequent the same wells.

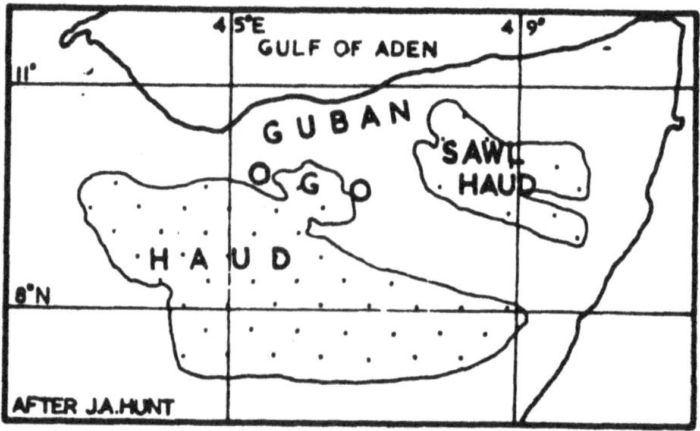

Map 2. Topographical zones of Northern Somaliland.

Thus in a variety of types of well the Ogo provides the home-wells for those lineages which in the dry seasons customarily inhabit it. And generally, except under severe drought, its wells give sufficient water for the needs of all livestock, especially for grazing camels, and for all human consumption.

The third zone, the Haud (correctly *hawd*) into which the Ogo descends to the south, is less favoured in water resources. Here the soil is generally red, and rolling plains extend for hundreds of miles covered by tall grass after the rains, and in places interrupted by belts of thick scrub. Although it lacks permanent water, this region is perhaps the most important pastureland of the north, and its rich grasses provide excellent fodder for camels. Like the southern part of the Ogo highlands, the Haud is intersected by numerous valleys and natural depressions[1] which flood after rain to become small temporary lakes.[2] Here tall Acacias grow and the seasonally flooded basins are the sites of small semi-permanent trading settlements and the oases of the Haud. The agricultural villages of the north-west are similarly based on such basins, and where they do not occur naturally, artificial ponds are dug. For the pastoralists, however, pools in the Haud provide water for human consumption, and for the less hardy livestock—sheep, goats, cattle, donkeys, and horses. When they dry up, as they usually do quickly unless the rains are particularly abundant, resort is had to the shallow wells[3] in which water can be found close to them. These are generally wells to which individuals, or brothers claim and maintain exclusive rights. They dry up periodically and often yield little or no water and only at great expense in digging. Like the ponds with which they are associated, they are used to satisfy the needs of man, of the weaker stock, and of an odd milch or young camel, but never for the full watering of the herds of grazing camels.

To counter its deficiencies in water resources in some parts of the Haud artificial basins have been excavated by individuals using hired labour, by lineage-groups, and by the Government. Some are lined with cement and hold thousands of gallons of water after they have been filled by local rain. From them empty forty-four gallon petrol drums are filled and taken out to water the flocks in the pastures by motor transport. Water thus distributed by vehicles provides a lucrative source of income in the dry seasons, and extends the grazing range of sheep and goats. Moreover, the construction of such privately owned storage tanks has often political significance. For since they are built only with Government sanction they sometimes serve to establish nuclei of infiltration of alien lineage-groups. Thus built by the members of one lineage, a tank becomes a grazing centre for people of that group and creates Government sanctioned rights to water in a

[1] Called variously *dooḥ* and *bohol*.

[2] Known in the east as *balli* and in the west as *har*.

[3] *Laas*; in the west, *beeyo*.

region where they may only recently have begun to pasture their animals.

I have dwelt at some length on the water resources of the three zones because in northern Somaliland access to water is crucial. From what has been said, it will be evident that in general rights to water depend upon its scarcity and the difficulties which have to be surmounted before it can be utilized. Along the coast, water is not usually a problem, and those lineages which retire to the Guban in the dry seasons to water their camels do not usually claim there prescriptive rights to water, except sometimes at large deep wells. Although water is again fairly abundant in the central highlands it is not so widely available and the permanent home-wells at which those lineages of the Ogo and Haud water their camels are usually less widely distributed and generally owned by particular groups. In the Haud, however, but for the recently introduced storage tanks, there are no permanent watering places. What wells there are, are seasonal, shallow, and not particularly abundant in water. Their use moreover is restricted to the watering of small stock and not extended to the grazing camels. Thus unlike the other two zones, there are no home-wells in this region. While in general it is in relation to the availability of pasture and water at different seasons in these zones that groups move, the home-wells essential for watering in the dry seasons, and particularly for the watering of the camels, are the main centres about which movement takes place.

III

Throughout these three topographical zones there are four main seasons, two wet and two dry. In the Ogo and Haud the main rains (*gu*) fall in the spring, beginning about April to the south and west, and May in the north and east, and generally coinciding with the advent of the south-west monsoon. Above all others in the year, spring is the season of plenty, when fresh green grass abounds and milk is plentiful. The breeding of most livestock, particularly of camels, is regulated so that most of the young are born after the spring rains when good supplies of grazing can generally be expected.

About June or July, when the south-west monsoon winds are at their height and dust is everywhere, the dry season of *ḥagaa* commences. According to the extent of the spring rains in the preceding season, the vegetation and pastures dry up more or less rapidly, and the dry season pattern of watering starts.

A short hot period at the end of *ḥagaa* heralds the arrival of the autumn (*dayr*) rains which, falling about September or October provide a subsidiary breeding season. The south-west monsoon drops and veers to the north-east. The *dayr* rains fall most heavily on the northern coast and last sporadically until December, or January when the main dry season (*jiilaal*) commences. This normally is the harshest season of the year, when stock may die of thirst, and debilitation, and man's life is likely to be endangered. At best, people manage to live just at subsistence level and no more. But if the *dayr* rains have been heavy and widespread, the dry season regime of watering may be arrested until the fresh growth of green grass and foliage is exhausted, and the vegetation again becomes brown and the earth dry.

Thus the cycle of the year is the rotation of the four seasons and the annual system of movement conforms to it. And through their livestock the pastoralists are very conscious of their close dependence on their sparse resources. As one poem has it, 'livestock are the growing grass'.[1] They are also very much aware of the extent to which their lives are regulated by the rhythm of the seasons, and of the delicate balance between subsistence and famine. A well-known and often quoted proverb states 'Abundance and scarcity are never far apart; the rich and poor frequent the same houses.'[2]

It will readily be seen that the seasonal distribution of rain through the three zones produces two overlapping ecologies. In the coastal central highlands cycle the *dayr* rains are the main wet season falling about December or January along the coast. A subsidiary rainy season (*gu*) falls in the northern highlands in May. The main rains of the highlands-plains cycle however, are the *gu* rains of March and April falling largely in the Haud. And here the *dayr* rains falling in September and October, and generally most heavily in the highlands, are seldom as extensive as those of spring.

From the table showing the seasonal distribution of the principal northern clans with which we are concerned in this book, it will be seen that two groups move in the Guban-Ogo circuit.

[1] *Ḥoola waa doogga soo baḥaye.*

[2] *Barwaaqo iyo abaar baaysu jiraa laba biḍḍaamoode; baḍaaḍe iyo nin 'ayḍ ihi guryaha waays beddelayaanne.*

DISTRIBUTION OF MAIN NORTHERN CLANS

CLANS (Clan-family affiliation is indicated in brackets)	ZONES OF MOVEMENT			REMARKS
	Coast	Central Highlands	Southern Plains	
'Iise (Dir)	Guban	Ogo	Haud	Two main divisions: 'White 'Iise' move between coast and Ogo, 'Black 'Iise' graze highlands and Haud and reach far into Ethiopia.
Gadabuursi (Dir)	Guban	Ogo	Haud	Haud groups reach far into Ethiopia and French Somaliland.
Habar Awal (Isaaq)	Guban	Ogo	Haud	'Iise Muuse of Berbera District graze mainly between the coast and highlands; Sa'ad Muuse of Hargeisa District between highlands and Haud.
'Iidagalle (Isaaq)		Ogo	Haud	
Habar Yuunis of Erigavo District (Isaaq)	Guban	Ogo		
Habar Yuunis of Burao District (Isaaq)		Ogo	Haud	
Habar Tol Ja'lo (Isaaq)	Guban	Ogo	Haud	Concentrated mainly in Erigavo, Burao, and Las Anod Districts.
Ḍulbahante (Daarood)		Ogo	Haud	Those lineages usually grazing along the Nugal Valley are called *Reer Nugaaleed*; those of the Ogo and Haud are known as *Reer 'Aymeed* or *Reer Oodeed*.
Warsangeli (Daarood)	Guban	Ogo		Mainly in Erigavo District, and reaching into Somalia.

These are the Habar Yuunis of Erigavo District, and the Warsangeli of the same District. The Habar Yuunis of Burao District, the Ḍulbahante of Las Anod District and the 'Iidagalle of Hargeisa District move almost entirely in the Ogo-Haud cycle. The remaining 'Iise and Gadabuursi of Borama District, the Habar Awal of Berbera and Hargeisa Districts, and the Habar Tol Ja'lo of Erigavo, Burao, and Las Anod Districts, move through all three zones. None of these movements are independent of each other—all fall within the same seasonal rhythm. Except in time of war groups are not spatially separated from each other but interpenetrate and inter-mingle in the pastures through which they are impelled to move by the seasonal distribution of rain. To a certain extent, therefore, the two circuits distinguished as separate systems of movement are artificial. Yet this is a convenient way of regarding the highly complex overall pattern of movement.

With the spring rains of April, the central lineage-groups which, from December or January to March, have been wintering on the high plateau (Ogo) and northern Haud, move southwards to the new grazing which the rains promise. Scouts are sent out by individual families, hamlets, and groups of hamlets, to report where rain has fallen and where pasture is plentiful. Then the hamlets move with their flocks and new temporary settlements form in regions of good grazing. At the same time the grazing camels move south at longer range in search of new pasturage. And where grass is plentiful the settlements either of hamlets with the flocks, or of camel-camps, which collect in it, may spend several weeks or even months in one place. Usually, however, as the grazing is exhausted much sooner than this, they have to move fairly frequently from pasturage to pasturage.

While this southern movement into the Haud is underway, those groups which winter on the coast near their coastal home-wells move up, filling the social vacuum left. As the coast becomes unbearably hot and desiccated at this time, they usually begin to move into the comparative cool of the Ogo highlands where some spring rain has already fallen or is expected, and where other sporadic rains have fallen prior to the main wet season. There is thus in all the three zones a general movement towards the south and the Guban-Ogo cycle coincides with the Ogo-Haud cycle since, to a large extent, those whose home-wells are in the Ogo plateau, have after the spring rains deserted it for the Haud plains.

Month	*Season*	*Climate*	*Social Activities*
April	*iilaal/gu*	N.E. Monsoon drops. Hot period before rains.	Watering stops. Movement away from wells towards summer pastures. General movement to south. Food abundant; most livestock produce now; marriage and general expansion in social life.
May	*gu*	Rains later in north and east.	
June	*gu*	Rains tailing off, S.W. Monsoon rising.	Pasture losing its freshness
July	*gu/ḥagaa*	Very hot and dusty, winds high.	Camels out in far grazing, grass drying up.
August	*ḥagaa*	Wind and dust, but rain on high plateau.	Hamlets with flocks falling back on wells.
September	*ḥagaa*	S.W. Monsoon dropping, hot, sporadic showers.	Harvest and time of plenty for western cultivators. Camel watering.
October	*ḥagaa/dayr*	N.E. Monsoon with autumn rain, heaviest on coast.	Movement away from wells, from highlands to Haud and to coast. Stock breeding, milk plentiful.
November	*dayr*	N.E. Monsoon blowing strongly, rain ceasing.	Grazing away from wells.
December	*dayr/jiilaal*	Main dry season, occasional showers on coast.	Watering begins as pastures dry up. Grazing prolonged by water from trucks.
January	*jiilaal*	Cold, harsh conditions.	Hamlets falling back on wells.
February	*jiilaal*	Very poor conditions.	Food scarce; camels, if still out in far grazing, are watering.
March	*jiilaal*	Hot period preceding rains.	People and stock concentrated near wells.

If the spring rains have not been widespread and heavy, as the pastures dry up after two or three months the dry season regime of *ḥagaa* commences. Those hamlets which have been in the southern Haud fall back on the basins and seasonal wells, and the watering of the sheep and goats begins. The grazing camels, however, may stay on in the Haud, from which if dry, they return regularly every two or three weeks to the home-wells in the higher plateau. As the summer dry season advances and the vegetation becomes more and more desiccated and exhausted, seasonal sources of water in the Haud plains dry up and a further movement back towards the central highlands becomes necessary. Here the central and southern lineage-groups mingle with northern coastal groups still in the highlands. Under pressure on their flanks and at the same time attracted towards their winter stations by the autumn rains, those whose home-wells are on the coast, move back towards them. And these *dayr* rains, falling in the centre about September or October, may arrest the northwards withdrawal of those in the Haud towards their home-wells in the highlands. For if rain falls heavily in their vicinity as they move north they will stay in the new pasture until it is exhausted and they are forced to converge on their winter quarters. Then the winter dry season pattern of *jiilaal* begins in earnest. As soon as all vegetation is burnt-up, the two zones, Guban and Ogo, are occupied mainly by those clans and lineages whose dry-season home-wells are located in them and except for grazing camels the Haud is virtually deserted. With the new *gu* rains falling about April in the Ogo highlands and Haud plains and later on the coast, the cycle of movement begins again.

The cycle of movement varies from year to year in relation to the distribution of rain and growth of vegetation. But in its general form it remains fairly constant, except in years exceptional for their lack of rain or for its concentration in a restricted area. As has been observed, the use of water from storage tanks, and its transport to the pastures by motor truck now enables the nomadic hamlets to stay longer away from the home-wells in the dry seasons. It does not, however, directly influence the pattern of movement of the grazing camels for they are never watered except at the deep home-wells of the highlands and coast. Yet, on the whole, this is a factor of increasing importance in the cycle of movement, and motor transport is sometimes, though certainly not commonly, even used in place of burden camels to move the nomadic hamlets to areas of grazing.

In the spring, about April or May, movement is thus from the highlands to the Haud in the centre, and in the extreme north from the burnt coastal plain to the highlands. This distribution more or less persists, with some return from the south to the Ogo home-wells until the *dayr* rains of September or October. Then the northern lineage-groups retire to the coast. As *dayr* rapidly gives place to *jiilaal* those lineages whose home-wells are in the central highlands return from the south to them. Thus the sequence of displacements through the three zones, Guban, Ogo and Haud, corresponds to the seasonal distribution of pasturage and water in them.

In this description I have considered only how ecological and climatic factors impel movement. For Somali always discuss pastoralism in terms of the distribution of grazing and water and the primacy of these factors must be evident to anyone who has lived in northern Somaliland. Not because they are unimportant, but because they are subsidiary, I have left out of account such considerations as diseases of stock and man, the occurrence of tick-infested areas inimical to the stock, regions where after the rains malaria is seasonally prevalent, and various other factors. I have also omitted to mention the necessity to satisfy the salt requirements of live-stock. But this is rarely a problem, for where salt is not naturally present in saline grazing or in the topsoil, it can readily be obtained by trade.

While primarily dictated by the distribution of grass and water, patterns of movement also to some extent reflect social factors and particularly the character of the relations prevailing between pastoral groups. Hostility between lineages tends to force them apart, and, if the ecological conditions permit, causes them to adjust their movements so that as far as possible contact is avoided. In these circumstances kinsmen tend to concentrate in a region for mutual support and lineages become temporarily localized to a much greater degree than they are under more peaceful conditions. And often, although not always, in relation to fighting administrative direction may affect movement.

IV

Before considering the identity of a clan in relation to its home-wells and permanent settlements, and the movements of its component segments through the year, something more must be said of the activities characteristic of the different seasons. Although they divide the year into four quarters, *gu*, *ḥagaa*, *dayr*, and *jiilaal*, the pastoralists also speak of *gu* and *jiilaal* as the two halves of the year as we speak of summer and winter. Or they speak of fresh grazing (*doog*) and drought (*abaar*) as the two seasonal poles about which their lives revolve. Sometimes, again, the division is phrased in terms of grazing (*daaq*) and watering (*aroor*).

Gu is the season of joy and plenty; rain falls, grass springs up, stock bring forth their young, milk is abundant—especially the delicious camel's milk, and food is again relatively plentiful. When after good rains these conditions hold the pastoralist speaks of abundance and plenty (*bashbash iyo barwaaqo*).[1] These words are on everyone's lips, and when water, grass, and milk are everywhere abundant, men hesitate to say too much of their good fortune. It is beyond speaking of: to express too much delight is inadvisable lest God replace fortune by disaster. After a few weeks diet of camel's milk, people who in the rigours of the dry season regime had become thin and weak recover their strength and vigour. This seasonal physical change is very noticeable and parallels a similar variation in the condition of livestock. And from living on the edge of starvation and having reluctantly to sell off livestock to purchase food to keep alive, the pastoralist becomes again self-sufficient, and often has for a brief time more than enough. At this time of year few stock are sold and since milk is plentiful few beasts are killed for food except to entertain guests or for ceremonial occasions. At the same time a man has more leisure to spend at home without having to worry ceaselessly over the care and watering of his stock.

It is after the rains particularly, that lineage-group meetings and councils are called to discuss matters which have arisen during the preceding seasons and to debate future policy. Sacrifices are made by lineage-groups in honour of their founding ancestors and in praise of local saints and the great saints of the Dervish Orders. Religious activities generally increase, and are usually at their height at this time of year when food and water are plentiful. This is traditionally too, a fitting time for the coronation of a new clan Sultan when appropriate entertainment and hospitality can be provided. To some extent also this reflects a weak and not highly developed association between clan leadership in the office of Sultan and rain and prosperity which I consider in a later chapter.

In *gu*, debts incurred in the preceding seasons are settled with newly-born stock. Marriages contracted in the previous *jiilaal* or *dayr* and for which the first instalment of bride-wealth has been paid are concluded with the settlement of the remainder. For the

[1] *Bashbash* is apparently onomatopoeic for wet and luxuriant grass and vegetation. *Barwaaqo* is a combination of *bar* raindrop, and *waaq* one of the pre-Islamic Cushitic titles for God.

northern pastoralist, *gu* is the season of marriage, for the cultivators in the west, *dayr* after the harvest. Even age is reckoned in the number of *gu's* a person has passed through. Dances are frequent and young unmarried men go from settlement to settlement to look at the unmarried girls and to sing to them. Thus camel-boys herd their stock near a nomadic hamlet and serenade its girls enticing them to join in dancing. The girls reply in song, generally obliquely, for the convention is that no direct reference should be made to love. While the girls mount their own dance, the two dancing groups may intermingle but the women remain shy and bashful. And although occasionally stopped by the intervention of a pious sheikh or *wadaad*, such mixed dancing is always very restrained. For there is nothing of that easy pre-marital intercourse common in many parts of Africa. An exceedingly high value is placed on virginity in women at marriage which the Somali practice of infibulation is designed to ensure.[1] Thus while suppressed excitement at such dances may run high, it does not culminate in the girls and youths going off to sleep together. The very idea that this could follow is abhorrent to the Somali pastoralist.

The rains and the abundance of food bring leisure for talk and discussion, especially in the 'coffee-shops'—where only tea is sold[2]—of the trade villages and towns, where elders often gather when they are not otherwise occupied in the interior. The health of the stock, prospects of the season, lineage politics, Government policy, and many other topics of vital import to the pastoralist are discussed. Old injuries and insults are remembered and feuds revived, for there is more leisure to raid and to loot stock. Yet it would be contrary to the facts to suggest that in *gu* fighting is

[1] Girls are infibulated usually when they are between eight and ten years' old (and sometimes earlier), the vulva being sewn together, usually by a Midgaan woman. A portion of the clitoris is excised to make the girl clean (*ḥalaal*) in a Muslim sense. This is conducted usually individually and without much ceremonial. The aim is to prepare a girl for marriage and to safeguard her virginity until that time. The excision of part of the clitoris may be made separately at an earlier age.

[2] These are called *makhaayad* and there is at least one in every trade centre. There must be several thousand in the British Protectorate alone. Tea (*shaah*, *kaakhaawi*), is now universally drunk in northern Somaliland, but coffee, which is properly the Arabic *kaakhaawi*, is said to have been the favourite beverage before the introduction of tea from India. Tea, which has the consistency of soup, and is nutritious and sustaining, is prepared by boiling up together tea, milk, water and sugar. A great deal of sugar is used and a man will often do a day's work on a single cup of tea in the morning, waiting till the evening before eating meat and rice or grain.

more frequent than at other seasons of the year. For war and feud occur throughout the seasons, but in *gu* the link between immediate cause and immediate effect may be more distant than in the dry seasons when fighting starts from necessity to gain access to water and grazing. In the rainy seasons on the other hand, conflict tends to result from the desire, often long matured, to revenge previous wrongs and to satisfy honour and 'name', as the pastoralists put it.

The dry seasons have very different associations. *Jiilaal* particularly is lamented for the trouble and toil which it brings. In Ḍulbahante country there are proverbially twelve scourges proper to *jiilaal*, and whether or not they all apply in one season to every individual, the notion that they may indicates how the harshness of the season and the rigours of its demands on man and beast are felt as compared with *gu*. For in *jiilaal* a married man is almost always pre-occupied with the watering of both his flocks and his camels and spends little time at home with his family. The physical exertion thus involved may be heavy, and is accompanied by the constant nagging worry of finding sufficient water, and the fear that wells may dry up. Lineages moreover are often contending for sparse resources and a man's difficulties are increased when he has to time his movements between hamlet and camel-camp to avoid contact or engage in battle with hostile groups. Thus although there is little leisure for vicarious plundering or for raiding for glory only, fights are common. Indeed the pastoralists equate war and drought (*'ol iyo abaar*) and oppose these conditions to those of peace and plenty (*nabad iyo 'aano*). Quarrels over insufficient water and pasture may develop into extensive lineage-group or clan wars. Indeed in the winter of 1956 amongst the Ḍulbahante, the wooden camel-watering trough[1] was proverbially regarded as a symbol of friction and bloodshed. In one case near my camp, two men quarrelled over the use of a trough and one was shot and this provoked a minor lineage-group feud.

Under *jiilaal* conditions, previous injuries, taunts, unrequited blood-debts, and other differences are all contributory factors, which are readily touched off when men are hungry and weary and least disposed to temporise. A small incident, such as that cited, readily leads to murder and to a train of homicide in a feud between lineage-groups.

[1] *Qabaal.*

Thus in the long series of campaigns between the Habar Tol Ja'lo and Ḍulbahante from 1951–57 to which reference is made in a later chapter a typical incident occurred at Galgal in the winter of 1952. Galgal is a small watering-place in the Ain region of the east of the Protectorate and traditionally within the sphere of Ḍulbahante movement. Parties of four Ḍulbahante primary lineage-groups, converged on the wells where they met groups of the Habar Tol Ja'lo, Maḥammad Abokor, already watering at what they regarded as their wells. The Ḍulbahante were refused access, and after retiring, sent back a caravan of burden camels protected by a covering force armed with rifles. A quarrel quickly developed and a fight ensued in which nine Ḍulbahante lost their lives and three were wounded. The Habar Tol Ja'lo lost two men, and five were wounded. This

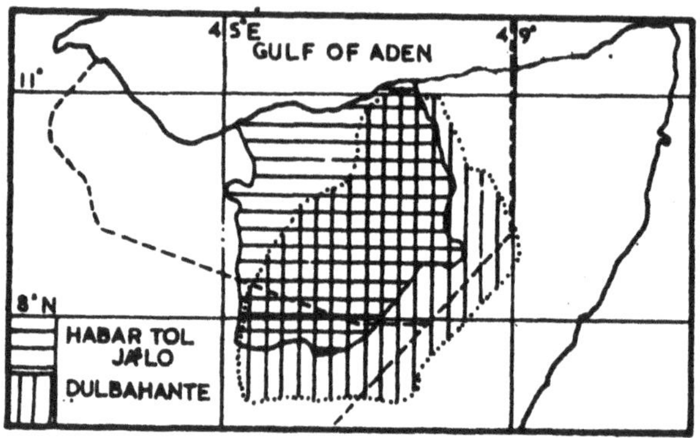

Map 3. Interpenetration of Habar Tol Ja'lo and Ḍulbahante clans.

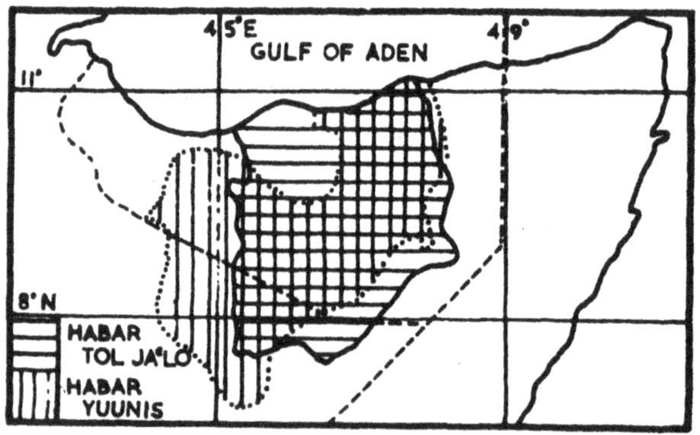

Map 4. Interpenetration of Habar Tol Ja'lo and Habar Yuunis clans.

dispute was temporarily patched up by government intervention but soon led to a further series of battles.[1]

This is a very brief characterization of what the different seasons mean in the social life of the pastoralists as they move with their livestock through the year.

V

The main areas of movement of those northern clans with which we are most concerned have already been shown. In the yearly cycle, most clans have a fairly regular pattern of movement. In the dry seasons, they are concentrated near their home-wells over which they have primary rights but which, where water is abundant and relations friendly, they may share with lineages of other clans. Thus in the dry seasons lineage-groups are normally at their minimum extension and densest concentration. At the same time, corresponding to their different water requirements, the separation between the grazing camels and hamlets with the flocks, is most marked. But after the rains, when the grass is green, agnates are widely deployed in the pastures, where they meet, and in the absence of hostilities, mingle with members of other clans.

It has already been observed that generally only at the level of the clan is there some degree of association between people and a particular stretch of territory. From the total annual movement of component lineages, the general seasonal distribution of a clan—at least between its maximum and minimum extension—can be plotted. Thus some indication of the range of annual movement of the Habar Tol Ja'lo and Ḍulbahante clans, and of the Habar Tol Ja'lo and Habar Yuunis is shown on page 46. And some idea of the character of movements at a lower level of segmentation—that of the primary lineage-group—may be gained from the sketch maps on pages 48-54. These show the main areas of densest concentration of three Ḍulbahante lineages in Las Anod District over the period April 1952 to March 1953. The maps are drawn from District Office records and give necessarily only a very approximate outline of the actual distribution. For it must be remembered that out of a large number of lineages

[1] A Habar Tol Ja'lo account of the cause of the Galgal incident, however, runs as follows. When a Habar Ja'lo caravan approached the wells to draw water it was refused access by the Ḍulbahante, but since the Habar Ja'lo were superior in strength they disregarded the Ḍulbahante and began to draw water. The latter then summoned reinforcements and a fight began.

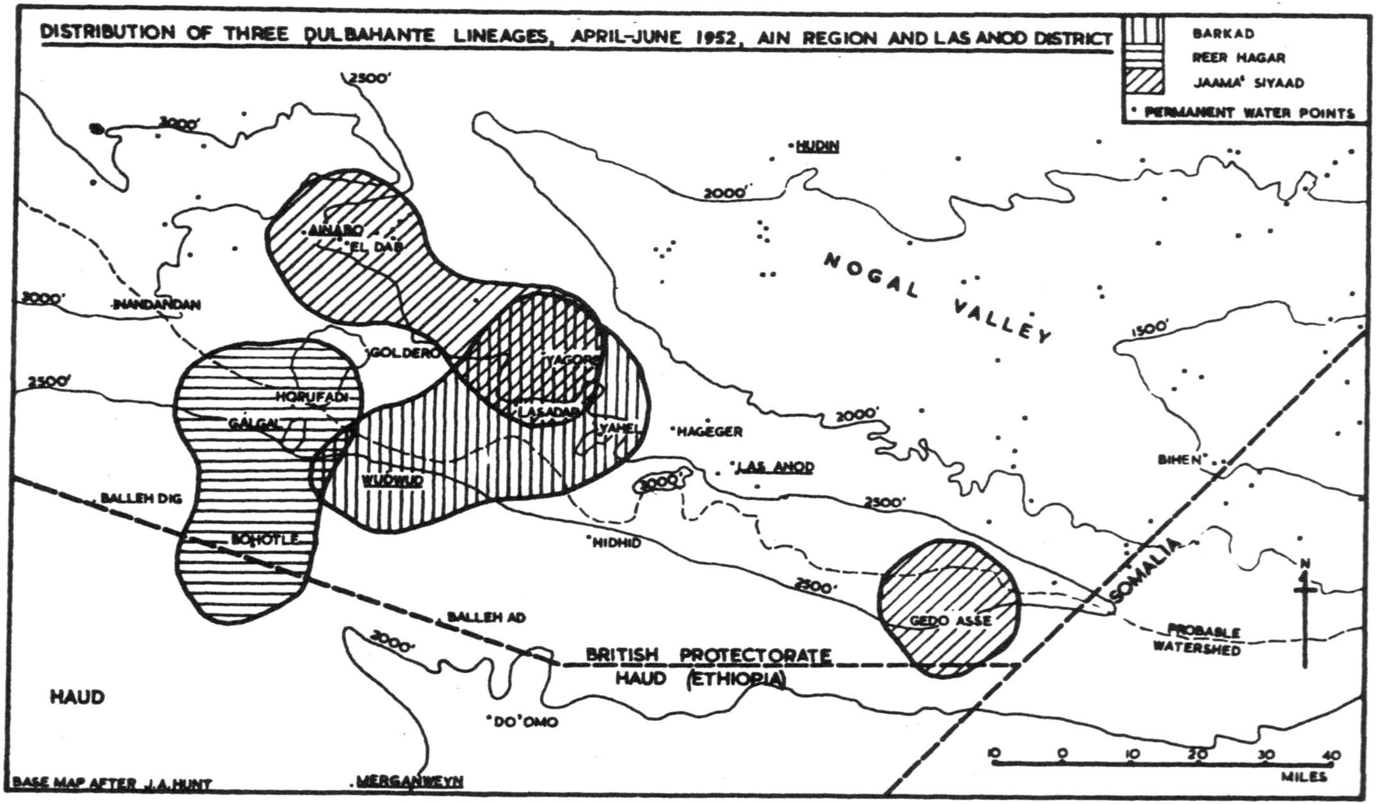

DISTRIBUTION OF THREE DULBAHANTE LINEAGES, APRIL–JUNE 1952, AIN REGION AND LAS ANOD DISTRICT
BARKAD
REER HAGAR
JAAMA' SIYAAD
PERMANENT WATER POINTS
NOGAL VALLEY
HUDIN
AINABO
EL DAB
INANDANDAN
GOLDERO
YAGORI
LASADAR
YAMEL
HAGEGER
LAS ANOD
HORUFADI
GALGAL
WUDWUD
BALLEH DIG
BOHOTLE
HIDHID
BIHEN
SOMALIA
GEDO ASSE
PROBABLE WATERSHED
BALLEH AD
BRITISH PROTECTORATE
HAUD (ETHIOPIA)
HAUD
DO'OMO
MERGANWEYN
MILES
BASE MAP AFTER J.A. HUNT

Map 5

of the same and different clans in this general area, the movements of the three Ḍulbahante lineages shown have been selected and others disregarded. So that areas on the maps shown as unoccupied were in fact being pastured by the livestock of other lineages. Moreover, information on the movements of the same lineages in the following year (1953-54) showed an entirely different pattern of distribution, although within the same general area.

In the area pastured by its livestock no clan or lineage has a specific title to grazing backed by ritual or mystical sanctions. Pasture is not subject to ownership but the right to graze in an area depends upon its effective occupancy. For ultimately, the final justification for remaining in a region of pasturage is the power to repulse invaders by force. Thus God provides pasture and man uses it. Wells, on the other hand, except where water is extremely plentiful and easy of access, are not only used by man, but also opened and maintained by him. By their labours specific watering rights are conferred on the individuals and groups who initially dig and subsequently keep them in repair. Thus in all cases of contested ownership, claimants lay stress upon the energy, labour, and expense involved in their construction. And when not in use wells which are the sole property of individuals or groups are usually covered over, marked with a lineage brand (such as that used for camels), and often also surrounded with a thorn fence. Thus titles to water are established and made known to all. Yet despite their existance and wide recognition, in the last resort such specific rights to water can only be upheld by force of arms.

As fixed points, the wells to some extent define the loci of pastoral movement and, like anchors, limit any entirely irregular nomadic distribution. Yet to describe the northern pastoral Somali as transhumant would be to imply a much more regular and restricted pattern of movement than they in fact exhibit. In these circumstances it is perhaps best to speak of restricted nomadism, although such a term conveys little of the dynamic character of pastoral Somali life.

While pasture is thus not owned, and clans do not occupy determinate territories at all seasons of the year, usage backed by effective fighting potential, and now administrative recognition creates some degree of customary association with particular areas. And this is most rigidly defined through the rights which attach to home-wells, and to villages and towns, where some

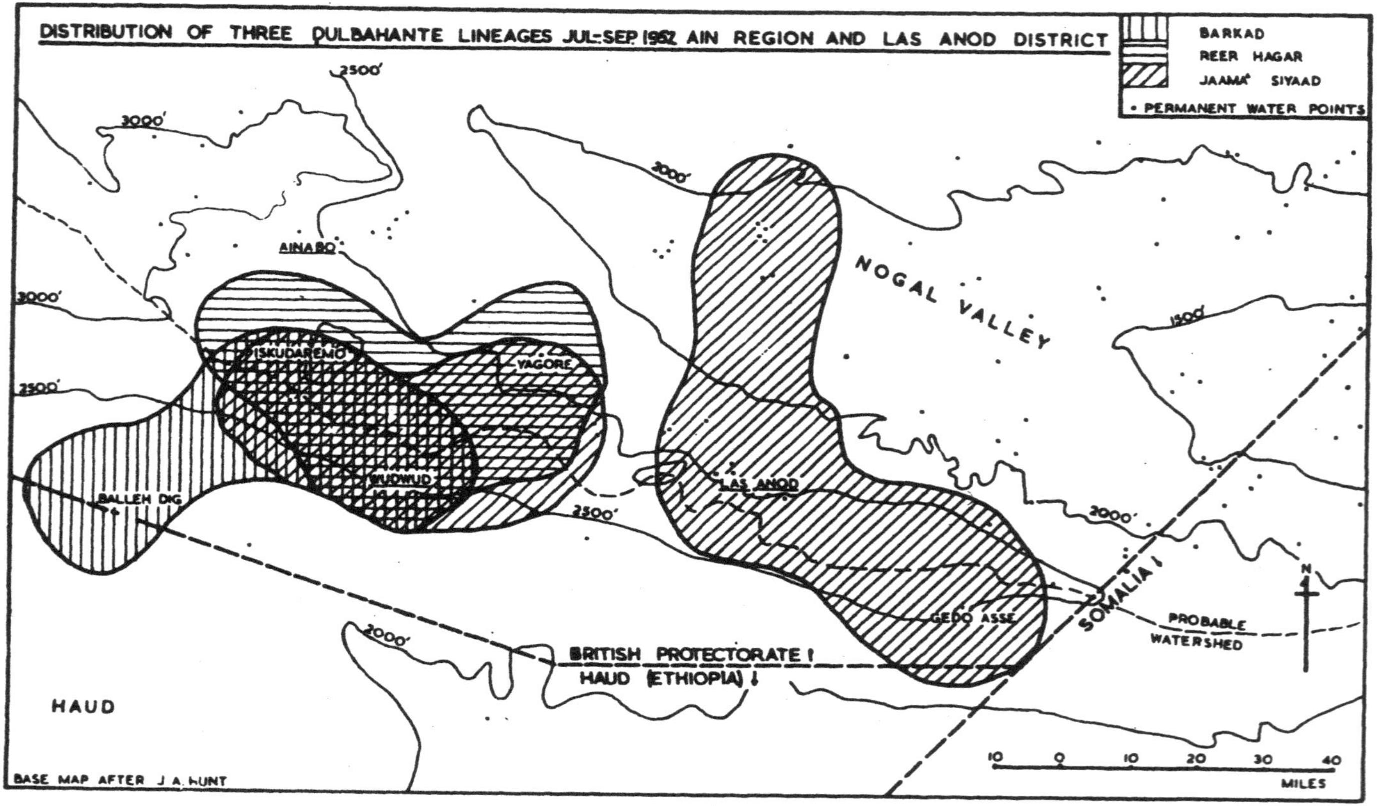

DISTRIBUTION OF THREE DULBAHANTE LINEAGES JUL-SEP 1962 AIN REGION AND LAS ANOD DISTRICT
BARKAD
REER HAGAR
JAAMA' SIYAAD
• PERMANENT WATER POINTS
2500'
3000'
2000'
AINABO
3000'
NOGAL VALLEY
1500'
2500'
ISKUDAREMO
YAGORE
WUDWUD
BALLEH DIG
LAS ANOD
2500'
2000'
GEDO ASSE
SOMALIA
PROBABLE WATERSHED
N
2000'
BRITISH PROTECTORATE
HAUD (ETHIOPIA)
HAUD
10 0 10 20 30 40
MILES
BASE MAP AFTER J. A. HUNT

Map 6

members of any clan are more or less permanently settled. So that in relation to wells and places of permanent settlement there is some, though ill-developed, sense of territorial extension. But claims that customary usage has established boundaries to pasturage, are almost always only brought forward in times of scarcity and famine, and when one clan is pressing upon another. Yet it may well be true, as Somali often maintain, that in the past prior to European administration the territories of clans were more distinct in their definition than they are today. For the blurring of frontiers, and the degree of interpenetration in the pastures, which is characteristic today, are viewed by some as the consequence of increased competition for ever shrinking resources. Thus under pressure from the Habar Tol Ja'lo expanding to their north, the Ḍulbahante claim that formerly their north-western boundary was the Sarar Plain now grazed mainly by Habar Tol Ja'lo. And there is good evidence that they have in fact been forced to move south. Those Ḍulbahante lineages which formerly grazed in the Ain region and which were accordingly called *Reer 'Aymeed* today pasture their stock mainly in the scrub-lands of the northern Haud where they are known as 'people of the bush' (*Reer Oodeed*). This migration illustrates the primacy of force, and the fact that usage only establishes an effective association with territory where it can be maintained by political and military supremacy.

In this connexion the attitudes of clans and lineages towards the British Protectorate Government's scheme to establish grazing reserves are revealing. The intention, which has already been implemented in a few areas, is to close regions of pasturage for several seasons to allow badly overgrazed land to regenerate and to further soil conservation and anti-erosion measures. The clans concerned viewed the scheme as a means by which they might be able to secure definite grazing rights sanctioned by Government. And to the extent to which they saw it as a possible means of securing boundaries against the incursion of rival clans, they were enthusiastic. But where it meant acknowledging the common grazing rights of other clans they were less in favour of it.

It is necessary thus to emphasize that although settlements and home-wells give some definition to clan extension and to the distribution of smaller lineage-groups within the clan, they do not establish an absolute localization. The nature of the country, the lack of rain and pasture, and the fitfulness of the seasons, all pre-

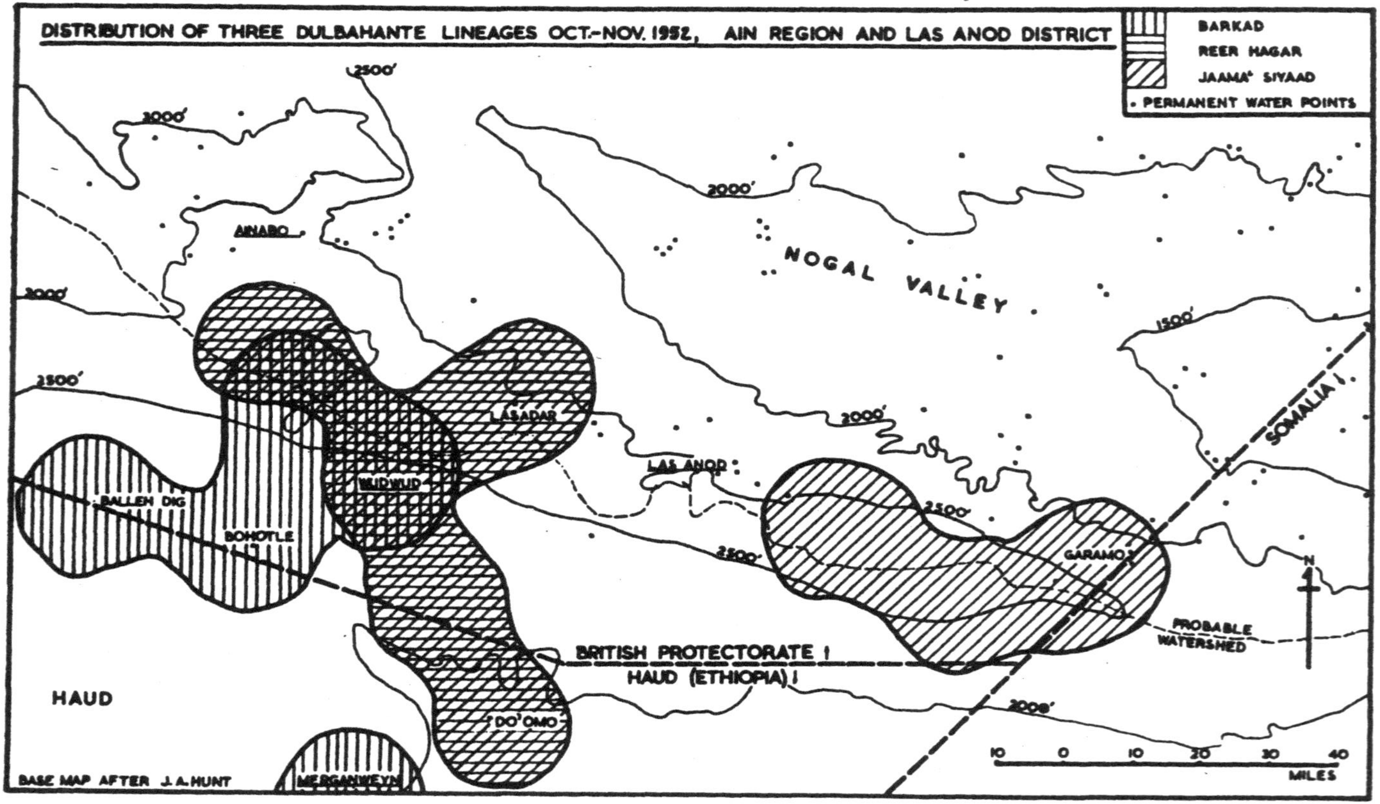

DISTRIBUTION OF THREE DULBAHANTE LINEAGES OCT.-NOV. 1952, AIN REGION AND LAS ANOD DISTRICT

BARKAD
REER HAGAR
JAAMA' SIYAAD
PERMANENT WATER POINTS

2500'
3000'
2000'
AINABO
NOGAL VALLEY
1500'
2000'
2500'
LASADAR
LAS ANOD
WUDWUD
BALLEH DIG
BOHOTLE
2500'
2500'
GARAMO
SOMALIA
PROBABLE WATERSHED
BRITISH PROTECTORATE
HAUD (ETHIOPIA)
HAUD
DO'OMO
2000'
MERGANWEYN
10 0 10 20 30 40
MILES
BASE MAP AFTER J. A. HUNT

Map 7

clude any absolute definition of this kind. Nor is the composition of any town or village unchangingly constant over the years. And settlements also move. The dust tracks which serve as roads and which spring up in new directions every few years, are a testimony to the amorphous and changing character of movement in response to the distribution of water and grazing. With new displacements, advances and withdrawals, well ownership changes, and wells also dry up and may be abandoned. This is particularly true of the shallow seasonal wells of the northern Haud.

At Wudwud, for example, a seasonally flooded basin and watering place for sheep and goats in the northern Haud, there is a large cluster of wells mainly individually owned. Traditionally these were first dug by the 'Ali Geri primary lineage of the Ḍulbahante clan. As other groups of the Ḍulbahante *Reer Oodeed* came in force to water in the region, the 'Ali Geri turned to water further north in the region of Lasadar where water is more abundant. Today few 'Ali Geri regularly water at Wudwud and the wells, of which there are probably over a hundred, are mainly used by the Barkad, Jaama' Siyaad, Yaḥye, Reer Hagar, and Hayaag—all primary lineages of the Ḍulbahante.

To seasonal wells of this kind dug and maintained by individuals, most men have titles in many and widely scattered areas. Thus the pastoralist of the Haud and highlands has often a title to twenty or more wells of this type. By this arrangement a high degree of freedom of movement and a wide choice of pasture are possible.

Corresponding to the greater work involved in their opening, maintenance and use, rights to the deeper home-wells in the highlands are tied to agnation. They are usually those wells in which the members of a primary lineage-group and rarely, dia-paying group have primary rights. But, their use is often extended to members of the same clan and sometimes to members of different clans. This frequently means the purchase of water by people of clans or lineage-groups other than those who hold the titles to the wells, and in some cases, regular contracts are made between groups to allow watering. For all these reasons, the home-wells cannot be regarded as points of absolute localization in the dry season distribution of clans.[1] While they are, relatively speaking

[1] 'The home-wells of the British Protectorate have been carefully mapped by Mr J. A. Hunt, a geologist and administrative officer with a long experience of northern pastoralism. Mr Hunt has also recorded all the main seasonal movements of the northern clans over the period 1944–50. See his *A General Survey of the Somaliland Protectorate, 1944–50*, 1951, Map No. 41, and pp. 160—67.

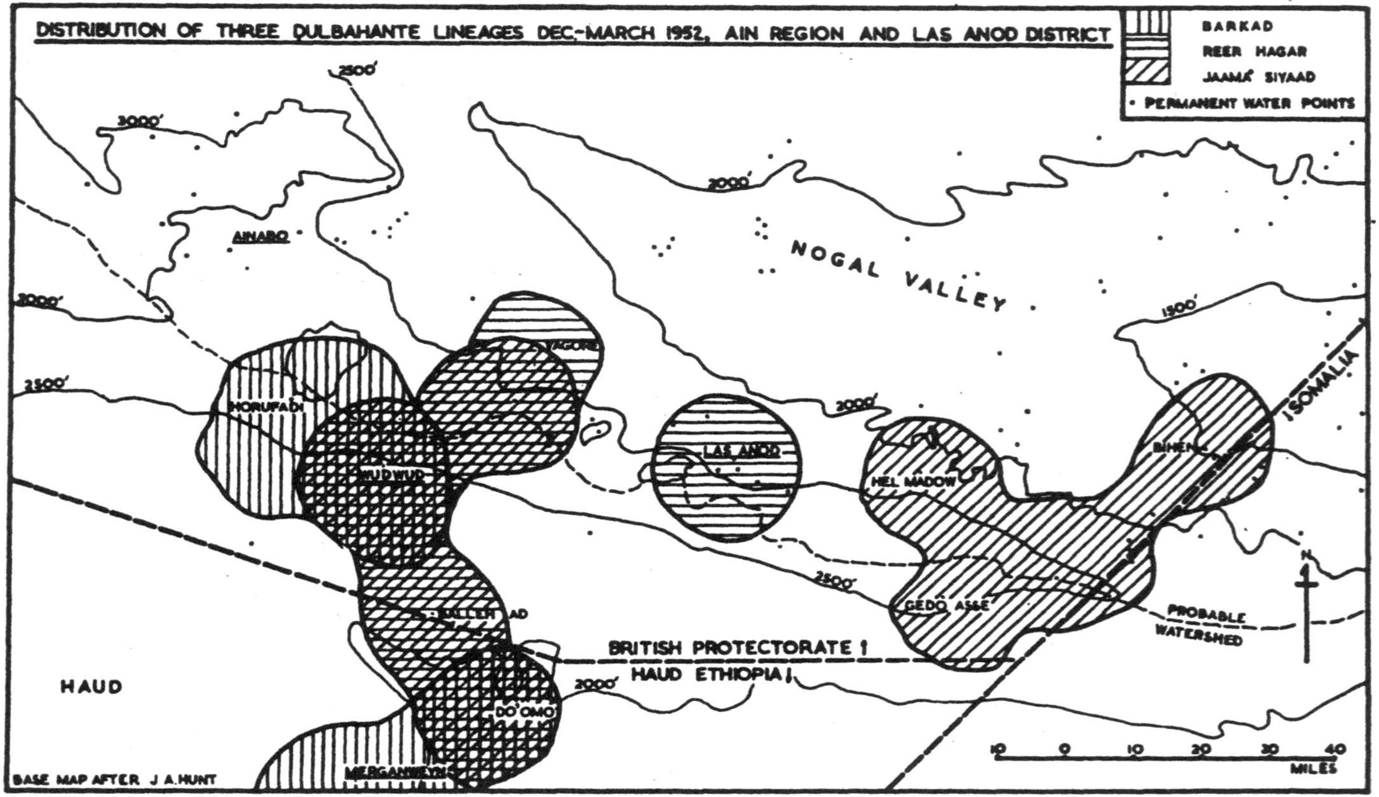

DISTRIBUTION OF THREE DULBAHANTE LINEAGES DEC.-MARCH 1952, AIN REGION AND LAS ANOD DISTRICT

BARKAD
REER HAGAR
JAAMA' SIYAAD
• PERMANENT WATER POINTS

NOGAL VALLEY
AINABO
LAS ANOD
HEL MADOW
GEDO ASSE
BIHEN
HORUFADI
WUDWUD
DO'OMO
MERGANWEYN
BRITISH PROTECTORATE
HAUD ETHIOPIA
PROBABLE WATERSHED
ISOMALIA
HAUD
3000'
2500'
2000'
1500'
10 0 10 20 30 40
MILES
BASE MAP AFTER J. A. HUNT

Map 8

fixed points in movement giving some definition to the seasonal cycle of displacements over the pastures, they continue to exercise this function only as long as there is not a general, but not necessarily irrevocable, clan movement away from them. Above all by spreading their titles to wells, clans and smaller groups, achieve the maximum utilization of their sparse resources within the general field of movement of other groups. This situation is explicable only in terms of ecological factors.

3

Pastoralism and the structure of Grazing Encampments

If clans and larger lineage-groups are fairly regular in their displacements through the seasons from year to year, the same cannot be said of the nomadic hamlets and camel-camps which are the basic units of movement. The apparent regularity at the level of the clan is thus only a generalization from the more irregular pattern of movement of its component units. That movement at one level appears different in character to that at another may seem paradoxical, but it is, after all, only a matter of the various levels of abstraction which we adopt in description.

With its flocks of sheep and goats, the nuclear family is called *ḥaas*. This term connotes weakness: it refers to the demanding water requirements of the flocks, and to the fact that the family consisting of a mother and her young children is primarily thought of as a group particularly vulnerable to the exigencies of the climate. The word *raas* is also used. This expression refers to the internal perimeter at the base of the nomadic hut and denotes the nuclear family as a group living in, and moving with, the nomadic hut (*aqal*). Each married woman, periodically accompanied by her husband, moves with the hut and burden camels necessary for its transport. Ideally two or three camels are sufficient for the transport of the nuclear family, the hut, and all its effects. Not every family, however, possesses enough burden camels to move it comfortably. And in these circumstances, close agnates generally, and cognates and affines, share camels when required to do so.

The loading and un-loading of the camels, and the erection and dismantling of the nomadic hut with its curved wooden supports and grass and skin coverings, are women's work. In these tasks a wife is assisted by other women—as well as her daughters—who happen to move with her. And although all this is strictly the province of women, when haste is called for, men do not hesitate to lend a hand.

The management of the sheep and goats which a husband

DISTRIBUTION OF LIVESTOCK

A. Nomadic Ḍulbahante

	No. of Wives	*Camels*	*Sheep and goats*	*Cattle*	*Gardens*
1.	2	6	60	—	—
2.	3	108	430	30	—
3.	2	36	200	—	—
4.	1	24	120	—	—
5.	4	200	1,400	20	—
6.	2	84	300	—	—
7.	2	35	160	—	—
8.	2	126	180	14	—
9.	1	40	150	—	—
10.	2	60	250	—	—
11.	1	44	200	—	—
12.	4	40	300	—	—
13.	3	55	160	—	—
14.	2	60	150	—	—
15.	3	100	1,000	—	—
16.	2	100	200	—	—
17.	1	40	120	—	—
18.	2	500	1,100	—	—
19.	2	500	1,100	—	—
20.	2	50	100	—	—
21.	1	24	100	—	—
22.	1	60	60	—	—
23.	1	20	50	—	—
24.	2	300	1,100	—	—
25.	2	14	50	—	—
26.	2	80	600	—	—
27.	3	60	120	—	—

B. Nomadic 'Iise

	No. of Wives	*Camels*	*Sheep and goats*	*Cattle*	*Gardens*
28.	3	20	400	—	—
29.	1	4	—	—	—
30.	4	170	400	200	—
31.	2	11	120	—	—
32.	1	12	120	—	—
33.	1	4	50	—	—
34.	4	20	400	10	—
35.	3	15	470	—	—
36.	2	25	360	—	—

allots to each wife, for her own and her children's sustenance, is largely in her hands. Here a married woman is assisted by unmarried daughters still living at home, and sons too young to be out with the grazing camels. Yet, although this is essentially women's work, and men often affect disinterest in the numbers and health of their flocks, these are their property over which they have primary rights of possession and disposal. To this stock attached to the nuclear family may be added a few milch camels from the main herds. And especially after the rains when the grazing is good and the camels have recently calved, many nomadic hamlets have milch beasts (*geel guri*) with them. The size of the flocks of sheep and goats naturally varies with the wealth of the husband, as in a general way, do the number of his wives. The unit adopted in enumerating them is the *tiro*, a flock of about a hundred head of stock. Both sheep and goats are penned and herded together.

From the figures shown in the table it appears that a wife and young family of four or five children require a flock of at least fifty to sixty head. For rarely more than half any flock are in milk at the same time. And at the end of the dry seasons, before the onset of the anxiously awaited rains, milk is usually very scarce and many a family hard put to survive.

The flocks are milked in the early morning, then let out to browse close to the hamlet under the watchful eyes of girls, and occasionally small boys too young to be with the camels. Girls as they tend the flocks, busily work bark fibre into rope, sit chatting in the shade, or play with friends.[1] At dusk as Venus appears in the sky, the flocks are led into the pens, counted and then milked by the women and children.[2]

In the eastern Haud at the beginning of the dry season, sheep and goats water at shallow wells. Here the work entailed requires less co-operation than that involved in the more arduous watering of the camels from deep wells. For it is largely a family matter in which a man and his wife, or wives, brothers, and more rarely close agnates, help each other. Yet although the assistance of a large number of kinsmen is not necessary, the actual labour may be considerable. I have been present at shallow wells in the

[1] The shepherd or shepherdess is called *aḍijir*—from *aḍi*, sheep and goats, and *jir* to stay with.

[2] From this association with the penning of the sheep and goats in the evening, Venus is called *maqal ḥiḍḥiḍ*; from *maqal* lambs and kids, and *ḥiḍ*, to shut in, or enclose.

northern Haud when it took four days to water a hundred sheep and goats in small groups, and the wells had to be dug by day and by night to yield water. The digging is done by men while the women drive the flocks up to the wells and supervise the animals as they drink from wooden troughs, metal basins, and other receptacles.

Although men exhalt the husbandry of camels above that of sheep and goats leaving much of the care of the latter to their women-folk, the management of the flocks is in some ways more exacting than camel-herding. In the dry seasons, the sheep and goats have to remain within a radius of a few miles from water. And at their height, the nomadic hamlets are normally even closer to permanent water than this, but the grass round the wells is usually severely over-grazed. The problem is therefore to find adequate pasturage and at the same time to keep within striking distance of water. Often a choice has to be made between passable grass but fairly distant water, and poor and virtually non-existent grazing with water close at hand. Only rarely in the dry seasons can both be found in the same place in sufficient quantities.

The nuclear family moves with its sheep and goats, burden camels, and milch camels and cattle, if any, setting up camp in nomadic hamlets where water resources and pasture permit. The hamlet comprises a variable number of nuclear families—but rarely more than four in peace-time. The huts are arranged within a common thorn fence (*ood*), divided into internal compartments in which the stock are penned at night. The following table indicates the numbers of nuclear families in hamlets based

Number of huts per hamlet	Number of hamlets
1	5
2	14
3	16
4	17
5	3
6	3
Total Hamlets	58
Total Huts	182

Median number of huts in a hamlet 2.6

on an analysis of three grazing settlements to which reference is made below.

Each wife has generally a separate pen for her stock, although sometimes the flocks of co-wives are penned together. But more commonly, where a widowed mother lives in the same hamlet with her son or married daughter, her sheep and goats are placed in the same pen with those of her children. And sometimes the flocks of the wives of two brothers living in the same hamlet share a common pen.

II

As a social unit the hamlet is called *reer*, and in its physical aspects as a structure of huts and fences is known as *guri*. The word *reer* denotes a social group, or even people in general, and is also the general expression for a lineage as I shall show in a later chapter. Each married woman or widow has her own hut (*aqal*)[1] and usually, flock of sheep and goats. As a social unit, and particularly as a domestic group, the hamlet has no formally installed leader. In the discussion of types of hamlet structure which follows it will be seen that the basis of every hamlet is a nucleus of close male agnates, often brothers, or an extended family. But the smallest hamlet is made up of a nuclear or polygynous family. Every adult free-born male speaks in council and the effective leadership of the hamlet depends upon its kinship structure. Where the hamlet has a permanent composition and is not merely as sometimes a temporary grouping of kinsmen it is led by the eldest agnate of most forceful character and personality. This informal position of leadership is most clear-cut when the hamlet consists of one nuclear or polygynous family or of an extended family under the authority of the father. It is least definite where the hamlet consists of a group of close agnates, but not brothers, and it is here particularly that force of character, ability, and general qualities of leadership cause one man's counsels to prevail over those of his peers. The emphasis placed on seniority in age and on experience is evident in the title given to the man who in any particular hamlet tends to direct its affairs. Whatever its kinship composition, its leader is always referred to

[1] Amongst the eastern Ḍulbahante the word *qoys* is used to designate a single house. So that to ascertain the number of nuclear families in a particular hamlet one asks the number of *qoys*.

as 'elder', or 'old-man' (*oday*), as in the expression 'elder of the hamlet' (*odayga reerka*).

Thus constituted as essentially a domestic group of a man with his wife or wives, with his father and brothers and their families, or only the latter, or more frequently of close agnates within the dia-paying group with their families, the hamlet is itself an unstable unit. Here I do not only refer to those changes in social alignment which correspond to different phases in the progress of a man from birth to death. The 'developmental cycle'[1] is not alone responsible for all the variations in hamlet structure, and does not automatically produce a regular series of changes in hamlet composition as a man progresses from youth to death. For all men do not leave the hamlet of their father when they marry, nor do all brothers separate on their father's death. And quite independently of changes in hamlet attachment occasioned by marriage or death within a developmental sequence, the composition of hamlets is constantly altering. At one time a man's several wives may be in the same hamlet, at another the husband may decide to separate them and they may move as independent and widely dispersed units. Again men attach their families now to one group of close kin, and now to another. A man may reside with a particular full or half-brother on one occasion and with another at a different time. Moreover while several agnates of the same dia-paying group may choose to move together for a time, at another time they may choose to separate and move with others. Here personal relations and preferences, and changing qualities in individual relationships are just as important as any regular sequence of residence patterns corresponding to changes in status in an individual's life. Thus the composition of hamlets fluctuates partly in accordance with domestic affairs, individual convenience and preference, and lineage-group politics. The female kin of a man's wives come to visit and temporarily attach themselves to his hamlet. A widowed mother, or father, moves amongst the hamlets of married sons. When, therefore, in a later section of this chapter I refer to 'types' of hamlet constitution I wish only to give the reader some indication of the kinds of kin who commonly move together as a domestic group. No greater definition than this is intended. Nevertheless, as a social unit

[1] Cf. Fortes, *The Web of Kinship among the Tallensi*, O.U.P. London, 1949, pp. 63–77; and in *The Developmental Cycle in Domestic Groups*, ed. J. Goody, Cambridge, 1958, pp. 1–15.

with a particular configuration of kin the hamlet has generally much greater identity than the temporary settlements of hamlets which form in an area of pasture.

Although each nuclear family is largely independent economically of others moving with it in the same hamlet, there is considerable over-lapping of duties particularly in the care of stock, and, when food is scarce, sharing of resources. Burden camels are commonly shared in movement, and in fetching water and provisions. And in the watering of the flocks, members of the same hamlet help each other. Thus, although not so close-knit a body as the nuclear family the hamlet has a certain identity and economic exclusiveness in relation to other hamlets and larger units. In contrast there is little co-operation of this kind in the grazing settlement. Its stability is largely a function of the local grazing and water available. Dissociation into its component hamlets moving to new pastures follows reports of rain and better grazing elsewhere. And in the dry seasons, unless when concentrated round the wells, a settlement's life is apt to be especially short. For the exhaustion of pasturage soon forces some groups to move off in search of better grazing. Thus save in time of war the settlement does not generally move as a unit. More typically individual families and hamlets, and sometimes groups of hamlets, move to the areas where their scouts have reported water and grass to be plentiful.

A day's march (*geedi,* the word is also applied to a group on the move), twelve to twenty miles or so, starts at dawn, or earlier. The huts are dismantled and loaded with the other baggage on the burden camels while it is still dark. Men walk beside or lead the camels which are not ridden. Only rarely is a wounded person or cripple seen mounted on a camel. Unless there is particular cause for haste, a halt is called as the heat increases to its maximum about mid-day. And if, for some special reason, it is necessary to move further the same day, the march is resumed about three o'clock and continued until dusk. When attack is feared, movement by night is often favoured. The seasonal return from the pastures to the wells entails several halts. These allow the stock to be watered—water may have to be brought by camel—and to recover strength by browsing on what grass is available. At the same time supplies of food—such as rice, dates, sugar, and tea are replenished. And in addition to providing for the family and flocks, the men must also attend to the watering of their grazing camels. For men from the hamlets have to go to to the wells to prepare for the arrival of the camels and stay to see to their watering. As the groups withdraw from the pastures the advance is made in stages. Thus for example, in February 1956, parties of the Barkad who from the previous spring had been grazing their stock near the Anglo-Ethiopian boundary in the north-eastern Haud, moved back some sixty miles northwards to their home-wells in three stages. At each halt they stopped for several days.

The settlement, or encampment of hamlets, is known as *degmo* from the verb *deg*, to settle or pitch camp. Its size and permanence are usually directly related to the amount of grazing present, and in the dry seasons to the availability of water. For these are the two necessities for settlement and for which there are no substitutes. Except during fighting, settlements as large as a hundred hamlets are very rare, even where the pasturage is lush. Those that I camped amongst rarely exceeded fifty hamlets in number, and most were smaller. Often some thirty hamlets settled temporarily in one region occupy an area of about twenty square miles with a density of over twenty persons per square mile.[1] And within a general area of settlement the distance between individual hamlets varies from a few hundred yards to a mile or so. In time of peace settlements themselves are spaced largely in relation to the distribution and density of pasturage. Since local rain produces widely scattered grazing, settlements of the same clan may be as many as, or more than, twenty miles apart. But wherever pasture and water permit, isolated hamlets occur between the main encampments.

To illustrate how where they settle hamlets are grouped by lineage affiliation, I describe a typical settlement in which I camped at Haradig in Ḍulbahante country.[2] This encampment had the structure shown for only three weeks. It then split up bit by bit, component hamlets moving elsewhere in search of better grazing. The season was March 1956, at the end of *jiilaal* in the short hot period

[1] From the estimate of the total population of the British Protectorate the overall density is ten persons per square mile. For French Somaliland the figure is eight; for Somalia eight; for Libya three; for Algeria ten; and for the Sudan eleven. Although the figure calculated for the British Protectorate as a whole may give some indication of the carrying capacity (in Mijerteinia in the north of Somalia, the density is less than two per square mile), it gives a very inaccurate image of the distribution of the people over the land. Large tracts of country are frequently deserted, at least in some seasons, and where people are temporarily encamped their concentration is as shown much greater.

[2] 'Haraḍiig', lit. 'the pools of blood', referring to a battle which took place here between the insurgent army of Sheikh Maḥammad 'Abdille Ḥasan and British forces. Haraḍiig lies to the east of Ainabo.

which precedes the onset of the spring rains. Rain had actually been seen falling to the south and this prompted people to move off in pursuit of it. The hamlets were concentrated round the two deep wells of Haradig where parties of camels from the far southern pastures were watering at regular intervals. The map shows the distribution of hamlets by primary lineage-groups. Of the twenty-eight in the area, seventeen were Jaama' Siyaad, one Jaama' Siyaad and Barkad, five Barkad, four Yaḥye and two Hawiye Reer Fiqi Shinni. The Hawiye Fiqi Shinni live with the Ḍulbahante but remain genealogically and structurally distinct from them. In their external relations they identify themselves with the Ḍulbahante; amongst the Ḍulbahante they are structurally equivalent to a primary lineage-group such as the Barkad. But no attempt is made to postulate common agnatic descent with their stronger Ḍulbahante hosts. The relationships of the three Ḍulbahante primary lineage-groups are shown in the genealogy at the end of the book.

From the distribution of hamlets shown it will be plain that within the orbit of movement of a clan there is a marked tendency for men of the same primary lineage-group to camp together where they settle temporarily in the pastures. Similar patterns of settlement are found in every encampment. And when threatened by hostile groups, lineages are even more clearly localized and more densely concentrated. Thus earlier in the same winter when the Habar Tol Ja'lo and Habar Yuunis were at war and parties of both clans were grazing their stock in the Haud, their settlements were sharply demarcated. Tension ran high and a gap of land was left unoccupied between their rival encampments.

It is only under such conditions of hostilities that a settlement of nomadic hamlets acts as a determinate corporate group. And it does so not because the grazing encampment of itself generates a sense of territorial unity, but because its members are agnates. It is kinship, not vicinage, which gives groups unity and cohesion.

Where war and feud are absent a settlement has little corporate identity. It is simply one particular, transitory configuration of kinsmen with their flocks in the pastures. An encampment is no more than a place of temporary human habitation in the unoccupied plains or desert. The constituent hamlets are separate herding units and there is no appointed leader for the settlement as a whole. Within it, the distribution of nomadic hamlets by primary lineage-group is congruent with the solidarity of the primary lineage-group in other respects, particularly in the

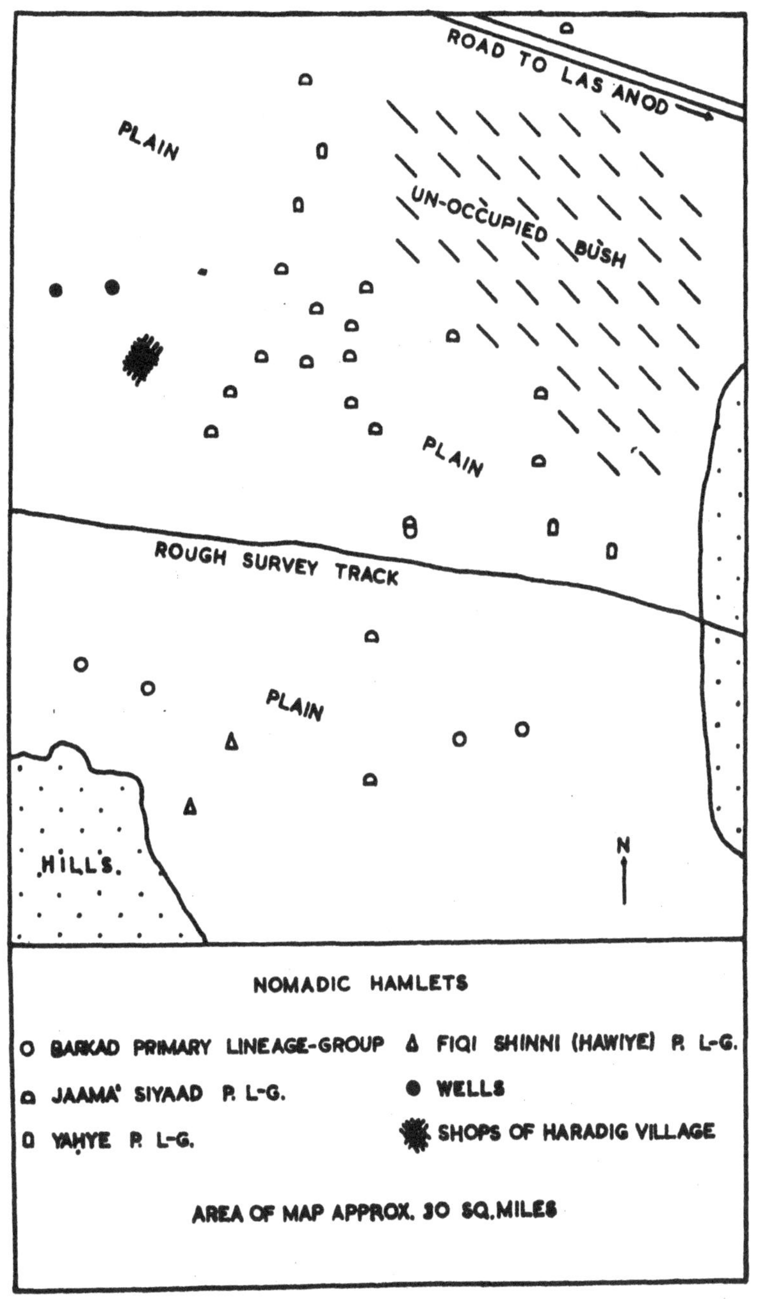

Map 9. Distribution of nomadic hamlets in Haradig region, March, 1956.

watering of camels from wells in the dry seasons. And except when lineages are localized in time of war all the members of a lineage are never concentrated in one single settlement but widely deployed in the pastures with their stock. Even those of the same dia-paying group are often distributed widely in different areas and ephemeral encampments within the general area occupied by a clan.

III

Having shown how agnates of the same primary lineage place their hamlets together where they settle temporarily in a region of pasturage we now examine the kinship structure of component hamlets. The information in the table is drawn from Haradig settlement and from two other typical nomadic Ḍulbahante

	Hamlets whose male members are agnates	
A.	Man, with or without widowed mother (or wife's mother) and with wife or wives.	16
B.	Extended family of brothers, with or without father.	8
C.	Kinsmen, other than brothers, of the same dia-paying group.	15
	Total agnatically structured hamlets.	39
	Hamlets including affines or cognates.	
D.	Affines living with nucleus of single or extended family.	7
E.	Affines living with nucleus of agnates within the dia-paying group.	6
F.	Other relationships.	5
	Total hamlets whose male members are not all agnatically related.	18
	Total hamlets 57	

encampments. The kinship ties shown are those which link the male heads of nuclear families in the hamlets. In some cases, a few of which are quoted below, wives are also kin so that the unity of the hamlet founded on the agnatic connexion of its male members is reinforced by links through women.

This small sample illustrates the degree of variation in the kinship composition of the nomadic hamlet. The commonest arrangement is of a man with his wife or wives (28% in the sample). Also of frequent occurence are those hamlets which consist of male agnates of the same dia-paying group with their spouses (26% in the sample). The extended family, a restricted agnatic grouping within the dia-paying group, has a lower incidence (14%). As the figures show there is a fairly high incidence of hamlets including affinally and other non-agnatically related men (31.6%), as against 68.4% with an entirely agnatic composition. Within this second class of hamlet structures the same trends exhibited by the first group of agnatically organized hamlets are evident. For here the commonest patterns of grouping are those in which affines live attached to a single or extended family nucleus, or to a nucleus of men of the same dia-paying group. The patterns of hamlet composition contained in the sample are illustrated in the following examples.

A

I take first the case of a man living with his wife or wives and their children.[1] In a Ḍulbahante encampment at Hidhid (Las Anod District) in January 1956, one hamlet was led by a man of the Barkad lineage, Reer 'Ali Shirwa'. There were two huts, one occupied by his wife of the Hawiye Reer Fiqi Shinni, and the other by his widọwed mother, of the Ogaadeen clan (Daarood). The sheep and goats of the two women were in the same pen and the hamlet had four burden camels.

B

As an example of a hamlet occupied by an extended family I quote that of two brothers of the Reer Faaraḥ Hagar who shared the same settlement at Hidhid. Each brother is the son of a different mother[2] and the elder (A), leads the hamlet. His wife is of the Ḍulbahante Khayr 'Abdi primary lineage-group.

[1] Where the several wives of a man are grouped in one hamlet the hut of the first married (the 'big house' *minweyn*) is usually immediately to the right of the main entrance to the kraal as one enters it.

[2] Siblings by different mothers are referred to as *waa is ku aabbe, waana kala hooyo* ('of the same father but different mother').

The wife of the second brother (B) is of the Ḍulbahante Hayaag. Both the mothers (C and D) live with the two sons, and each pens her flock with the sheep and goats of her son. Each mother has a separate hut (*buul*—the small hut of a widow).[1]

C

Of the common hamlet structure based upon an agnatic core of men of the same dia-paying group the following is an example. Three huts were occupied by men of the Barkad, Reer Maḥamuud 'Ali Shirwa' lineage, distributed as shown in the diagram.

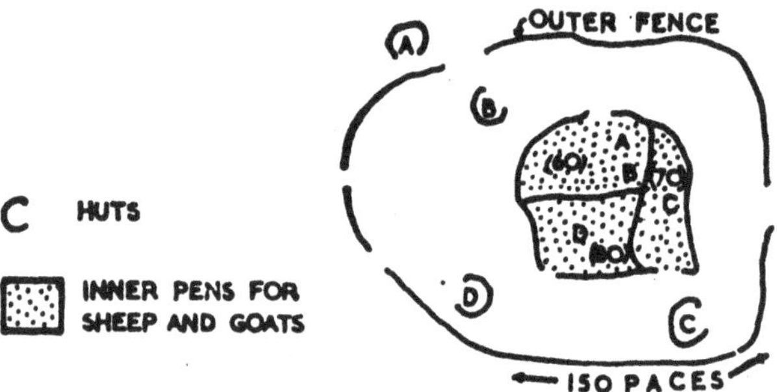

Figure 1. Plan of a nomadic hamlet.

Hut B belongs to the widowed mother of A. Their sheep and goats are herded together and they share the same burden camels. The wives of A and D are sisters of the Habar Tol Ja'lo clan, C's wife is Ḍulbahante, Reer Wa'ays Aadan. I have chosen to illustrate this hamlet because it is typical of many and because it shows how often a newly married man (A) begins by placing his hut outside the general fence of the hamlet. This practice is common though not universal whether a newly married man is living with his own or his wife's kin. In the former case it is explained in terms of the newness of the marriage and of the wife's gradual incorporation into the group. The relationships are as shown.

[1] The *buul* is in fact the much depleted and worn original bridal hut (*aroos*). Over the years with use, the marriage hut falls into decay as parts are given away to newly married female kin, particularly to daughters.

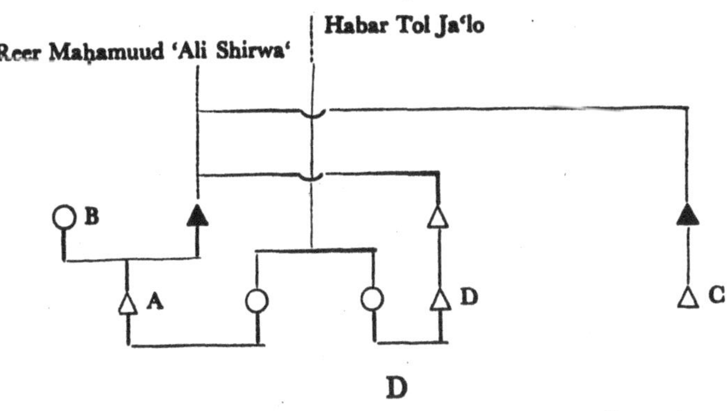

D

The commonest arrangement which includes affines is when a man comes to live temporarily usually, but occasionally permanently, with his wife's kin. While virilocal marriage is the norm, it sometimes happens that a man begins his married life in the hamlet of his wife's father. But this procedure does not correspond to any special type of bride-wealth payment. And marriages thus begun with the residence of the husband with his wife's kinsmen commonly change to virilocal residence after the wife has borne her first child. Only rarely does a man permanently live with his wife's agnates after the birth of his children. If a man does do so there are normally special reasons, and these are discussed below (pp. 82–83).[1]

A typical instance of a man living with his wife's agnates is afforded by a hamlet of the Barre Muuse lineage in an encampment at Qararo, between Bohotleh and Balleh Ad on the boundary between the British and Ethiopian Haud. There were four huts and the hamlet was led by A of the Barre Muuse. His wife, B is of the Habar Yuunis (Isaaq) clan. A's brother C, and the latter's wife D, of the Ḍulbahante Khaalid, occupied another hut. Other young unmarried half-siblings of A and C lived in a separate hut with their widowed mother E of the Marreḥaan (Daarood) clan. The remaining hut was that of F of the 'Ali Geri (Ḍulbahante) lineage married to G, the sister of A and C.

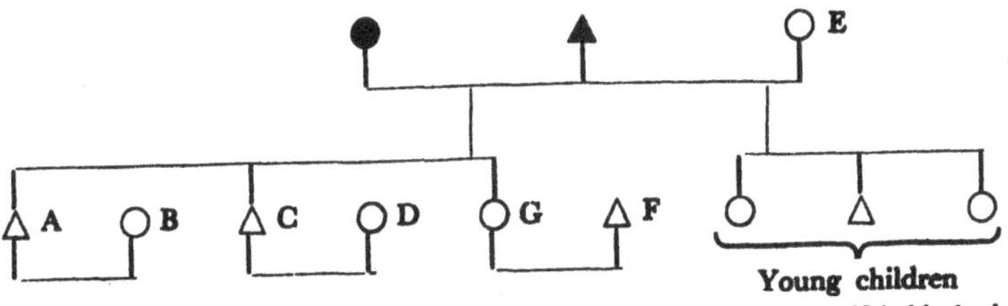

[1] When a man lives either temporarily, or permanently, with his wife's kin he is described as *inanlayaal*, lit. 'living with the girl'—from *inan*—girl, and *la-yaal* 'he lives with'.

Each family grouped in a hut had its own sheep and goats penned separately. There were also five cows attached to the hamlet and six burden camels.

E

In this example, chosen to illustrate a hamlet comprising men affinally linked to an agnatic core of members of the same dia-paying group, agnatic and affinal ties supplement each other. The hamlet was in the settlement at Hidhid and was of the Barkad primary lineage-group. There were six huts. The leader was A (Barkad) with his wife (B) of the Habar Tol Ja'lo clan. Her widowed mother C lived in the next hut. A third hut was occupied by A's son D, with his wife (E) of the Ḍulbahante Jaama' Siyaad. A's brother F lived in a fourth hut with his wife (G) of the Majeerteen clan (Daarood). The

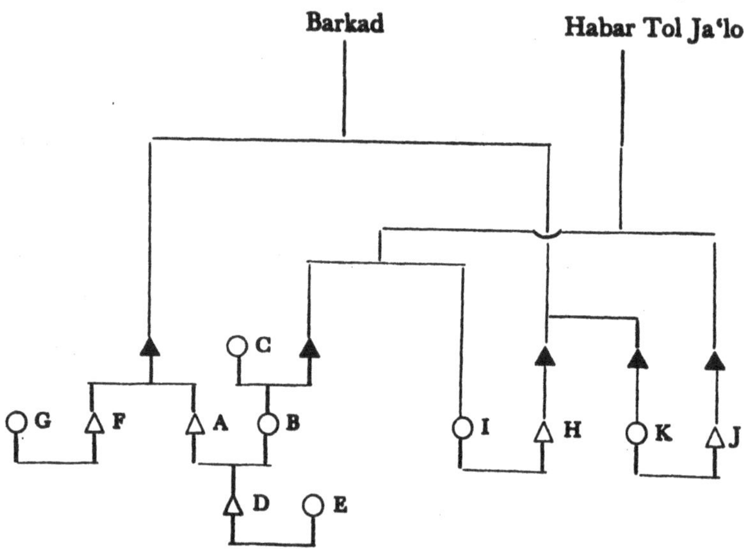

fifth member was H of the same dia-paying group of Barkad as A, with his wife (I) of the Habar Tol Ja'lo, a kinswoman of A's wife. Both women are of the same lineage. The last family is that of J of the Habar Tol Ja'lo, whose wife (K) is of the same lineage of Barkad as the other agnates. Each family had its own flocks separately penned and there were only four burden camels for the whole hamlet.

F.

Finally I cite an instance which includes relationships other than those already illustrated. This type of hamlet grouping although uncommon shows how in extreme cases more remote kinship ties are recognized and stressed to provide a basis for co-residence. This particular example utilizes a matrilateral tie to supplement and cement a weak agnatic relationship which otherwise would be unlikely to be used as a principle of hamlet solidarity. The hamlet contained four huts and was one of those in the encampment at Hidhid. The elder of the group was A of the Hayaag. His wife (B) is of the Reer Wa'ays Aadan. The next family was that of C also of the Hayaag, with his wife (D) of the Ḍulbahante Reer 'Ali Geri. A and C although of the same primary lineage-group (Hayaag) are of different dia-paying groups, but they are also matrilaterally related. For they are both the sons of a common mother (E),[1] of the Reer Wa'ays Aadan, who, when I lived in the settlement, was staying in a separate hut beside her son C. E was originally married to A's father, but when he died she was taken in widow inheritance by C's father. The last male member of the hamlet was F of the Ḍulbahante Reer Faaraḥ Hagar, and attached to the others by his (in 1956) recent marriage to G of the 'Ali Geri through C's wife D, of the same lineage. His attachment is thus through a double affinal link.

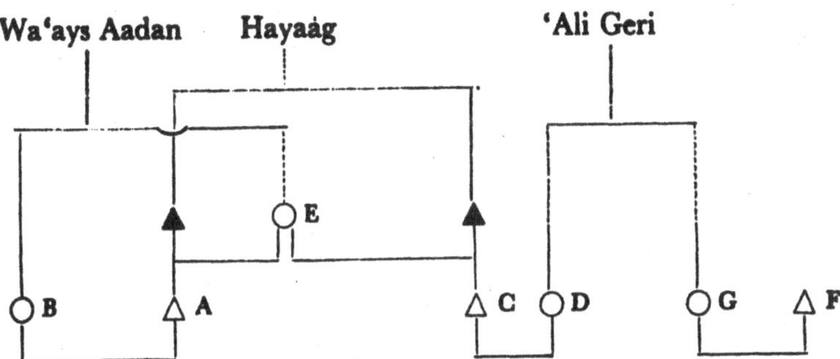

But for C, whose sheep and goats were herded with those of his mother (E), each member of the hamlet had his stock penned and herded individually. There were seven burden camels.

These six cases have been chosen to illustrate those residence patterns in hamlets which to a greater or lesser degree appear to be most common. In a system of shifting agnatic attachment hamlets are relatively stable units. Their constituent members form a domestic rather than a political unit. Yet the two spheres of grouping overlap as the high incidence of hamlets based on agnatic ties within the dia-paying group shows. In a political context Somali do not in any case sharply distinguish between the relations of brothers, or of father and son, and those of more

[1] Siblings of the same mother but different father, *waa is ku hooyo, waana kala aabbe*.

remote agnates. And where a distinction between the close kinsmen of the extended family and the wider circle of agnates of the same dia-paying group is made, it is often phrased in terms of the greater number, and therefore greater value to the individual's safety, of the latter. For although it is mainly within the restricted range of kinsmen whom we might describe as of the family, that bride-wealth, dowry, and the family estate, are distributed, property rights in an extended sense are subject to wider agnatic ties. I am not of course suggesting that an individual's relations with his father and siblings are not unique. But the boundary between relationships within the extended family and outside it in the sphere of extended agnation is not sharp. For the small family circle within which agnation is generated is not isolated from the larger orbit of lineage and political relations. In the contribution and distribution of blood-wealth within the dia-paying group every male member counts as a unit. A man pays for his young un-married sons, counted also as male units, but adult siblings usually pay individually. Thus the extended family is not recognized as a single unit in this respect.

IV

Having discussed the husbandry of sheep and goats and the distribution patterns and composition of the nomadic hamlets, I now turn to the subject of camel husbandry.

The grazing camels (*geel ḥer*) herded in the camel-camps are in the charge of camel-boys (sg. *geeljire*)[1] ranging in age from about seven to twenty years. Only on rare occasions is a married man out with them. This is the case for example when a man has no stock of his own and works for someone else, or when he lacks sons and younger agnates to whom the care of his herds would normally be entrusted. The camel-camp itself is simply a circular thorn kraal (*ḥero*) protecting the stock penned in it at night from wild beasts and other marauders. It may contain only one herd. But usually the camels of close kinsmen are herded together, and the stock of brothers, cousins, father and sons etc. are managed communally by a group of youths and penned at night within a common kraal. Camel-camps which contain more than one herd are divided internally into compartments. A typical kraal is illustrated below. The compartments into which they are divided

[1] 'Those who stay with camels' cf. *aḍijir*, shepherd.

are known as *kadin* from the entrance (*kadin*), the gap in the kraal fence by which the animals enter and leave, and which at night is closed with branches and bushes. And a *kadin* is also the unit of enumerating camels. It may comprise from sixty to over a hundred head of stock but it usually indicates between eighty and a hundred beasts.

The grazing camels are mainly females but most herds contain at least one stallion (*barqab*) whose behaviour, especially in the mating season, is a constant source of amusement to Somali.[1] The milch camels—adult beasts in milk—are known collectively as *geel irmaan* and distinguished from the remainder of the herd known as *gaane*. The latter include all camels not in milk; dry adult she-camels, younger unserved females (sg.*qaalin*), and calves (sg.*nirig*) as well as males (*awr*).

In direct contrast to a man's desire for male descendants the birth of a she-camel is preferred, for as Somali say, she will increase the herds. And the precious milch stock are always the first to be watered at the wells in the dry seasons. Some of the male camels are trained as beasts of burden, others are selected for breeding, and some again are castrated (*awr gool*) and fattened for slaughter at feasts and religious ceremonies.

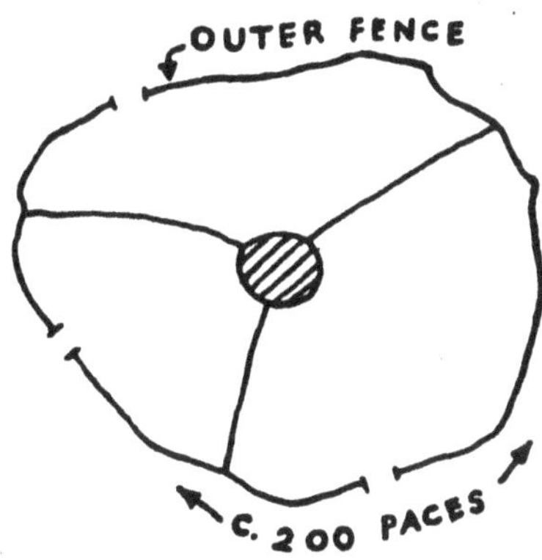

Figure 2. Camel camp containing three herds (sg. *kadin*). The camel-boys sleep at night in the clearing (*ardaa*) in the centre of the ring.

Like the hamlet the camel-camp is not a permanently stable unit with a constant composition of kin. Periodically some of the herdsmen of a camp move their stock to a new area to form a new camp with other kinsmen. Moreover, once established, a camel-camp rarely stays in the same place for more than a few weeks

[1]Selective breeding is normally practised.

unless the pasturage is particularly good, or unless movement is prevented or delayed by the presence of a hostile force of superior strength.

The camel-boys live almost entirely on camel's milk; only rarely is there water to drink. In the dry seasons when few beasts are in milk the rule is that what little milk is available should be shared amongst all the herdsmen of a camp. Thus, irrespective of the milk production of the individual herds, all the milk is pooled and distributed amongst the herd boys. The youngest drink their fill of the frothy liquid first. Occasionally game may be caught and roasted, or the camel-boys of several camps may club together to kill a camel for roasting over a shallow trench. When after the rains the pastures are green and many beasts are in milk their lot is enviable. For the milk of newly calved camels grazing on fresh pasturage is particularly delicious and justly esteemed by the herdsmen. But in the dry seasons their life is exceedingly hard. Milk is in short supply, and the camel-boys are always on the move to and from the wells, covered in dust and half bemused. Nor do they have huts or shelters to protect them from the elements. In all seasons they sleep together at night on a bed of grass (*ardaa* or *gole*) in a clearing in the centre of the kraal from which they guard the camels. Hence they are known as *ardaa wadaag*, those who 'share the same mat'. This expresses the unity of those herdsmen whose stock move together and who stay together in the same camp. But although they form a herding unit, each camel-boy is naturally most concerned for the welfare of those camels in which he has a share. And their economic solidarity, but disparity of private interest, is recognized in the proverbial saying 'the camels are common to the herdsmen, but they are also separate'.[1]

Like the sheep and goats the camels are milked in the early morning shortly after sunrise before they go out to browse, and again in the evening about two hours after sunset, when they have been mustered in the pens and counted. During the day, with their attendant herdsmen, the camels graze some distance from the camp. As the heat increases they seek the shade, if there is any, and the boys doze and chat. Wherever camels move, soft sandy pits occur where the beasts have rolled on their backs in the earth to scratch and rid themselves of ticks. This is an attention which the herdsmen also readily provide for their stock.

[1] *Geeljire geela waana is ku jirtaa, waana kala jirtaa.*

When they have reached the age of seven or eight years, and sometimes earlier, boys are sent out with their brothers and cousins to look after the camels. Their life, as has been said, is a hard one, particularly in the dry seasons. Indeed the camel-camps are in effect the initiation schools for the nomadic life. For amongst the northern Somali there are no age-grades or age-set organizations. While boys are circumcised sometimes shortly after birth, or more usually about the age of puberty, this is an individual act, although sometimes two or three boys of about the same age may be circumcised together. It is designed to make a boy clean (*ḥalaal*) in a religious sense and to prepare him for marriage. But no special instruction is imparted and circumcision is not attended by the performance of ritual, although while the penis is healing it is most important that no woman should see it lest it fester and refuse to heal. Uncircumcised boys are called collectively *buuryaqab* and are considered unclean (*ḥaaraam*) in a Muslim sense. But this condition has little practical importance except that men, especially those who pray very regularly, may object to eating meat killed or prepared by an uncircumcised youngster.

In a camel-camp the eldest herdsman is its natural leader (except in the case of a hired servant), but there is no formal differentiation of roles or offices. The young lads sent out to the camps are trained to go without water and to live on milk alone. They learn the art of camel-husbandry, the care of the stock, and their water and pasture requirements. They are taught which are the best grasses, and which pasture is noxious and to be avoided. Thus they learn to adapt themselves to living with the herds, to seek the best grazing, to deal with sickness and to count, water and milk the camels. To illustrate the care and affection which the camel-boys lavish on their stock I mention an incident which occurred while I was in one camel encampment. In extreme drought and heat few camels were in milk and the camel-boys were living just at subsistence level with no water to alleviate their thirst. One morning a young camel-herd came to my tent to beg water, not, as he emphasized, for himself, but for two young camels which were sorely in need. My companions amused by the boy's solicitude for his stock, did not lose the opportunity of pointing out how this incident typified the pastoralist's regard for his camels.

The herders quickly learn to appreciate the necessity of being always on the alert and of treating strangers with suspicion. Here I speak from bitter experience of the difficulties involved in extracting information on the number and size of the herds. Even when I was with close friends, near kinsmen to the camel-herds, our questions were only answered after many assurances of good intentions had been given and after much cajolery.

All this training fits them for the stern routine of the dry seasons when the camels have to be led to the wells about every three weeks. Not infrequently taking seven to eight days, this means a return journey of over a hundred miles to and from the wells each fortnight and often more, and is in addition to local movements in the pastures. In many cases the herders walk well over a thousand miles a year.

I describe below the kinship structure of a typical settlment near Balleh Ad in Ḍulbahante country in the northern Haud in February 1956. The camels were then grazing in the abundant high grass of the wide basin—parts of it marsh in the rainy seasons—and watering some sixty miles distant at Yahel and Yagore in the Nugal Valley to the east of Ainabo. Other herds were coming from upwards of thirty miles further south and were making the return journey of about two hundred miles at least once a month. And longer treks to the wells sometimes have to be made.

There were twenty-eight camel-camps in the settlement, belonging to the Hayaag, Reer Faaraḥ Hagar, and Reer 'Ali Geri, all primary lineage-groups of the Ḍulbahante. Their relationships are shown in the genealogy at the end of the book.

The sketch map shows how men of the same lineage-group tend to set up camel-camp near each other. As in the encampments of nomadic hamlets this lineage distribution is particularly marked in time of war. Moreover, like the former, the settlements of camel-camps have no unity based on territorial association. Men of the same primary lineage-group herd their camels close to each other where they graze because they are agnates, just as for the same reasons they help each other in the watering of the camels.

V

The kinds of kin who herd their camels in the same camp have provisionally been stated to be brothers, fathers and sons, and agnates of the same dia-paying group. The incidence of these three varieties of camel-camp composition is indicated in the table which refers to the settlment at Balleh Ad.

It will be seen that the more common arrangements are those where either a man herds his camels alone, or herds them with those of his kinsmen of the same dia-paying group. These kin-groupings, it will be recalled, are also those which occur most

A.	Camels of one man herded separately	9
B.	Camels of an extended family of brothers with or without the father	2
C.	Camels of kinsmen of the same dia-paying group	16
D.	Camels of kinsmen of different dia-paying groups	1

frequently in the structure of the nomadic hamlet. Experience of camel-camps in other settlements and amongst other northern clans leads to the conclusion that these are in fact the most common patterns of association. It is to be noted that none of the camps at Balleh Ad contained the camels of an affine; for indeed it is rare for a man to place his camels permanently with kin other than those of his own dia-paying group. Yet affines are often present as members of a nomadic hamlet. Before I discuss the significance of this distinction between the structure of nomadic hamlets and camel-camps I give some examples to illustrate the types of camel-camp distinguished in the table.

A

Camel-camp No. 13 (numbers refer to the map) contained the stock of a man of the Reer Warfaa 'Ali Geri, with his hundred camels in one pen (*kadin*). In charge of them were two of his sons. The owner's hamlet lay some sixty miles off near the wells where his camels were watering.

B

Camel-camp No. 3 contained the stock of two brothers (A and B) of the Reer Faaraḥ Hagar, Reer Maḥamuud 'Igaal. The camels were in separate pens and the camel-boys were A's three sons (C, D and E) and F, a younger kinsman whose relationship to the others is as shown. B's sons were still too young to be out with his camels.

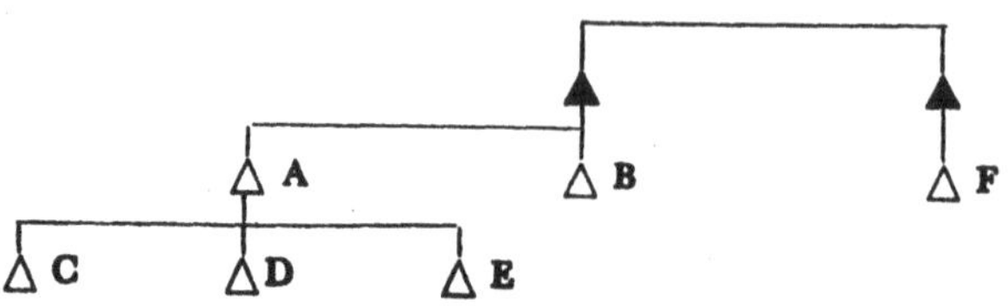

The hamlets of the two brothers—each living in a separate nomadic hamlet—lay some thirty miles to the north, and their camels were watering a further thirty miles beyond.

C

Camel-camp No. 1 consisted of three pens with the stock of two brothers, A and B, and of their father's brother C. The last had a hundred and fifty camels, B a hundred and twelve, and A ninety.

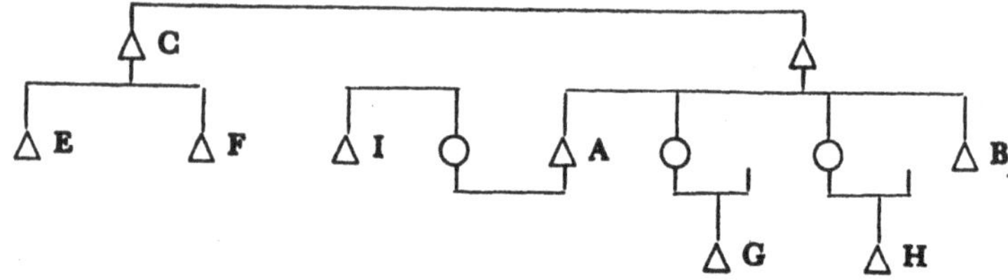

The camels were watering at wells some 60 miles to the north while the hamlets lay thirty miles to the north. C's camels are in the care of two of his sons, E and F. A and B had no boys old enough to be with their stock which was in the charge of two sisters' sons (G and H) and one wife's brother (I).[1]

Because of its interest in including the stock of a Midgaan bondsman, I cite another example of this type of camel-camp. Camp No. 17 contained the stock of four men, with the exception of the Midgaan, all of the Reer Hagar, Reer Ismaa'iil 'Igaal lineage. A had one hundred and thirty-seven camels in the charge of his three sons, B, C and D. The Midgaan, who works for A, had four camels in the charge of his son. E, the son of A's dead brother F, had a hundred and eighteen camels tended by his sons, G and H, and by his younger brother I who has a joint share in the stock. The last pen contained thirty-one camels belonging to J, a member of the same dia-paying group as A and B. His camel-boys are his younger brother K and his son L. The relationships of these men are illustrated in

[1] As in most other patrilineal societies the mother's brother (*abti*) stands in a relationship of particular intimacy and friendship with his sister's son. By attaching themselves to him as camel-herds, the sister's sons are in a position to enjoy their mother's brother's generosity and kindness. The services rendered by a wife's brother on the other hand are given rather from a sense of duty being classed with the dowry returned by the woman's kin in exchange for her bride-wealth.

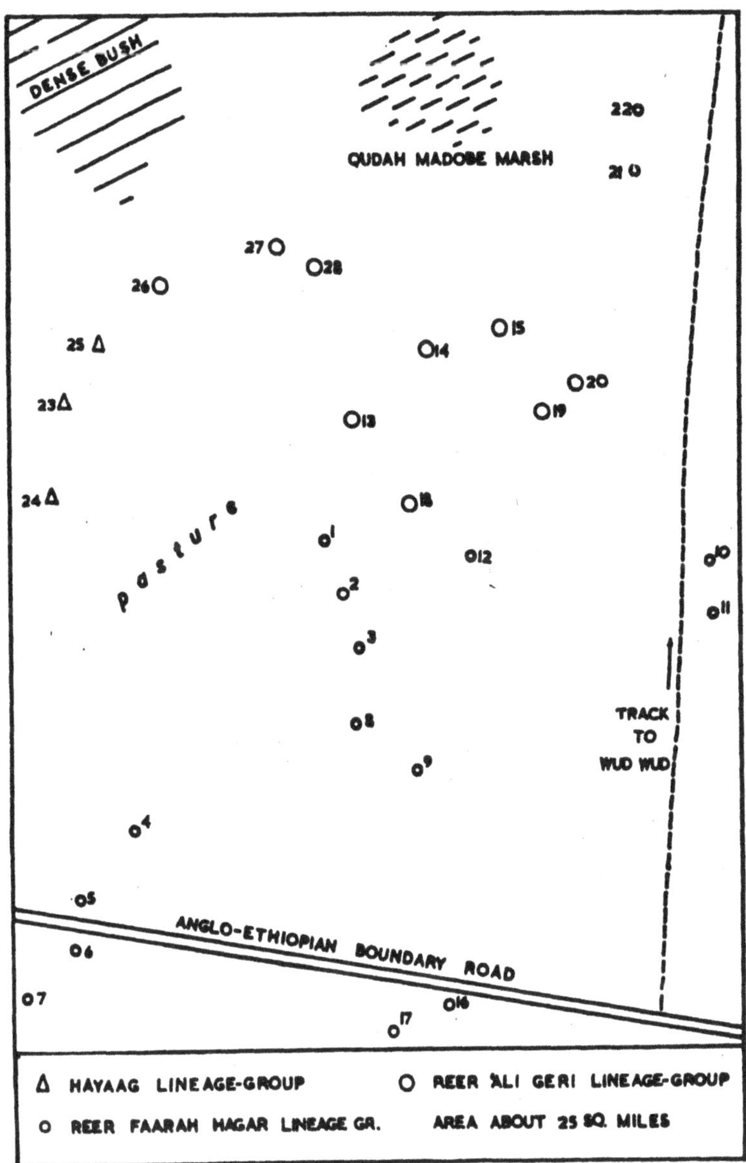

Map 10. Balleh Ad. Ḍulbahante camel-camps, February, 1956.

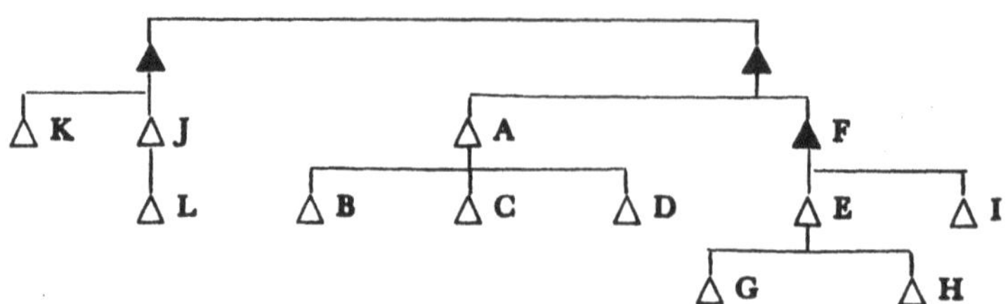

the genealogy (the Midgaan, who is not included genealogically with his protectors, is omitted).

The camels were all watering in the same region as those of the previous camps. One of the owners had his hamlet there; two were in a separate encampment to the north-east; and one lay to the west.

D

Where members of different primary lineage-groups of the same clan are in alien territory amongst a different, and potentially hostile clan, they naturally tend to band together for safety, particularly when they lack affinal or matrilateral ties to their hosts. But within a clan it is unusual for members of different primary lineage-groups to place their stock in the same camps unless they seek support from one friendly group against the threat of hostility from another lineage. Camp No. 7 at Balleh Ad was an example of a stock-group containing the camels of men of different primary lineage-groups. There were camels belonging to four men of the Reer Hagar. A had over two hundred camels. B's camels shared a pen containing one hundred and thirty-five head with those of C. D, a son of A, had a separate pen for his twelve beasts. The remaining men whose camels were in the camp are E, and F, both of the Reer 'Ali Geri primary lineage and G, of another primary lineage-group ('Ali Garaad). The camels of each were separately penned, reference to the map (p. 79) shows

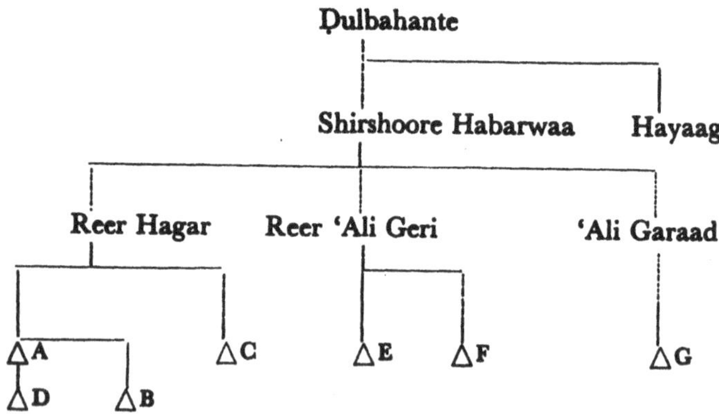

how these three men having chosen to settle on the southerly edge of the encampment, joined their closer kinsmen of the Reer Hagar rather than more distantly related clansmen (the Hayaag) in other camps.

VI

In some of the camel-camps discussed above it was noted that men whose camels were in the same camp lived with their flocks and families in different hamlets. The table records the location of the nomadic hamlets of the camel-owners of Balleh Ad settlement at the time I visited them.

It will be seen that while the camels of some seventy-two men were in the same settlement, the hamlets in which they lived with their wives, children and flocks, were distributed over eleven different and widely spaced regions. Indeed of the twenty-eight camps, in only fourteen cases were those whose camels were herded together living in the same hamlets. From experience of other encampments of which Balleh Ad is typical it can be stated generally that those men whose camels are herded together do not necessarily share the same hamlet. For the fluidity of movement which the ecological conditions require makes it impossible for every hamlet to have a corresponding camel-camp. Thus in composition each of the two units is very often independent of the other. And although their movements are from time to time

Location of hamlets of men whose camels were in Balleh Ad settlement.	Number of men
Hidhid	17
Muuse Godeer	12
Merganweyn	3
Lasadar	20
Dalama Une	2
Bohotle	6
Hellmirale	2
Wudwud	5
Do'omo	1
Yahel	2
Higlole	2
11.	72

co-ordinated, particularly in the dry seasons, the camel-camps and nomadic hamlets are two separate herding units. A man may move his wife or wives and their children from one group of kinsmen in one hamlet to another in a new hamlet without making any re-allocation of his grazing camels. And brothers or other men of the same dia-paying group may move in separate hamlets while their camels are herded in common. Moreover, herds are moved from one camp of kinsmen to another without producing any change in the composition of the hamlets of their owners. All this indeed, is self-evident for, as I have said, the hamlets are often many miles distant from the camel-camps and each out of contact with the other often at least for days, and sometimes for weeks on end.

There are, however, certain limiting factors which more rigidly circumscribe the composition of the camel-camps. In the nomadic hamlets the choice of association is wider. Thus none of the camps in the settlement described contained affinally related men. But about a third of the nomadic hamlets in our sample include men affinally or otherwise non-agnatically related to an agnatic core. Of these the majority were newly married husbands living with their wives' kin. When a man comes thus to stay for a matter of months, or for one or two years, with his wife's people he brings with him the sheep and goats, and burden camels necessary for her support (if these are not provided by his wife's kin), but he leaves his camels behind in the care of his own kin who have joint rights in them. For a man to transfer the custody of his camels from the care of his own to his wife's kin is tantamount to a renunciation of his lineage affiliation. While cases of this kind do occur they are very rare amongst the pastoralists. A man may, for example, fall out with his own people and seek the sanctuary of his wife's kin, or for other personal reasons, he may prefer to live with them rather than within his own lineage. Thus a man of the Habar Tol Ja'lo married a woman of the Ḍulbahante Reer Faaraḥ Hagar and lived uxorilocally with them. When he died some of his children returned to their own clan, but one son chose to stay with his mother's people and brought his stock, including his camels, to herd with theirs. But while assigning him a protected status in their wars with the Habar Tol Ja'lo, the Reer Faaraḥ Hagar do not, however, accept responsibility for his blood-wealth. It is to be noted here moreover, that when a man thus deserts his own kin to live with his wife's agnates, he normally retains his own genealogy, and his children belong to his own clan and lineage and not to those of his wife. Such a position is ambiguous: for to a certain extent a man has dual status in both kin-groups without being a full member of either. As long as he lives with his wife's lineage-group he will be protected, but unless he also pays blood-wealth with them he is excluded from blood indemnification. But if he pays blood-compensation with his wife's kin he must cease paying it with his own agnates and they can no longer regard him as a full kinsman whose life they will fight to defend or avenge. The insecurity and ambiguity of the position explain why amongst the pastoralists it is so rarely assumed.[1]

The inclusion of affinally and matrilaterally related kin in the nomadic hamlets, but the exclusion of their camels in the camel-camps, can also be seen to reflect ecologically controlled factors. For, as has been seen, in relation to their different water and grazing needs, the camels are separated from the flocks. The former move at long range, generally far from the hamlets in which the bulk of the people of a lineage are concentrated. They have greater mobility and are in more extensive contact with the herds of other lineages and clans. But although they are more resistant to climatic conditions, they are more vulnerable to attack and they are more valuable than the flocks. The youths who tend them and defend them should need arise, are largely youngsters far from the main fighting potential of their lineage-group. It is thus consistent with security needs that affines and other non-agnates should be admitted to the better protected hamlets and excluded from the more vulnerable camel-camps.

Over his camels a man has primary, but not absolute, rights of possession. For the camels of the individual members of a dia-paying group constitute their joint stock-wealth as a group. Camels are branded, and the brands (sg. *sumad*) are those of lineage-groups usually dia-paying groups—not of individuals. Sheep and goats, on the other hand, bear the brands of their individual owners. Yet in terms of the contract binding the members of a dia-paying group in joint responsibility for homicide, individual herders have an interest in all the stock of the dia-paying group. And while it is true that this applies to all wealth generally, including sheep and goats, ideally it is in camels that wealth is

[1] On the status of protected persons living with their affines or otherwise, see below, pp. 186-93

reckoned and collective responsibility expressed. Thus at all levels of grouping in the lineage system, as one lineage is mobilized in opposition to another, the members of the respective groups speak of 'their camels' as against those of their opponents. Somali say 'when we are of the same treaty (dia-paying group) or of the same lineage-group, camels are common to us all'.[1] And whenever camels are stolen by raiders the immediate rallying cry for support is 'Agnates', (*Tolla'ay*). In response to this call, a man's kin come to his aid, and action is initiated to recover the lost stock or to make a reprisal.

It is, moreover, in camels that blood-wealth is reckoned, and the value of a person's life translated into terms of wealth. A man's life is normally valued at a hundred, and a woman's at fifty camels.[2] On this score a man is worth a hundred camels, and a camel a hundredth part of a man. This equation expresses the relation between the social value of a man, and of a woman, and wealth in camels.

In an extended sense camels are associated with male kinsmen. Men care for camels, women tend sheep and goats. And in respect of camels particularly Islamic principles of inheritance are ignored to the exclusion of the rights of female heirs. Sometimes women come to own sheep and goats, and town property in their own right, but it is exceedingly rare for a woman to possess full rights of ownership in camels. Indeed it is so rare, that when in special circumstances this happens it is a topic of widespread conversation and comment. All stock are inherited, but men take much greater interest in acquiring rights in camels than they do in sheep and goats. During his life a youth grows into rights in his father's herd. Ideally at birth his father gives him a camel-calf called his 'navel-knot' (*ḥuddunḥiḍ*). And as he grows into manhood he receives occasional gifts of camels from his father and elder brothers. Thus the 'navel-knot' she-camel is the nucleus of his own herd, and, as his responsibilities increase with his years, he acquires increasing rights in camels. At marriage his rights are usually formalized and a portion of the family estate allotted to him as bride-wealth. But this does not necessarily mean that thereafter his camels are herded separately from those of his father or brothers. Again on the father's death, those stock which remain in the estate are apportioned amongst

[1] *Intii is ku ḥeer ah, ama intii is ku qolo ah, geelu waa innaga ḍeḥeeyaa.*
[2] This is discussed more fully in Chapter VI.

the sons and other heirs (father's, brothers etc). And here although he has privileged rights, an elder brother may waive his entitlement in favour of unmarried younger brothers, arguing, that since his bride-wealth has already come from the estate, he has enjoyed a just share.

Somali view the increase of their herds over the generations as paralleling the extension of their lineages. The herds of a clan are viewed as the inherited patrimony of its founder. Thus Sheikhs Daarood and Isaaq are regarded by their respective descendants as the sources of their herds. While the growth of the flocks is thought of similarly, there is less interest in them in this respect for their main value lies in fulfilling subsistence needs.

As well as providing milk and ghee, sheep and goats are often slaughtered for meat, particularly in the dry seasons when other food is scarce. Some are exported on the hoof to Aden, and this with the export of their valuable skins, constitutes the most important external trade asset of northern Somaliland. In the internal economy their skins[1] are exchanged in the dry seasons for sugar, tea, rice, sorghum, and dates etc. Camels are slaughtered less frequently, and generally only on important ritual or religious occasions. Here male camels are usually killed, or she-camels which have completed their calving life, which normally lasts about fifteen years. Thus the slaughter of a young she-camel before her bearing life is over, marks a special gesture of abnegation and is reserved for occasions when it is desired particularly to impress God, or the saints, or an honoured guest. From these considerations it is plain that although camels are in no ordinary sense sacred, and are used for carriage and to provide milk and skins, their general significance transcends mere subsistence or consumer value. Sheep and goats, on the other hand, whatever their actual use, are thought of primarily as a means of subsistence. Yet of course camels, sheep and goats, and other stock, are interchangeable, both directly, and in terms of money. The distinction between the social values of the two types of livestock can probably best be suggested by stating that the pastoralists work on a camel standard. For it is in camels that bride-wealth and blood-wealth are reckoned and ideally paid. Moreover, members of a lineage think of their joint rights in terms of camels rather than in terms of sheep and goats. And, as has been noted, the value of a man's life is phrased in camels. Their position is summed up

[1] In 1957, a sheep-skin was valued at about three shillings.

in statements such as 'camels beget children, settle blood-debts, and provide milk and transport'. After horses they are the most prized of Somali wealth and the pastoralist never tires of extolling the merits of his herds or of boasting of their numbers. It will be seen that this evaluation is consistent with the composition of the two herding units and accords with the agnatic grouping of the herds of camels.

From what has been said a more accurate distinction can now be made between the two basic herding units. The nomadic hamlet is essentially a domestic group, the camel-camp is not. It is an appendage of the hamlet, a reservoir for excess milch stock, and a repository for potential burden camels and stallions. But it is far more than this for it contains the capital resources of the pastoralist, not only of the individual, but in an extended sense of the lineage. And it is in the visible possession of camels that agnation is affirmed.

VII

This discussion of the composition of camel-camps and hamlets has led to some consideration of the values which the pastoralist attaches to his stock and I give here a few examples of typical camel-songs (*hees geel*). As well as being praised in serious poetry (*gabay* and *geeraar*) camels are sung to at all times; by the camel-boys at night in the camps, in caravans on the way to buy or sell provisions or to bring water, at the watering of the herds at the wells, and on the long marches to them. Of the following camel-songs two are sung on the way to the wells, and the third as the camels are watered after their long trek to them. The last song is part of a cycle sung at the different stages of watering and refers to the help given by men of the same lineage at the wells.

I

Saddeḥ boqol iyo
Three hundred and
Siddeetan habeen
Eighty nights
Oo sidkeed yahay
Of carrying
Sabool sugi waa
A poor man cannot wait
Aan se kugu simayn
But I could let you wait.

This song refers to the long period of gestation of the camel, the singer suggesting that only a man of property could wait till his camels calved.

II

Shan bilood iyo
Five months and
Shan habeen bay
Five nights she
Shurinaysooy
Has averted her face
Hawd ku sheellayd
And hidden in the Haud
Waa shinkeedii
It is her time
Maaḥda sharafka leh
To drink water pure
Loogu shubi jirey
As crystal (from the wells)

Here the singer records that his camels have been able to spend as long as five months in the far-grazing away from the wells, but that now the time of watering has come. This shows a year of good rains and grazing.

III

Hadday tubantahay
If they are standing ready (the camels)
Waa tolla'ayoo
Then the clansmen must rally
Looma kala tago
And no man leave till all are watered.

This is one of the songs sung as the camels are watered and men sling up the spilling buckets from a deep well. It is a work chant and part of a cycle of songs, as I have said, associated with the whole process of the watering and the co-operation of agnates.

VIII

In this and the previous chapter we have considered the Somali pastoral economy in relation to the arid conditions under which they live. We have constantly had to acknowledge the degree to which Somali pastoralism is accommodated to the prevailing ecological conditions of the country. And for those who are unfamiliar with northern Somaliland it is necessary to reaffirm that, despite apparently large herds of livestock, the Somali pastoralist lives frequently on the edge of starvation. For while there appear to be too many livestock for the impoverished land to support, there are insufficient for the needs of an ever-increasing population.[1] Moreover, despite remedial measures, erosion continues to deplete the scant pastureland available. The deterioration of pastures is particularly marked in the areas near the home-wells of the Ogo highlands which have to support the grazing movements of the coastal groups as well as those of the highlands and Haud. The effects of the shrinking and increasingly inadequate natural resources are seen in the very slight excess in drought conditions which is enough to upset the delicate balance between land and people and lead to famine. Except in good years, temporary famine relief measures are now a regular necessity, at least in the British Protectorate.

There is thus by any standards keen competition for shrinking resources and a necessarily tight adjustment of the economy and system of husbandry to the environment. The difficulties of the harsh environment have been met by the separation of the grazing camels from the sheep and goats with the formation of two separate herding units making for the maximum utilization of the resources available. This division which conforms to ecological requirements is also accompanied by a distinction in the values which attach to the two types of stock. Sheep and goats have importance mainly in subsistence while camels have greater social value since in addition to their subsistence uses they are regarded primarily as a medium for the regulation of most aspects of social, political, and religious life. In a sense camels represent agnation, for to a large extent social relations are a function of joint interest and joint rights in them. In conformity with this, agnatic kinship, which underlies the structure of both

[1] That the population is increasing is indicated by a Net Reproduction Rate of 1.3 calculated from figures given by A. M. Morgantini (1954) for the municipal populations of Somali. This result was obtained by using the formula NRR = 0.3536 + 0.001996 (FR), to correlate the Fertility Ratio with the Net Reproduction Rate. It can, however, only serve as a general indication that the population is increasing since the population statistics on which the calculations are based refer only to municipalities which may not be fully representative of the total (rural and urban) population. I am indebted to Professor J. C. Mitchell for making this analysis.

camel-camp and nomadic hamlet, is especially important in the former. While the hamlets are essentially domestic groups of kinsmen, the camel-camps contain the capital resources of lineages.

In relation to their ecology, the Somali have developed a system of grazing where no firm titles attach to pasturage except those which depend upon force. Thus the individual stock-herder has an optimum degree of freedom in his movements with his stock. As long as his water requirements are met (and titles to wells are spread widely) the only restriction placed upon his range of movement is the necessity to defend himself and his livestock against the threat of hostility. It is here, as well as in the watering of camels from deep wells, that the co-operation of kinsmen is essential.

In a region of grazing, transitory encampments form in which men of the same dia-paying or primary lineage-group tend to cluster together with their flocks or to herd their camels in adjacent camps. With their ephemeral character such settlements produce no sense whatsoever of local unity, of ties to locality. Their only solidarity, most marked in time of war, is that which derives from clanship and contract. Thus vicinage is unimportant but kinship vital. This again, may be viewed as conforming to the ecological conditions which require constant movement and prevent the development in the pastures of residential grazing units with any degree of stability.

In the following chapter which deals with permanent settlement in trade-villages and towns, in religious communities, and in cultivating villages, I discuss the extent to which this pastoral system is modified by new conditions.

4
Settlement and Cultivation

I

It was shown in the previous chapters that within the territory grazed by a clan, although primary lineage-groups are not geographical units, people of the same lineage tend to camp side by side where they are temporarily gathered in a region of pasture. This distribution which brings people of the same lineage-group together with their livestock, particularly the camels, in which they have a collective interest is especially marked in time of war. The same tendency for lineages to provide nuclei of settlement is found also in the villages and towns which to some extent demarcate the nomadic movements of the pastoralists, and in the cultivating centres in the north-west of Somaliland.

The villages (sg. *tuulo*) and towns (sg. *magaalo*) which are the centres of trade are widely scattered and vary greatly in size from minor settlements of less than a hundred permanent inhabitants to the larger towns such as Hargeisa with a population of about 30,000–40,000, Jibuti with about 30,000 (of whom 15,000 are Somali), and Berbera with a population which fluctuates between some 15,000 and 30,000. Galkayu, the largest town in northern Somalia, has a municipal population of only 8,000 persons. Town populations fluctuate with the seasons. The number of their inhabitants is generally greatest in the dry months when they attract nomads from the interior as temporary settlers. In the rainy seasons the movement is away from the urban centres when temporary town-dwellers are drawn out with their stock to the pastures. The population of the ports also varies with the trade winds. From October to March during the north-east monsoon when the coast is open to dhows from Arabia, the Persian Gulf, and India, Berbera sometimes attains a population in the region of 30,000 people, while in the south-west monsoon this may drop below 20,000.

The pastoralists who thus form a transitory element in towns live for the most part in their nomadic huts (*aqal*) erected on the periphery of the urban centres. The more permanent townsmen who are occupied as shop-keepers, livestock merchants, importers and exporters, petrol retailers and mechanics, and government officials, etc, live mainly in stone (*daar*) or mud and wattle houses (*'ariish*), and now, to some extent, in government-constructed brick dwellings.

All such permanent or semi-permanent centres—for many small villages are deserted after a few years and spring up elsewhere—are of necessity situated in close proximity to water. Where wells are shallow, or are exhausted after a few years, villages die out and new settlements appear in more favoured regions. The instability of all but the largest administrative capitals is reflected in the regular abandonment of old roads and tracks and the cutting of new ones to the new centres.

All settlements are based on trade and are the markets where the produce of the interior—largely sheep on the hoof, milk, meat, ghee, skins, and gums, is sold or exchanged for imported cloth, sugar, tea, rice, sorghum, dates, hardware, and other trade commodities. In regions of dense grazing, merchants set up temporary shops in grass shelters and follow the main nomadic movements by camel and trade-truck. In a region occupied by several lineage-groups there is usually at least one merchant of each lineage relying mainly on his own kinsmen for custom and giving them generous credit. Debts are settled periodically by the members of small lineage-groups in concert and, as has been pointed out, usually after the livestock have calved in the spring when accounts are closed in lambs or kids.

In the centre and the east of northern Somaliland, where there is little or no cultivation, villages are often as much as forty miles apart. But in the west, particularly in the agricultural regions of Hargeisa and Borama Districts of the British Protectorate, they are more frequent and less widely spaced. An important commodity of trade here is the locally grown sorghum of which a large proportion is purchased by merchants for sale in other regions.

Few of the present towns of northern Somaliland with stone buildings are more than fifty years old, and most have developed even more recently, often from earlier and more modest settlements of nomadic huts. Apart from the coastal centres occupied during the Egyptian period and the now mainly deserted mediæval ruins, the only old towns with a tradition of several centuries of continuous occupation as urban centres are Harar in Ethiopia, and the dying town of Zeila'. Both as has been said, were founded many centuries ago by Arabian immigrants and unlike modern northern towns, grew into cosmopolitan centres whose citizens had a strong sense of identity based on dwelling in the same place and largely independent of ethnic origin or lineage affiliation. Even as late as 1949, what was left of the mixed urban population of Zeila' (the Reer Seyla') was recognized by the British Administration as a distinct and autonomous community outside Somali clanship and was allocated a stipended headman (Akil).

Such ancient cosmopolitan centres are exceptional. The majority of northern Somali towns are of recent formation, and, inhabited mainly by Somali, have little or no sense of corporate identity as urban centres. Their members live and act not so much as citizens of a common urban community but as members of distinct and rival lineages. And in comparison with the continuing strength of lineage affiliation the importance of any ties based on other principles of association is slight. Independently of agnatic connection vicinage has little practical significance. Indeed, where there are bonds of common interest and solidarity between neighbours they are generally those between agnatic kinsmen who live in close proximity. For in towns the tendency for people of the same lineage to live side by side where they settle is still strong. This localization of kinsmen is most marked in the smaller settlements of the interior where little or no Government control is exercised in the disposition of dwellings. It is also clearly seen in the structure of the clusters of nomadic huts, occupied largely but not entirely by transitory settlers, which lie on the peripheries of large towns some distance from the more central, permanent mud and wattle, stone, and brick buildings. In Las Anod, for example, the Administrative headquarters of the Ḍulbahante in the east of the British Protectorate, the area of the town composed of movable nomadic huts is divided into two distinct territorial divisions along the lines of lineage cleavage. One division contains predominantly people of the Faaraḥ Garaad segment of the Ḍulbahante clan, while the other is inhabited by people of the opposed Maḥamuud Garaad lineage.[1]

Even with Government planning in the lay-out of large towns, the permanent stone, and mud-and-wattle dwellings tend to be

[1] For the relationship of these large Ḍulbahante lineages see the genealogy at the end of the book.

grouped in quarters (sg. *ḥaafad*) roughly according to the lineage affiliation of their inhabitants. In almost all northern Somali towns there is certainly a strong tendency for people of the same lineage (or clan where several clans jointly occupy a town) to cluster together. But to a considerable extent, as I have indicated, this is distorted by town-planning and the allocation of building sites by Government. Nevertheless, even where there is not a strict localization of kinsmen, when a fight occurs in a town people of the lineages concerned attempt to gather together in separate areas as far removed from their enemies as possible.

The desire of people to match the area in which they live with their lineage affiliation is only one aspect of the continuing strength of clanship in urban settlements. For although permanent towns-people are to some extent divided into new occupational categories (as e.g. clerks and officials, merchants etc) which do not relate to clan affiliation, their political and economic loyalty remains vested in their lineages of birth. Urbanization in northern Somaliland is very different to that in other more heavily industrialized African territories with larger European settler communities. The mere fact of residence in a town, even a town as large (by Somali standards) as the capital of the Protectorate, while it brings him into contact with a wider range of individuals many of whom are not kinsmen, does not lead a Somali to sever his ties with his own pastoral agnatic kinsmen. For except in the commercial port of Jibuti in French Somaliland there is in fact little or no economic or political discontinuity between town and interior in northern Somaliland. Towns are primarily the markets for the interior and to an important degree are the centres of pastoral politics.

Most influential elders and sheikhs spend much of their time in the towns and those who can afford to hold town property which they occupy for part of the year at least. For quite apart from anything else, it is important for leaders to represent and watch over the interests of their lineages in administrative headquarters. In addition to participating in court cases in which their groups are concerned, a great deal of time is spent in wrangling with the elders of other lineages and with the administrative authorities over payment of blood-compensation.

Important elders resident in towns usually move out into the interior in the wet season when the pastures are at their best and men like to be as near their camels as possible. At this time a man tends to move his town family into the grazing areas where his children can enjoy the fresh rich milk from his herds and flocks. Elders are often also called out into the interior at other times to settle disputes amongst their agnates, to take part in lineage councils, to collect compensation or distribute it, to broadcast Government policy and to direct clan fighting; so that even those who spend the dry seasons in towns have one foot with their kinsmen in the pastures.

Towns in northern Somaliland are thus in no sense independent fastnesses in a nomadic environment. They are indeed, on the contrary, the very nerve centres of pastoral politics and of crucial importance in the nomadic political system. Many feuds have their direct origins in towns, and, even when they have not, fighting is frequently directed from villages and settlements where the resident elders control lineage politics. Thus there is in fact no sharp division economic or political, between the pastoralists (*Reer guuraa*) and permanent town-dwellers (*Reer magaala*) although the latter often taunt the nomads calling them uncouth Beduin. Far from lying outside, or on the periphery of pastoral nomadism, towns are the principal centres about which the system revolves.

Residence in a town does not thus dis-establish the force of clanship and contract, for it does not rupture the economic bond which link agnates. Permanent townsmen, in most cases still have livestock, particularly camels, in the charge of their kinsmen in the interior. Lineage rivalries are as clearly defined and as important in town life as they are outside it. And since there is continuity in structural relations between town and rural area lineage rivalries in one automatically produce the same rivalries in the other. Thus a riot in the town of Burao in the Protectorate in 1956 between Habar Tol Ja'lo and Habar Yuunis clansmen was simply one urban incident in the long train of hostilities between the two clans which I discuss more fully in Chapter VIII. Many of the new activities which are part of town life simply offer wider scope for lineage jealousies and conflict. To take a minor instance, there is lineage friction over the allocation of trading licences and 'coffee-shop' licences. And where interest is shown in municipal elections it tends to reflect agnatic principles of solidarity.

Yet despite this close interdependence between urban centres and the rural environment, the new classes which towns have produced in trade and in the Government service have promoted the growth of new aspirations and new patterns of thought. There is a growing desire on the part of many permanent townsmen, not only of the new educated élite, to break away from their lineages and dia-paying groups for they find their continued demands increasingly irksome. Many, in seeking to emancipate themselves from the pastoral system, claim that they are not responsible for all the actions of their kinsmen whose consequences they have to share. It will be seen that here there is a contradiction between the traditional role of towns in the pastoral system and the new ideas and aspirations which are to some extent developing. Since towns are better policed than the interior town-dwellers feel less need for the support of their kinsmen who traditionally provide their only security when their rights are threatened. In this new direction there is some evidence of a growing, though still very weak, sense of membership of an urban community or residential district as opposed to lineage allegiance. And of course with these new trends it is in towns that the new nationalist political parties which we describe in Chapter IX find their strongest support. But the influence of these modern trends even in party politics is still slight in comparison with the strength of lineage solidarity. I emphasize here the fact that town and interior form one economic and political system in which the same structural principles govern social relations and leave until later consideration of the new political movements.

II

The pervasive character of the pastoral system is also seen in the local organization of the cultivating communities founded by the religious orders (sg. *tariiqa*)[1]. These are to a much greater extent isolated and self-contained settlements established according to the ideals of Muslim brotherhood and unity opposed to the sectional interests of Somali lineages. But, as I shall show, although they achieve a greater degree of residential unity based on common religious values and sedentary cultivation, the political affiliation of their members remains subject to agnation, and within the community houses tend to be distributed by lineage.

1 *Tariiqa* (*Ar. ṭariiqa*) means literally 'The Way' in the sense of the 'path to God' and indicates a particular direction of religious devotion in Islam. The settlements are also commonly known in Somaliland as *jamaa'a*. For a fuller discussion of Somali Sufism and the Dervish Orders see below, pp. 218-28.

Thus, although there is a sense of common identity independently of agnatic connexion, it is weakened by the external economic and political ties of the members of the community with their pastoral kinsmen along the lines of clanship. Despite the fact that members of such an autonomous sedentary community are bound together far more closely than the inhabitants of a town, like the latter they retain their economic and dia-paying solidarity with their kinsmen. In the arid conditions of northern Somaliland *tariiqa* communities are few; there are probably fewer than twenty in the whole of the British Protectorate, but in the riverine regions of southern Somalia where cultivation is extensively practised there are many more.[1]

I illustrate the economic conditions of such northern religious settlements and their relation to the pastoral system by discussing the community of the Dandaraawiya Order at Sheikh in the centre of the British Protectorate. The settlement lies to the west of the town of the same name and occupies some few hundred acres of land enclosed within a roughly circular thorn fence and thus distinguished from the grazing land of the Habar Awal and Habar Yuunis clans of the district. In years of good rain sorghum is cultivated but the subsistence economy of the members ('brothers', *'ikhwaan*) is based on cattle husbandry and subsidiary occupations in the adjoining town. Each domestic group has one or two fields for cultivation and access to the common grazing land of the *tariiqa*. Most families in the wet seasons send at least some of their cattle into the interior with their close agnates who are pastoralists. Many people have sheep and goats and camels herded with their agnates in the interior. The majority of the male heads of families follow secular callings (see table) some working in the adjacent town. This fact is regretted by the heads of the settlement who complain that, in the old days, in the time of the founder, men devoted their lives to religion to a greater extent than they do today. In 1955 there were some 280 people living in the settlement of whom thirty-nine were married men, sixty women, and one hundred and eighty-one children. Of the thirty-nine adult heads of families, only ten depended exclusively upon their livestock and cultivation. The remaining twenty-nine had additional sources of income gained mainly in secular occupations.

The settlement was founded by Sheikh Aadan Aḥmad of the Habar Awal clan about 1885. Sheikh Aadan who had gone to Mecca

[1] In British Somaliland settlements of the Qaadiriya Dervish Order are found at Hudin, Wudwud, Qaruro, DobaGudud, Geditale, Berato, Gubato, Suqsudde, Gebile, Hargeisa, and elsewhere in the west. There are two farming settlements of the Dandaraawiya; that at Sheikh described here, and another at Hahe in Burao District.

about the age of twenty and there come under the spell of Sayyid Maḥammad Dandaraawi's[1] teaching, returned to the Protectorate to propagate the Dandaraawiya Order and was recognized by the founder as regional sheikh for the Habar Awal. The Sheikh obtained a grant of land with the agreement of the local Habar Awal and Habar Yuunis elders and with their help and co-operation began the task of establishing a religious settlement and of extending the local teaching of religion. During his lifetime, Sh. Aadan enjoyed a great

Occupations of male members of Tariiqa

Government *Qaaddi* (Kadi)	3
Men of religion (*wadaads*)	3
Teachers (Government)	4
Other Officials	4
Domestic Servants	3
Masons	1
Carpenters	2
Traders	4
Shopkeepers	5
Total	29

reputation for piety and wisdom and was frequently approached to act as an arbitrator in the settlement of lineage disputes outside the settlement. His stone tomb where annual sacrifices are held, is in the centre of the community. The present head of the community is Sheikh Maḥammad Ḥusseen a lineal descendant of Sheikh Aadan, who also practises as a Government Kadi. The settlement is no longer a centre of missionary activity; few new converts to the Order and admissions to the community take place, and if anything its strength is dwindling rather than increasing.

Those living in the settlement are subject to a much more strict observance of the rules of the Dandaraawiya Order than its adherents outside.[2] The community is governed by a council (*majlis*) composed of the elders and sheikhs and presided over by Sheikh Maḥammad Jirde. In contrast to the normal Somali practice,[3] women are

[1] The Sayyid died in Mecca about 1908. He was a staunch supporter of the British and during the insurrection led by Sheikh Maḥammad 'Abdille Ḥassan (see p. 226) from 1900–1920 his followers in Somaliland co-operated with the Administration against Sheikh Maḥammad's followers of the Saaliḥiya order.

[2] The Dandaraawiya Order is more puritanical and strict in its rules than the other *tariiqas* followed by Somali.

[3] Somali normally explain their failure to observe the veiling of women in terms of the exigencies of the nomadic life where it is considered unpractical for a woman who is herding the flocks and loading burden camels to be veiled. In towns the wives of wealthier merchants and officials tend to wear the veil as a mark of social distinction.

supposed to wear the veil and are expected to adhere more strictly to the religious law than they normally do in the interior. Women who infringe the rules of the community are summoned with their husbands before the council and some of their personal possessions, such as jewellery, may be confiscated and sold for the benefit of the community's funds. Quarrels between women may be punished by plastering the disputants with cow-dung. Men who quarrel are subject to fines, and the final sanction is expulsion from the community with loss of cultivating and grazing rights in its fields. Men marrying into the *tariiqa* are examined by the elders to determine whether or not they are suitable for admission. In addition to the normal free and obligatory gifts of alms (*sadaqo*) and (*seko*),[1] I was told that a monthly tax was levied on all members of the community. This and other sources of revenue accrue to a central fund which is used for giving alms to the poor, meeting the expenses of hospitality, maintaining the mosque and tomb, and providing feasts at the annual ceremonies in honour of the saints.

It is clear that the settlement as a community has a degree of unity which cuts across the various ties of clanship which divide its members. Its autonomy as an extra-lineage organization, however, is limited. For while I was told that when a member of the community injures another member the affair is settled internally, it was admitted that homicide in the community would involve the lineage-groups of the persons concerned. And while they deplored it, the elders of the *tariiqa* acknowledged that membership of the community did not absolve the 'brothers' from their blood-compensation responsibilities to their lineages. For although it is condemned, the practice is to pay blood-wealth by lineage affiliation and dia-paying group. The Shariah is said in the past to have been observed more strictly when the settlement was a sanctuary in which men could find refuge from their own agnates provided they were considered suitable for admission to the *tariiqa*. Thus during the ravages of the armies of Sheikh Maḥammad 'Abdille, when the Administration withdrew to the coast and poverty and chaos were general in the interior, it was claimed that the community was unmolested and provided sanctuary to the impoverished.

In terms of the religious ideal of brotherhood which the *tariiqa* seeks to achieve, members of the settlement when asked their genealogy sometimes reply '*tariiqa*'. The opposition of this ideal to the reality of clan ties is formulated in assertions, such as that the

[1] These are the Somali pronunciations of the Arabic *ṣadaqa* and *zaakat*.

settlement has no genealogy (*abtirsiinyo*) or that its genealogy is the 'chain' of names of the saints (*silsilad al-baraka*) through whom God and the Prophet have revealed the *tariiqa*. This is the list which records the names of those saints who revealed God's purpose to the founder of the Order, and instructed him in the path which he should follow and teach to others. After the name of the founder follow those of his successors to whom he gave authority to transmit the *tariiqa* and to administer it locally[1]. It is their mystical charter which the sheikhs of the community oppose to their clan genealogies with the political segmentation which they imply.

The houses of the settlement, mostly of mud and wattle, are grouped in a rough semi-circle round the tomb of Sheikh Aadan and the mosque in the centre. These are distributed largely by lineage-group. Families of different clans and lineages are linked by affinal and matrilateral ties so that the settlement as a whole has a close-knit kinship structure differing in this respect from that of the nomadic settlement. It includes men of different clans —not simply of different dia-paying or primary lineage-groups —living permanently in the community and bound to its agnatic core by affinal and cognatic ties. As will be seen from the table, the majority of members are Habar Awal and Habar Yuunis clansmen. Minority groups, such as a few Ḍulbahante and others far from the regions in which their clansmen live in strength, participate in the blood-compensation pacts of those to whom they are married. Some pay compensation with the Habar Yuunis and some with the Habar Awal. The distribution by lineage of the fifty-eight houses in the community is shown in the table.

Although agnation is effective in determining the residential pattern of the community, and although in cases of homicide or general strife the community is divided by conflicting lineage ties, it has considerably greater identity as a territorial unit than does a village or town. Such corporate unity as the *tariiqa* possesses, is founded on the one hand on religious identity; for all the

[1] In this case the chain is Sh. Maḥammad Ḥuseen (present head)—Sh. Nuur Guuleed—Sh. Aadan Aḥmad (the founder)—Sayyid Maḥammad Dandaraawi (d. 1908)—Sayyid Ibraahiim ar-Rashiid (d. 1873)—Sayyid Aḥmad ibn Idriis (founder of the Aḥmadiya d. 1836)—Sayyid 'Abdul Wahhaab al-Tazi—Sayyid 'Abdul 'Aziiz al-Dabaq (both from the Maghreb)—Sayyid 'Abdul 'Abbaas el-Khaddar (a mythical personality associated with Alexander the Great)—The Prophet Maḥammad.

Distribution of Houses by Lineage-group

Habar Awal unspecified	4	
H. A. Deereyahan	12	
H. A. Aadan 'Iise	12	
H. A. Reer Sahal	1	
	29	50.0%
Habar Yuunis		
Sa'ad Yuunis	4	
H. Y. Gunbuur	1	
H. Y. Muuse Ismaa'iil	1	
H. Y. Muuse 'Abdalle	14	
	20	34.5%
Others:	9	15.5%

members are 'brothers' rather than 'cousins'.[1] On the other, unity stems from corporate rights in cultivation and grazing and permanent settlement. Rights in land and religious unity in the self-contained *tariiqa* settlement thus produce an identity of interest and action cutting across lineage divisions and are cemented by a web of affinal and cognatic relationships. In these circumstances a more developed system of authority and sanctions arises than that found in the typical organization of the nomads, for, at least to some extent, the religious head, the sheikh of the *tariiqa*, has political authority. I shall consider this development more fully in a later chapter. That religious unity is involved and not simply corporate rights in cultivation is shown by the structure of the cultivating villages in the west of northern Somaliland which we must now consider.

III

Although gaining in popularity through the profits which can be made in a good year, cultivation is still despised by the Somali pastoralist however much he may covet the income of a farmer.[2] In the eyes of a Ḍulbahante or other herdsman of the north-east,

[1] *Ilma' adeerro*—members of the same lineage, agnates other than siblings and father's and sons. See below, pp. 134-5.

[2] The cultivators are known as *Reer qodaal* 'diggers', (from *qod* to cultivate, or as *Reer beereed*, 'gardeners', (from *beer*, to plant) in opposition to the pastoralists, *Reer guuraa*.

those who till the land are poor in spirit and in livestock, for cattle and ploughing oxen replace camels to a considerable extent. To the pastoralist camel-rearing and fighting are the proper pursuits of men, and the cultivators are derided as weak (*masaakiin*) and unwarlike. The mutual contempt between nomad and cultivator is often phrased in terms of the relative excellence of camel's and cow's milk. Such insults are usually levelled between entirely pastoral clans such as the Ḍulbahante and partly agricultural clans such as the Habar Awal where differences in economy serve as a convenient vehicle for the expression of the rivalry between the two clan-families (Daarood and Isaaq) to which they belong.

DISTRIBUTION OF LIVESTOCK

Jibriil Abokor Cultivators

	No. of Wives	Camels	Sheep and Goats	Cattle	Gardens
1.	1	1	10	5	1
2.	2	5	10	7	2
3.	1	—	30	15	1
4.	2	6	—	5	1
5.	1	1	40	4	1
6.	1	—	14	6	—
7.	1	6	—	4	—
8.	2	6	—	12	1
9.	1	1	30	1	1
10.	2	20	100	30	3
11.	1	10	40	20	1
12.	1	7	—	5	1
13.	2	10	40	20	1
14.	2	2	14	12	2
15.	1	1	20	6	1
16.	1	1	30	4	—
17.	2	1	30	10	1
18.	1	1	—	3	1
19.	2	10	40	13	1
20.	1	1	30	2	1
21.	1	11	30	5	1
22.	1	1	30	—	1
23.	1	1	—	6	2

Cultivation, as has been said, is possible on the high ground in the fairly fertile soil of north-western Somaliland where in some places the annual rainfall is as much as twenty inches. The most westerly of the northern cultivating Somali are the Bartire, Yabarre, and Geri (all Daarood)[1] inhabiting the Jigjiga-Harar region of Ethiopia where they form a Somali wedge amongst the agricultural Galla. From the Galla and from these Daarood clans cultivation has been adopted by the Gadabuursi (Dir) and by the Sa'ad Muuse segment of the Habar Awal clan (Isaaq) of the British Protectorate. Cultivation was introduced into this region of the Protectorate about the turn of the century,[2] and the first farms were established by religious settlements (*tariiqas*). The region is thus one of culture change where to some extent Galla words and institutions associated with cultivation have been adopted by Somali. In addition, through cultivation and the formation of territorial groups, ties to locality are beginning to develop. And these provide an additional principle of unity to that of agnation which eventually they may challenge.

Cultivation is accompanied by cattle husbandry.[3] Most of those who own gardens have few camels as will be seen from the table showing the wealth in livestock of a number of representative individuals. Their settlements are based on natural or artificial basins which provide water for domestic use and for the cattle which never move far from the villages—unless they are taken out to good grazing in the summer months near permanent water. Since they require watering at least every four days in the wet seasons as well as in the dry, their movements are much more circumscribed than those of the sheep and goats, or camels. And except where they are sent out to graze near a water-hole in the care of a group of cattleherds (*lo'jir*) they pasture near the settlements during the day and are penned at night within the outer fence of the homestead. But for rinderpest, cattle diseases are few in the north. This affliction is well known and a form of immunization is practised by giving healthy beasts a light infection.[4] Selective breeding is not highly developed but the climate ensures that most calves are born after the spring rains. The

[1] See Lewis, 1955, pp. 21–4.

[2] The total area under cultivation in British territory is estimated at some 140,000 acres. See *Colonial Reports, Somaliland Protectorate, 1954–55*, 1956, p. 14.

[3] Cattle are of the Zebu type (*Bos indicus*), and in this region are a cross-breed of the Eastern Somali short-horn with the lyre-horned Ankole Zebu of Ethiopia.

[4] See R. G. Mares, 1954, p. 474.

majority of bulls are castrated for ploughing and broken to the yoke when they are about two years of age.

Shifting cultivation is not practised although a village settlement may move a hundred yards every few years to a fresh site. The gardens which surround the villages remain permanently attached to them. The plots distributed amongst the heads of nuclear families range between a quarter of an acre and an acre in extent, although some are larger. There is no definite pattern of crop rotation, although a man may allow one field to lie fallow one year, planting it the next. Commonly the whole demarcated holding is not ploughed but only a portion of it, the rest lying under grass to provide pasture for young stock. The stover which is left after the harvest also makes valuable grazing for cattle in the dry winter months.

Many cultivators are also transhumant pastoralists. Most men have flocks, and less commonly camels, as well as cattle and a garden; and, if in addition to his plot and oxen, a man has only a few sheep and goats and is completely sedentary, he usually has brothers or other close agnatic kinsmen with camels and flocks. Many of the settlements indeed expand about harvest time or later in the autumn or winter (*jiilaal*) as families with sheep and goats return from the southern grazing and camels are herded closer to the home-wells. But during the spring and summer months of good grazing, some settlements are deprived of as many as half their full populations, filling up again as the flocks and herds return about harvest time. Frequently, moreover, a man settles one wife, her children, and flocks, on a farm which he works while sending another wife, family, and flocks in summer to the southern pastures. When a man owns camels as well, they are sent out to the far grazing in the care of herdsmen recruited from within the same range of kinship connexion as those of the pastoralists. The practice whereby a married man does not himself usually herd his camels, allows the head of the nuclear family to give most of his attention to his farm, being actively concerned with the camels only when they return to the home-wells for water in the dry seasons. If his presence is then necessary the camels are watered at wells as near the settlement as possible.

The agricultural settlement or small village (*tuulo*) is generally larger than the nomadic hamlet and contains from four to twenty or more huts and nuclear families. I discuss the kinship structure of these below. The settlements are really small, permanent villages without in most cases shops or merchants. But the houses are simply nomadic huts (*aqals*) although often larger and more solidly constructed than those of the pastoralists. Some of the larger settlements, however, occasionally contain one or two mud-and-wattle houses of the type common in the permanent trade centres. Often they include also a mud-and-wattle mosque or Quranic school (*mal 'aamad*), built by public subscription and labour, and used for all religious activities such as sacrifice to local saints and the observance of the Muslim calendar festivals and the weekly service of the local Sufi brotherhood.

IV

In contrast to agricultural practice in the farming regions of southern Somalia where in some cases much of the labour of cultivation is performed by serfs (*boon*) in north-west Somaliland the division between sedentary cultivators and nomadic kinsmen is not one of serfs and nobility. Although, as I have said, agriculture is scorned by the pastoralists, those who till the soil are not servants or bondsmen but simply pastoralists who have adopted cultivation.

The main crop is sorghum with some cultivation of Indian corn as a secondary crop. The fields are ploughed before the *gu* rains of April and May. The wooden plough (*nugi*) is drawn by a pair of oxen (*qindi*)[1] and is similar in construction to that used in Ethiopia.[2] Not every farmer has his own oxen and many have to hire a team from a neighbour or kinsman. In 1957 a day's hire of a plough and pair of oxen cost about six shillings (East African). The cost varies with the season being highest before the spring rains when there is keen competition to plough the land.

Channels are dug by hand or ploughed on all sloping land round a plot to direct as much rainwater as possible on to it. Throughout the growing season these channels are maintained and new ones made to divert any adjacent surface water on to the land. The seed is sown after the rains. The fields are carefully tended during growth and periodically weeded by hand. This is followed by inter-row ploughing to clear channels to bring rainwater round the roots of the crop. When the crop is well grown, light raised platforms are erected on which children perch wielding rope slings to scare away

[1] Cf. Amharic *gindo*.

[2] See the illustrations in G. W. B. Huntingford, *The Galla of Ethiopia*, London, 1955, p. 72.

birds which attack the plants and cause considerable damage. At night, marauding wild-pig—another scourge—are kept at bay by guards mounted beside a fire.

When the sorghum ripens about September or October, the stalks are cut fairly low down with a hooked knife and piled in heaps. The heads are then severed, and collected on a piece of clear, level ground for threshing. They are threshed by a party of kinsmen and neighbours (*guus*)[1] beating with heavy curved wooden sticks, and paid for their labour in food and the promise of reciprocal help. The beating is regulated by the singing of songs; the leader starting the song and the others joining in in unison and keeping to a regular rhythm for some five minutes when they pause for a rest. Like the songs sung to the oxen while ploughing, these contain many Galla words although independent Somali versions also exist.

If for immediate sale or barter, the grain is put in bags; if it is to be kept for some time, it is stored in pits near the homesteads, and the season's yields vary with the size of holdings between four to twelve 200-lb. bags of grain. The crop is normally harvested in stages according to need and the availability of labour. Since a party of from six to a dozen men can easily fill about six bags in a day one or two flailing parties are often sufficient to thrash the whole of a man's yearly harvest.

The success of the harvest is mainly dependent upon the rainfall and the effect of a severe drought is often disastrous. But a late-sown crop, when ripe, may be blighted by cold winds in an early winter. Apart from the attacks of birds and wild pig which can usually be controlled fairly easily, the only major scourge are locust swarms. Their advent is still largely unpredicatable and in spite of the efforts of Locust Control officials they may completely devastate the crops.

To a considerable extent sorghum is grown as a cash-crop. Even if grain will be required later for planting and domestic consumption by the producer, when prices are high at the time of harvest, he is likely to sell more than he should in order to obtain ready cash. He then satisfies his subsequent needs by purchasing grain when the market price has fallen. After the harvest, the cultivator often needs money in order to replenish his stores and equipment and to buy clothes for himself and his family. And unless he possesses a considerable number of livestock he is more dependent upon ready cash for his trade needs than the pastoralist who can utilize sheepskins or obtain credit by promising to settle his debts in young lambs and kids after the rains. In any

[1] Cf. The Galla expression *guza*, of similar meaning.

case, what the spring (*gu*) months of April and May are to the pastoralist, the autumn (*dayr*) months of September, October and November are to the cultivator. Thus in the west, harvest time is the season of dancing and marriage, when people have more leisure for relaxation and social activities.

There are no harvest festivals and no rites or religious services specifically connected with cultivation. Local saints, however, are petitioned to bless the fields and, particularly when birds molest the crops are solicited through gifts made to the custodians of their tombs to safeguard the growing sorghum.

For the western cultivator, in addition to providing ready money,[1] sorghum, with milk, ghee, meat and trade commodities, is a vital part of his diet. The pastoralist who eats grain or imported rice—preferring the latter when it is cheaper—obtains these by trading the produce of his flocks and herds. But the cultivator who is generally self-sufficient in sorghum, may lack milk, on which alone when plentiful, the pastoralist can subsist. The price of locally grown sorghum fluctuates according to the seasons, production, and imports, from other countries (mainly Ethiopia). From a peak of about sixty shillings (East African) a bag before harvest, the price drops to about thirty shillings later in the year when the market is flooded.[2] The heads of the sorghum plant thus provide a staple in the diet of the cultivator. And stalks left behind in the ground, with those left after the heads have been severed, provide valuable stover for cattle in the winter months (November-April) when the grazing is at its poorest.

V

The land in which cultivating settlements are today densely settled in the west of the British Protectorate is land previously pastured by those who now cultivate. When, following the example of the local religious settlements, lineages of the Sa'ad Muuse and Gadabuursi began to adopt cultivation from their neighbours in Ethiopia, they established permanent villages where before they had lived in nomadic hamlets. The adoption of agriculture did not, as in southern Somalia, coincide with the

[1] The prestige value of camels is indicated by the fact that cultivators often spend a portion of the money obtained from the sale of their crops in buying camels.

[2] After the very poor harvest of 1955 in British Somaliland, a two hundred pound bag was selling at the unprecedented figure of one hundred shillings. The Government was forced to make a bulk shipment from the Sudan.

occupation of foreign territory previously occupied by others, nor did it involve settlement in new areas.[1]

At a series of meetings between the lineages concerned and representatives of the Administration about 1930, limits were set to the areas open for cultivation and the regions of Sa'ad Muuse and Gadabuursi cultivation were approximately determined. The division between the land cultivated by these two groups roughly follows the Borama and Hargeisa District boundaries. The southern limit to cultivation was fixed in Hargeisa District by a line running generally some few miles south of the main Hargeisa-Borama road. South of this line cultivation is prohibited and the clearing of the ground and firing of the bush is a punishable offence. In the interests of both cultivator and pastoralist and to conserve the soil in this arable region cultivation is strictly controlled by the Government.[2] New land for cultivation is only allocated by the Administration after consultation with farmers and pastoralists and in relation to the rival claims of different lineage-groups.

As has been seen, amongst the pastoralists uncultivated land is not owned nor are prescriptive rights necessarily asserted to it except in time of war and then often only in relation to scarcity of water and grazing. Thus, ultimately, the only effective method of maintaining rights to pasture and water is through superior force. The rights of the numerically dominant group in an area are always recognized whether or not they are contested by an actual appeal to force. The criterion of effective occupation thus determines grazing rights, since their continued enjoyment depends upon the ability of those occupying an area to maintain their position. In the same way, the rights of the cultivating groups in this region of arable land depend upon their effective occupation of it. Thus when cultivation was adopted primary rights were acquired by the Gadabuursi clan and Sa'ad Muuse sub-clan as collectivities since they were, and still are, numerically, and therefore politically dominant in the region. Within these units rights were distributed amongst those lineage-groups which prior to the adoption of agriculture customarily pastured their livestock in the region. In proportion to their greater numbers and greater strength larger lineage-groups gained more holdings.

[1] The arable regions of southern Somalia, as has been shown (above p. 25), were wrested from pre-Somali populations by northern Somali settling in the south where land was obtained by conquest.

[2] Cultivation and use of Land Ordinance (Laws, Cap. 119). In practice, areas for cultivation are demarcated at the discretion of District Commissioners in response to local agreements amongst those concerned.

Lineage-groups are not, however, regularly arranged on the land according to their genealogical propinquity any more than lineages amongst the pastoralists are territorially distinct units. The present distribution of land-holding units derives from the previous distribution of lineages in the pastures. The pastoral structure has as it were been 'frozen' to produce the present pattern of agricultural holdings. And as amongst the Sa'ad Muuse there were various minority groups, loosely assimilated politically but genealogically distinct,[1] so these are now found scattered in autonomous cultivating settlements with their own holdings and also living as affines and cognates in the farming villages of the numerically and politically dominant Sa'ad Muuse.

It is important to note that although a new economy has been adopted the pattern of pastoral political ascendancy has not changed. Amongst the cultivators as much as amongst the pastoralists it is still force of numbers which establishes a lineage as politically dominant in relation to others. There is no ritual or religious attachment to the earth and, perhaps in keeping with the manner in which cultivation has been adopted (by settlement not by conquest), no concept of groups having political dominance through rights in land irrespective of their numerical strength. For, as has been said, the politically dominant groups are the Gadabuursi and Sa'ad Muuse and their segments, and these now own most of the land precisely because they were and still are numerically strong.[2] The minority communities enjoy security of tenure amongst their stronger hosts but they are still politically weak because of their numerical deficiency. In payment of compensation and in the ultimate analysis in resort to arms, the larger dominant groups have more power and influence at their command, and this is apparent in the settlement of disputes between them and the weaker minority communities. I shall discuss the position of these more fully presently.

In the Sa'ad Muuse sub-clan of the Habar Awal clan, the primary lineage-groups most heavily engaged in agriculture are the Jibriil Abokor, Ḥusseen Abokor, 'Abdalle Abokor, and Ugaaḍ Abokor all of Hargeisa District. Their areas of settlement are roughly as follows.

[1] These are mainly the Akisho (of Galla origin) and the Tol Ja'lo (Isaaq) (not to be confused with the Habar Tol Ja'lo) and the Madigaan (Dir.).

[2] As amongst the pastoralists, the members of a numerically and therefore politically dominant lineage are known as *gob*—which may be loosely translated as aristocrats—in opposition to the members of weaker lineages derogatively referred to as *gun* (lit. the bottom). These terms are discussed more fully below, p. 192.

The Jibriil Abokor lands extend from Dila to Dubur (near Teiso), the 'Abdalle Abokor from Dubur to Hara Adaḍ, and the Ḥusseen Abokor from Hara Adad to Hargeisa. Mixed with these but mainly with the 'Abdalle Abokor are the less numerous Ugaaḍ Abokor. The Jibriil Abokor are the most westerly, their farms mingling with those of the Gadabuursi near Kalabayd where the boundary between Habar Awal and Gadabuursi cultivation runs. From this point westwards, Gadabuursi farms extend to Borama and beyond it.

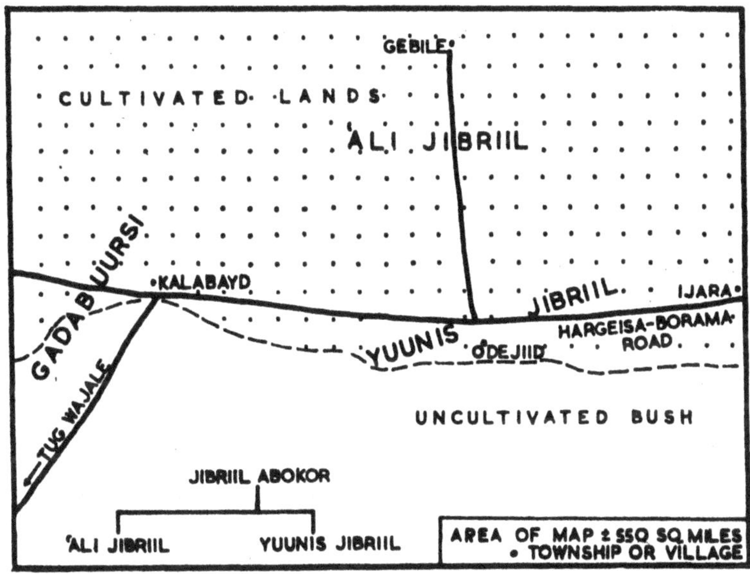

Map 11. Distribution of Sa'ad Muuse and Gadabuursi in the region of Gebile.

Within the areas predominantly cultivated by one primary lineage-group there is a degree of localization of the immediate lineage segments. Thus in the Jibriil Abokor cultivating area, segments of the next order are distributed largely, but not entirely, as separate land-holding units. For example, as the map shows, in the Gebile[1] region there is a fairly clear-cut territorial division between the 'Ali Jibriil and Yuunis Jibriil lineage-groups; these being lineage segments descended from 'Ali and Yuunis, two sons of Jibriil Abokor. Each of the two areas shown is occupied predominantly by one of the two lineages. But within

[1] The township of Gebile, seat of a Subordinate and Kadi's Court, lies some thirty miles to the west of Hargeisa.

these areas farming settlements are not distributed strictly according to their lineage affiliation. Quite apart from the foreign minority communities mentioned above (Akisho, Tol Ja'lo, Madigaan, etc) and from minority groups of other segments of the Habar Awal clan, and of other Isaaq clans, all the members of segments of either 'Ali or Yuunis Jibriil are not settled in contiguous farms.

An illustration is afforded by an area of some fifty square miles which I surveyed lying between Gebile and the main Hargeisa-Borama road. In this region there are thirteen farming settlements of which six are Reer Dalal ('Ali Jibriil), four Yuunis Jibriil, two Warrakiyo (Akisho), one Madigaan, and one Habar Awal Afgaab Muuse[1] (descended from a brother of Sa'ad Muuse). While the Yuunis Jibriil farms are clustered together on the southern edge of the region, where the land of the 'Ali Jibriil shades into that of the Yuunis Jibriil, the Reer Dalal segments which include people of four different dia-paying groups are scattered widely and not all in the same place. Although Gebile may be said to be the centre of the Reer Dalal, and is so regarded, some Reer Dalal settlements lie scattered five miles to the east of Gebile towards Arapsiyo, and also near Wajale across the border in Ethiopia. There are even settlements of the Yuunis Jibriil in the heart of this predominantly 'Ali Jibriil region. While there is thus some tendency for the localization of the immediate segments of primary lineage-groups, below this level settlements are not rigidly arranged on the land according to their lineage-group. Dia-paying groups are not necessarily local units.

A similar territorial structure is found amongst the cultivating Gadabuursi of Borama District. Here cultivation was adopted about the same time (about 1910) and in some places earlier than in Hargeisa District. The Gadabuursi Reer Maḥammad Nuur, for example, are said to have begun cultivating in 1911 at Jara Horoto to the east of the present town of Borama. The larger segments of primary lineage-groups are again roughly localized although there is considerable over-lapping. Thus, well-known segments of primary lineage-groups such as the Jibriil Yuunis,[2] Aadan Yuunis Makaahiil Deere, and Reer Faaraḥ Nuur occupy fairly distinct areas of cultivation.

It will be seen that in this region of cultivation primary lineage-groups and their immediate segments have tended to become established as territorial units. But within these divisions smaller

[1] The genealogical segmentation of the Jibriil Abokor is shown below, at the end of the book.

[2] Not to be confused with the segment of the Jibriil Abokor (Habar Awal clan) of the same name.

lineages and dia-paying groups are not absolutely localized. Few settlements contain all the living male members[1] of the descent groups with which they are associated and which are numerically and politically dominant in them. Nor are settlements of members of the same small lineage-group or dia-paying group always adjacent to each other. Normally they live within the general area occupied by the immediate segment of their primary lineage-group but they are often several miles apart within it and nearer to more distantly related agnates with whom they may co-operate in the management of a common water-hole. Here there is some evidence of the development of a sense of vicinage as distinct from only agnatic solidarity.

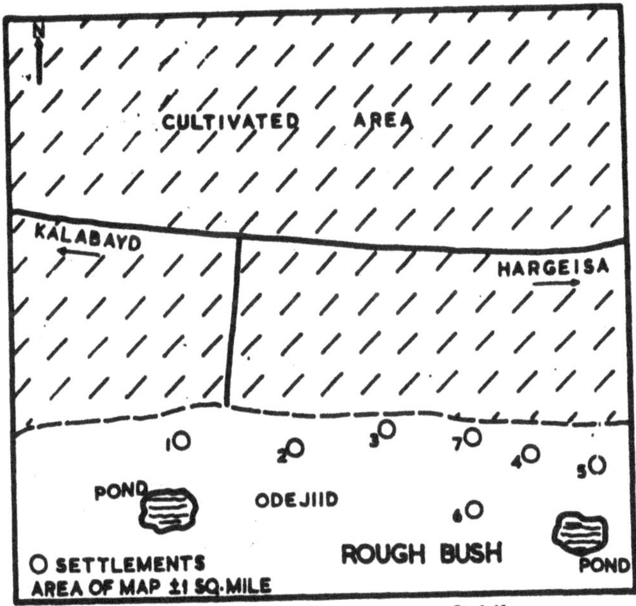

Map 12. Odejiid Region, near Gebile.

The seven settlements of Odejiid, some ten miles to the south of Gebile, provide a good example. Their distribution is shown in this map. The total population of married adults in the summer of 1956 was one hundred and sixty-one. The largest village was number VI with a population of 32 married men and women; the smallest, number VII, contained a nuclear family of one man and wife with their unmarried daughters living in two separate houses. Settlements III-VII share one common pond, while I and II share another,

[1] Marriage is mainly virilocal, as amongst the pastoralists.

although as will be seen from the kinship chart (page 113), settlement II is more closely related to Nos. IV and VII than it is to I. With the exception of that of the Akisho (III), all these settlements are of the Bah Kooshin segment of the Bah Gadabuursi (Jibriil Abokor) dia-paying group. So that the division in use of water-holes does not correspond to the division of the dia-paying group into its two internal segments, the Baha Lo'doon and Bah Kooshin.[1] The two ponds are managed by the two groups separately, they are dug out each year by the communal labour of the settlements concerned, and, in the dry season when water is scarce, guarded against intrusion by a rota of watchmen.

The fields lie round the settlements stretching northwards towards the main Hargeisa-Borama road. They are not fenced off from each other, but the extent of each individual's holding is indicated by local landmarks, bushes, stumps of trees, and lines of aloes. But boundary disputes are common. The regulation of these by the local settlement elders will be discussed in a later chapter.[2]

As stated earlier, since the threshing of the grain requires more labour than an individual himself can perform, work parties (*guus*) are mustered, composed of kinsmen and neighbours. The following examples illustrate the composition of such flailing parties.

Settlement II at Odejiid (see genealogy) is occupied by Yuusuf Buuḥ, his unmarried children, and by 'Umar and Maḥammad Ḥassan married sons of Yuusuf's diseased brother Ḥassan Buuḥ. 'Umar and Maḥammad share one field inherited from their father. Yuusuf shares two fields with his unmarried sons. During the harvest season of October, 1956, Yuusuf summoned a party of ten for a day's flailing. As an old man and the head of the settlement Yuusuf did not actually work himself and was content merely to urge on the labourers. These consisted of his son 'Ali, his dead brother's son 'Umar Ḥassan, and eight other agnates of his lineage, the Reer Geelle Kooshin. These were all youths who counted from three to four generations to a common ancestor with Yuusuf within the Geelle Kooshin lineage. The composition of the *guus* was thus in this instance entirely agnatic. The party was regaled with sorghum cooked in fat in the morning, and then worked till dusk filling seven bags of grain. There were frequent breaks and rests, the main one about mid-day when tea was served and poured out by Yuusuf Buuḥ himself as host. After the day's work all were offered cooked osrghum, and some given a little grain to take home to their families.

[1] See below, p. 154.

[2] See below, pp. 233-37.

GENEALOGICAL RELATIONSHIPS OF ODEJIID SETTLEMENTS (I–VII)

(*Agnatic relationship of principal settlement elders*)

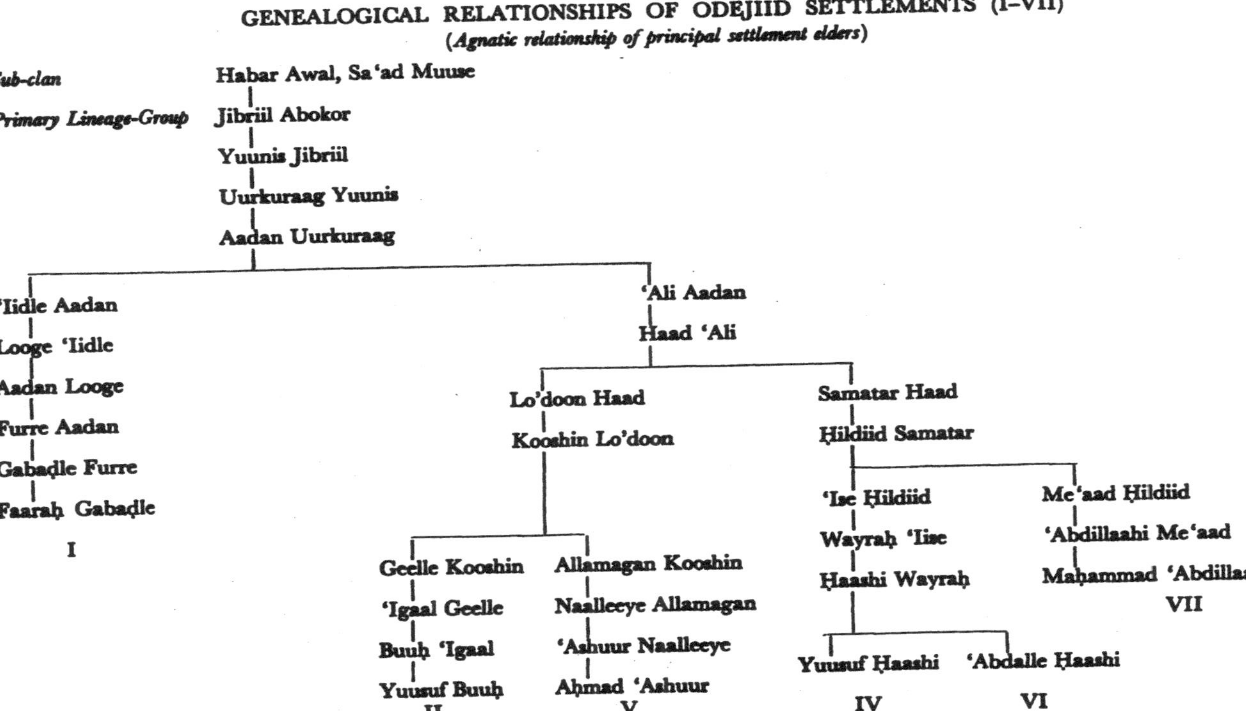

Those who had come some distance stayed the night and returned to their homes, which all lay within a ten mile radius, the following morning.

At a similar flaying party held by 'Abdillaahi Kaahin (No. 13, of settlement VI at Odejiid) there were fourteen thrashers including 'Abdillaahi himself. Of these, eleven were agnates of the Reer Haad 'Ali—the lineage-group which embraces all the agnates of settlements II and IV-VII—of whom seven, including 'Abdillaahi and his son, were from his own settlement. The remainder were from the other settlements at Odejiid. Three were affines from the Akisho Warrakiyo settlement III united by kinship and common interest and sharing the same water-hole. The labourers were similarly provided with food but paid no wage.

As has been indicated, the farming settlement is physically a small village enclosed within a common thorn fence and divided by numerous paths running between its component houses. The fields in which the villagers have cultivating rights are scattered round the village within easy walking distance. Each nuclear family, or closely related families within the same range of relationship as those of the pastoral hamlets, pen their stock separately within the village and close to their huts. Most of the agnatic members of settlements, joined them about the same time, or are the sons of the original settlers. Each settlement does not therefore have a 'founder'. Nor, as I have said, are there any ritual ties to the land. There is no hierarchical organization in the cultivating village any more than there is in the pastoral hamlet. There is no village chief or headman and no formally constituted council. But the heads of all the component nuclear families constitute an informal council regulating the internal affairs and family disputes of the settlement. Yet, as in the nomadic hamlet, in most settlements, there is at least one elder whose leadership, in no way rigidly defined and with the power to influence through advice and not to give orders, is generally acknowledged by the members of the village. He is always a man of the numerically dominant lineage round which the settlement is formed.

Each village does not possess a separate name as a territorial entity. But since the various regions of the country (amongst the nomads as well as the cultivators) are given local names which usually refer to some prominent geographical or topographical feature,[1] the general location of a particular settlement can be

[1] E. g. Odejiid, correctly *Oodejiid*, from *ood* bush, and *jiid* line or path, the name referring to the fact that this region marks the southern limits of cultivation and

specified. In the north-west of Somaliland many local names are apparently of Galla origin and, according to tradition, date from the time when, prior to the advent of the Somali, this region was occupied by the Galla.

However, the continuing importance of clanship as opposed to the incipient and yet weak force of local contiguity is seen in the fact that men describe themselves not in terms of their place of settlement but in terms of their lineage affiliation. Thus farmers of the Odejiid region do not refer to themselves as 'the people of Odejiid' (*Reer Oodejiid*) but as Reer Ḥildiid Samatar, or whatever their lineage happens to be. Their social relations are defined first by their lineage affiliation and only secondarily by the particular region in which they happen to live. Political and jural status is still governed by clanship and contract without direct relation to spatial distribution in particular settlements. For the dia-paying political unit to which a person belongs is never localized in only one cultivating village.

I have stated that every settlement amongst the cultivating northern Somali has an agnatic core whose members are numerically dominant in it. When, as in most cases, the settlement is of the numerically dominant lineage of the region, its members enjoy higher status and generally stronger rights in land than those of foreign minority groups. This is the case whether the latter are simply accreted to the dominant lineage in a settlement, or whether they are living separately in their own villages within the area occupied by the dominant land-holding lineage. Before discussing the land rights of minority groups I compare the kinship structure of two typical settlements one of the numerically dominant group, and one of a minority.

I take first settlement No. VI at Odejiid as exemplifying a village of a dominant lineage. This settlement of the Yuunis Jibriil segment

---

bush clearance. Gebile is from *geb*, a river bank, and means the place by the river. Las Anod, correctly *Laas 'Aanood*, the place where the wells (*laas*) are milky (*'aano*). El Afweyn, correctly *'Eel Afweyn*, the well (*'eel*) with the large mouth. Odweyna, correctly *Oodweyna*, the place where there is much large bush. Kalabayt, correctly *Kalabayḍ*, from *kala* apart, the place where the road forks. Innumerable other examples of this kind could be given. Only rarely does a place-name refer to a person. An instance is the town of Sheikh, so called after the famous Sheikh 'Abdillaahi Sheikh Quṭub whose descendants, the Reer Sheikh Aw Quṭub are scattered in the Ogaden, but whose shrine is at Sheikh in the Protectorate amongst the Habar Awal. Sometimes though not often, a waterhole which has been dedicated to God in the name of a lineage ancestor, and thus declared the property of God (*waqaf*) bears the name of the man concerned.

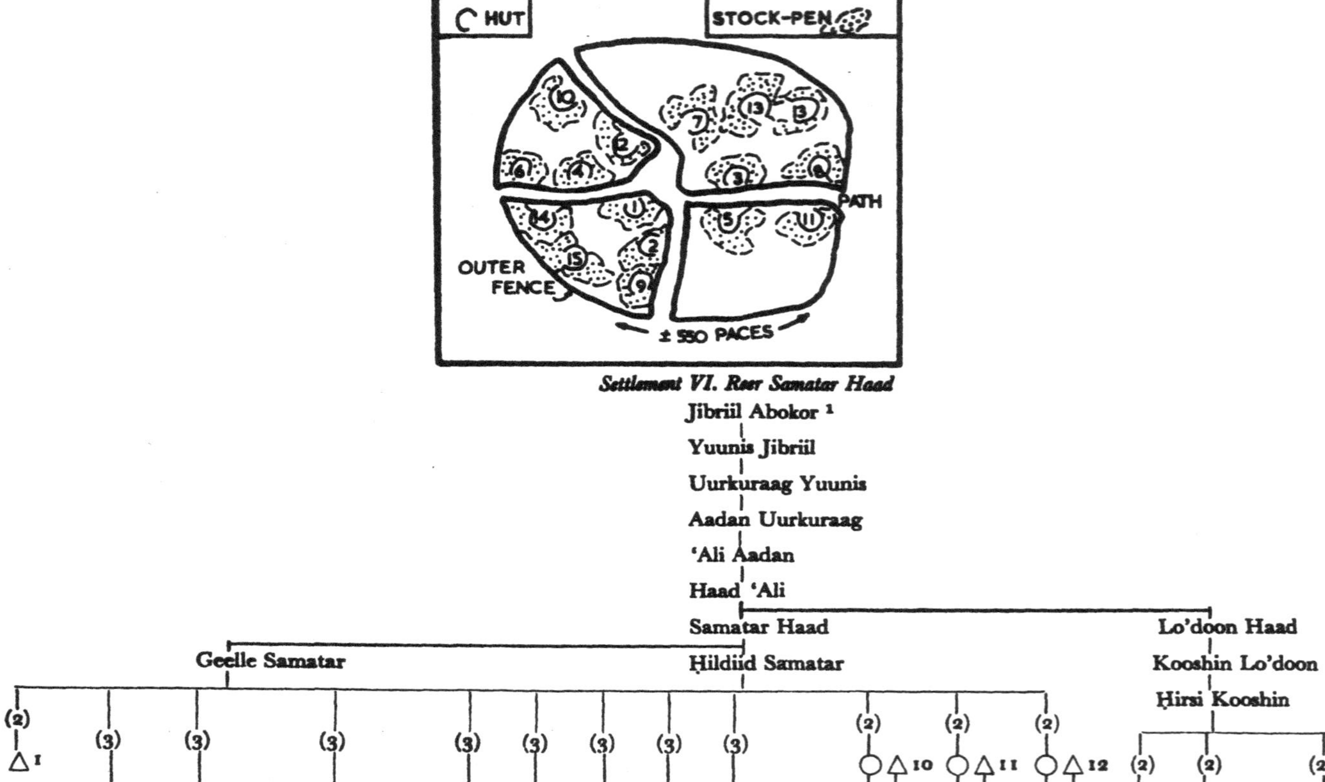

Settlement VI. Reer Samatar Haad

[1] The numbers in brackets refer to the number of generations counted in the descent lines from a living head of a family to an eponymous ancestor.

of the Jibriil Abokor contains sixteen houses distributed roughly in four quadrants within the village.

Each house has its own attached enclosures for cattle and sheep and goats and the whole village is intersected by paths. The clearings within the outer fence are used mainly as store pits for grain. In 1956 the settlement had a total adult population of thirty-two; fifteen adult married males, and sixteen married women, and one widow.

The settlement, as such, has no name, but its people are referred to as Reer Samatar Haad from the name of the politically dominant lineage to which, as will be seen from the kinship chart, the majority of its agnatically related male members belong (seven out of eight). One man (13) belongs to the Reer Lo'doon Haad lineage connected to the Samatar Haad as shown; to him are attached affinally two others (14 and 15). The remaining five married men and heads of nuclear families are linked affinally to the Samatar Haad lineage, four to the Ḥildiid Samatar and one to Geelle Samatar. Although there is thus a large proportion of affines (46.7%) as against 53.3% agnates, the composition of the settlement is based on the agnatic core of Samatar Haad. The most influential man in the village (8) is a man of religion (*wadaad*). He is by no means the richest of the elders, since he only owns a modest number of livestock, and one field, and has only one wife. But backed by his knowledge of religion. and his membership of the dominant lineage his forceful character and personality give his opinions considerable weight in the settlement. The sheikh of the village (14) of the Gadabuursi, 'Ali Yuunis, is affinally related to the agnatic core. The richest, but not the most influential villager (13) of the Reer Lo'doon Haad with two wives, has two fields and a considerable number of stock including ten camels. During the rains while he stayed in the settlement tending to his fields, he sent his first wife with her young children and flocks and camels out into the southern pastures across the Ethiopian border. They returned in September before the 1956 harvest. Both he and the nominal leader of the settlement (8) are men of about the same agé. But the latter enjoys greater prestige on account of his greater learning in religion—he plays a prominent part in all religious activities and in the weekly Sufistic services—and because he belongs to the Samatar Haad, the dominant lineage.

A good example of a cultivating village of an alien minority group is that of the Warrakiyo Akisho (III) whose only kinship ties with the dominant Yuunis Jibriil are by marriage and cognation. There are sixteen houses with thirteen male heads of nuclear families and sixteen married women of whom two are widows living with their unmarried children in the settlement. One man (1) has two wives and two houses. Of the thirteen heads of nuclear families eleven are agnates (84.6%) of the Warrakiyo lineage (Akisho); and two (15.4%)

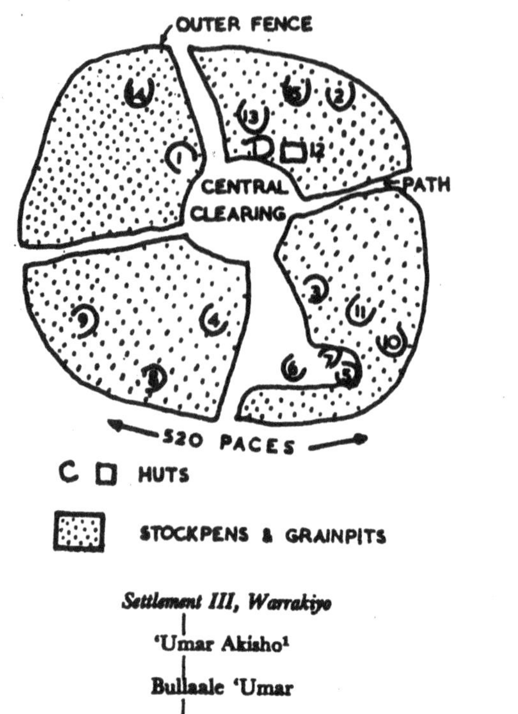

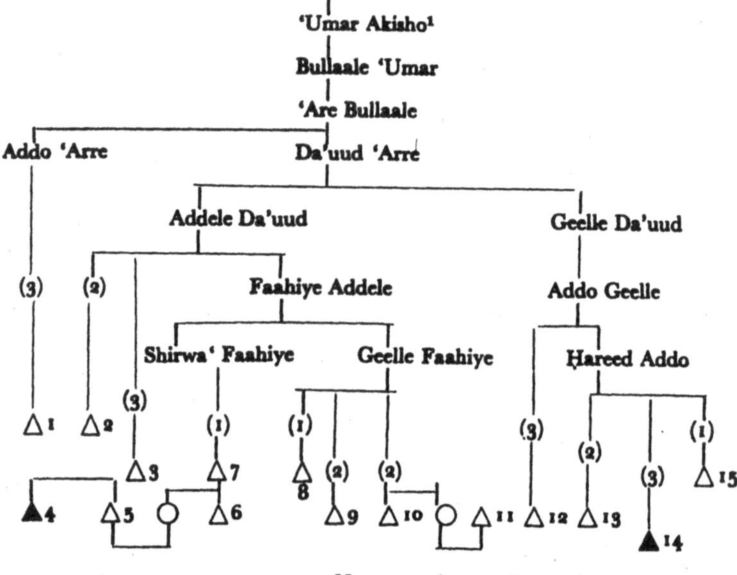

Nos. 14 and 4 are deceased.

[1] The numbers in brackets refer to the number of generations counted in the descent lines from a living head of a family to an eponymous ancestor.

are affines living with their wives' agnates. There is also one family of orphaned children living cognatically within the settlement into which their father had married.

The more strongly agnatic character of this settlement reflects the alien status of its members. They have a sense of identity and exclusiveness in opposition to people of the Yuunis Jibriil by whom they are considered to be slightly inferior. Since the Yuunis Jibriil segments are stronger, attachment to the Warrakiyo Akisho is not so attractive.

Again the settlement has no formal head, but the eldest man in the settlement(7) who is almost blind and is probably about eighty years old, is recognized as being the leading elder. The history of his family's marriages illustrates how members of such alien communities as the Warrakiyo are linked matrilaterally and affinally to the dominant Yuunis Jibriil. Both his father's mother and his own mother were of the Yuunis Jibriil as are his own wives. Both his sons are married to women of the Jibriil Yuunis. It will be seen that this old man belongs to the Warrakiyo lineage which is most highly segmented and numerically dominant in the settlement.

As stated in an earlier chapter, one of the defining characteristics of the primary lineage-group is that it is exogamous. Thus in this region out of seventy marriages which I recorded only three (4%) were between members of the same primary lineage-group, in this case within the Jibriil Abokor. As the Jibriil Abokor settlements are linked by agnation and do not normally intermarry, marriage takes place between them and the minority settlements. These are thus linked to the villages of the dominant lineage by a web of affinal ties. Thus in Warrakiyo settlement III the three affines who are heads of nuclear families are all of the Yuunis Jibriil lineage. And out of twenty marriages contracted by Warrakiyo male agnates of the settlement, eighteen (90%) were with Yuunis Jibriil women of the surrounding settlements. In many of the latter, men of the dominant Yuunis Jibriil have married Warrakiyo Akisho women as well as women of other minority communities within the region, and women of other lineages (some within the Habar Awal clan) from outside. As I have indicated, cognatic ties also link the minority settlements to those of the dominant lineages and these proliferate over the years.

VII

When the arable land in the north-west of the Protectorate was originally apportioned amongst the various lineages concerned (including the foreign minority groups—Akisho, Madigaan, Tol Ja'lo etc) the superior rights of the numerically dominant Sa'ad Muuse (Habar Awal) and Gadabuursi were acknowledged in the allotment of holdings. The informal rights which customary grazing of an area tends to create backed by the sanction of numerical strength crystalized in the new rights to land for cultivation. The minority communities which historically may have had prior rights were accepted on sufferance by the larger and stronger and probably more recent Sa'ad Muuse and Gadabuursi. Men of these dominant groups, however, acknowledge the rights to land of the weaker alien communities. But while Akisho, Tol Ja'lo, and Madigaan clansmen claim that they have absolute rights to the land where they exist in autonomous settlements, land disputes indicate that their rights are subject to a continuance of good relations with the numerically superior lineages amongst which they live. Thus the Sa'ad Muuse, and the Gadabuursi similarly in their region, speak of the whole area of cultivation as theirs. And while they are genealogically, and to some extent socially and politically distinct, amongst their stronger neighbours, the minorities tend nominally to be identified with them in external relations. This is evinced in friction between the Gadabuursi and Jibriil Abokor. The extensive affinal and cognatic ties which link the minorities to the dominant lineages are regarded by the latter as attempts to establish mutual ties where common agnation is absent. Through having the status of affine (*ḥidid*)[1] as opposed simply to that of clients or protected strangers (*magan*), the minority groups are placed in a superior and stronger position.

There is no system of tribute, nor do the minority settlements perform special duties for those of the dominant lineage. Each settlement of a dia-paying group is, as I have indicated, autonomous under the leadership of its own elders, subject to the residential ties which link the members of contiguous settlements together especially in relation to the communal maintenance of a waterhole. The Akisho, Tol Ja'lo, and Madigaan minorities have their own independently constituted dia-paying groups under headmen recognized by the Government. They are not generally involved in blood-compensation contracts with their more powerful neighbours. But it is admitted that in the event of hostilities they may seek assistance from their stronger affines and

[1] See below Chapter V.

cognates. This represents a recognition of their numerical deficiency and that without help from their neighbours they could not adequately defend their position against external aggression.

More specifically, the character of land-rights depends upon political status. Although dia-paying groups are not localized but distributed in several not always contiguous settlements, political viability and rights to land depend upon the ability to pay blood-compensation independently. Those minority lineages such as the Akisho, Tol Ja'lo, and Madigaan which pay blood-wealth independently and which are recognized as autonomous dia-paying groups therefore enjoy rights in land almost as strong as their numerically dominant neighbours. The principle that in the last analysis military supremacy is the source and guarantor of rights could only threaten their security of tenure were they involved in general strife with the stronger Gadabuursi or Sa'ad Muuse amongst whom they live. And even then, despite the fact that land is not registered, the Government would undoubtedly defend their land against usurpation.[1]

It is thus only those minority communities not organized in independent dia-paying groups, and directly under the protection of the dominant Sa'ad Muuse or Gadabuursi, which have merely usufruct rights in land. The following case demonstrates their insecure position. The Kharrab segment of the Habar Yuunis clan were for many years attached to the Sa'ad Muuse Jibriil Abokor, paying blood-wealth with the Reer Dalal lineage. When their protectors adopted agriculture they followed suit and came to farm some fifty holdings under the tutelage of the Reer Dalal. When a series of disputes occurred between the subordinate Kharrab and superior Reer Dalal a sneering comment that the Kharrab were little better than bondsmen (*sab*) led them to sever their connexion with their protectors. After three years of negotiations to clear up outstanding debts, the Kharrab left the Reer Dalal relinquishing all claim to the land they had farmed. Of a group so closely attached to the Reer Dalal (though genealogically distinct) that they did not intermarry, only one Kharrab farm now remains in the region.[2]

Similarly in the various settlements associated with particular segments of an autonomous dia-paying group, alien members of other dia-paying groups, whether of the stronger Sa'ad Muuse and Gadabuursi or weaker minorities, do not enjoy much more than usufruct rights to land. Here their land rights depend upon

[1] Since this was written land registration has been introduced.

[2] For this illustration and much valuable discussion on land tenure I am indebted to Mr J. A. Brown, sometime District Commissioner, Hargeisa.

the character of their association with the land-holding lineage in the settlement. Thus abandonment of his natal lineage and dia-paying group for that of the settlement in which he lives, places a man in a strong position and gives him a title to land which he can pass on to his descendants as long as they continue to live in the same community and participate in its dia-paying arrangements. As the examples cited have shown, cultivating settlements often contain extraneous aliens who have married into the land-holding lineage of a village and who share in its blood-compensation agreements. But, marriage to a landed lineage confers upon a man cultivating rights only for his children by his wife of that lineage. His rights, and the rights of his children, lapse if he divorces the woman and marries again outside the settlement. Such matrilaterally entailed rights moreover cannot be disposed of without the consent of the elders of the land-holding lineage. In fact, if matrilateral male heirs to land wish to dispose of their holdings, they have often to surrender them and receive scant compensation.

As has been indicated, land, like camels and livestock in general, remains within the agnatic group on the death of the holder. The provisions of the Shariah are not applied, except perhaps in a few very limited cases in towns where a Government Kadi is at hand to apportion the estate according to the religious law. But even in towns only in rare cases is inheritance of property contested (out of 992 cases before Government Kadis' Courts in 1956 only nineteen concerned inheritance, i.e. less than two per cent). Women are normally excluded from inheriting land except where limited rights have been granted to a husband as client of a land-holding lineage.

Where a man leaves several male descendants, but only a small plot, it is usually farmed by the first-born son who should share the produce with his siblings. If a man leaves several gardens[1] and only two or three sons, each is given one holding, the largest being the prerogative of the eldest. When a man has two or more wives he divides his land between them for their use and that of his children. When a man has only one small field and more than one wife, the land is not divided into several plots, but the harvest is shared amongst his families by different wives. That the first wife and her children expect a larger share than the others leads

[1] As in the case of the pastoralists, the family estate is frequently divided on the marriage of the sons and before the father's death.

frequently to disputes. Where a man leaves adult sons by one wife and young children by another, the former assume the management of the estate. But if they show any tendency to exclude their younger half-siblings from their entitlement to a share in the harvest, the local settlement elders are not slow to intervene. For when a man has not apportioned the family estate before he dies it is divided by the elders of his lineage with the approval of the elder sons. It is the duty of the elders to continue to superintend the management of the estate in which as agnates of the landholding group they have an interest, and to see that it is administered fairly in accordance with local custom.

Agnation in principle confers a perpetual right for a man to lineage-group land. As long as he continues to act as a member of his natal lineage and to share in its activities, paying blood-wealth with it and supporting it when called upon, he continues to have a right to inherited land even when residing away from his agnatic kinsmen. I am not however, certain how long such rights can be sustained to a field left uncultivated. My impression is that should a man desert his natal settlement and holding, and appoint no-one to work it for him, his agnates would press him to relinquish the land. In any case, few people absent themselves indefinitely from their homes without maintaining contact and continuing to share the debts and responsibilities of their dia-paying group.

Since land is the main source of wealth to the cultivator, and since his kinsmen have an interest in his wealth through the rights and obligations of clanship and through the contractual agreements which bind the members of a dia-paying group, a man has primary but not absolute rights in lineage land. Land rights are tied to agnation and in an extended sense land is the estate of a patrilineage. As in the case of livestock, men regard their rights in land as an inherited title. Thus the individual member of a land-holding lineage has greater freedom in the disposal of his land than those who enjoy cultivating rights only through being connected affinally, matrilaterally, or by contract to a landed lineage.

VIII

At the beginning of Chapter II it was argued that some knowledge of the ecological and economic setting of pastoral Somali society is essential if the nomadic political constitution is to be understood. In discussing structural political relations in later chapters we shall constantly be concerned with spatial relations between groups and economic competition for the sparse resources which the Somali pastoralist has at his disposal. Thus in relation to pastoral Somali politics this chapter and the two preceding ones have dealt with the main features of the economic structure and territorial organization. For the pastoral economy is the setting of northern Somali political institutions and political relations ultimately relate always to this economy.

It is necessary to emphasize that in northern Somaliland town and rural community are not separate spheres of action. There is generally no discontinuity between rural and urban society for both town and interior form part of a common pattern of life dominated by pastoral values. Indeed, as trade-centres the typical northern towns are the focal points of the pastoral system. Territorially, like the home-wells, they give some definition to the dispersion of lineages in the pastures. But despite their greater stability as compared with that of the ephemeral grazing settlements in the pastures, towns generate little residential solidarity amongst their inhabitants. Yet their more heterogeneous constitution extends the bonds of clanship and contract and of economic co-operation in trade and leads to the recognition of wider agnatic ties which in the pastoral situation tend to be nullified by internecine rivalries.

The continuing importance of clanship in towns is evident in the tendency towards the localization of kinsmen in separate wards, and in fights which break out between individuals only to assume a lineage character. Above all it is apparent in the management of pastoral lineage affairs from the towns and even in the organization of the new political movements which we consider in a later chapter. Yet these new political movements are one aspect of a reaction against this pastoral agnatic determinism, and an indication of a growing desire, particularly in the main urban centres, to escape from the bonds of clanship and blood-compensation contracts. These new developments reflect the influence in the urban setting of such factors as more widespread educational facilities, a minimal development of industry and new trades, the urban practice of Islam, and perhaps most significant of all, the greater degree of security which more effective police control affords the town-dweller.

The structure of the cultivating settlements in the west of northern Somaliland represents the 'fixing' of pastoral patterns of territorial distribution. Here dia-paying groups are not concentrated in single areas but deployed, though less extensively, as they are among the pastoralists. Thus in neither the cultivating nor the pastoral environment are dia-paying groups localized units, although in time of war they tend to assume such distinctive territorial formations amongst the pastoralists. I have argued that this follows from the dispersion of kinsmen which the ecology dictates and which amongst the agriculturalists has merely become stabilized by settlement. And whereas among the nomads land as pasturage is open to all, here it becomes an agnatic commodity. There is not, however, a general correlation between territorial distribution and lineage affiliation except at the higher levels of segmentation, as for example, at that of the primary lineage-group or its immediate segments.

Among the pastoralists political dominance in terms of the ability to defend sparse resources for animal husbandry is generally conferred by numerical superiority. Among the cultivators in addition to this, lineages are also dominant in relation to rights in land for cultivation. But, if by giving rise to agnatic holdings settlement continues to support agnation, it also creates a new principle of territorial unity which is opposed to patrilineal solidarity. For it is vicinage rather than clanship which is commonly the basis of the local corporate interests which unite contiguous settlements in the use of a common water-hole. Here there is evidence of some degree of local solidarity based on common residence in the same area. This is in strict contrast to the situation of the pastoralists where corporate activities are governed solely by clanship and contract and not by ties of vicinage. The special character of the cultivating settlements moreover appears to be reflected in another respect in which they differ from the pastoralists. Lineage disputes among the cultivators are of less frequent occurrence and there is a wider range of conflict settled by local elders without direct recourse to self-help or to Government intervention. This conclusion is supported by District Office records which reveal a smaller incidence of lineage fights among the cultivators and is reflected in the taunts which the pastoralists level at their less belligerent countrymen. I note here, leaving it to a later chapter to elaborate, that settlement seems to create conditions conducive to a more formal structure of authority; and at least one in which local elders wield greater power than they do in the pastoral situation. Certainly local cultivating communities maintain law and order without recourse to violence even between members of different dia-paying groups where among the pastoralists self-help or administrative intervention would be required.

Residential solidarity is taken a stage further in the few religious settlements (*tariiqas*) of the north. Here residential ties are supplemented by the ideal of religious unity, of 'brotherhood' in a religious sense. This results in a more formal administrative structure within the community and in the development of formal organs for controlling its life. It is of course, in the community as a whole, as a religious corporation, that rights in land are vested. For the community's lands have been in effect dedicated to God as a trust (*waqaf*) by the lineages amongst which it is established. The system of blood-wealth payment practised by Somali is generally known to be contrary to the strict interpretation of the Shariah[1] and this conflict between religious ideals and customary practice is at its most acute in the religious settlement. Here it is particularly regretted by the devout that clanship and dia-paying group affiliation still regulate homicide. Religious identity has usurped some of the functions of agnation, but blood-group solidarity which is the most decisive criterion of political allegiance remains that of the pastoral morality founded on agnation. And with the present economy and the existing ecological conditions the force of clanship triumphs.

[1] See below, pp. 217-8.

5

Clanship and the Paradigm of the Lineage System

THE preceding chapters have shown how the possession of livestock is tied to agnation and how clanship is the political principle regulating competition for sparse resources. It has been necessary to devote considerable space to the structure of the local units because these are based on political clanship. In later chapters we shall be concerned with the processes of social control; with the means by which lineage political relations are regulated. But before we can proceed further we have to examine the principles of lineage segmentation and the way in which lineage segments are articulated in the lineage system. Thus it is clanship and the morphology of the lineage system which form the subject of this chapter.

Somali politics are founded on the implicit values of agnation supplemented by the explicit bonds of contractual agreements amongst agnates. It is political contract which calls forth, marshals, and formalizes the implicit bonds which unite men of the same lineage. Political relations at every level of lineage segmentation have generally this two-fold character. In the following chapter I shall show how contract (*ḥeer*) is superimposed upon agnatic kinship (*tol*) to form political units whose members are united in the payment of blood-wealth and common political responsibility. This process is most binding and occurs most commonly with the dia-paying group; but as occasion demands it is also applied at other levels of segmentation within the general field of clanship.

I

Politics are in principle governed by agnation (*tol*). A person's membership of a lineage and of the total lineage structure within his clan-family is established by the genealogy which links him through male ancestors to the eponym of the clan-family. In naming, the Muslim Arab practice is followed of giving a son or daughter as surname the first name of the father, so that each generation bears a new first-name and it is thus that the genealogies which record agnatic descent are built up. A man called Ḥassan Jaama' bears a son 'Ismaan Ḥassan and a daughter Khadiija Ḥassan. 'Ismaan in turn marries and begets sons Yuusuf and Faaraḥ. These are then connected to their grandfather (*awow*), by the agnatic genealogy, Yuusuf and Faaraḥ, 'Ismaan, Ḥassan Jaama'. When Khadiija marries her agnatic genealogy stops since her children are born to her husband's line. The word 'genealogy' (*abtirsiinyo*)[1] which Somali equate with the Arabic *nasab* (which they also employ) is a compound of *ab* or *aabe* (father agnatic generation), *tiri* (to count, or reckon), and *sii* (to give), and means literally 'reckoning of agnation'.

It is a matter of family pride to teach children their father's genealogy. This duty usually falls mainly on the mother and the ease with which small children of eight or nine years can recite their genealogies up to their clan-family ancestor is astonishing; especially since the genealogy may include well over twenty names, some of which are repetitive. Everyone knows his genealogy up to the eponym of his clan-family. Beyond this point, descent is ultimately traced to the line of the Prophet Maḥammad or to noble Arabian familes closely associated with his. Prominent elders, Akils, and Sultans, generally know the genealogical relationships between their clan and other clans of the same clan-family for this knowledge is important in their management of clan affairs. They know the proximity of their relationship to other lineages within the clan and to other clans within the clan-family. They know their connexion with members of another clan of the clan-family without having to work genealogically to the point at which they share a common ancestor. Younger persons less well-versed in the genealogical segmentation, have to follow through their own genealogies until they reach a common ancestor to determine their relations with someone else. It is too, usually only elders and sheikhs or men of religion generally (*wadaads*), who are familiar with the genealogy of their clan-family ancestor to the point at which it joins the lineage of the Prophet Maḥammad or of his 'Companions'.

The portions of the genealogies which link Somali lineages to noble Arabian families connected with the Prophet have religious rather than secular functions. Although there is frequently

[1] The expression *abtirsiimo* also occurs.

political enmity between, for example, members of the Daarood and Isaaq clan-families, it would be quite impossible for all the Isaaq to unite against all the Daarood dispersed over a vast area and intersected by clans of other neutral clan-families.[1] The sections of the genealogies above clan-family ancestors which bridge the gap between Somaliland and Arabia, the source of Islam, have primarily religious significance. And here, although it is not intended in this book to present a full account of Somali Islam, it is necessary to say a little of the Somali cult of saints.

In principle, ancestors of a lineage-group, at various levels of segmentation, are venerated by their descendants in periodical sacrifices made in their name to God and the Prophet.[2] Usually every year a feast-day (*mawliid*) is recognized when members of a lineage assemble to hold a communal sacrifice (*Rabbibari*)[3] in praise of their ancestor. This is usually arranged in the summer months between April and July, when milk is plentiful and grazing abundant, allowing large parties of herdsmen to congregate in the same area of pasture. These ceremonies are often not performed at the actual place of burial of the lineage ancestor which may be unknown to many and is often far from the area in which the nomadic hamlets and camel-camps are gathered. Thus the shrines of ancestors do not necessarily localize groups and the ancestor cult is practised in conformity with the needs of nomadism described in previous chapters.

The religious significance of lineage ancestors is largely a function of the number of their descendants and corresponding political importance. It is particularly at the level of the clan-family ancestor that the ancestor cult is most developed. So that where social cohesion is at a minimum, religious power is at a maximum. This again is correlated with the fact that, above the

[1] Where, however, in the same region different Daarood lineages are in contact with different Isaaq lineages conflict often flares up between those of each clan-family. This is the case in Jigjiga District of Ethiopia where a dispute between Daarood and Isaaq individuals readily develops into a feud between all the Isaaq and all the Daarood of Jigjiga.

[2] Lineage ancestors are in effect regarded as Sufi saints and their veneration thus finds a natural place in Somali Islam. See my 'Sufism in Somaliland: A Study in Tribal Islam', *B.S.O.A.S.* 1955/56.

[3] Literally, 'to beseech God', from *bari*, to pray or ask for, and Arabic *Rabbi*, one of the many names for God. The expression *Allaahbari* (with the same meaning) is equally common. Both words express the idea of sacrifice to God as a plea or petition. The more pure Somali expression *ḥus* is generally used in preference to the Arabic *mawliid* when a sacrificial ceremony is performed in honour of a close ancestor or a deceased kinsman.

clan-family ancestor, descent is traced to the founders of Arabian Islam, validating the Muslim practices and beliefs of the Somali. It must be noted however, that all the saints (sg. *weli*, pl. *awliyo*), venerated by Somali are not lineage ancestors. Many of the most important saints in northern Somaliland have no significance as the founders of descent-groups and are venerated solely because of their miraculous works and for the part they have played in the introduction and spread of Islam in Somaliland. The most notable of these rank in Somali eyes with Sheikhs Daarood and Isaaq, the founders of the corresponding clan-families. I should also stress that the cult of saints, whether of lineage ancestors or of saints outside the lineage system, in no way eclipses the authority of God or the Prophet but is simply a more direct approach to the primary sources of religious power. In the numerous religious ceremonies at which I have participated the pre-eminence of the Prophet and the ultimate power and glory of God were never disputed.

Genealogies above the clan-family ancestor, establishing connexion with the founders of Islam, are, as I have said, known generally only to elders and men of religion whose business and pride it is to conserve the genealogical relationships of their clans to the Prophet's line (*Quraysh*). Many religious men carefully cherish these genealogies written in Arabic on a scrap of paper tucked between the pages of a Quran or other devotional book. There are in fact few who, without refreshing their memories by glancing at such manuscripts, can recite the whole of their genealogies to Quraysh. The Qurayshitic genealogies hallowed with Divine Blessing are sometimes incorporated in manuscript hagiologies including poems in praise of the saint (sg. *qasiida*)[1], accounts of his blessing (*baraka*) of his miraculous works (*karaama*), and various biographical details. In a few cases these have been printed in Arabic in Egypt or Aden; but printed copies are generally rare in northern Somaliland. These hagiologies are read or recited in the services performed on saints' days and on the occasions of pilgrimage (*siyaaro*) to the saint's tomb. They are of course used when, for any reason, the saint is petitioned to intercede with God to grant a special favour.

[1] These are generally written in Arabic and follow the standard Muslim pattern. But some are composed in Somali or a mixture of Arabic and Somali ('*wadaad*'s writing') and recorded in Arabic. Many composed in Somali have become part of the very extensive corpus of Somali folk-literature. For a typical example see Lewis *B.S.O.A.S.* 1958, pp. 144–45.

It is not necessary to discuss Somali Islam further except to illustrate my statement that as political solidarity decreases with genealogical span, religious power increases. The most widespread and important cults of lineage saints in northern Somaliland are those of Sheikh Isaaq and Sheikh Daarood. In the case of Sheikh Isaaq, the cult centres particularly at the Sheikh's magnificent domed tomb at Mait in Erigavo District of the British Protectorate. The annual birthday celebration (*mawliid*) is held locally amongst the Isaaq wherever they happen to be, and also at the tomb itself which is an important place of pilgrimage, usually on the 20th of the Muslim month of *Safar*.[1] There are also many shrines (sg. *maqaam*) in different parts of the country, often attached to a mosque dedicated to the Sheikh, whose power even the Daarood acknowledge. A similar cult surrounds Sheikh Daarood whose importance is naturally greatest amongst his descendants.[2]

II

For religious purposes clan-family genealogies are conserved in Arabic but otherwise genealogies are preserved orally and passed on from generation to generation. The genealogy of an elder of the Reer Faaraḥ Hagar shown illustrates our terminology of segmentation. The genealogy is typical of the highly segmented series of lineages into which many segments of a clan are divided.

[1] In every region occupied by the Isaaq, the saintly clan founder is weekly commemorated every Thursday with the reading of his *manaaqib*. As well as numerous manuscript hagiologies there are several printed histories of which one of the most recent is the *Amjaad* of Sheikh Ḥusseen bin Aḥmad Darwiish al-Isaaqi as-Soomaali, printed in Aden 1375 A.H. (1955 A.D.) Sh. Isaaq of Arabian origin is regarded as one of the main founders of Somali Islam. For a Somali account of the life of the Saint see 'Ali Sheikh Maḥammad, 1954, p. 22ff.

[2] Sh. Daarood is buried some twelve miles to the S.E. of the village of Hadaftimo in Erigavo District of the British Protectorate. The tomb is a much simpler construction than that of Sheikh Isaaq. The Sheikh's *mawliid* is usually celebrated in the month of *Soonfur*, the Arabic month of *Shawaal*. Every Friday Sheikh Daarood is celebrated locally with the reading of his *manaaqib*. Daarood is considered both by his descendants and by the Isaaq to have preceded Sheikh Isaaq by perhaps about two centuries. But some Daarood sheikhs connect him with Sheikh Ismaa'iil Jabarti, the well-known Arabian saint who died in 806 A.H. (1403 A.D.) and is buried at Bab Siham in Zabid in the Yemen. They in fact regard Daarood as the son of Ismaa 'iil Jabarti although this means that Daarood succeeded Sheikh Isaaq by almost three centuries. One hagiology sustaining this tradition in circulation in Somaliland is the *Manaaqib . . . al-Jabarti* of Sheikh Aḥmad bin Ḥusseen bin Maḥammad, printed in Cairo, 1945. The examination of the historical basis of these conflicting claims is outside the scope of this book and will be considered in a forthcoming publication.

The Ḍulbahante clan in fact comprises about fifteen primary lineage-groups.

These are shown in the fuller genealogy at the end of the text. The primary lineage-groups are in turn segmented into some fifty dia-paying groups of which only a few examples are detailed in the genealogy. In a few cases small primary lineage groups which are not highly segmented act as dia-paying groups. This for example is true of the Hayaag, Yaḥye, and Ḥaamud Ugaas and others. So that our model of segmentation applies fully only to those large lineages which are most highly ramified and which

Levels of Segmentation

Daarood Ismaa'iil	*Clan Family*
Kablallaḥ Daarood	
Koombe Kablallaḥ	
Harti Koombe	
Si'iid Harti (Ḍulbahante)[1]	*Clan*
Muuse Si'iid	
'Abdalla Muuse	
Habarwaa 'Abdalla	
Shirshoore Habarwaa	
Faaraḥ Shirshoore	
Aḥmad Faaraḥ	
Aadan Aḥmad	
Hagar Aadan	*Primary lineage-group*
Faaraḥ Hagar	
'Igaal Faaraḥ	
Maḥammad 'Igaal[2]	*Dia-paying group*
'Ali Maḥammad	
Aadan 'Ali	
Nuur Aadan	
'Abdi Nuur	*Individual elder*

[1] The nickname 'Ḍulbahante' means literally 'he who conquered all the lands'.

[2] From 'Igaal Faaraḥ's sons stem eight lineages divided into two uterine groups, the Bah Hawiye (400) and the Bah Ugaaḍ (1,500).

include all the orders of division we have distinguished. I discuss this again later in the chapter.

Every ancestor who begets several sons is a point of segmentation into lineages, into corporate agnatic political groups. Every ancestor is at once a point of unity and division since through his sons his descendants are divided into separate descent-groups but united in him as one lineage-group.

The system of units which we have distinguished as clan-families, clans, primary lineage-groups and dia-paying groups suggests a more stable hierarchy of segmentation than actually exists. Like the classical lineage systems of the Nuer[1] and to a lesser extent of the Tallensi[2] what is most characteristic of the Somali system is its relativity and its flexibility. Within his clan-family a man belongs to a wide range of segments of different orders. But the points of unity and division at which political solidarity most frequently emerges are those of clan, primary lineage-group, and dia-paying group.

In conformity with this shifting system of political affiliation there are no words in Somali to designate specific orders of segmentation. The four terms, *qabiil*,[3] *qolo*, *jilib*[4] and *reer* which are commonly used to refer to different levels of grouping, and which have been consistently misinterpreted by most writers on the Somali, can legitimately all be applied to the same genealogical and political unit in different contexts. Generally speaking, apart from its restricted use to designate the descendants of a living man, *reer* means lineage in an extended sense. Thus the Ḍulbahante clan is a lineage (*reer*) of the Daarood clan-family and smaller units within the Ḍulbahante are lineages (*reers*) of the Ḍulbahante clan, and so on down to the minimal unit which consists of a man and his sons. The Arabic loan-word, *qabiil*, is generally restricted in use to the larger units such as clans, sub-clans, and primary lineage-groups. But here again its use is entirely relative. What, in relation to a smaller unit is referred to as a *qabiil*, in relation to a larger unit is spoken of as *qolo* or *jilib*. If a man of the Ḍulbahante, referring to his relations with other members of his clan, describes his *qabiil* as Ḍulbahante, his *qolo*

[1] E.E. Evans-Pritchard, *The Nuer*, Oxford, 1940.

[2] M. Fortes, *The Dynamics of Clanship among the Tallensi*, O.U.P., London, 1945.

[3] Cf. Ar. *qabiilah*. In Somali *qabiilla* also occurs.

[4] In distinction to the other terms, all meaning 'group' in a general sense and particularly 'agnatic group', *jilib* means literally a joint or division, as e.g. a knee-cap. The word also connotes strength and prominence.

as Barkad (a primary lineage-group) and his *jilib* as a smaller Barkad lineage, he may in another situation refer to Daarood as his *qabiil* his *qolo* as Harti (see genealogy at end of text) and finally his *jilib* as Ḍulbahante. None of these terms can be assigned any precise or fixed significance except by reference to other units. All are relative terms within the hierarchy of segmentation based on agnatic connexion.

A man is a member of one lineage only in opposition to another. There is thus little need of an abstract terminology of segmentation: all political relations between agnates can be described exactly in terms of descent from a specified ancestor. The word *reer* prefixed to an ancestor indicates all his descendants. And this is the formula most generally used in the designation of lineages by reference to their eponymous founders.

Since politics are in principle a function of genealogical proximity, genealogical distance—'the number of ancestors counted apart'; as Somali say[1]—defines the political relations of one man or group with another.

Thinking genealogically of their political (and social) affiliation it is always the point at which genealogies converge in a common ancestor that is significant, where as Somali say 'they come together' (*meeshii ay isu yimaaddaan*). As has been shown, the term for genealogy (*abtirsiinyo*) means reckoning of ancestors in the male line, or of agnation. All agnatic kin who can trace descent from a common ancestor by a number of generations differing by only one ancestor call themselves reciprocally *adeer*. At the closest point of genealogical connexion this term is used reciprocally by a man or woman and his or her father's brothers.[2] The children of brothers call themselves reciprocally *ina' adeer* (from *inan*, son and *adeer*; the plural is *ilma' adeerro*), and this term is extended to all agnatic kin, other than siblings, who count back the same number of generations to a common ancestor. Strictly speaking, if two persons in tracing descent from a common ancestor differ by two or more generations they should refer to each other as *awow*, the restricted meaning of which is 'grandfather' or 'grandson'. But in practice a young man speaking to an older agnate of whose exact genealogical connexion he is uncertain will call him *adeer* or *ina' adeer*. By a polite convention, even when genealogically unrelated, people are often addressed as *ina' adeer*

[1] *Immisa awow yey kala tirsanayaan.*
[2] A man's father's sister is called *eeddo*.

in the sense of 'clansman'. The following diagram illustrates the terminology.

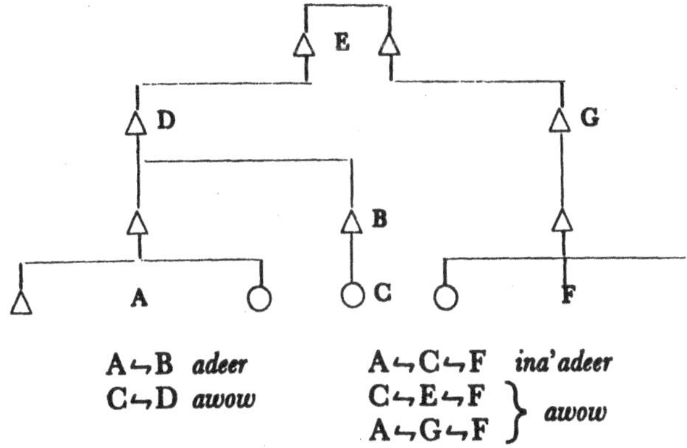

The appropriate term of kinship relationship and the corresponding rights and obligations binding agnates are determined by counting the number of generations which separate them. The answer to this calculation is the greater or greatest number of generations which one counts before reaching an ancestor common to the others. Agnates separated equally by two generations are called *ilma' adeerro run ah* (lit. 'true cousins'), by three generations *ilma' adeerro labaad* (lit. 'second cousins') by four generations *ilma' adeerro saddeḥaad* (lit. 'third cousins'), and so on. These terms for agnates express increasing degrees of remoteness and a corresponding diminuition in social solidarity. Similarly, people describe their kinship connexion in terms of the generation to which they count back to share a common ancestor. Thus people speak of community of social relations being defined by descent from a 'third ancestor', 'fourth ancestor' (*awowga afraad*) and so on.

To determine a person's agnatic and political affiliation one asks 'What is your agnatic group?' (*Tol maad tahay*) or more commonly (*Qolomaad tahay*).[1] This question is then followed up by a series of enquiries to reach a lineage socially (and politically) significant to the questioner. Agnation, and with it political distance or proximity, may either be traced through the smaller units to the larger, or from the larger to the smaller. In the former case one asks 'Who are your agnates?' and is given in answer some lineage within the clan such for example as Reer Faaraḥ

[1] From *qolo*, group.

Hagar. Then one says 'And after Hagar?' following the genealogy up. In the reverse direction, once given a large group such as say the Daarood clan-family, one then asks 'Of the Daarood who are you?' (*Daarood yaad ka tahay*), receiving for example the reply 'Ḍulbahante'. The same question is then repeated until the socially significant group is reached. Normally when a person is asked his lineage, he gives in reply the lineage structurally equivalent to that of the questioner. Thus, if a man of the Ḍulbahante while on a visit to a town in Isaaq country is asked his lineage, he may say 'Ḍulbahante' or even 'Daarood'. There would be little point in giving in reply to a questioner of another clan or clan-family, the minimal political unit, for it would be unknown and not structurally equivalent. When, however, the same question is asked within a clan, as for example, within the Ḍulbahante, a man gives his primary lineage-group, Reer Hagar, Barkad, Jaama'Siyaad, or whatever it happens to be. Within his primary lineage-group, he gives the minimal political unit, which is his dia-paying group. This procedure of establishing connexion along the lines of genealogical cleavage well illustrates the relativity of affiliation which is one of the most characteristic features of lineage systems such as that of the Somali.

Agnation is a given element in Somali politics. A person is born into a lineage. In principle a man cannot ever completely sever his ties with it or change his genealogy which represents his political affiliation and the range of kin towards whom he has obligations and upon whom he depends by the mere fact of agnatic connexion. A woman's position is slightly different and will be more fully examined presently. At the moment it is sufficient to point out that marriage transfers a woman's procreative powers temporarily to the lineage of her husband but her connexion with her own agnates is never completely severed. Marriage is mainly virilocal, but a wife is only lightly attached to her husband's group; she retains her own genealogy and her agnates continue to be largely responsible for her actions just as they do not fully surrender their rights to her as a potential bearer of children. Uxorial and genetricial rights are transferred in marriage, but not absolutely.[1] Consequently a woman is torn in two directions, through birth to her own agnates, and through her husband's children to his lineage.

[1] These terms are adapted from Dr L. Bohannan's rights *in uxorem* and *in genetricem*, see L. Bohannan, *Africa*, vol. xix, 1949, pp. 273–87

III

The concept of agnation (*tol*) centres on all that is binding and absolute. The verb *tol* means to bind together, or to sew, and Somali ideas of the constraining force of agnation are expressed in numerous sayings such as that 'Agnates are bound together' (*tol waa tolane*). Various proverbs contrast the strength of agnation with affinal and matrilateral ties, with that is, relationships through women. Agnation is like iron, like the testicles it cannot be severed or cut off voluntarily, whereas links through women are compared to those of a rope or the hair which can if necessary be broken. Thus the expression *ḥayn iyo ḥiniin*, literally the cloth worn by women round their limbs and the testicle, distinguishes kin traced through women, and male agnates. The number of proverbs which emphasize the all-pervasive force of agnation are many but I give two further examples each illuminating in a different context. A well-known saying has it that 'A limb is broken when the advice of agnatic kinsmen is disputed' (*talo tol oo la diidaa tagoog jabay leedahay*). Another frequently quoted proverb attributed to a man of the Ḍulbahante who had been offered a gift of horses (the most prized Somali stock) to deny support to his kinsmen says 'Of agnates and wealth, I chose (to support) my kin' (*tol iyo fardo, tol baan doortay*).

Tol means then agnates (or agnation) in an extended sense, the range varying with the political context, but generally always within the sphere of agnatic connexion. Close agnates within extended clanship (*tol*) are often distinguished as *ḥigto* or *ḥigaal*, and these words have again the sense of binding and of holding together.[1] We have now to consider how affinal and uterine ties (especially the latter) operate within the framework of political agnation.

IV

Since the concern of this book is with politics, and not with marriage and kinship, we do not need to pay much attention to

[1] These words are from *ḥig*, near. There is also a noun *ḥig* which means a species of alloe (Sansevieria Abyssinica) and also the second milking of live-stock. I was not able to discover any connexion between these usages. *Ḥig*, meaning near or close, occurs in the expression *ḥigsiisan*; a wife's sister or other close female agnate married by a man after his wife's death. The expression means 'the one given next'.

the affinal relationships created by marriage. Affinal ties are not normally a basis for political affiliation or cleavage. Nevertheless affinal ties are not simply unique for the individual, they do not fall entirely within what Fortes calls the 'web of kinship'[1]: to some extent they link lineages.[2] For marriage involves the temporary surrender of a woman's fertility (genetricial rights as well as uxorial rights) by her natal lineage to the lineage-group of the husband. Divorce which is frequent[3] breaks marriage and the wife's genetricial and uxorial rights revert to her lineage to be transferred anew in successive marriages and payment of bride-wealth.

The corporate character of marriage is reflected in the traditional right which a man has to succeed to the widow of a dead brother or other close agnate. Widow inheritance (*dumaal, waa la dumaalay*)[4] creates a new marriage with a new but often reduced payment of bride-wealth and children are born to the new husband and not to the deceased. Similarly if a wife dies (especially if she dies young or without children) the husband has a strong claim to his wife's sister or close female agnate (as *ḥigsiisan*)[5] paying again a reduced bride-wealth. But in the British Protectorate widow inheritance and the sororate are not now extensively practised partly, apparently, through the effect of the Natives Betrothal and Marriage Ordinance of 1928 which empowers a woman, betrothed against her will, to register her refusal to marry before a District Commissioner. Registration of refusal immediately nullifies the legality of the betrothal. Out of 135 marriages recorded only eight (5.9%) involved widow inheritance and only 3 (2.2%) sororatic marriage.

[1] M. Fortes. *The Web of Kinship among the Tallensi,* O.U.P. 1949.

[2] This and other aspects of marriage are discussed more fully in my *Marriage and the Family in Northern Somaliland.*

[3] The following table gives the total number of divorces recorded in 135 marriages (the numbers ending in death rather than divorce are not shown) in three samples.

Clan	Marriages	Divorces	Percentage
Nomadic Ḍulbahante	75	19	25.3%
Nomadic 'Iise	26	5	19.2%
Cultivating Habar Awal Jibriil Abokor	34	2	6.0%
Totals:	135	26	19.3%

[4] Literally, 'the deceased brother's wife has been taken in marriage'.

[5] See above, p. 137.

In its corporate aspects marriage is effected by a reciprocal transfer of property between the wife's and husband's families. A proportion of about two-thirds of the bride-wealth (*yarad*) is usually returned as dowry (*ḍibaad*).[1] The dowry consists of the nomadic hut with its effects and sufficient burden camels for its transport, and, in addition, often a flock of sheep and goats and some camels. Not infrequently some of this stock are of those originally given as bride-wealth. This is taken mainly by the husband but a small proportion may be distributed amongst those close kinsmen who contributed to the bride-wealth.

Marriage itself, as an individual contract binding a man and woman as husband and wife and giving the man rights over his wife as a partner and mother of his children is effected not by the exchange of *yarad* and *ḍibaad* but by the husband's promise to make a personal gift called *mahar* to his bride. This gift is promised before a sheikh or *wadaad* and forms the main part of the marriage ceremony. Without *mahar* no relationship between a man and woman is marriage. The personal dower is often small in value: it rarely exceeds a fifth part of the bride-wealth and is sometimes no more than a few pounds in value. Although *mahar* must be promised at the marriage ceremony it is rarely paid then. Indeed, frequently the husband only fulfills his obligation when he divorces his wife. Thus held in suspense, a woman's personal dower is in effect a surety against divorce and is in fact often so regarded by Somali. Yet quite frequently, the *mahar,* though promised, is not even paid on divorce and thus in many cases remains a theoretical transaction. But nevertheless it is the husband's undertaking to give his wife the dower to which she has agreed that constitutes marriage as a legally binding contract between two individuals.

It is however, the exchange of wealth, usually mainly in livestock and largely in camels, which establishes the affinal link (and in the next generation the matrilateral bond) between their

[1] Known also in north-western Somaliland as *diiqo*. In fifty-five marriage transactions which I recorded the smallest bride-wealth among the pastoralists was three camels for which no dowry was given in return. The largest was a bride-wealth of fifty camels and two horses for which the corresponding dowry given to the husband consisted of thirty camels, four fully laden burden camels, and one rifle.

Amongst the cultivators the lowest bride-wealth I recorded consisted of three cattle for which the dowry given in return was twenty-four Rupees (i.e. 36 Shs.). The largest bride-wealth was one of twenty cattle with a corresponding dowry of twelve cattle and four laden burden camels.

lineages. Any gift from affines is called *ḍibaad* and any gift to them during the marriage is *yarad.*

A man speaks of his affines (*ḥidid*) as a group and the link between the individual families is generalized on each side and viewed as a link between the respective lineages imposing duties and obligations on both sides. The affinal link, however, does not give rise to formal political relations. It is not of itself a direct political alliance; and affinal ties have no direct part in the morphology of lineage segmentation. Yet they provide a useful subsidiary social bond on the strength of which a man can expect hospitality as a kinsman (not merely as a guest) from a lineage to which he is either linked personally as an affine or through the affinal ties of another member of his lineage. To this extent the affinal link has a corporate character in all satisfactory marriages where a generous bride-wealth has been countered with a generous dowry. It might be thought that affinally linked lineages cannot fight. This is not so. Indeed many lineages which make war and feud upon each other are heavily intermarried. But in battle, a man will always seek to spare his wife's agnates, at least her close kin, and if captured they will be accorded preferential treatment. The bond is important too in providing a channel of information between affinally linked yet hostile lineages; and affines often play a major part in negotiation and in the settlement of disputes.

Since dia-paying groups, meaning here the formal, relatively stable, minimal political units, are exogamous and since marriage very rarely takes place within the primary lineage-group,[1] extended agnation is cut across and reinforced by affinal ties. Thus people are at once agnates (in an extended sense) and affines. But when they act politically as corporate groups they do so through agnation. Exogamous lineages refer their refusal to marry internally to their relatively small numbers and correspondingly strong agnatic identity. In discussing the historical development of lineages, I was often told that as the lineage extended and ramified constituent segments began to inter-marry where before they could not because they were 'too small in numbers'. Conversely, marriage is relied upon to bridge the gaps in loose agnatic kinship by the creation of affinal ties. Thus,

[1] Amongst the Majeereen clan of northern Somalia, the Shariah sanctioned practice of the marriage of first patrilateral cousins is said to be making some inroads. But such marriages even in the towns of the British Protectorate are exceedingly rare.

though rare today, it was in the past formerly apparently quite common to settle a dispute between lineages not only with the payment of blood-wealth but also by giving a nubile girl without bride-wealth to create affinal links of amity.[1] But as has been said this does not mean that hostility in the future is impossible. When individuals are a party to dia-paying political alliances where they have no agnatic connexion, intermarriage becomes important in cementing the bonds of alliance without kinship and in enhancing their status to that of kinsmen, if only of affines. This process, of which we have already had examples amongst the western cultivators particularly, will be considered further in the next chapter.

V

Affinal ties are thus not directly a part of lineage morphology. But the matrilateral ties to which they give rise in succeeding generations are of great significance in lineage segmentation. Here it is necessary to distinguish between those ties which connect a lineage to the patrilineal kin of its founding ancestor's wife and those which, within patrilineal descent, differentiate collateral segments according to the matriliateral affiliation of their founding ancestors. The former relationship between one lineage and that of its ancestor's wife is only exceptionally the basis of a political alliance and has little importance in formal political relations. The latter on the other hand is part of the substance of lineage morphology and extremely important in northern Somali political structure. To avoid confusion I refer to this second link as a uterine relationship.

Although matrilateral ties of the first kind are seldom the basis of formal political unity they do sometimes establish political links between lineages which are not patrilineally related. Here the pattern for the relationship is that between a man and his mother's brother (*abti*), a link which has corporate significance in the sense that not only the two individuals but their lineages stand to each other in the relationship of sister's son to mother's brother. As has been shown the bond is one of informal friendship and even indulgence particularly on the part of the mother's brother's group. The few cases in which this corporate social

[1] This additional amount of compensation is known as *samirsiis* from *samirsii*, to satisfy.

bond is given a specific political value concern groups which claim direct lineal descent from immigrant Arabs and thus are agnatically strictly outside Somali genealogical structure. Thus it is through their ancestor's marriage to a daughter of Dir that the Daarood clan-family who claim direct lineal descent from Arabia are linked to the other Somali clan-families. And similarly while other Somali regard the Isaaq as lineal descendants of Dir, the Isaaq themselves acknowledge only a matrilateral connexion, maintaining their claims to independent agnatic descent from Arabia.[1] Other examples of groups claiming direct patrilineal descent from Arabia and linked matrilaterally to Somali lineages also occur sometimes at a lower level of segmentation and here the relationship is more specifically political in character. A typical case occurs with the Ḥeebjire segment of the Gadabuursi clan. This lineage which acts as a Gadabuursi segment sometimes claims patrilineal descent from Sheikh Fiqi 'Umar, many of whose other descendants are widely scattered in Somaliland,[2] and acknowledges only a matrilateral tie with the Gadabuursi.

It would be pointless to quote other examples of a linkage which though occasionally the basis of formal political unity is rarely so, and has in general very slight significance in comparison with the uterine ties which at all levels of segmentation unite and divide lineages. In considering the importance of these in lineage morphology it is appropriate to start from the position within the polygynous family for as Somali say 'When a son is born the agnatic line extends' (*wiil dalayaa baa ab durug*). We have already seen how lineages develop lineally and how the genealogies extend over the generations. But we have now to consider how the uterine cleavages which divide siblings according to their matrilateral affiliation in familial relations later become points of cleavage and alliance in the lineage system. Islamic law permits a man to have as many as four wives at any one time, and although there are relatively few men who practise polygyny to this extent there are many who have two wives, and a considerable number who have three. Thus in a sample of one hundred and twenty-seven married men between the approximate ages of thirty and sixty years, seventy-two (56.6%) had one wife; thirty-seven (29.1%) had two; twelve (9.4%) had three; and six

[1] Cf. above, p. 12.

[2] See further Lewis, 1957, pp. 91–3.

(4.9%) had the legal maximum of four wives. Of this sample fifty individuals were cultivators of the Jibriil Abokor lineage and the others pastoralists of the Ḍulbahante and 'Iise clans; the latter showed a considerably higher degree of polygyny. At the same time, with the high divorce rate, especially amongst the pastoralists, there are a large number of successive marriages. Indeed in my experience it is uncommon for a middle-aged man not to have married at least twice whether in concurrent or successive unions.[1] Polygyny and successive marriage thus give rise to groups of siblings sharing a common father but having different mothers. From the point of view of subsequent lineage morphology whether these sibling groups derive from concurrent polygynous marriages or from successive unions is irrelevant.

Thus if, for example, Maḥammad marries three wives, Khadiija, Aamina, and 'Ambaro, either concurrently or in successive unions, and each bears him children, then the three uterine families (*baho* sg. *bah*) are referred to as Bah Khadiija, Bah Aamina, and Bah'Ambaro as shown. Collectively all the children are classified as and call each other siblings (*walaalo*, sg. *walaal*). More specifically they are said to be of the same father but different mothers (*waa is ku aabbe, waanna kala hooyo*). Within each uterine family the children share a common father and

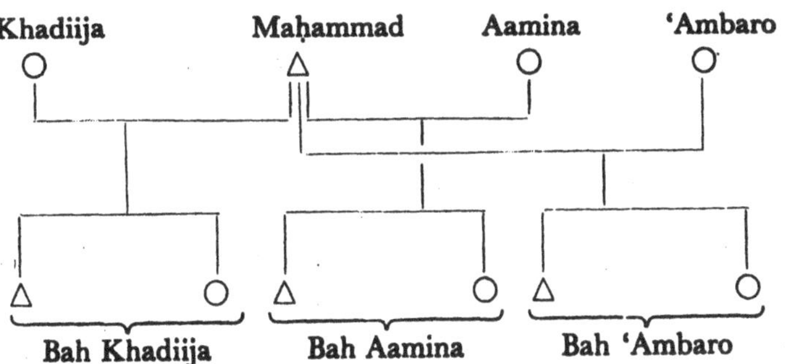

[1] The table shows the overall frequency of plural marriage in three samples of adult men.

	Ḍulbahante	Jibriil Abokor	'Iise	Total
Married once	3	14	1	18
Married twice	5	6	4	15
Married thrice	8	3	—	11
Married four times	1	—	3	4
Married five times	3	—	1	4
Married six times	2	—	—	2
Married seven times or more	2	—	—	2
Average marriages	3.1	1.5	2.9	2.4

mother (*waa is ku aabbe, waanna kala hooyo*). In the hierarchy of relationships this is the most binding and intimate. Correspondingly, in the wider lineage structure outside the family, cleavage and association of collateral lineages following the uterine affiliations of their ancestors occurs at every level of segmentation. Siblings who share only a common mother (*walaalo hooyo*) belong to different lineages (except when a divorced woman marries a man of the same lineage as her previous husband, or through widow inheritance) and this relationship however important it may be in personal kinship relations has generally no political significance.

VI

We can now apply these processes of linear generation and of uterine segmentation in an extended sense to understand the structure of the lineage system. Not all families of the same generation produce the same number of sons, nor do they increase as lineages through successive generations at the same rate. Proliferation within the lineage system is uneven. This is expressed in Somali by saying that one group 'increased' (*wuu batay*)[1] at the expense of another. The numerous and stronger group is described as *far'amay*[2] or (*farabatay*) whereas the less numerous and weaker group 'has not multiplied' (*ma tarmin*).[3] These terms refer to the relative numerical strengths of groups and contain the implications of growth and ramification in much the same way as Somali speak of similar processes in plant growth. The genealogical equivalents for collateral lineages, one of which counts a greater number of generations to the common apical ancestor, are *laanḍeer* and *laangaab*, the 'long' and 'short branch' respectively (from *laan* a branch; and *ḍeer*, long; and *gaab*, short). In fact, although these terms refer specifically to a disparity in the number of generations reckoned to the same apical ancestor, they are used loosely to distinguish a large lineage-group (*laanḍeer*) from a smaller collateral group (*laangaab*).[4] Members of two such unequally balanced collateral

[1] From *badnan*, plenty, abundance, increase.

[2] *Far'* means progeny, increase, expansion, ramification, and *far'amay* that which increased. Cf. Arabic *far'*. The purer Somali expression *farabatay* is a combination of *far* finger, and *batay*, increased.

[3] From the verb *tar*, to branch, to multiply etc. and also to help. *Ma tarmin* is the negative.

[4] The expression *laanhoose*, 'bottom branch' occurs with the same sense.

lineages refer to each other as 'cousins' (*ilma' adeerro*) in respect of their descent from a common ancestor. But those of the 'long branch' take special pride in their longer genealogy which records their numerical superiority. Where there is a significant difference in the number of generations counted by the members of two lineages to a common ancestor, those of the 'long branch' are usually the more numerous and therefore more powerful. They possess the 'decisive strength' (*ḥoogroon*).

To take an example. The Ḍulbahante number some 100,000 men, women and children, and are divided into some fifty dia-paying groups. From the genealogical chart of the clan, where the approximate male strengths of component groups are shown, it will be seen that there is a general correspondence between genealogical span and numerical strength. In the genealogy, only the ancestors of lineages today in existence are shown. From the eponym Si'iid Harti (nicknamed 'Ḍulbahante') descend four lineages, the Muuse Si'iid, Maḥammad Si'iid, Aḥmad Si'iid, and Yunnis Si'iid. Of these, the descendants of Muuse Si'iid comprise the majority of the Ḍulbahante clan highly segmented into numerous lineages of every order of segmentation. The Aḥmad Si'iid ('Hayaag') are a primary lineage-group about a thousand strong and the other collateral lineages are all small, insignificant, and incapable of independent political action. Living members of these small groups trace descent to Ḍulbahante through only a few generations. Because it is larger, the Hayaag lineage has a longer genealogy and its living members trace descent from the clan founder through some eight generations. In the next generation, that of Muuse Si'iid's sons, 'Abdalle's three brothers, Maḥammad, Abokor and Barre, are the ancestors of small lineages, whose members count only a few generations back to the clan-founder Ḍulbahante. Thus, for example, a man of the Reer Maḥammad Muuse counts only ten ancestors to Ḍulbahante.

The same process of differentiation occurs at every generation all through the clan genealogy. The point at which there is greatest proliferation in the genealogical tree is at the generation descended from Shirshoore Habarwaa where his three sons, Faaraḥ, Maḥamuud, and 'Abdi are the ancestors of highly segmented lineage-groups. Indeed Faaraḥ Shirshoore and Maḥamuud Shirshoore have given rise to two great congeries of lineages of the order of sub-clans. Following the segmentation down, it will be seen that the 'long branches' of the Faaraḥ Shirshoore (called Faaraḥ 'Garaad') are the Reer Hagar Aadan and the Reer 'Ali Geri of which the segmentation of only the former is shown in detail. The 'long branches' of the Maḥamuud Shirshoore (Maḥamuud Garaad) are the Jaama'

Siyaad (whose detailed segmentation is not shown) and the Naalleeye Aḥmad. Members of these lineages count from fifteen to twenty generations to the clan eponym, whereas those of the smaller 'short branch' lineages tend to count at every generation a lesser number of ancestors to the clan-founder. Thus, men of the Reer Barre Muuse count only some ten generations to the same ancestor (Ḍulbahante) which a man of the Reer Faaraḥ Hagar reaches only after counting between fourteen and eighteen generations. Other examples are included in the chart where a triangle affixed to a descent line indicates a living male member of a group and shows the number of generations which he counts to the group ancestor shown in the genealogy. At every generation in the genealogy ramification and segmentation are co-ordinate with numerical strength. The larger a group the more highly it is segmented, and usually, the longer its genealogy.

This correlation is found in every Somali lineage. In the genealogy of the Jibriil Abokor segment of the Sa'ad Muuse lineage of the Habar Awal (Isaaq) clan shown, the same process applies. The Jibriil Abokor comprise some 40,000 males and females and are segmented into about twenty dia-paying groups. As in the genealogical chart of the Ḍulbahante, I have shown the actual descent of some individuals through descent lines to indicate the number of generations which the members of different sizes of unit count to the eponym Jibriil Abokor. In considering a smaller unit than a clan, I have been able to show internal segmentation in greater detail. Thus the lineages descended from Geelle Qayaad (the Qayaad being a part of the dia-paying group composed of the three lineages Qayaad, Ḥildiid, and Yuusuf) are small groups whose ancestors are only two or three generations removed from living men. Within the Jibriil Abokor, the two largest groups of lineages are those descending from Yuunis Jibriil and 'Ali Jibriil respectively. The former have a male strength of some 5,500 while the latter boast 12,000 males. The 'Ali Jibriil are the 'long branch'; from 'Ali's sons stem most of the Jibriil Abokor. Following the segmentation down it will be seen that at every level between Ismaa'iil 'Umar and Lo'doon Elmis the 'long branch' derive from the first left-hand ancestor in the chart. In the generation of Lo'doon Elmis's sons the development into further lineages proceeds mainly through Qayaad Lo'doon. Thus at every generation some lineages ramify more highly than others and 'long branches' are distinguished from 'short' ones. Members of the stronger 'long' lines count a greater number of ancestors to the eponym Jibriil Abokor than do the weaker 'short' ones.

There is thus a demonstrable correlation between the numerical strength of a group and its genealogical span. Clearly, however, for a line to continue requires reproduction through an approximately equivalent number of generations whether it is a small (*laangaab*) or a large (*laanḍeer*) segment. If there are living members of two groups one of which counts some twenty generations to a common ancestor, and the other ten or a dozen, it is reasonable to assume that the names of ancestors which are not important points of segmentation have been forgotten. And this is what appears to happen. This would explain also why sometimes in the upper portions of genealogies different informants offer different names in tracing descent from a common ancestor. There is, for example, occasionally confusion in filling in the names of ancestors between the founder of a clan and of a clan-family. Thus in the upper sections of genealogies names which are not significant because their descendants are no longer alive tend to be forgotten.[1] When one enquires, for example, the sons begotten of a clan-ancestor, many people only remember those ancestors who are politically significant as founders of structurally important extant lineages. Others are forgotten and may only be dimly recalled by clan elders and Sultans well versed in the history of a clan. In giving their clan genealogies, it is always the main lines of descent—the 'long branch' portions of the genealogies—which are followed through and given prominence at the expense of subsidiary descent lines. There is often thus confusion and discussion in deciding the seniority by birth of the sons of any important apical ancestor, and it is the name of the ancestor whose descendants are most numerous and most important rather than the first-born (*'urad*) whose name is normally given first.

All this suggests that ancestors who are not structurally important tend to drop out of the genealogies as a lineage proliferates over the generations. As some lineages expand, others dwindle, and some die out. This explains too, why, where there is doubt as to the genealogical placing of a lineage, it is usually of a small, insignificant group, and not of a large flourishing lineage. While I do not wish to go far into the complex subject of the historical content of Somali genealogies, it seems that the genealogical tree is as a whole extending with the population, for the increasing population requires an ever expanding lineage system. It is a continually segmenting system, at least in the 'long branch' lineages which are its growing points. As I have explained, from the way in which they are described in the sixteenth century (in the *Futuuḥ al-Ḥabasha*)[2] we know that what are

[1] Cf. the discussion in E. E. Evans-Pritchard, *The Nuer*, pp. 198–200.

[2] See above, p. 15.

today clan-families were then structurally 'clans' and other lineages then important seem to have virtually disappeared. When a group develops much more quickly over the centuries than other collateral segments, the balance of segmentation is upset and a whole highly ramified cluster of lineages may assume a higher structural position. This would appear to explain why, for instance, the Isaaq who are structurally now a clan-family and claim independent Arabian origins are still regarded by other Somali pseudo-historically as a clan of the Dir. For if we accept the whole burden of Somali tradition, the Isaaq are of Dir origin although they themselves deny it—and through their increase they appear to have become formally differentiated as a separate clan-family. This is what their separate traditions of origin proclaim, whatever their true historical content. I shall have more to say shortly of this imbalance between the strength of lineages and their position in the larger genealogies of clans and clan-families.

It would thus appear, that over time as the lineage system develops, as some groups expand and others contract, the genealogies are at least to some extent telescoped to conform with the existing system of structural relations. Names disappear in the genealogies of small groups which do not proliferate. This is not, however, how Somali view their genealogies. For them the genealogies as well as representing the existing structure of formal political relations also tell a historical record. Not only are they a political manifesto but also the history of a line. When I argued with Somali that names which are not points of bifurcation in the system tend to drop out this suggestion was strongly repudiated. How, one is asked, can a person forget the names of his ancestors which as a child he has learnt by heart to remember. The disparity in genealogical span between small and larger lineages is explained in terms of differential procreation. Somali point out that of a group of brothers each does not have the same number of descendants and that God may favour the line of one while another languishes without many descendants. They point to the fact that a living man with many marriages may have four or even five generations of descendants while another brother has only one or two. This they consider explains the disparity in generations between 'long branch' and 'short branch' lineages and not the telescoping of genealogies by the elision of ancestors' names. But these objections and explanations do not, I think, completely explain such genealogical differences. Moreover, when a man boasts of his long genealogy, of being *laanḍeer* and *gob*—an aristocrat—he does not do so only because of his pride in the string of names which connects him to a distant ancestor. His pride is a reflex of what his genealogy implies, and indeed derives from the strength of his lineage.

VII

The irregularity of genealogical expansion and the differentiation into 'long' and 'short' branches may be represented by means of a simple paradigm.

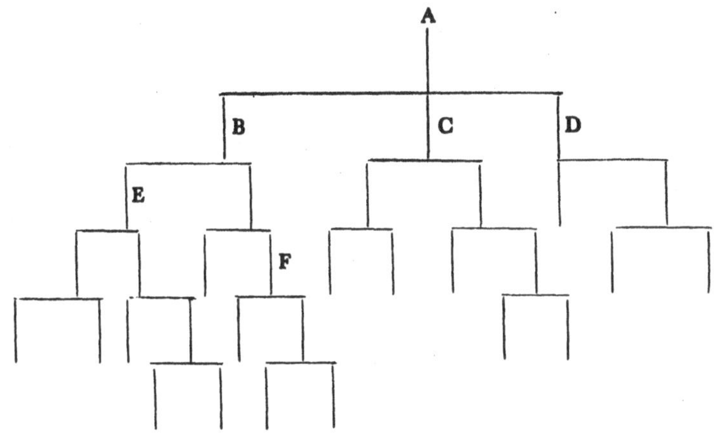

In the diagram, a large lineage A is segmented through proliferation into three subsidiary lineages, B, C, and D. Of these, B is the 'long branch' in relation to C and D. C is the 'long branch' in relation to D, and D is the 'short branch' in relation to both C and B. These terms refer directly to genealogical segmentation but also correspond to differences in man-power and fighting potential. Lineage C, despite its strict genealogical equivalence to B, is 'structurally' equivalent to lineage E a segment of B. Similarly D is equivalent in size and fighting potential to lineage F although genealogically it stands opposed to the whole of B of which F is only a minor segment. Whereas in principle, because of their genealogical position, the members of C or D should regard the members of B as an undifferentiated whole, in fact they do not do so. What I propose to call the 'size factor' supervenes and alters the political significance of groups in contrast to their strict position in the genealogies. For all practical purposes the people of lineage-group C regard themselves as a unit opposed not to the whole of B but to its structurally equivalent segment E. Similarly, the members of lineage E regard themselves as a unit in opposition to lineage-group C and so on. When, however, all the members of A unite in opposition to some external threat they do so along the lines of genealogical cleavage. But internally they are differentiated by size and fighting strength as well as by genealogical proximity. When internally B unites as a unit in opposition to D, the members of that small lineage will seek to ally themselves with other stronger groups to counter the strength of their opponents. Preferentially they will ally with C.

In the internal segmentation of lineages, where they are equally, or approximately equally divided according to strength, the pattern of allegiance is that defined by their strict genealogical position. Thus in the diagram

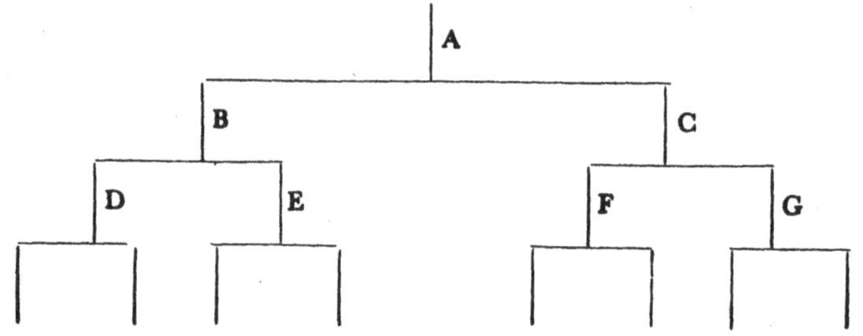

the members of E act as a corporate unit in opposition to D, and similarly the members of G as a unit opposed to F. Lineage B is a unit opposed to Lineage C consisting of the segments F and G. This model of segmentation applies where genealogical cleavages correspond to numerical strength. Here the opposition is between 'long branches' which descend from a common ancestor, where in each segment there is a regular sequence of differentiation into smaller units of equivalent size.

It will be seen that in their cleavage by agnatic descent the genealogies record generally an unequal division of power. The second paradigm of segmentation shown in the diagram above represents only a fraction of the true picture of Somali lineage development. The first diagram with its cleavage into 'long branch' and 'short branch' lineages is a closer representation of the reality of lineage segmentation and political affiliation. Our terminology of segmentation into clans, primary lineage-groups, and dia-paying groups, is only an approximation to the facts of genealogical division. The most highly ramified lineages have all these orders of segmentation and more; the less ramified sometimes have only a division between dia-paying group and clan. The possibilities of cleavage at different levels are much greater in the more highly bifurcated lineages than they are in the smaller. Thus in the Ḍulbahante genealogy, the Hayaag lineage-group, for example, is genealogically equivalent to the whole of the Muuse Si'iid although their strengths are in the ratio one to forty. The Hayaag act within the Ḍulbahante clan as a dia-paying group and primary lineage-group at the same time. Externally they are Ḍulbahante, along with the other segments of the clan. Thus in spite of their relative genealogical positions, the Muuse Si'iid are in no sense 'structurally' equivalent, except when all the segments of the clan unite in opposition to another clan as Ḍulbahante. In the context of external relations the Hayaag become structurally equivalent to the Muuse Si'iid with all its sub-divisions and in spite of the difference in their strengths, while internally they are lineage units of a different order.

Such inequalities occur at every level of segmentation and in every clan and lineage. Segmentation by agnatic descent does not give rise to a simple hierarchy of balanced descent groups. At every generation, lineage segments of similar strength are not counterpoised. Fighting potential in a society based on self-help is all-important and is coordinate with size. Amongst the nomadic clans with their rich wealth in livestock compensation is paid according to the male strength of every group and children are included in this reckoning. So that male strength represents the fighting power of a group and also its ability to pay compensation and act collectively as a corporate political unit. Hence the significance of the 'size factor' is very important.

To take another illustration again from the Ḍulbahante. Within the Faaraḥ Garaad congeries of lineages, the Barkad and Bah 'Ararsame do not stand politically opposed to all the descendants of Aḥmad Faaraḥ, although this is what their genealogical position implies. On the contrary, they are structurally equivalent to constituent units such as Naalleeye Aḥmad, 'Ali Geri, Hagar Aadan and other like units within it. Equally, other dia-paying groups and primary lineage-groups stand structurally opposed to others at different levels and points of genealogical segmentation. The Hayaag are equivalent to the Naalleeye Aḥmad, to the Khayr 'Abdi and to others, and all these to other equivalent units in different genealogical positions. A quarrel between individuals of the Barkad and 'Ali Geri is likely to develop into a feud between the two lineages but this does not mean that all the Aḥmad Faaraḥ necessarily unite with the 'Ali Geri against the Barkad.

Here the 'size factor' intervenes and interrupts segmentation according to strict lineal genealogical principles. Structurally equivalent groups of comparable size and strength oppose each other to some extent irrespective of their genealogical positions. Genealogical proximity is not always the determinant of political unity where units of equivalent size oppose each other. But, of course, where the segmentation is even and regular, where there is genealogical cleavage into equivalent units through a range of segmentation, genealogical proximity does control group relations. Thus in the Ḍulbahante clan, to a certain extent all the Faaraḥ Garaad stand opposed to all the Maḥamuud Garaad, and a fight between constituent lineages of each may spread to a general cleavage between these two large lineages. Here, generally, the more distant units are genealogically, the greater the likelihood of extended strife between the larger units of which they are segments. Thus strife between a segment of the Ḍulbahante and a segment of the Habar Tol Ja'lo is more likely to lead to fighting between the Ḍulbahante as a unit opposed to the Habar Tol Ja'lo as a unit, than is strife between one group of Faaraḥ Garaad and one segment of Maḥamuud Garaad to a general war between these two segments of the Ḍulbahante. Similarly, the probability of generalized tension within the Faaraḥ Garaad is less than between it and the Maḥamuud Garaad and so on. The smaller a unit the greater is its cohesion, and the larger a unit the more likely is it to split into hostile groups following the lines of genealogical cleavage.

VIII

In the foregoing we have seen that although agnation and genealogical proximity are in principle the basis of political cohesion uneven development makes lineages genealogically equivalent structurally disparate. Birth places lineages in a certain position relative to each other in the genealogical hierarchy. But irregular growth alters the balance between them. It is here that uterine divisions amongst apical ancestors are extremely important in constituting additional lines of cleavage, and of

a. Maritime range and Guban Coastline to the west of Mait.

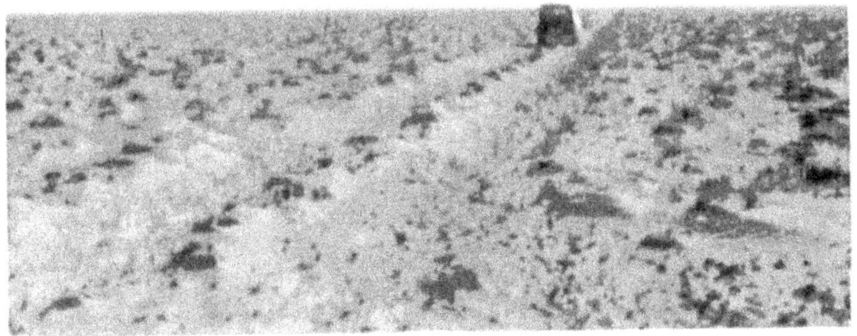

b. A barren stretch in the Ogo Highlands to the south-east of the Protectorate.

a. Sheep and goats waiting to be watered at Wudwud in the Northern Haud.

b. Camels watering at Ainabo wells.

a. Laden burden camels of a hamlet grazing in the Haud.

b. Men working at the wells.

a. Family setting up camp.

b. Girls at a well on the coast to the west of Berbera.

a. Water containers being filled at the wells.

b. Girls inside a hamlet.

Somali Sheikh.

a

b

a and *b* Demonstrations at Hargeisa in April 1956 called to show the depth of public feeling over the return to Ethiopia of the Reserved Areas. Note that in *a* women participate, and in *b* that men are wearing white fillets signifying deep sorrow.

Somali District Commissioner speaking with lineage elders.

unity. Just as siblings are divided amongst themselves according to their uterine descent so are lineages in terms of the uterine divisions between their founders. Thus, for example, in our simple paradigm (p. 149) in the internal relations between the three lineages B, C and D, the weaker lineages C and D will tend to unite in opposition to B and they may do so through uterine ties real or putative. Where this occurs the members of a lineage allied through a common mother call themselves Bah Khadiija, say, giving the name of the mother or her clan.[1] Here the points of division are not agnatic ancestors but their mothers and the recognition of the uterine link as a political principle provides, as it were, a lateral system of unification whereby unevenly balanced agnatic segments can achieve approximate numerical parity. The uterine alliance of lineages through real or putative common uterine descent operates at all levels of the lineage system paralleling the processes of agnatic segmentation. It is as much part and parcel of the system. Such uterine alliances work within the bonds of agnation which they supplement by providing a further means of differentiation into political units. Lineages divided internally by uterine links are united externally by their common agnatic descent. Thus uterine ties divide members of lineages at one level while they are united at a higher level by common agnatic descent.

Thus to take an example from the Jibriil Abokor cultivators of the west of British Somaliland. The Jibriil Abokor Reer Haad 'Ali lineage[2] is split into two dia-paying groups, the Bah Gadabuursi and the Bah Khadiija, according to the uterine descent of its component lineages. The Bah Gadabuursi dia-paying group is further segmented into two loose putative uterine divisions, the Baha Lo' doon and the Bah Kooshin. In this case the prefix *bah* indicative of putative uterine alliance, is prefixed to the names of the dominant lineage segment in each of the two alliances of lineages, that is to the Lo' doon and Kooshin respectively. Lo'doon and Kooshin are in fact father and son as will be seen from the genealogy, and the distinction between the two putative uterine groups is largely between descendants of Lo'doon through Kooshin and his descendants by other sons. Within the Bah Gadabuursi dia-paying group, a man's first loyalty is either to the Baha Lo'doon division or to the Bah Kooshin. In a situation which involves both segments equally both unite as the Bah Gadabuursi dia-paying group which in turn is a segment of

[1] The word *habar*, literally old-woman, or mother, is applied similarly as a prefix to denote a uterine alliance

[2] See above, p. 113.

STRUCTURE OF BAH GADABUURSI DIA-PAYING GROUP (JIBRIIL ABOKOR)

Jibriil Abokor
Yuunis Jibriil
Uurkuraag Yuunis
Aadan Uurkuraag
'Iidle Aadan — 'Ali Aadan
Ḥaad 'Ali

Khalas Haad — Lo'doon Haad — Samatar Haad — Ḥargeeye Haad — Khayre Haad — 'Agdeer Haad — 'Igaal Haad — Liibaan Haad

Bah Khadiija dia-paying group (c. 2,200 males)

Nuur Lo'doon — Ḥargeeye Lo'doon — Rooble Lo'doon — Kooshin Lo'doon — Ḥildiid Samatar

Geelle Kooshin — Shire Kooshin — Wa'ays Kooshin — Ḥirsi Kooshin — Allamagan Kooshin

Bah Gadabuursi dia-paying group (*c. 1,700 males*)

A. *Baha Lo'doon*[1]

Reer Khalas Haad (Gebile, Galole)
Reer Ḥargeeye Lo'doon (Shabelle)
Reer Nuur Lo'doon (Gebile)

B. *Bah Kooshin*

Reer Geelle Kooshin (Odejiid)
Reer 'Iidle Aadan (Odejiid)
Reer Rooble Lo'doon (Gebile)
Reer Shire Kooshin (Shabelle)
Reer Wa'ays Kooshin (Ijara)
Reer Ḥirsi Kooshin (Odejiid)
Reer Allamagan Kooshin (Odejiid)
Ree Ḥildiid Samatar (Odejiid)

[1] Names in brackets indicate the areas of densest concentration of the lineage segments concerned.

the Reer Haad 'Ali. Through this lineage affiliation is traced to the primary lineage-group, the Jibriil Abokor and eventually to the clan, the Habar Awal. And as a member of the Habar Awal clan a man is a member of the Isaaq clan-family as opposed to the Daarood or Hawiye.

Consider now an example at a higher level of segmentation. In the genealogy of the Ḍulbahante clan it was seen that in the number of their descendants the most important sons of Shirshoore are Maḥamuud and Faaraḥ Shirshoore. This left out of account the genealogically equivalent but numerically very disparate lineages descended from four other sons of Shirshoore. These are the Ḥusseen Ugaas, Ḥaamud Ugaas, Maḥamuud Ugaas, and Ḥassan Ugaas of which the last named is the largest. The last three of these lineages in 1955 were separate dia-paying groups, but at the level of Maḥamuud Garaad and Faaraḥ Garaad they unite as a loose political alliance, putatively on a uterine basis, called Bah Ugaas. In fact, they tend to throw in their lot with either the Maḥamuud Garaad or the Faaraḥ Garaad according to the situation and in accordance with what appears most advantageous to them.

Similarly in the Isaaq clan-family, component clans are divided into two uterine divisions as shown in the genealogy. The first division is between those lineages descended from sons of Sheikh Isaaq by an Ethiopian woman–the Habar Ḥabuusheed–and those descended from sons of Sheikh Isaaq by a woman of the Magaadle clan—the Habar Magaadle. Indeed most of the largest clans of the clan-family are in fact uterine alliances. The Habar Tol Ja'lo (or Habar Ḥabuusheed) are in origin a uterine alliance of the lineages descended from Sheikh Isaaq's four sons Aḥmad (nicknamed 'Tol Je'ele'—he who loves his agnates), Muuse, Ibraahiim and Maḥammad. The name is currently shortened to 'Habar Ja'lo' and the majority of the clan stem from the descendants of Muuse through his son Abokor. Ibraahiim's descendants—the 'Sambuur'—form a small group living mainly in Burao and Erigavo Districts of the Protectorate. Similarly, Maḥammad's descendants—the "Ibraan'—are a small unimportant scattered group. This is also true of the slightly larger but equally dispersed Tol Ja'lo, descended from Aḥmad. These as we have seen amongst the Jibriil Abokor[1] have a certain autonomy, but they are numerically insignificant in comparison with the descendants of Muuse.

Referring again to the genealogy of the Isaaq clan-family, the Habar Awal clan is a uterine *bah* alliance which originally included the Ayuub, named after Awal the first-born and more prolific of the

[1] See above, p. 120.

two brothers Awal and Ayuub. The Ayuub have now, however, increased sufficiently in strength to break away at least to some extent from the descendants of Awal (the Habar Awal clan) who still, however, retain the name of the uterine alliance. Awal and Ayuub according to some traditions are of the same mother; according to others Awal though born by a different mother was suckled by the mother of Ayuub. Garḥajis and Arab are both sons of Sheikh Isaaq's first (Magaadle) wife. The descendants of Garḥajis, Da'uud (eponym of the 'Iidagalle clan) and Si'iid (ancestor of the Habar Yuunis clan) are known collectively as Habar Garḥajis, a *bah* alliance which sometimes includes the Arab clan. The Habar Yuunis will on occasion ally with the 'Iidagalle as Habar Garḥajis in opposition to the Habar Awal. The Habar Yuunis themselves are a *bah* alliance of all the descendants of 'Arre Si'iid. Yuunis, the first born son of Ismaa'iil, whose descendants are the most numerous, has given his name to the alliance although his own descendants are not as numerous as those of his brothers Muuse and 'Abdalle.

It will be seen that in the case of the Isaaq clan-family, uterine cleavage is of the utmost importance in the structure of the largest descent-groups (clans). Even the uterine division between those clans of the Habar Ḥabuusheed and those of the Habar Magaadle has occasionally some political significance. Thus when the Habar Yuunis and Habar Tol Ja'lo are at war, although they cannot count on the support of all members of the two divisions, the Habar Yuunis taunt their Habar Tol Ja'lo rivals by saying that they are not Somali at all since their mother was Ethiopian. Similar uterine cleavages occur at every level in the structure of the Isaaq clans as much as they do amongst the Daarood and other Somali. Further examples will be found in the genealogies at the end of the book.

Real or putative uterine alliances are thus as much a feature of the Somali lineage system as is agnatic segmentation.[1] To express the formation of such an alliance the verbal form *bahayso* is employed as in the statement, 'they formed a uterine alliance' (*wey is bahaysteen*). Ideally, alliances of this kind are made where there is genuine common uterine descent, or at least descent from mothers of the same clan. But many political unions are struck across agnation without this justification, and to a corresponding degree without honour. These are known as *gaashaanbuur*, meaning literally 'pile of shields' and referring explicitly to the aim of

[1] M. Fortes, *The Dynamics of Clanship among the Tallensi*, 1945, pp. 198–206 describes such uterine segments as 'matrilaterally defined' matri-segments within the patrilineage.

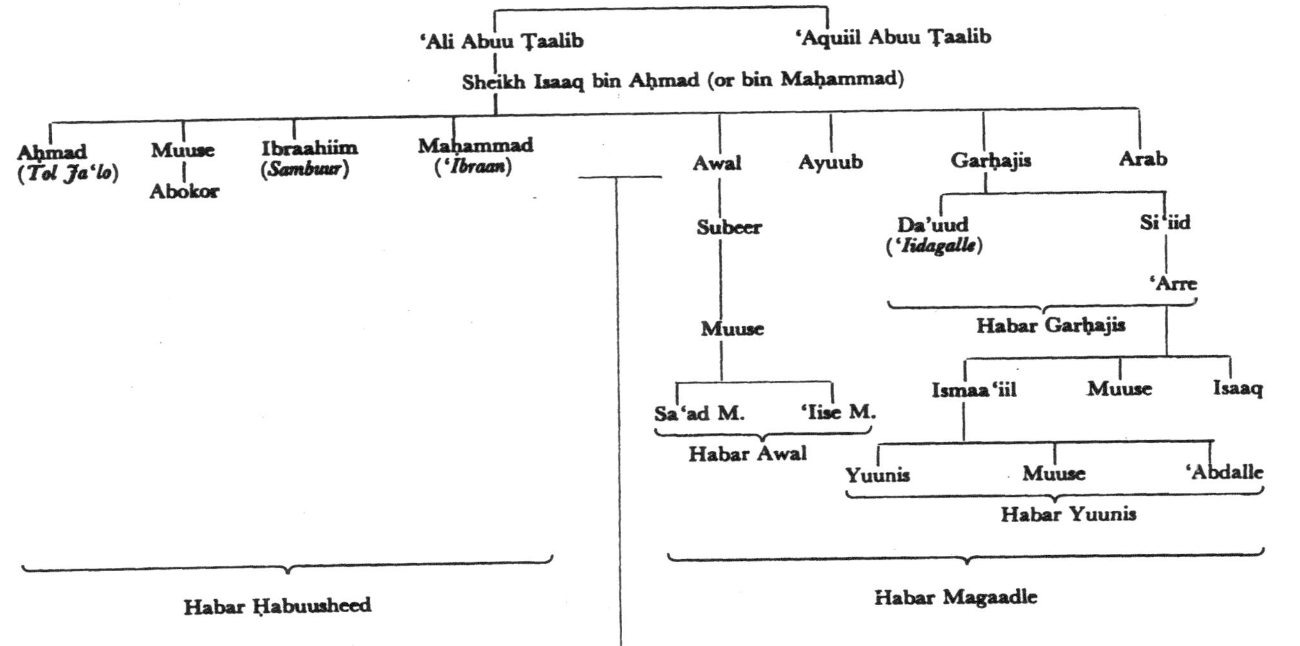
'Ali Abuu Ṭaalib
'Aquiil Abuu Ṭaalib
Sheikh Isaaq bin Aḥmad (or bin Maḥammad)
Aḥmad (*Tol Ja'lo*)
Muuse
Abokor
Ibraahiim (*Sambuur*)
Maḥammad (*'Ibraan*)
Awal
Ayuub
Garḥajis
Arab
Subeer
Da'uud (*'Iidagalle*)
Si'iid
'Arre
Habar Garḥajis
Muuse
Ismaa'iil
Muuse
Isaaq
Sa'ad M.
'Iise M.
Habar Awal
Yuunis
Muuse
'Abdalle
Habar Yuunis
Habar Ḥabuusheed
Habar Magaadle

the alliance to acquire fighting strength and with it political power.[1] Since this is an extra-lineage process and is not an integral part of lineage morphology but only a political regrouping of unequally balanced lineages, I defer discussion of it to the following chapter. Normally there is no re-adjustment of the genealogies; the genealogies are not manipulated to redress the balance of uneven natural development. In fact, sometimes in taking down genealogies I was asked whether I wanted the names of the lineage segments as they were paired off in uterine and non-uterine alliances, or in the order of their natural position within the genealogies. For the Somali these are two separate systems, not to be confused.

IX

At the beginning of this book I stated that kinship provided the first key to an understanding of Somali politics. In this chapter I have sought to give a formal account of the morphology of the lineage system and of the structural processes which produce segmentation in it. Clearly segmentation has two aspects; a historical one and a contemporary one. The lineage system is an on-going structure, continually developing by segmentation over the generations as the population expands. In this historical process, ancestors, as reference points of contemporary segmentation in the day-to-day relations between lineages, change their significance as segmentation proceeds. A name which at one point in the history of the system represents a primary lineage-group, may, in time, come to represent a clan or even eventually clan-family. What are today clans were at some stage in the past lineages equivalent in size and character to existing primary lineage-groups or dia-paying groups. Growth in the system is irregular; some lineages expand with historical segmentation, while others contract and even disappear. This historical process provides the framework of contemporary political lineage relations. Groups unite and divide by reference to points of historical cleavage. Fission and fusion in contemporary relations follow the lines of historical bifurca-

[1] The verbal form is *gashaanbuurayso*. Thus 'they formed a political alliance' is '*wey is gashaanbuuraysteen*'. The word is a compound of *gaashaan*, shield, and *buur* hill, or heap, mountain etc. It will be appreciated from what has been said in previous chapters that shields are no longer generally current in northern Somaliland and that rifles have replaced spears to a large extent.

tion and development. Uterine cleavages are inherent in the system. Uterine ties are remembered or invoked to strike alliances across agnatic cleavages to redress the balance of irregular growth and uneven proliferation. And in some cases coalitions are created within the framework of loose, or extended, and even non-existent agnation, without always the benefit of uterine connexion.

The agnatic generation recorded in the genealogies which every child learns by heart and which ideally prescribes the limits of his political affiliation is, as it were, the main theme of Somali politics upon which actual political relations are at any point in time a variation. The morphology of the lineage system is the frame-work of clanship of the division of people into corporate but not localized unilineal descent-groups. A man has political unity with others at different levels and as a member of different orders of grouping according to the context of hostility. What begins as a dispute between two individuals of different dia-paying groups may, if they are of different clans, spread to a feud between clans united for the time being as corporate political groups. In principle, within the clan dia-paying groups oppose dia-paying groups, primary lineage-groups primary lineage-groups, and within the clan-family clans oppose clans. But the simple model of agnatic segmentation with equipoised units at every level is distorted by the recognition of irregular growth and by the importance given to the uneven distribution of man-power and fighting potential. These inequalities are counteracted partly by uterine ties which act as a built-in compensating mechanism, and partly by alliances (*gaashaanbuur*) outside kinship.

Thus political unity is implicit in agnation, and its range varies according to the context of opposition. Yet agnation in itself does not create political units united in collective responsibility for their members' actions although normally it provides the basis of political unity. It is here that the second fundamental principle of Somali politics, that of contract, enters. To call into effect the implicit values of agnation contractual agreements are made at every level of segmentation. In this respect the dia-paying groups differ from other orders of lineage because in them contractual political agreement is localized. Dia-paying groups are the most stable political units. It is at this level of lineage segmentation that contract most frequently operates. But political relations are not restricted only to this level. When any order of lineage, be it clan, primary lineage-group, or dia-paying group, acts as a corporate political unit against another, it generally does so in terms of a contractual treaty binding all its members. In every context, prolonged political solidarity implies contractual agreement.

6

Clanship and Contract

I

Clanship and contract are fundamental principles in the constitution of Somali political units. For clanship alone does not explain political solidarity, nor does contract act by itself except in exceptional cases. It is only in terms of the two taken together that it is possible to understand the political institutions of the northern pastoralists. Thus where agnatic kinsmen are parties to a political contract Somali speak of *tol ḥeerleh*, 'agnates bound by treaty'.

To understand how these two distinct principles interact and jointly contribute to the political solidarity of groups it is first necessary to consider the meaning of the word *ḥeer*. This word usually translated 'custom' has more specific connotations.[1] Its closest equivalents in English are compact, contract, agreement or treaty in a bilateral sense. Thus several men or parties are said to be of the same *ḥeer* (*waa is ku ḥeer*) when their relations are regulated by an agreement, either directly entered into by them or accepted as a legacy from their ancestors.[2] For contractual obligations may be entailed by a prior agreement binding the ancestors of persons or groups. And agreements can be contracted into and contracted out of. As need arises the terms of

[1] The agnatic framework of nomadic Somali society, if not fully understood in its segmentary implications, has long been appreciated. One of the earliest writers to stress the lineage character was G. Ciamarra, *Camera dei Deputati, doc. xxxviii, Relazione sulla Somalia Italiana*, allegato B, Rome, 1911. Much has similarly been written on Somali 'custom'. The most notable contributions are E. Cerulli, 'Il diritto consuetudinario della Somalia Italiana settentrionale,' *Bollettino della Società Africana d'Italia* anno xxxviii, Naples, 1919; M. Colucci, *Principi di diritto consuetudinario della Somalia Italiana meridionale*, Florence, 1924; A. C. A. Wright, 'The interaction of law and custom in British Somaliland and their relation with social life,' *Journal of the East African Natural History Society*, 17, 1–2, 1943, pp. 66–102. As far as I am aware, however, the first indication in the literature of the true nature of Somali *ḥeer* is contained in a paper by J. G. S. Drysdale of the Protectorate Administration ('Some aspects of Somali rural society today', *The Somaliland Journal*, 1955). Most writers, and there have been many, have failed to appreciate the fundamentally contractual nature of *ḥeer* and its interaction with agnation.

[2] 'There is an agreement between us' (*ḥeer baa innagu ḍeḥeeya*) is a common way of stating this position.

contracts are abrogated, existing treaties modified or rescinded, and new agreements made. The majority of *ḥeer* agreements binding groups relate principally to collective defence and security and to political cohesion in general.

By extension, *ḥeer* means customary procedure founded upon contractual agreement. In its widest sense, as for example in describing general cultural features of Somali life such as habits of dress or food, custom is usually referred to as *'aado* (Cf. Arabic '-a-d-t). But I have also heard *ḥeer* used in this sense and been given to understand that it is the traditional expression for custom as opposed to the more recent Arabic loan-word.

Several other uses of the word serve to further elucidate what Somali understand by *ḥeer*. The rope placed over the roof of the nomadic hut to give it stability and either fastened to the ground on each side or secured by stones, is called *ḥeer*. Similarly, the verbal form means 'to surround' as for example in the phrase 'we are surrounded by an enemy party' (*'ol baa innagu ḥeerraa*). Thus the implication of binding, fastening, and of securing underlies all these usages. Clanship (*tol*) it will be recalled, has similar implications. Both concepts emphasize security and cohesion. The difference is that *tol* solidarity derives from agnatic status in the lineage system, and *ḥeer* from egalitarian contract. Both are complimentary. *Ḥeer* then, denotes a body of explicitly formulated obligations, rights and duties. It binds people of the same treaty (*ḥeer*) together in relation to internal delicts and defines their collective responsibility in external relations with other groups.

II

The most important delicts are those of homicide (*dil*), wounding (*qoon*), and insult (*ḍalliil*), the last embracing a wide range of infringements of rights, from adultery to defamation. The corresponding compensations are *mag* (or the Arabic *diya*), *qoomaal*, and *ḥaal*. The Arabic expression *ḥaq* is also used specifically of wound-compensation (*qoomaal*) and of right, justice, and equity in general.[1]

Compensation for physical injuries and homicide is based on the Shariah, being assessed by sheikhs and Government Kadis

[1] The Arabic loan-word *qaynuun* is used generally for custom or law, especially civil law, as applied in a Government court.

according to standard Shafi'ite authorities.[1] The Shariah tariffs apply generally with local variations and the specific compensation rates embodied in the *heer* treaties of different groups are based upon them. Although the rates most generally current today in northern Somaliland are 100 camels for the homicide of a man and fifty camels for a woman (or their equivalent in other currency), in parts of French Somaliland and northern Somalia local agreements have established lower values of blood-wealth.[2] But in principle, all Somali accept that another man's life is worth 100 camels although compensation may in practice only be exacted under threat of retaliation or through Government intervention. It is claimed that formerly, prior to foreign administration, the unit within which blood-compensation was regularly paid was the clan, and that between clans compensation was only offered to fend off retaliatory action. But it is difficult to establish the truth of this. What is clear is that, prior to the advent of foreign rule, blood-compensation could only be exacted by the threat of force. Strong groups could refuse to pay compensation owing to weak groups who, unless they wished to engage in a war which would be likely to destroy them, found it expedient to settle their blood-debts with their stronger rivals. In a later chapter I shall show how this tradition of the ultimate power of might continues even today under modern administration.

To some extent there is a degree of correlation between the nature and amount of blood-wealth paid and the structural distance of the parties concerned.[3] Thus the Gadabuursi formerly accepted that within their clan blood-wealth had to be paid in

[1] The most commonly used work is al-Nawawii's *Minhaaj aṭ-Ṭaalibiin*. For other Shariah Texts see Lewis, 1956, p. 150.

[2] Several years ago in the British Protectorate a standard exchange rate for camels paid in blood-compensation was accepted. A compensation camel was given a value of nine sheep (ewes). In 1957–58 the value of a blood-wealth camel varied between 45 and 50 Rs; thus full compensation was worth between £337 10/- and £375. According to the current market value of camels, however, a good young she-camel may fetch 100 Rs; and fifty camels valued at this amount be paid in place of the statutary 100 beasts each valued at 50 Rs. Indeed the quantity of camels required is now usually unimportant provided that their total value is that of full blood-wealth. And money (or other currency) is frequently substituted today as part or even the whole of the blood-price.

[3] Between groups, killings on one side normally cancel out killings on the other. It is frequently a large discrepancy between the score of deaths which leads to the continuance of a feud.

livestock where stock were available. Although it might be difficult to find 100 camels, especially amongst the agricultural Gadabuursi, the equivalent value in other livestock, in cattle, sheep and goats, was preferred to payment in money. But between the Gadabuursi and 'Iise clans there was no objection to the substitution of money even where the group paying compensation possessed ample livestock. Prior to 1900 again, the Gadabuursi and 'Iise clans, who are frequently at strife, had an agreement (*ḥeer*) that between them the compensation payable for a man's life was ten she-camels, ten cows, 100 sheep and goats, and one nubile girl fitted out for marriage and complete with all her household equipment.

Between Somali and other neighbouring peoples structural distance is reflected in a further reduction in blood-compensation. In French Somaliland between Somali and Danakil ('Afar) blood-wealth for a man stands at fifteen she-camels. In Harar Province of Ethiopia the rate between Somali and Galla is seventy head of cattle.

Within the dia-paying group, as will shortly be seen, the members' solidarity is reflected in an evaluation of blood-compensation generally lower than that paid externally between dia-paying groups. Outside the group, between closely related lineages, compensation is often increased to an amount in excess of the statutary rate to discourage blood-shed where clanship solidarity is weaker. Thus in the Ḍulbahante clan within each of the Faaraḥ Garaad and Maḥamuud Garaad groups of lineages, each with its own Sultan, the compensation for homicide is 120 camels in the case of a man, and sixty in the case of a woman. But between the Maḥamuud and Faaraḥ Garaad the value is the normal one of 100 and 50 camels respectively.

Where compensation higher than the statutary tariff is paid, the additional amount is referred to as *samirsiis* which means to give 'satisfaction' or 'to effect conciliation'. This procedure is frequently resorted to where a person of high status is killed or where the circumstances of a homicide are particularly disgraceful. If, for example, an elder is murdered who enjoys universal respect, not only within his own dia-paying group and clan, more than 100 camels' compensation is often demanded and usually obtained. This assumes of course that either through Government intervention, or fear of reprisal, or for other reasons, the guilty group is under pressure to effect a settlement.

Similarly, a killing between two lineages which have just concluded a treaty of peace is a much graver affair than a killing between groups which are already at war. In these circumstances hostile acts which disrupt or threaten to disrupt peaceful relations between groups who desire to remain on friendly terms require more than the ordinary amount of compensation. Thus when three men of one clan were killed by bandits of another the aggrieved lineages claimed three full blood-wealths of 5,000 Rs. each[1] and three additional payments of 500 Rs. The latter claim was referred to as compensation for insult (*ḥaal*) or *samirsiis*. It was paid at once but the blood-wealth took several months of negotiation before it was settled. In this case the claimants held that the attack was a gross affront since the two clans normally have little contact and are at peace. The clan to which the bandits belonged was held responsible even though the latter were operating independently and not with the approval of their clansmen.

But the circumstances of a killing are sometimes so outrageous that they lead at once to concerted reprisals, the desire for immediate revenge preventing any thought of negotiation. The Gadabuursi are traditionally the enemies of their militant neighours the 'Iise. Many years ago, when a treaty of peace was being negotiated between the two clans by emissaries of both sides, a famous Gadabuursi elder and arbitrator was treacherously murdered by an 'Iise youth while he was praying. This at once aroused such passionate resentment amongst the Gadabuursi that all thoughts of settlement were forgotten and a general war broke out which is still remembered for its bitterness and violence.

To some extent as I have shown, the amount of compensation payable for homicide depends upon the status of the person killed. In many cases, and perhaps generally however, the death of a child requires the same compensation as that of an adult. Thus the Gadabuursi even exact payment of full blood-wealth for a miscarriage caused by a blow inflicted on a pregnant woman. If the foetus is recognisable as male or female, blood-wealth is claimed accordingly.

It is often maintained that Somali make no distinction between deliberate and accidental homicide in the amount of compensation held to be payable or in the way in which it is paid. This is

[1] Equivalent to £375 sterling. The rupee which no longer exists in coinage is still often used as a unit of enumeration. It is equivalent to 1 shilling 50 cents (East African currency).

not strictly true. Between hostile groups whether a killing is accidental or premeditated is of little moment. But within a small, closely integrated group such as the dia-paying group, some consideration is often given to the circumstances of death. Thus in some dia-paying group treaties accidental death carries a lower blood-wealth than deliberate murder. And especially between close-kin, although the amount of compensation payable may remain the same, accidental deaths are more susceptible of amicable settlement than premeditated homicides.

How are untraditional accidents accommodated within this scheme? Some time ago it was agreed by the clans of the British Protectorate that a fatal traffic accident should not give cause for claims for blood-money. And in principle, claims for compensation in such cases do not proceed under the Shariah but may be filed as civil cases concerning individuals. Nevertheless, sometimes group responsibility is accepted and blood-wealth paid out of court. Thus in Jigjiga, in 1942, a man of the Arab clan (of the Isaaq clan-family) driving a trade truck knocked down and killed a man of the Bartire clan (Daarood). Blood-wealth was claimed but when it had not been paid four months after the accident the Bartire retaliated by murdering the most important Isaaq elder in Jigjiga. This abrupt action reflects the structural distance of the parties, since both clans are of different and rival clan-families between which there is traditional enmity.

I have already indicated that in some circumstances intention is taken into account in the valuation and payment of compensation whereas in others it is not. But invariably Somali go to great lengths in attributing the responsibility of a person's death to the action of others. At his own expense a Sultan erected a masonry well in a town. He had hoped to make a profit on the sale of water from the well. But the enterprise proved a failure, and the well was left derelict without a parapet round it. One dark night a man of another clan fell down the well and was killed. His clan claimed blood-wealth from the Sultan's clan but public opinion was divided as to the legality of this claim. A court of Somali elders ('Akils' Court')[1]

[1] 'Akils' Courts' were established under an ordinance of 1921 with a minimum quorum of three and a full court of five members. These courts had only civil jurisdiction although 'on receipt of written authority from a District Court', they were empowered to 'enquire into and decide: (a) any point of native law and custom; (b) any question relating to the value of *yarad* (bride-wealth) or *ḍibaad* (dowry) paid or to be paid; (c) any matter affecting the value or amount of stock or property transferred, or paid over, or alleged to have been transferred, or paid over, on account of a tribal or other settlement'. These 'Akils' Courts' have since been replaced by 'Subordinate Courts', see below, p. 169.

ruled that compensation should be paid, but the British Administration, disturbed at the repercussions which this might have in future cases, held that no damages should be paid. Eventually, after a great deal of discussion and dispute, the Sultan paid 300 Rs, the compensation at that time payable by the Government to the family of a man killed by a Government vehicle. But this was not a popular decision.

III

Settlement can be effected by payment of compensation between lineages at every order of segmentation, either when the parties themselves wish to make peace (*nabad*)[1] or when they are forced to do so by Government intervention. The sanctions which control the payment of compensation differ according to whether the lineages concerned are or are not bound by treaty. Except between those close kinsmen who inherit together and who commonly assist each other in payment of bride-wealth and who share the bride-wealth received when a girl is married, all delicts concern groups. Political and jural responsibility is defined by contract within agnation. The extent to which the individual is politically and legally identified with his contractual group of kin is well shown in the following case. A man administered a drug of his own preparation to a fellow clansman. When the patient subsequently died, investigation by other herbalists showed that the drug was injurious although it had been thought to be beneficial. No one disputed that the deceased had taken the drug willingly. Yet clan elders with the assistance of elders of another clan ruled that since the herbalist had not first obtained the consent of the deceased's kin before administering the drug he and his dia-paying group should pay blood-wealth to the kin of the deceased. The consent of the patient alone was not considered sufficient and compensation was paid. Many similar cases could be quoted to show how rigorously binding *ḥeer* contracts are. Moreover, even after the death of individual claimants, unsettled blood-debts in one generation carry forward to succeeding generations.

[1] This word, which is part of the standard Somali greeting 'Is it peace?' (*ma nabad baa?*), indicates absence of tension or worry, the opposite of emotion. Where a bereavement is recently suffered there is no *nabad*. The word *heshiis* means an agreement, an appeasement, an acceptable settlement reached by bargaining. The verbal form is *heshii*.

Leaving aside for the moment the effect of Government intervention by invitation, complaint, or direct intervention, unsettled disputes are taken by the disputants before an *ad hoc* panel of arbitrators (*guddi.*) I shall discuss the composition and function of such informal courts of arbitration more fully in the next chapter, only indicating here their general characteristics. Between groups which are not parties to a common contract this informal court of arbitration has no means of enforcing its findings (*gar*).[1] In these circumstances, settlement thus ultimately depends upon the readiness of the disputants to make peace and to some degree on the skill of the arbitrators in obtaining an acceptable compromise. Within the confines of contract, however, the solidarity and common treaty obligations of those concerned force them to settle unless one party wishes to secede from the contractual group. For unlike the procedure between dia-paying groups where the disputants themselves generally seek arbitration, within a dia-paying group elders see that disputes are settled. The elders of a dia-paying group by tying him to a tree and threatening to kill his livestock may force a recalcitrant member to fulfill his duties or to honour a contractual obligation. And the final sanction invoked is expulsion from the group. It is the enforcement of sanctions within the dia-paying group which marks it off as a distinct political and jural unit.

Where within a contractual group there is disagreement over the settlement of a debt or over the authority of the elders, the group usually splits, one party withdrawing from the contract and often paying money to do so. Thus for example, in one case when two segments of a dia-paying group renounced their treaty, the seceding group paid the other £70.

The procedure outlined above, with self-help remaining ultimately the final arbiter, persists within the modern judicial organization. In the British Protectorate, cases of assault or homicide which come to the notice of the Government are examined in the first place according to the terms of the Indian Penal Code.[2] If, under this code, a prosecution for homicide results in a conviction and the accused is hanged or sentenced to imprisonment for a period in excess of ten years, no blood-wealth is awarded or usually claimed. But if, as often happens, mainly through the difficulty in obtaining evidence from kinsmen of the

[1] Literally judgement, decision etc, from *garo* to understand or know.

[2] Applied under the Somaliland Principal Order in Council, 1929.

same dia-paying group, the case for the Crown fails, blood-compensation is claimed by the injured group. The case then becomes what the Administration rightly terms a 'Political Case' since it concerns not individuals but lineage-groups. Such cases are a source of endless casuistry and a never-ending bane to District Officers who spend much of their time attempting to settle them. Those claiming compensation may require members of the accused group chosen for their probity and good character to swear fifty oaths to the effect that no member of their lineage is implicated. The defendants are then left to choose between swearing the oaths, paying the blood-wealth required, or of returning them to their opponents. If the claimants testify by fifty oaths to the truth of their allegation they are entitled to payment.[1] Sometimes the swearing of the divorce oath is similarly employed to exonerate the defendant from guilt or prove the case for the plaintiff.

In cases of assault tried under the Indian Penal Code, when a fine is imposed by a Government court a proportion may be paid as compensation to the aggrieved party. The latter are then also able to file a suit claiming additional compensation in a Subordinate Court.[2] Here the plaintiff has resort first to a Government

[1] This is the Somali interpretation of the Shafi 'i *qasaama* procedure. See J. W. D. Anderson, *Islamic Law in Africa*, London, 1954, p. 372.

[2] The former Akils' Courts were abolished and replaced by Subordinate Courts by the Subordinate Courts Ordinance of 1944. Under the terms of the Ordinance Subordinate Courts are empowered to enforce 'the native law and custom prevail-within the limits or among the tribal community'. In a criminal case a Subordinate Court can impose a fine, imprisonment, with or without hard labour or (now only in the case of juveniles) corporal punishment subject to the limitations imposed by its warrant. Warrants issue from the Governor. Appeals lie to the District Courts and finally to the High Court. Most of the principal townships of the Protectorate have a Subordinate Court and often also a Kadi's Court although in some instances these two functions are combined in one court. In practice, Subordinate Courts have only very limited jurisdiction in criminal matters, and, apart from hearing claims referred to them by a Kadi's or higher court, much of their work concerns infringements of township regulations, and breaches of the peace in towns etc. Each court has usually several Assessors or Judges who are appointed as authorities on Somali custom.

As well as assessing wound-compensation, Kadis are empowered to administer the Shariah (under the ordinance of 1944) in matters of personal status. They have no formal criminal jurisdiction. In practice most of their time is taken up with matters relating to marriage, divorce, claims for maintenance by a divorced wife and so forth. They also to a lesser degree administer the provisions of the Shafi 'i Code in inheritance. But as has been stated in a previous chapter only a few town Somali accept fully the Shariah regulations in the inheritance of property. Live-stock tend to be inherited to the exclusion of female heirs in conformity with the agnatic principle.

Kadi's Court where damages are assessed according to the Shariah. Injuries have previously to be examined by a Government Medical Officer who sends the claimant to the Kadi with a note of their nature. The latter then assesses damages referring to Shafi'i text-books. Such an assessment for physical injuries may amount to considerably more than full blood-wealth. But when a claim for the Kadi's assessment is laid before a Subordinate Court, the judges are not bound to adhere strictly to the Shariah evaluation. They often tend to reduce the amount of the award if the injuries claimed for are only of a technical nature. Here the Court Assessors are guided by their knowledge of custom (*ḥeer* in general) with which they temper the strict interpretation of the Shariah.

In cases of theft where the thief is apprehended or a charge of theft proved, the provisions of the Indian Penal Code are also generally applied.[1] But even when a conviction is obtained the plaintiff usually seeks restitution by filing a civil case against the culprit and his lineage, particularly where livestock are concerned.

However strange their procedures, the foreign courts are now part and parcel of the nomadic life and accepted as such. Government has in fact become a third party in the system of relations between rival lineages. Within this total and complex system, contractual agreements for offence and defence remain basic principles in the organization of Somali politics.

IV

Contractual obligations are typified in the small lineage-groups which we have called dia-paying groups. These units of which there are some 360 in the Protectorate, vary in man-power between some 300 and 3,000 males. Everyone is born into a dia-paying group and everyone has by birth affiliation in one. But contracts can be rescinded and new ones created; ideally this should always be within the limits of agnatic connexion.

It is only through membership of a dia-paying group that one has political and jural status. An individual cannot himself act as a viable and independent political unit. He cannot alone pay 100 camels should he kill someone, nor can he meet other large

[1] About 1920 when the normal Somali practice of requiring a thief to return the article stolen (sometimes twice over) proved ineffective, the Administration was asked to apply the Indian Penal Code.

amounts of compensation without the assistance of others. Thus one criterion of the viability of the dia-paying group is its ability to discharge collectively the blood-debts of its members. Yet the ability to meet compensation obligations satisfactorily is not the sole criterion of solidarity. Many large dia-paying groups could easily act as several lesser groups in payment of blood-wealth but choose not to split up. I discuss the stability of dia-paying groups later in the chapter and only wish here to stress the fact that the fundamental criterion of political and jural viability is the power to discharge blood-debts without impoverishing the joint resources of a group. The importance of being able to meet blood-debts as an alternative to suffering reprisals is illustrated in the following case. The Akisho, as has been seen, are a minority group of Galla origin scattered amongst the Habar Awal in the west and centre of the British Protectorate. A man belonging to one small group of Akisho living in subject status with a lineage of the Habar Awal clan murdered two youths of his protectors. He was found to be mad and was sentenced by a Government court to life imprisonment. His protectors, however, still claimed blood-wealth for the two killings. The murderer's lineage was small and its members pleaded that they could not pay compensation. But the offended lineage ignored these excuses and continued to insist. Since the Akisho concerned were indeed unable to pay damages they left their hosts and fled across the border into Ethiopian territory.

The dia-paying group is an agnatic lineage or alliance of agnatic lineages and is thought of as having a dominantly male character. Daughters of the group leave it on marriage to join the lineages of their husbands. But married women are not fully incorporated into the dia-paying groups of their husbands. The responsibility for their safety and for injuries committed by them lies partly with their own agnates. This is consistent with the fact that a woman's ties to her lineage of birth are not fully severed on marriage and is reflected in the relatively high frequency of divorce.[1] To some extent the practice varies from clan-family to clan-family. Amongst the Isaaq of the Protectorate generally, if a married woman is killed whether or not she has borne children, her agnatic kin and her husband's agnates divide her blood-wealth equally between them. Similarly, when a married woman is guilty of homicide, her husband's agnates and her own contri-

[1] See above, pp. 137-38.

bute equally to the blood-wealth due. The husband, however, with his kin is solely responsible for small delicts committed by his wife. Amongst the Daarood and 'Iise on the other hand, a married woman's agnates are solely responsible when she kills someone, and conversely receive her blood-wealth if she is killed. But if a murdered woman leaves children they are entitled to share with her own agnates in her blood-wealth. In small amounts of compensation for which a married woman is liable payment is made out of her own personal dower (*mahar*), or paid by her children if they are adult, or in some cases again, paid by her husband. For it is usually considered shameful if a husband is not prepared to meet small liabilities on the part of his wife.

Generally, amongst both the Isaaq and Daarood, I believe, if a wife kills her husband blood-wealth is paid by her agnatic kin to his agnates and the children of the deceased usually receive the largest single share (the *jiffo,* see below). This particular contingency is regarded with amusement by Somali as it is so blatant a reversal of the normally dominant role of the male in society. I give one example. A *wadaad* of another clan living with the Ḍulbahante, had two wives, one of whom was a Ḍulbahante woman. Jealousy between the co-wives led to a quarrel between this woman and her husband which ended in his death. The case was complicated by the fact that there were few witnesses to the act and the woman's lineage paid only a reduced compensation (*jiffo*) to the children who were left without a father. This settlement is also partly a reflection of structural distance and the 'size factor' since the deceased husband's lineage were a minority living amongst the more powerful Ḍulbahante.

If a man kills his wife, full blood-wealth is usually paid by his dia-paying group to that of the woman. Cases of this kind are certainly rare although I have heard of instances.

V

Individual dia-paying groups vary enormously in the details of their arrangements for collectively paying blood-compensation and compensation for other delicts. Usually the full blood-price is divided into two portions. The larger (*mag ḍeer*), 'the greater blood-wit' is paid and received by all the members of the group as a whole. The smaller (*jiffo*), rated frequently at thirty-three and -a-third camels (the 'third' is of course paid in other currency), is paid and received by the immediate kin of the party responsible for homicide or from whom a member has been killed. The 'immediate kin' are usually male agnates descended from a common ancestor of the third or fourth ascending generation.

This two-fold distribution of responsibility corresponds to the internal structure of the dia-paying group. The subsidiary '*jiffo-paying groups*' meet all compensation due from or to them independently of each other up to the amount of the *jiffo* and the members of each unit are described as of the same *jiffo* (*jiffo wadaag*).[1] *Jiffo* is literally the metal ferule at the base of the spear's

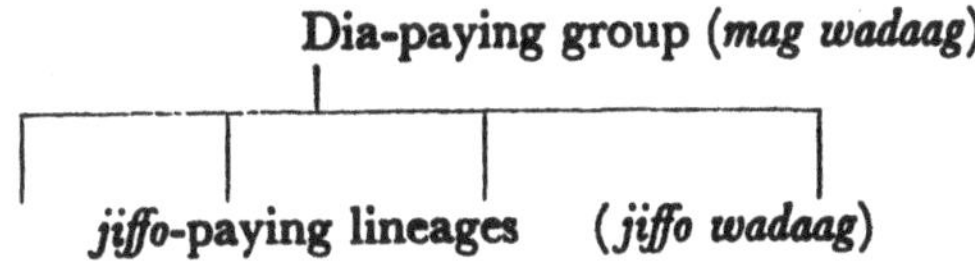

shaft and has the sense of pin-pointing the responsibility for homicide or other injury. Within the dia-paying group, it indicates the small lineage directly concerned. In payment of full blood-wealth (*mag*) the *jiffo*-groups combine as *mag wadaag*. This is one way of describing those who pay blood-wealth in concert and who thus form a dia-paying group. Its members are said to be of the same treaty (*ḥeer*), or of the same blood-price (*mag*), or again of the same compensation (*ḥaq*). These are simply different ways of indicating that a body of agnates acts collectively as a dia-paying group in terms of a common treaty. The members of a dia-paying group may also describe their collective solidarity in terms of 'the same division'.[2] This expression means literally forming 'one place', and what is one place in the distribution and contribution of compensation above the value of the *jiffo* splits up into internal divisions (*meelo*) in payment and receipt of amounts below the *jiffo*. This terminology corresponds exactly to the division of the group as a whole (those who are *mag wadaag*) into *jiffo*-paying sub-divisions.

All dia-paying groups consist of *jiffo*-paying components. Each group has by the terms of its treaty its own standard of *jiffo* which may be higher or lower than thirty-three-and-a-third camels, but is often this amount. Where compensation is claimed against the group for an amount less than the *jiffo*, the *jiffo* lineage concerned

[1] *Wadaag*, means 'together' or 'in concert'.

[2] In Somali, *waa is ku meel.*

settles its debt without help from other sections of the dia-paying group. For outstanding debts above the *jiffo* the dia-paying group as a whole pays collectively. Here different methods of collecting and distributing compensation are followed. Amongst the northern and central pastoral clans who are generally rich in livestock the assessment of the proportions in which compensation is contributed or distributed is based on the male strength of the *jiffo*-paying subdivisions. In this system, male children are counted as male adults and each *jiffo*-group's responsibility is assessed according to the number of men and male children in it. The assumption is that concern or liability is a direct function of male strength. This procedure is known as 'penis-counting'.[1] But amongst those clans and lineages in the north-west who are partly agricultural and have less stock (e.g. the Jibriil Abokor, Gadabuursi, etc) payment is generally assessed on the basis of family or *jiffo*-group stock-wealth. This method is called 'wealth reckoning'.[2]

In payment of compensation, whether for homicide or assault, the amounts actually contributed (and conversely received) by the members of the dia-paying group—including the person or persons directly concerned—tend to vary with the size of the group. Often the larger a group is the less each individual has to pay. When for example a man of a group some few thousand strong kills an outsider the murderer with other members may pay no more than a few shillings. On the other hand, in the receipt of blood-wealth, the bereaved family usually receives the largest single portion of the blood-wealth; often as much as twenty to thirty camels or their equivalent in other livestock, goods or money. Where lineages larger than the basic dia-paying groups are united temporarily in payment of compensation, the amounts paid by individual members may be infinitesimal. Thus, while exchange of blood-price removes immediate enmity between lineages it often provides little econonic deterrent to continued bloodshed.

Within the dia-paying group, homicide is regarded as particularly dis-honourable (although not subject to specific ritual sanctions) and the rates of compensation are adjusted to reflect the unity of the group and dastardly character of the action. Either the amount of compensation within the group is lowered in relation to that paid externally or else it is increased above it. The former is the commoner procedure and means that a man's

[1] *Qoora tiris.*

[2] *Ḥoola tiris, baaho,* or *qabno.*

life is rated at less than 100 camels within his dia-paying group. Frequently the rate payable is that of the *jiffo*.[1]

VI

I now offer some examples of *ḥeer* treaties of dia-paying groups. It will be appreciated that the morphological principles of lineage segmentation described in the previous chapter operate in the internal lineage structure of the dia-paying group as much as at other levels of segmentation. Lineal segmentation, uterine divisions, and alliances outside agnation all occur in the structure of dia-paying groups. Examples embodying the use of these different principles of association will be given in the course of the chapter. My first examples of *ḥeer* codes concern groups with a simple, lineal segmentation.

Ḥeer codes today are submitted in the form of petitions to the local District Commissioners and, at least in the British Protectorate, District Offices maintain a file of local clan and lineage-group treaties. Since the collective jural and political solidarity defined in these agreements is recognized by the Government, *ḥeer* becomes a source of law. The petitions which record *ḥeer* are generally written in Arabic, or in the local Somali version of it ('*wadaad's* writing')[2] and now-a-days also in English. They bear the signatures (or thumb-prints) of the elders of the parties to the agreement and are often couched in ambiguous language, so that whether by design or accident they are frequently difficult to interpret and give rise to much casuistry and counter-petitioning. Dia-paying treaties are often also directly recorded by District Officers to guide them in their interpretation of 'political cases' and to ensure that their record of agreements is up-to-date. Generally, however, as soon as an existing treaty is altered or rescinded and a new one ratified, the latter is communicated to the local District headquarters.

It will readily be appreciated that *ḥeer* is not static and that it is constantly being revised in the light of new conditions. Some of these relate to the fragmentation of groups which have become too large and unwieldy to continue as manageable units. Others

[1] But in most cases the amount of compensation contributed by the culprit himself is greater when a delict has been committed within the group than when it has been committed outside it.

[2] See my 'The Gadabuursi Somali Script', *Bulletin of the School of Oriental and African Studies*, 1958, xxi/1, pp. 135–40.

derive from fission following quarrels and disputes, rivalry for political control amongst leading elders, and new and more advantageous attachments. Others again, stem from incessant fighting involving directly only one section of a group, when other segments object to having to share constantly in blood-debts for which they are not directly responsible. I discuss the viability of dia-paying groups and the forces which cause them to divide and to hold together further below; here I only wish to indicate how fluid *ḥeer* is and how new *ḥeer* codes are made as occasion requires.

Ḥeer agreements are made at lineage-group councils (sg. *shir*) summoned for the occasion. At these, all adult males have the right to speak. The heads of all the families concerned, or their representatives, assemble to promulgate a common treaty by whose terms they bind themselves to abide. They lay down in detail the delicts and punishments which they wish to recognize amongst themselves and establish the principles by which they will act externally as a collective political unit. They decide the proportions in which they will pay and receive compensation for external actions and the amounts payable in internal disputes. Thus those concerned are provided with a legal and political constitution and established as an independent jural and political unit. The proceedings begin with prayers led by sheikhs and *wadaads* and end in the same way.

As far as I am aware, these political and juridical contracts were not recorded in writing prior to the advent of foreign administration. They were apparently only conserved orally and in the memory of those concerned, but they were no less binding. Colonial administration has merely offered an impartial mediator to whom treaties may be entrusted to become a source of law in the modern administrative situation. A remark in a paper by Cruttenden,[1] however, suggests that dia-paying contracts were sometimes lodged with the custodians of the shrine of a prominent saint. A saint's tomb is a sanctuary, and if this in fact were the general procedure prior to foreign administration (Somali say it was not), it would have offered a means of enhancing the validity of treaties.

My first example refers to the Ḥassan Ugaas lineage of the Ḍulbahante clan of Las Anod District in the British Protectorate. The

[1] 'Memoir of the Western or Edoor tribes, inhabiting the Somali coast of North-East Africa,' *Journal of the Royal Geographical Society*, 19, 1849, pp. 49–76.

Ḥassan Ugaas are currently estimated to number about 1,500 men. They comprise four main segments (*jilibs*) which act as *jiffo*-paying groups.

Ḥassan Ugaas

Yuusuf Haaruun Jibriil Haaruun Si'iid Haaruun Aḥmad Haaruun

A petition delivered to the District Commissioner and dated the 8th of March, 1950, states their *ḥeer* to be as follows:

1. When a man of the Ḥassan Ugaas is murdered by an external group twenty camels of his blood-wealth (100) will be taken by his 'next of kin' (i.e. his sons, brothers, father, and possibly uncles) and the remaining eighty camels shared amongst all the Ḥassan Ugaas.
2. If a man of the Ḥassan Ugaas is wounded by an outsider and his injuries are valued at thirty-three-and-a-third camels (a standard rate for non-fatal but quite serious injuries),[1] ten camels will be given to him and the remainder to his *jiffo*-group.
3. Homicide amongst members of the Ḥassan Ugaas is subject to compensation at the rate of thirty-three-and-a-third camels, payable only to the deceased's next of kin. If the culprit is unable to pay all or part, he will be assisted by his lineage.
4. In cases of assault within the Ḥassan Ugaas for which compensation up to the value of thirty-three-and-a-third camels is payable (i.e. according to the Shariah) only two-thirds will be paid.
5. *Ḥaal* of 150 shillings (East African) is payable to the person attacked[2] when a man of the Ḥassan Ugaas joins another to fight with a third.
6. If one man of the Ḥassan Ugaas insults another at a Ḥassan Ugaas council (*shir*) he shall pay 150 Shs. to the offended party.
7. If a man of the Ḥassah Ugaas marries a girl already betrothed to another man of the group, or a widow whom it is the customary right of another to marry, he shall pay *ḥaal* of five camels to the aggrieved party.[3]
8. If the Ḥassan Ugaas kill a man of another group they will pay his blood-wealth in equal shares (amongst the four lineages) by 'penis-counting' (*qoora tiris*).

[1] This is known as *jaa' ifo* (as distinct from *jiffo*) and is any non-fatal but fairly serious wound for which compensation is of the order of thirty-three-and-a-third camels, but may be more.

[2] When two men attack another of the same group this is known as *hiill* or *tuuto* and insult compensation is regularly payable. This is a common provision in dia-paying treaties.

[3] This refers to the Somali practice of widow inheritance (*dumaal*) where the children belong to the new husband and not to the deceased brother or close agnate. A reduced bride-wealth is normally paid.

9. Compensation for serious wounds valued at thirty-three-and-a-third camels or more, owing to a person of another group, will be paid collectively by all the Ḥassan Ugaas by 'penis counting'.
10. This *ḥeer* cancels all previous agreements of the Ḥassan Ugaas.[1]

My next example is of the Hinjiinle another dia-paying group of the Ḍulbahante, with an estimated male strength of some 580. There are three segments.

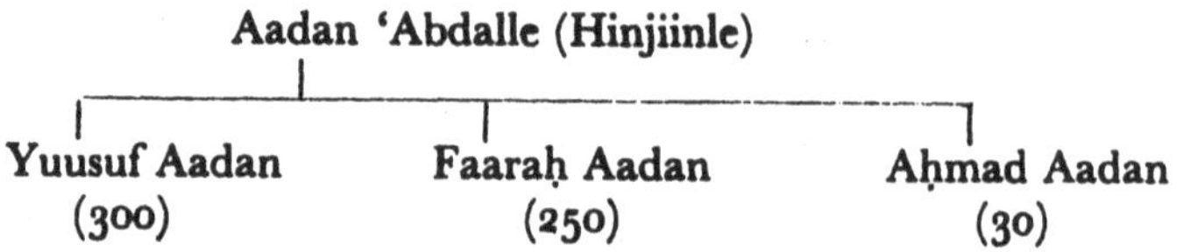

A statement lodged in the District Office, Las Anod, and dated the 8th September, 1954, records their treaty as follows.
1. If a man of our group is killed by another group his next of kin will receive fifteen camels as *jiffo* and the rest of the blood-wealth will be shared amongst the Hinjiinle.
2. When a Hinjiinle woman is killed by an outsider seven-and-a-half camels of her blood-wealth will be taken by her next of kin, and the rest shared amongst the Hinjiinle.
3. Where homicide occurs within the Hinjiinle the following procedure shall operate.[2] The murderer is liable to *barigooyo*;[3] all his property will be handed over to the next of kin of the deceased. If the murderer's property amounts to less than thirty-three-and-a-third camels, the difference will be paid by all the Hinjiinle in concert. If the killer or killers have no stock, a *jiffo* of thirty-three-and-a-third camels is to be paid by the Hinjiinle collectively to the next of kin of the deceased. The same *ḥeer* applies if a woman is murdered, except that here the amount is half that for a man, i.e. sixteen and two-thirds camels.
4. If one of the Hinjiinle kills a man of another group, he and his next of kin shall pay ten camels as *jiffo* and the remainder of the blood-wealth shall be paid by all the Hinjiinle.
5. Where a woman of another group is killed, five camels as *jiffo* will be paid by the murderer's immediate kin and the balance (forty-five camels) by all the Hinjiinle.

[1] For information on these treaties I am much indebted to the courtesy of Mr H. Y. W. S. Dickson, District Commissioner Las Anod, in allowing me access to the District Office files.

[2] Here, as in other places, I have paraphrased the actual wording in the interests of clarity in consultation with informants.

[3] In north-western Somali the pronunciation is *baḍigooyo*. Amongst the eastern Ḍulbahante the Cushitic post alveolar *ḍ* has been modified to *r*, see M. M. Moreno *Il Somalo della Somalia*, Rome, 1955, p. 11. The word means literally 'cutting off the entire property'.

The following example is from the Ḍulbahante Jaama' Siyaad primary lineage group. This particular treaty, binding segments of the Samakaab Jaama' lineage of the Jaama' Siyaad, does not describe the procedure for external payment of blood-wealth in detail, but relates mainly to solidarity in the settlement of lesser amounts. The lineages concerned are related as shown.

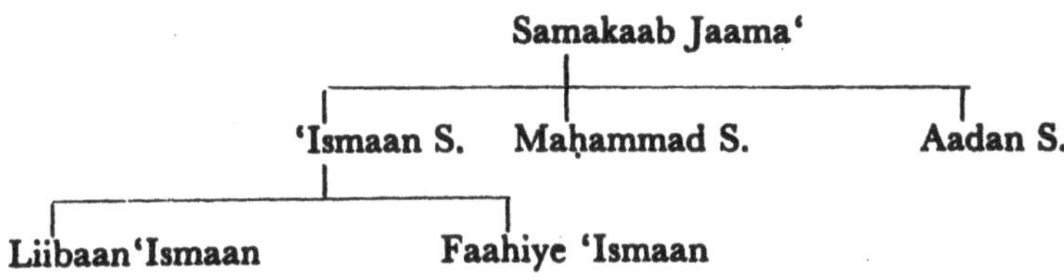

1. On receipt of a *jiffo* of thirty-three-and-a-third camels, twenty-five camels shall be taken by the 'family' (*raas*)[1] of the deceased, and eight-and-a-third by the rest of his segment.
2. Where a man of the Samakaab Jaama' murders another man outside the group, his segment shall pay thirteen camels and the remaining segments twenty-and-a-third.
3. If one man is killed by another of any of the segments, the murderer shall pay a *jiffo* of twenty camels and the remaining thirteen-and-a-third be paid by the other lineages.
4. In the case of a wound valued at *jaa'ifo*[2] and inflicted by another man of the Samakaab Jaama', only eight camels will be paid.
5. Where a man of the group inflicts a serious wound upon another outside the Samakaab Jaama' thirteen camels will be paid by the culprit and the remaining twenty-and-a-third by the other segments.
6. Where the Samakaab Jaama' receive wound compensation from an outside group, the wounded person is entitled to half the amount, and the remaining half shared by the Samakaab Jaama' as a whole.
7. If two men of the group attack another, compensation for insult shall be paid at the rate of one virgin four-year old camel.
8. The insult compensation for slapping a man with one's hand or with a shoe, is one four-year-old she-camel within Samakaab Jaama'.
9. Where a person is responsible for paying a fine in excess of three camels, he shall be helped by all the Samakaab Jaama'.
10. Amounts less than this will be paid by the culprit.
11. Three quarters of compensation for wounds shall be paid and received by the culprit and his lineage (i.e. *jiffo*-paying group).

[1] See above, p. 56

[2] i.e. a serious wound, but not a fatal one, for which the compensation is commonly thirty-three-and-a-third camels, see above, p. 177

12. There will be no remuneration for looking after the livestock of others.
13. This treaty is to express the solidarity of the Samakaab Jaama'. In payment of blood-wealth we are also associated with the 'Afi Faaraḥ and Diiriye Lineages.[1]

Every dia-paying group has its own body of law embodied in its *ḥeer* code. The categories of delict recognized are general and common to all dia-paying groups but the amounts of compensation payable and the proportions in which they are paid vary from group to group. None of the treaties quoted above contains a complete list of all the categories of delict which the members of a dia-paying group acknowledge. The corpus of law is modified as required and new provisions are incorporated in a *ḥeer* code while others may be excised from it. My final example illustrates this and concerns the introduction of new regulations in a dia-paying group treaty recorded by means of a supplementary petition. A letter from the Ḍulbahante Nuur Aḥmad dated 1946 and addressed to the District Commissioner Las Anod states as follows:

'The Nuur Aḥmad have agreed to the following *ḥeer*, and therefore there shall be no marriage within the Reer Nuur Aḥmad. If a man of the Nuur Aḥmad marries a girl of the Nuur Aḥmad he shall pay damages valued at twenty camels to the girl's father. A man guilty of illicit relations with an unmarried girl shall pay five camels in compensation (to her father). We have decided to make this agreement (*ḥeer*) because we do not want to have marriage amongst us.'

VII

To illustrate the principles discussed and the manner in which compensation is actually paid according to the terms of dia-paying group contracts I now cite some cases.

The first concerns a murder which occurred in 1955, near Odejiid, within the Bah Gadabuursi dia-paying group of the Jibriil Abokor cultivators. The Bah Gadabuursi, with a male strength of some 1,700 contains two internal uterine divisions, the Baha Lo'doon and the Bah Kooshin (see above p. 154). Each of these is made up of a number of small lineages. Each is independently responsible for debts incurred up to the amount of ten camels. But for compensation greater than this amount the two uterine divisions combine together

[1] These are two other segments of the Jaama' Siyaad primary lineage-group.

as the Bah Gadabuursi. Each group pays and receives compensation in proportion to its stock-wealth and at the moment since they are fairly equally balanced they each pay half-shares. Within the Bah Gadabuursi as a whole compensation for homicide is sixty camels in the case of a man and twenty-five in the case of a woman. In the case in question both the murderer and his victim were members of the Baha Lo'doon. After the killing, several arrests were made by the police and witnesses called for trial. But no evidence could be obtained and the charge had to be dropped. All the Bah Gadabuursi, however, together collected the equivalent of thirty-three camels which were given mainly to the sons of the deceased and to his close kinsmen, agnates within two or three generations. A small amount was also distributed amongst the elders who had settled the case. The murderer himself only paid the camel slaughtered at the burial ceremony[1] for the dead man.

The following case concerns the Bah Ogaadeen, one of the dia-paying groups into which the Reer Hagar Aadan primary lineage-group of the Ḍulbahante is segmented (see Ḍulbahante genealogy). The group has a total male strength of about 1,000 and is led by an unpaid Akil. The Bah Ogaadeen is a uterine alliance and comprises six *jiffo*-paying groups. A man of the Ugaaḍyahan Naalleeye Aḥmad (of the Ḍulbahante Maḥamuud Garaad) was killed by a man of the Bah Ogaadeen[2] (Faaraḥ Garaad). Since blood-wealth between the Faaraḥ Garaad and Maḥamuud Garaad lineages stands at 100 camels with no additional payment for 'satisfaction',[3] the Bah Ogaadeen paid the statutary 100 camels by 'penis-counting'. Each of the six constitutent *jiffo*-groups contributed according to its male strength. The segment responsible for the killing produced thirty-four camels, of which, being poor in livestock the murderer's family paid only six.

Another example from the Reer Hagar shows how compensation received by a group may be applied to patch up differences within it. The lineages concerned were the Reer Faaraḥ Hagar and the Reer Aadan Hagar, two of the eight lineages which descend from Hagar Aadan, the ancestor of the Reer Hagar primary lineage-group. The murdered man belonged to the Bah Ugaaḍ (some 1,500 males) segment of the Reer Faaraḥ Hagar. The Reer Aadan Hagar paid blood-wealth of 110 camels (ten of which were for 'satisfaction'), consisting of seventy young two-year-old camels and forty pregnant adults. The *jiffo* payable to the close kin of the deceased was thirty-three camels and the ten additional placatory beasts. Amongst the

[1] 'The camel for burial' or 'coffin camel' (*hashi ahanka*). This was nevertheless the largest single contribution made by any individual.

[2] For the relationships of the lineages see the Ḍulbahante genealogy at end of book.

[3] i.e. *samirsiis*, see above p. 164.

close kinsmen of the deceased these were divided as follows. The father of the dead man and his remaining sons took thirty-one camels: his two brothers (father's brothers of the dead man) each took six camels. This left sixty-seven camels unallocated. Since at the time there was enmity over an unsettled homicide within the Bah Ugaaḍ between two segments (who now pay blood-wealth separately), the remaining sixty-seven camels were used to settle this previous debt and paid to the aggrieved segment. Their acceptance closed the feud between the segments for the time being.

As a final illustration I quote the settlement of an assault inflicted on a man of the Barkad primary lineage-group by an 'Ali Geri raiding party. The settlement I describe was only achieved seven years after the assault had taken place and marked the end of a feud between the 'Ali Geri and the Barkad. It is in relation to this feud with the 'Ali Geri that the Maḥamuud Barkad (to whom the injured man belonged) with a male strength of about 2,000 are united as a single dia-paying group. The victim was severely wounded by his 'Ali Geri assailants and compensation for his injuries was assessed at 160 camels (valued at 12,000 shillings) by a Government Kadi.[1] Since in the intervening period there had been many incidents between the 'Ali Geri and the Barkad, when the case came to be settled it was found that the 'Ali Geri already owed the Barkad 9,000 shillings while the latter owed their opponents 12,000. This left 9,000 shillings outstanding for the 'Ali Geri to settle. This amount was paid to the Maḥamuud Barkad (inclusive of the 'Amir Barkad who pay blood-wealth with them). The wounded man received 3,000 shillings. Of the residue 2,000 shillings was divided within the dia-paying group amongst its various segments and a small amount used to provide hospitality for guests of another clan who had come as a deputation. The remaining 4,000 shillings were divided amongst all those of both the 'Ali Geri and Barkad who were present at the meeting which settled the dispute.

I cannot vouch for the accuracy of these figures as it is possible that my informants' memories may have betrayed them in some instances, but it is important to note that the elders involved in settling peace and in distributing compensation are invariably well paid for their labours. All those who participate in settling a dispute whether they are directly implicated or not, expect a generous reward for their trouble.

VIII

It is necessary now to give some attention to the question of the

[1] Note here how an assessment for serious wounds may exceed the statutary rate of compensation for homicide.

viability of dia-paying groups and to the forces which tend to make them split up into separate units, and conversely, to hold them together. The stability or instability of a dia-paying group is the result of the interaction of many different factors. Some of the most important of these are size, the structural context of hostility, the geographical location of segments, the distribution and strength of leadership within the group, and the balance or lack of balance within the group which may be due to the action of all or any of the factors mentioned and to others. At any point in time, any one or even several of these forces may assume prominence while others equally important in another situation or in another group may be unimportant. It is difficult, if not impossible, to assign a strict order of importance to these various considerations since what is significant in one situation or group may not be in another. It is difficult too to distinguish between the different factors and to decide which, in a given group at a given time, appears to have most effect on the structure of the group concerned. If anything, other considerations are generally subordinate to the need to maintain solidarity to meet an external threat, so that the structural context of hostility is generally the most important factor when the stability of dia-paying groups is considered as a whole. Yet the need for collective security may be met by a dia-paying group splitting up and constituent segments striking new *ḥeer* alliances. Some idea of how these different forces work can best be gained by considering particular examples. In the following cases I have tried to isolate what appear to be the most relevant factors in a specific situation.

Size in terms of male strength and stock-wealth, controls the ability either to retaliate, to resist attack, or to pay or to exact compensation. Limits are thus set to the minimum size of a dia-paying group. Below a certain male strength a group cannot function as a viable jural and political unit. Few dia-paying groups have a male strength of less than 200–300 and most are considerably larger. Other things being equal, the larger a group the greater its strength and ability to pay compensation, and generally the less each individual member has to contribute. The Barkad primary lineage-group consists of two dia-paying groups, the Maḥamuud Barkad and the 'Ali Barkad. The former as we have seen, has a male strength of about 2,000 and the latter only of some 200. The 'Ali Barkad generally pasture their stock in the Ain region of the Protectorate, whereas the Maḥamuud Barkad move mainly in the Nugal Valley. The Maḥamuud Barkad are currently divided into four large *jiffo*-paying groups each containing several lineage segments. Their unity as a dia-paying group is a reflection of their hostility to the 'Ali Geri. Prior to the 'Ali Geri feud (to which reference was made above, p. 182) these four *jiffo*-groups were independent dia-paying groups.[1]

But although size confers benefits, especially upon the larger segments, it tends ultimately to lead to unwieldiness and division. This is particularly the case when an external threat is removed. In the absence of external pressure smaller segments (*jiffo*-groups) within a dia-paying group frequently find their position difficult and attempt to break away as independent dia-paying groups. The leading elders of the more important *jiffo*-groups have more influence because they belong to larger segments. The policy of a dia-paying group as a whole tends then to be controlled by its strongest elements often to the detriment of its weaker segments. And large *jiffo*-groups are loath to allow smaller ones to break away when they benefit from their co-operation. Sometimes the larger groups use their power unjustly in the distribution and contribution of compensation within the dia-paying group as a whole. Incoming dues are often appropriated by the larger segments to the exclusion of the weaker groups, but the latter still have to contribute to compensation, often for actions in which they have no direct share. Thus for example, the Aḥmad Barre, one of the three segments of the Barre 'Abdille dia-paying group, notified the District Commissioner, Burao, in 1955, that they had broken away from the other two lineages and would in future act as an independent dia-paying group. They were apparently in difficulties and sought to gain the support of the Administration to effect the breach. In their letter to the District Commissioner precedents for such action were quoted. The other two segments were accused of causing trouble and provoking feuds with other groups

Barre 'Abdille

Aḥmad Barre — Samatar Barre — Nabad Barre

in which the seceding group had to share responsibility although it was not directly implicated. Reference was made to 'the hateful and abominable system known as dia-group which forces us to pay many dia-shares although our men had no part in the killings.' Another statement refers to the desire of the Aḥmad Barre to remain at peace and to divest themselves of 'the evils of the dia-paying group system'. It is worth noting here that the Aḥmad Barre were attacking the *ḥeer* system (as nationalist politicians do) and were seeking at the same time to replace one *ḥeer* by another.

[1] This is established by District Office records as well as by contemporary statements.

I have already cited the solidarity of the large Maḥamuud Barkad dia-paying group as an example of the effect of external hostility. But external pressure sometimes has the reverse effect and leads to the fragmentation of dia-paying groups. To some extent this depends upon the level in the lineage system at which hostility is directed. Thus for example, prior to the Ḍulbahante-Habar Tol Ja'lo clan wars which spread unity amongst all the Ḍulbahante segments, the Reer Faaraḥ Hagar formed a single dia-paying group within the Ḍulbahante in opposition to the collateral Reer Aadan Hagar. But once the campaign against the Habar Tol Ja'lo had opened, the enmity between the Aadan Hagar and Faaraḥ Hagar was forgotten and the latter split up into smaller dia-paying segments.

The influence of geographical distance is seen in the division between the Maḥamuud and 'Ali Barkad mentioned above. Similarly the Habar Tol Ja'lo Sambuur dia-paying group has divided; all those Sambuur grazing in Burao District pay blood-wealth separately from those left behind on the Erigavo coast. The Reer Ḥassan Aadan lineage of the Sambuur are genealogically closer to segments in Burao District, but since they now pasture their stock in Erigavo District they pay blood-wealth with other Habar Tol Ja'lo lineages there. Movement within the same region—and in the nomadic flux segments change their position as they move about—sometimes drives genealogically distant groups to ally together in payment of blood-wealth. Small scattered minority communities amongst the Gadabuursi and Sa'ad Muuse cultivators are as we have seen sometimes forced to form *ḥeer* alliances with their stronger patrons. Here agriculture, limiting movement, increases the importance of geographical proximity. I discuss the status of such dependent groups further in the next section.

The influence of the qualities of leadership of the elders of dia-paying group segments is also involved in the stability of the Maḥamuud Barkad and the instability of the Reer Faaraḥ Hagar. Similarly, although they have recently split up, the Barre 'Abdille segment of the Habar Tol Ja'lo were for long united when from their size they could easily have dissolved into separate groups. Their unity before their present division is a reflection of the stature and strength of following one of their principle elders. But the presence of several energetic and ambitious leaders in a dia-paying group tends often to disrupt its stability. Thus it is apparently the presence of a group of able and ambitious elders competing for power in the Habar Yuunis Reer Sugulle some 2,100 strong (male strength) which has led to the division of this lineage into several separate dia-paying groups ranging in male strength from 250 to 700. This tendency towards the disintegration of dia-paying groups, created by rivalry amongst the elders of their segments, seems to be encouraged by competition for appointment as Government headmen and Akils. But discussion of the position and powers of these dia-paying group headmen must be postponed until the following chapter.

The tendency towards fission created by sheer size may be exacerbated by internal factors such as friction within the group over payment of blood-compensation. Segments which are repeatedly involved in settling debts for which they are not directly responsible disclaim responsibility and seek to withdraw from an onerous contract. On the other hand, groups which from size alone should divide may not do so because no claims are being made against them. Thus about twenty years ago, the Habar Tol Ja'lo Ḥassan Daahir dia-paying group with the exception of one segment, left the coast and moved inland. In their migration the segments disintegrated considerably but their common *ḥeer* remained intact because no occasion for applying it arose.

It is indeed often directly in relation to a specific claim for compensation that groups split. This as we have seen may drive one segment to withdraw from a contract because it no longer wishes to pay compensation for acts in which it is not directly concerned. But fission may also be stimulated by the receipt of compensation. A segment to which damages are owing may seek to break away from other sections of the same dia-paying group to avoid having to share compensation with them. All these processes are reflected in *ḥeer* petitions in District Office files which bear testimony to the constant squabbles and manoeuvres within dia-paying groups, in spite of the *ḥeer* contracts which bind their members together and lay down common canons of jural and political responsibility.

IX

Everyone is at once a member of a widely ramifying series of lineages and of a contractual group, with which he pays and receives blood-wealth and which guarantees the security of his life and property. An individual or group may live temporarily, but rarely by choice permanently, with a foreign lineage and dia-paying group. This is sometimes the case, for example, when a man begins married life with his wife's people and is referred to as 'staying with the girl'.[1] Such individuals or groups, loosely attached affinally or merely guests (*marti*) to a lineage and dia-paying group other than their own, normally leave their camels behind in the custody of their own agnates. Their contractual obligations remain with their agnatic kinsmen unless they formally renounce their treaty and make a new one with those

[1] This is called *inanlayaal*, cf. above, p. 69.

amongst whom they live as foreigners. Amongst their alien hosts non-agnates are assigned a protected status described generally as *magan*. The protecting group does not accept full responsibility for the lives of those assigned this position, but gives only general sanctuary. Infringements of the *magan's* protected status bring dishonour. Thus when protected persons are molested, their patrons are obliged to vindicate their 'name' by seeking vengeance or the payment of compensation. This is due not to them, but to the lineage and dia-paying group of the guest or *magan*. In practice, however, there is often joint retaliatory action by the *magan's* protectors and by his own kin. The hosts are then entitled to claim insult compensation (*ḥaal*) from the aggressor for the affront to their honour.

This patron-protégé relationship is also the bond, formerly more important than it is today, struck by caravan traders passing through country occupied by foreign lineage-groups. Thus from Ḍulbahante country there were formerly two main caravan routes to the port of Berbera. One lay through Bohotle, to Burao, then through Sheikh to Berbera. Caravans of sometimes as many as several hundred camels carrying gum, *ye'eb* nuts,[1] ostrich feathers and ghee, and driving sheep and goats, and horses and camels for sale, made their way to the coast. At Bohotle they came under the protection of the Habar Tol Ja'lo; at Burao the Habar Tol Ja'lo handed over to the Habar Yuunis, at Sheikh they came under the protection of the Habar Awal 'Iise Muuse, and at Berbera they were protected by the Habar Awal Sa'ad Muuse, Reer Aḥmad. Another route lay through the Sarar Plain where the Habar Tol Ja'lo conducted the caravans as far as Berbera. Here the patronage of the Habar Tol Ja'lo, Reer Daahir was exchanged for the patronage of the Habar Awal, Reer Aḥmad. In this inter-lineage caravan trade, a protector was selected for his own good character and for the strength of his lineage and was paid a fee or given presents for his work. The protector and his group are usually referred to as *abbaan*.

To a limited extent this institution still operates, particularly in the case of foreign Asian traders and merchants settled in Somaliland, who, though they stand outside Somali politics as far as blood-feuds are concerned, appoint a salaried *abbaan* to represent them and to protect their general interests. The *abbaan* spends most of his time in the merchant's shop or place of business acting often as a care-taker.

Similarly standing outside Somali society, are the Midgaans,

[1] The fruit of the Cordeauxia edulis.

Tumaals, and Yibirs,[1] traditionally bondsmen of the northern pastoralists and practising various skilled but despised trades such as shoe-making, leather work, ironwork, and hairdressing. Formerly many Somali families and lineages had a few bondsmen (*sab*) attached to them as hereditary serfs and the Midgaans were prized as archers in battle. But now few Somali lineages have many *sab* bondsmen. In their internal relations the *sab* are segmented into lineage-groups on the Somali pattern but like Asian traders they can only have relations with Somali through their Somali patrons (*abbaan*). Formerly there was no intermarriage between freeborn Somali and *sab* and there is little even today. The Somali family or lineage to which they are attached, protects them in their relations with other Somali and is generally responsible for any damages which they inflict. In addition, the Somali patron may help his *sab* bondsmen to collect bride-wealth when they marry and generally stands surety for them. Blood-wealth for a bondsman is said formerly[2] to have been less than that for a noble Somali although I found little indication that this still holds true today. *Sab* traditionally do not have their own dia-paying groups of equivalent status to those of independent Somali. But sometimes they are explicitly a party to the dia-paying contract of their patrons. Now-a-days, moreover, there is a general tendency towards a partial emancipation; and many *sab* have left their traditional patrons to practise their skills in the towns. There is also a general movement amongst the *sab* to set up their own independent dia-paying groups with equivalent status to those of free Somali. Already this has been achieved by some sections amongst the Majeerteen of northern Somalia who now have headmen recognized by the Government. In the British Protectorate, however, this has not yet been attained and the non-viability of the *sab* is thrown into relief by Somali lineage-group fights in towns. When fighting breaks out amongst noble Somali the *sab* tend to take the part of their traditional protectors and to be divided amongst themselves accordingly.

In an entirely different category from either individual Asian immigrants or *sab* bondsmen are the many small groups of noble Somali scattered amongst stronger lineages and clans. Too small themselves to pay blood-wealth independently and often too far removed from their natal lineages to have effective relations with

[1] Collectively called *sab*.

[2] See Lewis, 1955, pp. 51–55.

them, they are driven to seek the protection of their stronger hosts. Where relations are completely severed with their lineages of origin this means that they have to enter into contractual agreements with those amongst whom they live. Lack of strength and therefore of political viability, drive such weak groups into alliances which betray their insecurity and attract little honour. The often quoted proverb 'Either be a mountain or attach yourself to one' (*ama buur ahaw ama buur ku tirso*) sums up their plight. Such arrangements where alliance is achieved by contractual treaty alone or by treaty in addition to weak kinship ties, are those mentioned in Chapter V and known as *gaashaanbuur*, 'pile of shields'. The expression refers to collective fighting strength in terms of the traditional weapon of defence, the shield (*gaashaan*). It is also currently applied to describe the British Commonwealth of Nations or the alliance of the Western Powers with the United States against Russia.[1] It is particularly in the sense of including weak *magan* groups outside agnation that *gaashaanbuur* has a derogatory connotation.

There are varying degrees of adoption and of incorporation within stronger lineages. These range in degree of dependent status with associated inferiority from neighbour (*deris*), appendage (*saar*[2]), followers (*soo raa'*), to pretenders (*sheegad*[3]). In the last relationship the attached group bound contractually assumes the lineage affiliation of its protectors and may claim a common agnatic origin. All these terms denote protected persons or groups and they are sometimes used indiscriminately to refer to any person or group with this status. They can best be understood from examples which show how male strength, fighting potential, and the ability to pay blood-wealth independently are the criteria which determine the status of affiliated groups.

The terms *deris* and *saar* are applied to the Madigaan (Dir), Tol Ja'lo (Isaaq), Akisho (Galla), and Habar Yuunis (Isaaq) and other minorities living amongst the northwestern cultivators. Most of these have their own dia-paying groups and Akils and are recognized by the Administration as autonomous units. Amongst the Gadabuursi and Habar Awal who are nominally their patrons they are not subject to disabilities in day-to-day life. As we have seen they inter-

[1] The Arabic *ḥulafaa'* is sometimes used as equivalent to *gaashaanbuur*.

[2] *Saar* is a general term applied to parasitic creepers such as the Somali plant *carmo*, Cissus spp.

[3] From the verb *sheeg* to say or tell, here in the sense of those who claim (pretend) to be what they are not.

marry freely and enjoy most of the rights of their stronger hosts. In external relations the minorities tend to side with their neighbours and are externally identified with them. But even when these minority communities are too weak to act as independent dia-paying groups, and when they or individual aliens have to enter the *ḥeer* agreements of their hosts, there is usually no question of genealogical assimilation.

So great is the strength of pride of lineage and passion to maintain lineage integrity that it is extremely difficult to evaluate those allegations of lineage heterogeneity which rival groups sometimes level at each other. But one well authenticated case occurs with the Reer Barre amongst the Habar Awal, 'Abdalle Sa'ad—Reer Aadan 'Abdalle, who are mainly nomadic. Amongst them, lived a group of Akisho dependents who in 1946 were involved in a fight with another segment of the Habar Awal, the 'Abdalle Abokor. When seven of the 'Abdalle Abokor were killed and only three Akisho the latter were required to pay the outstanding four blood-wealths to their opponents. They found themselves in difficulties and approached their Aadan 'Abdalle protectors asking for full incorporation in their lineage. There was much opposition at the time from other Akisho who had no desire to see one of their segments lose its identity. But in the end, the group of Akisho in question was fully adopted into the Habar Awal clan as a segment of the Aadan'Abdalle. They thus became true 'pretenders'. (*sheegad*).

Other minorities occur amongst many of the northern nomadic clans, and it is only where they are too small to pay blood-wealth independently that they enter into contractural alliances with their hosts. Amongst the Habar Yuunis Muuse'Arre in the east of the Protectorate are small groups of Madoobe, Minsalle, Turre and Jibrahiil said to be of Dir origin who are generally referred to as *magan*. The Gehayle who fall into a similar category although they have a Government recognized headman and claim Majeerteen descent, live mainly in the Erigavo District of the Protectorate. Similar minorities of Dir, Isaaq and Galla origin occur amongst the Ogaadeen.[1] But although groups may be so small and weak that they have to ally with their stronger hosts only rarely are they fully adopted into a lineage by a genealogocial fiction. Cases such as that of the adoption of the Akisho group mentioned above are relatively rare.

In a few instances, however, independent dia-paying groups of extraneous origin do claim kinship with the larger lineages and clans amongst which they live. Thus the Hinjiinle, whose dia-paying treaty was quoted in an earlier section, are said to be of Galla Akisho

[1] See M. Pirone, 'Le popolazioni dell' Ogaden' and 'Leggende e tradizioni storiche dei Somali Ogaden', *Archivio per l' Antropologia e la Etnologia*, Vol. LXXXIV, 1954.

origin although they now claim to be Ḍulbahante.[1] Another example of *sheegad* in the British Protectorate are the Muḥammad, a lineage some 800 strong whose members live in Burao and Erigavo Districts and act as an independent dia-paying group. Formerly they lived mainly with and supported the Habar Tol Ja'lo, Muuse Abokor, claiming to belong to the Bi'iid segment of that lineage. During the past few years they have turned to ally with the Warsangeli clan (Daarood) of Erigavo District and today claim Warsangeli origin. They assert that in the past they had wrongly read their genealogies but have at last found the truth. This claim of course, is regarded with cynical amusement by other Somali. The Reer Dood, a dia-paying group allied to the Habar Tol Ja'lo Maḥammad Abokor of Burao District and claiming kinship with them are also said to be *sheegad*. Their origin is disputed.

Finally a more equitable type of alliance occurs in the 'Iise clan. The clan as a whole is divided into the 'Three 'Iise' (*saddeḥda 'Iise*) and the 'Three followers' (*saddeḥda soo raa'*). There are six principal apical ancestors in the clan genealogy; Walaaldoon, Hoolle, Ileeye, Hoorroone, Uurweyne, and Wardiiq. Those lineages which descend from the three ancestors, Hoorroone, Uurweyne, and Wardiiq are said not to be of the same agnatic origin as the others. In particular the Wardiiq, in whose line the office of Sultan (*Ugaas*) for the clan descends, are admitted by some 'Iise to be of Habar Tol Ja'lo origin. And the 'Iise themselves make the distinction between those who are 'Iise by birth (*ḍalad*) and those who are 'Iise by adoption (*daqad*) even though they all act corporately as 'Iise.

I have quoted here those few well-authenticated cases of full genealogical adoption of which I have knowledge. There are no doubt others,[2] but in comparison with other segmentary lineage societies and for that matter with the Digil and Rahanwiin cultivating tribes of southern Somalia[3] the relative absence of genealogical fictions amongst the northern pastoral Somali is striking.

[1] This adoption is said to have taken place about 1920.

[2] The Gadabuursi clan are commonly alledged by the members of other clans to be of very mixed composition and there seems to be some evidence in support of this.

[3] It has been pointed out that the Digil and Rahanwiin tribes have an extremely heterogeneous composition. Many of their territorially defined political units contain elements of many different Somali clans—and also Galla—federated together through adoption in a dominant land-holding lineage which provides the skeletal framework of the group. To what extent the Digil and Rahanwiin have a contractual system similar to that of the northern pastoralists is not clear. Until a full analysis of Sab political structure is forthcoming it would be precipitate to attempt to explain the differences between their system and that of the northern pastoralists. It seems, however, that the Sab political system reflects the particular historical circumstances which distinguish them from their northern kinsmen. For, as I

It was indeed one of the first things which I noticed in my early months in the country when I became aware of the many small foreign minority communities scattered amongst stronger hosts but not genealogically identified with them. Compared with other segmentary lineage systems the infrequency of full genealogical assimilation amongst the northern pastoralists seems consistent with the fact that agnation is not the sole idiom in which political relations are cast. For contract, with or without the benefit of real or putative uterine connexion, can unite groups between whom no agnatic relationship subsists, and contractual alliances work within the framework of the lineage system to adjust the balance of power without normally disturbing existing genealogical relationships.[1] Thus pride of agnatic origin can be maintained and political expediency satisfied without full genealogical identification.

As has been said in an earlier chapter, small groups of uncertain origin and inferior strength such as the Akisho amongst the Habar Awal and Dir fragments amongst the Daarood and Habar Tol Ja'lo of the east of the Protectorate, are referred to derogatively as *gun* (lit. 'bottom') in contrast to their stronger neighbours (*gob*). *Gun* is a term of abuse and only used openly when the speaker wishes to antagonize those whom he derides in this way. The opposition between *gun* and *gob*, which might be translated loosely as aristocrats, refers specifically to the distinction between the puny and weak and the numerous and strong. But *gob* has a larger connotation since it is applied as a term of praise to honour the accomplishment of an admirable action. It is the word of praise given to a man whose deeds notably sustain the ideal values of the pastoralists. And since strength is one of the supreme Somali virtues the members of 'short branch' lineages are sometimes taunted as *gun* by their 'long branch' kinsmen who count themselves aristocrats (*gob*). This indeed is the sense of the proverb which blatantly announces that 'he who is weak in numbers is the son of lowliness' (*ninkii yari waa inan gumeed*).[2] It is moreover,

[1] This is discussed more fully below, pp. 298-300.

[2] This is a proverb of the Majeerteen clan, and also of the Ogaadeen.

have shown, in their present composition the Digil and Rahanwiin are a conglomeration of many diverse elements and many of northern origin welded together within the past few centuries in the expansion of the Somali from the north to the riverine areas of southern Somalia where agriculture has been extensively adopted.

significant to note that *gun* means also the stem or trunk of a tree and like the terms 'long branch' and 'short branch', is used equally of plant and lineage morphology.

X

The preceding discussion demonstrates the importance of contract as a political principle. It is possible to have treaty obligations and political solidarity without agnation. Yet, in general, Somali regard the two principles of clanship (*tol*) and contract (*ḥeer*) as complimentary, and agnation is viewed as the primary, all pervasive, force ordering social relations. Most commonly contract works within the field of clanship. The ideals of agnatic solidarity embodied in genealogies, extend throughout the whole field of agnation within which an individual belongs to a great number of different segments each represented by an ancestor in the genealogies. Collective action at one level in the system creates temporary divisions and alliances which, as it were, crystallize the genealogical range of clanship. But the genealogies are ideally permanent, they 'cannot be cut even by iron', and their continuity enables political solidarity to be mobilized at another level on a different occasion.

In its most general sense, common agreement or common custom (*ḥeer dulnimo*) not based on specific contracts, is distinguished from the formal codes (*ḥeer do'nimo*) which regulate the affairs of dia-paying groups. As new orbits of agnation are recognized in different situations with the formation of political groups at various levels in the lineage system, so specific contracts are made binding the groups concerned. Thus although, collective payment of blood-wealth is most frequently at the level of the small nuclear units which we have referred to as dia-paying groups, larger lineages form treaties of collective solidarity as occasion demands. These then become dia-paying groups at a higher level of segmentation.

Two things have to be distinguished here. First, there are the relatively stable alliances which groups of dia-paying groups forge to differentiate themselves from other more structurally distant lineages. This does not involve the creation of new and larger dia-paying groups but only the recognition by contract of a degree of common solidarity in opposition to more distant groups. This is usually achieved by an agreement to pay a higher price for a life where a killing takes place amongst the groups concerned than that applicable outside them. I have already pointed out how the dia-paying groups of the Faaraḥ Garaad segment of the Ḍulbahante clan are opposed to those of the Maḥamuud Garaad and how this is expressed through increasing the compensation payable for homicide from 100 to 120 camels. Between the Faaraḥ Garaad and Maḥamuud Garaad the value of a man's life stands at 100 camels, but within each this amount is increased by twenty camels. Similarly, within the Faaraḥ Garaad itself, the Reer Wa'ays Aadan, the Reer Faaraḥ Aadan, and the Reer 'Arraale Mahad Aadan are united in opposition to their stronger collaterals the Reer Hagar Aadan.[1] Although these are independent dia-paying groups with their own internal treaties the three lineages are contractually bound to pay 110 camels when one kills a man of another. The terms of this agreement are as follows: 'In a case of deliberate murder amongst the three lineages the murderer is either condemned (handed over to the Government) or required himself to pay with his close kinsmen twenty camels; the balance of a total value of 110 camels being paid to the close agnates of the deceased by the three lineages in concert.'[2] This example shows how lineages may differentiate between structurally distant dia-paying groups and structurally close groups by the terms of a general agreement. Such arrangements are usually relatively stable.

Less stable and more ephemeral are the occasions when to meet some general threat a large lineage, comprising many individual dia-paying groups, unites by contract. In this case a new and very large dia-paying group is temporarily created. When two whole clans are engaged in total war they are sometimes united against each other as two opposed dia-paying groups. Thus in one phase of the long-drawn out struggle between the Ḍulbahante (100,000) and the Habar Tol Ja'lo (100,000) clans, temporary *ḥeer* agreements were made binding all the members of each clan in collective responsibility for homicide against those of the other. When, however, hostilities reached such a pitch that there were many killings and many of the component segments were involved in payment of compensation for actions in which they were not directly implicated the general Ḍulbahante contract was rescinded. Again, in such situations of general clan hostility, collective responsibility is sometimes recognized by agreement after an occasion of bloodshed. During a riot in 1957 in Hargeisa (the capital of the British Protectorate) between members of the Arab clan (20,000) and the Sa'ad Muuse (100,000) sub-clan of the Habar Awal, one man of the Arab was killed. Since the affray had the character of a general mêlée, all the Sa'ad Muuse accepted collective responsibility. A bloodwealth of 100 camels was paid by

[1] See genealogy of the Ḍulbahante clan.

[2] Treaty lodged with the District Commissioner, Las Anod.

them in fifty portions corresponding to the fifty dia-paying groups into which the Sa'ad Muuse are divided. Individuals paid negligible amounts.

These examples have been cited to show how contractual agreements are struck at different levels in the lineage system as occasion requires. Like agnation, *ḥeer* is not a static principle, but dynamic within the framework of the lineage system. The range of agnation acknowledged and marshalled by treaty is constantly shifting as the direction of hostility changes. To a large degree this structural relativity is rooted in the dynamics of the nomadic life where competition for sparse grazing and water continually arises at different levels of grouping. It thus seems appropriate to regard the Somali political and jural contract as a mechanism for, as it were, knotting the diffuse ties of agnation as political unity is specifically required at different levels of segmentation. The general field of clanship is particularized where political solidarity has to be strengthened and the implicit obligations of clanship given specific jural and political meaning. It is for this reason that the smallest political units, the dia-paying groups, can be said to have only relative stability. Clanship provides the framework upon which contractual agreement as a political principle works. What in agnation is diffuse and elastic, is made definite and specific by contract. Political and jural units are defined by contract within agnation. Since contract can override agnation and join groups outside clanship its importance cannot be minimised. Contract unites and divides and this is recognized by nationalist politicians when they attribute their difficulties in creating a stable national patriotism to the force of *ḥeer*, rather than to the force of clanship (*tol*).

7

Authority and Sanctions

I

LACK of any stable hierarchy of political units is characteristic of the Somali social system. In conformity with this, there is no formal hierarchy of political or administrative offices. Each of the main orders of segmentation—dia-paying group, primary lineage-group, and clan—does not have a specific office of leadership associated with it. At every level of lineage allegiance, political leadership lies with the elders of the group concerned, and only at the level of the clan is there sometimes the special office of clan-head. The position of the 'Sultans' who often, but by no means always, lead clans will be considered presently.

At every level of segmentation, all adult men are classed as elders (*oday*, pl. *odayaal*) with the right to speak at the councils (sg. *shir*) which deliberate matters of common concern. Traditionally only *sab* bondsmen (Midgaans, Tumaals, and Yibirs) are excluded from direct participation in the political affairs of the noble Somali lineage to which they are attached. But now-a-days, through employment in government service or trade in towns, some *sab* have amassed considerable wealth and have increased their status sufficiently to gain admission to the councils of the lineage of their traditional Somali patrons.

In principle, all adult males have an equal say, since all can speak in the councils of their group. Naturally, however, the opinions of different men carry different weight. Here status differences refer to wealth, inherited prestige, skill in public oratory and poetry, political acumen, age, wisdom, and other personal characteristics. Religious knowledge and piety, as evinced through such meritorious acts as pilgrimage to Mecca, and the regular observance of the daily prayers and obligatory fasts, earn a man respect and prestige. Although the formal distinction is made between those who devote their lives to religion (*wadaad*) and those whose lives are primarily taken up with worldly affairs (*waranleh*, 'spear-bearer'), many individuals combine skill in both spheres and enjoy respect in both. Theoretically, and ideally, men of religion (*wadaads*) are supposed to stand outside lineage politics. But knowledge of religion and the formal marks of piety may enhance the position of an elder in clan politics.

Despite the fundamentally egalitarian character of Somali society, there are often considerable variations in wealth, as much in the interior in stock-wealth as in riches acquired through successful trade in the towns. Somali are well aware of the power which wealth brings, and at the same time, of the responsibilities which it entails in the suppport of poorer kinsmen. A rich elder does not lack a friendly hearing for his opinions from his less well-off kinsmen, and can usually rely on their support for his views in lineage affairs. Thus movements amongst the 'Iise Muuse lineage of the Habar Awal clan to establish a Sultan found a ready target in a rich clansman who, having amassed considerable wealth abroad, retired to Somaliland. Although the candidate eventually achieved the position for which he was championed, much of his fortune was dissipated in the process amongst his supporters. In this context the proverb 'when a rich man does not tell the truth people will say he does' is contrasted with that which states 'when a poor man tells the truth people may say he lies.'

In general, respect attaches to age and seniority of lineage. Age in itself, if accompanied by wisdom and long experience of politics and not weakened by senility, is an important factor in the attention paid to an elder's views in council. But men spent in years who have lost their virility, are not usually looked to for political leadership. In any lineage, the eldest member of the genealogically senior (*'urad*) branch, even when it is a 'short-branch' lineage, has automatically the duty of pronouncing the blessing in group ritual and the right to an especially coveted portion of any livestock slaughtered (the *hal du'o*). Despite these ritual privileges, however, he has usually less political importance than an aged elder within a group with many descendants and close kinsmen, or a senior man of the 'long branch' segment of the lineage-group. For these command respect for their opinions through the following which they can muster.

While the different qualities mentioned are all instrumental in determining a man's status and influence in council, it is difficult to rank them in any strict order of importance. A person's position is a reflection of a number of different qualities. What earns one man a favourable position in relation to his peers may not be effective in the case of another. Popularity and political influence are the result of a totality of different attributes important amongst which are hospitality (which should go with wealth), wisdom, and those various qualities of strength, courage and skill in political affairs which are summed up by the word *belaayo*. This word means 'disaster' or 'catastrophe', but what is disastrous to adversaries is often advantageous to one's self, and it is in this sense that *belaayo* is a term of praise for a man whose actions come near to the ideals of Somali belligerence, independence, daring and panache. When Somali refer to a person as *belaayo*, they mean that he fulfills their ideals of manly hardihood and distinction. And what wealth and weight of kinship may not ensure, agility in the conduct of affairs, and the skilful manipulation of jealousies and ambitions, may achieve.

II

The informal council (*shir*) summoned as need arises, at every order of segmentation, and attended by all the adult men, or their representatives chosen at smaller lineage-group *shirs*, is the fundamental institution of government. It has no formal constitution except that of membership of the lineage concerned, no regular place or time of meeting, and there are no official positions on it. All men are councillors, and all men politicians. Agreements are reached by majority decisions following the direction taken by the concensus of feeling at a meeting. Usually the participants sit in a rough circle in the shade of a tree, in the central clearing of a nomadic hamlet, or they may meet in a 'coffee-shop' in a village or town. Where a large lineage with a male strength of several thousand is concerned, delegates may be chosen to represent each of the component lineages and sent to a central meeting-place. Sometimes, however, all those concerned, even if they number several thousand, attend the council and form a large loose ring. Representatives may then be appointed for the smaller units and sent into the middle of the circle to thrash the matter out while their kinsmen sit listening in the outer-ring. Men sit or squat on the ground at a *shir* and when they wish to speak often rise to their feet. Although there may be a great deal of argument and wrangling, all those present are expected to behave courteously and breaches of good manners may be punished. Thus at a large Habar Awal *shir* which had met to discuss the rights of cultivators and pastoralists in the west of the Protectorate members of two of the lineages represented assaulted the elders of other groups present. The offenders were directed by the Sultan to pay insult compensation (*ḥaal*) to the affronted elders.

Sheikhs and *wadaads* are sometimes less influential in council proceedings when political action is being discussed. Their part is to consecrate the meeting by opening the proceedings with prayers and to close them with blessings. In this role they are particularly important at peace-councils (sg. *shir nabadeed*) summoned to effect conciliation between hostile groups. If conciliation is achieved, and an acceptable conclusion (*guddoon*) reached, they add the sanction and seal of religion to the proceedings with prayers such as 'May the peace of God go with us' (*Ilaahow nabad geli*), all those present adding 'Amen', and usually reciting the *fatḥa*.[1]

The *ad hoc* council disposes of the collective business of a group. *Ḥeer* contracts are promulgated within dia-paying groups and between them, or they are rescinded; peace-treaties are made, the decision to unite against another group is taken and an attack planned with the appointment of a battle leader; all these and other matters are dealt with by the *shir*. Similarly, councils apportion and collect compensation received by, or due from a lineage. They sometimes arrange also for the settlement of debts incurred collectively in trade. Lineage councils also debate Government policy and discuss matters which they wish to bring to the notice of the Administrations. In the dry seasons, the construction and maintenance of wells, and the regulation of watering are considered; and in all seasons movement to new grazing areas is debated. The installation of a clan Sultan requires the summoning of a very large council, preferably after the rains, when pasture and food are plentiful so that many thousands of clansmen can assemble in one area for several days to attend the various ceremonies, feasts, and dances appropriate to the occasion. The rainy season is also usually selected when the members of a lineage-group collect to honour their ancestor in communal sacrifice.

[1] The opening sura of the Quran. Those present recite with them and conclude the sura by crying '*fatḥa*', often several times.

III

At every level of grouping, lineages are led by their elders; different individuals having different powers of leadership according to the criteria discussed above. The dia-paying group has no specific office of political leadership attached to it. It consists simply of a group of elders who are close kinsmen. In principle, all are equally important. But men of outstanding character naturally tend to have greater influence in the policies of a dia-paying group than others less endowed. Indeed frequently several men are regarded as the unofficial leaders of their group. It is unusual to find only one individual with power and influence. Nevertheless, in their relations with the Administrations dia-paying groups have adopted the practice of electing individuals to represent them. In the eyes of those who nominate them, these delegates are simply emissaries, or go-betweens, and not infrequently are chosen specifically for their skill in dealing with administrative officials. They are generally called Akils (correctly *'aaqil*, pl. *'aaqillo*). The Indian loan-word *jawaabdaar*, dating from the period of administration of British Somaliland by the Indian Government through Aden, 1885-98, is also employed. *'Aaqil* is an Arabic borrowing (from the root '-q-l, mean- 'wise', or 'intelligent'), and Somali sometimes refer to their *'aaqils* as the 'heads' (sg. *madaḥ*) of the groups which they represent. Some Somali maintain that the Akils system of group representation was introduced during the period of Egyptian rule of the coast (1875-85), but since the word occurs in Burton's account (1856) the institution appears to have a longer history.[1] Yet if they did not introduce Akils for the first time, the Egyptian authorities certainly used them as spokesmen for the different lineage-groups.

The Akils system has been continued by the present Administrations in all the Somali territories, elders being selected according to their apparent qualities of leadership and good sense for appointment as stipended headmen. To bring the British Protectorate into line with the general devolution of authority and development of local government current in recent British Colonial policy, a system of 'Local Authorities' was introduced in 1950.[2] As an innovation this scheme was at first bitterly

[1] R. F. Burton, *First Footsteps in East Africa*, Memorial edition, 1894, vol. ii, p. 134.

[2] The Local Authorities Ordinance, 1950.

opposed, particularly by the heads of clans (Sultans) holding traditional titles. These dignitaries regarded it as an infringement of what little prestige and authority they customarily enjoyed and feared that their unique position would be lost. This resistance was gradually overcome, however, with what success will be presently seen, and the attempt made to 'balance-up' dia-paying groups and to introduce more order and regularity than actually exists by appointing at least one stipended Akil or 'Local Authority' for each large dia-paying group. In the Ḍulbahante clan for example, the majority of the fifty or so dia-paying groups have salaried Akils and some of the larger groups have several appointments. Thus the Bah 'Ararsame with a male strength of about 1,700 have one 'First class Akil' and one 'Second Class Akil'.

These functionaries are usually described officially as 'chiefs'[1], but this is a misleading title since it suggests a traditional position of authority which does not exist. In the Protectorate, the Local Authorities Ordinance does empower certain Akils to assist the Administration in maintaining law and order, in enforcing when possible Government orders and regulations, and in bringing persons guilty of crimes to justice. But the vesting of these powers in one person is largely untraditional and runs counter to the bonds of contractual solidarity which bind the members of a dia-paying group together and unite them against other political units. There is a further difficulty, in that although Somali make use of the principle of delegation in their traditional political organization (as in delegated representation at *shirs*, for example), they are mistrustful of anything but direct, face-to-face relations. It is then not surprising that as a whole Akils are severely handicapped in discharging their duties satisfactorily. It is perhaps surprising indeed that they succeed at all.

Although, despite a certain hostility towards Government, elders are attracted by the salary and title of the office, it is by its very nature not an easy one to fulfil satisfactorily. As soon as an elder is appointed as a Local Authority he is placed in a position of opposition to his fellow kinsmen of his dia-paying group. He becomes an administrative official, representing Government, and law and order. This may not be apparent as long as he is only acting as the emisary of his group to the Government, and as in effect, a friend at

[1] *Colonial Reports; Somaliland: 1952-53*, 1954, p. 40; *Rapport . . . Somalie, 1957*, 1958, p. 20; H. Deschamps, *Côte des Somalis*, 1948, p. 66.

court. But when his group are at fault and he is required to elicit the circumstances of a killing or raid, to collect evidence and to produce witnesses, and to find and bring to court the person or persons responsible, no matter how high his prestige and personal integrity, he naturally encounters difficulties. In these circumstances his position often becomes intolerable. It is true that in some situations, as for example when the member of a group responsible for a delict is unpopular, or a general ne'er-do-well, his kinsmen may be glad to hand him over to the Administration, but this is rarely the case. To some extent, the readiness or reluctance with which a person wanted in connection with a crime is surrendered to justice, depends upon the pressure to which his dia-paying group as a whole is subject. This again is a function of the situation and intensity of hostility, whether from other dia-paying groups or from the Government. If a group is under great duress, it may yet be prepared to produce though unwillingly, the individual responsible, and to hand him over to the Administration through its Akil. This is most likely to occur where the crime is committed within the dia-paying group. Examples of dia-paying groups which make explicit provision in their treaties for the surrender to justice of miscreants (especially murderers) have been cited in the previous chapter.

For these reasons, through the very efficiency and loyalty with which they discharge their traditional duties as elders, Akils tend to fail to fulfil the tasks set them by the Administrations. Thus they often have to be suspended from duty. The following case is typical. In the situation of tension between Habar Tol Ja'lo and Ḍulbahante clans, a prominent Habar Tol Ja'lo Akil was temporarily removed from office for refusing to co-operate with the Administration. He had been requested by a District Commissioner to accompany a party of police to arrest three men of his group who were wanted in connection with the murder of a Ḍulbahante clansman. Later the Akil's own son was arrested as a suspect.

In spite of these factors which militate against the success of the system as a means of local government, Akils and Local Authorities are now an established institution. Some, certainly manage to hold the respect of their kinsmen, and at the same time to discharge their duties as Government officials fairly satisfactorily. At least they provide a means of mediation between the central government and dia-paying groups, the advantages of which are not lost on the elders themselves. Indeed in the British Protectorate there is now rivalry between elders to achieve appointment. Quite apart from the attractiveness of a small but regular income, elders naturally view the system in terms of the advantages which may accrue to them personally and to their kinsmen, rather than in terms of the distasteful tasks which the Administration may require them to perform. Many indeed hope to enjoy the benefits while avoiding the disadvantages as skillfully as possible.

As was suggested in the previous chapter, the appointment of Akils and Local Authorities seems to weaken the stability of dia-paying groups. This is difficult to substantiate satisfactorily. But it appears that by singling out an individual elder and recognizing him as the leader of a group of equals, jealousies and rivalries are created or at least exacerbated which threaten the stability of the dia-paying group. Groups now vie with each other for recognition as independent dia-paying units, or where they already exist as such, clamour for the creation of further Akils' posts. Indeed to some degree the possession of a 'Local Authority' seems increasingly to be becoming the criterion of dia-paying group viability vis-à-vis the Administration. Yet at the same time, the very nature of Somali political segmentation gives the dia-paying group only relative stability. This means that artificial positions of leadership are created for groups which are inherently unstable.

IV

The office of Sultan for a clan, or sub-clan where the clan is large, is the only truly traditional titular political office in northern Somali society. The position corresponds to the distinctive character of the clan as a social unit, just as the clan is a more clearly defined territorial unit than are other orders of lineage grouping. In addition to the universally understood Arabic *Suldaan*, used particularly by the Isaaq, the position has several different titles. Purer Somali expressions are *Boqor, Ugaas* (particularly amongst the Ogaadeen and in the north-west of Somaliland), and *Garaad*, current in most of the Daarood clans other than the Ogaadeen. *Boqor* also means a belt; and I was told that its use as a title for the clan-head refers to the latter's unifying role and to the fact that he is conceived of as an intermediary binding his clansmen together. The word *Garaad* also means 'mind', 'wisdom', 'understanding' etc., (cf. *'aaqil*), and according to Basset[1] is a Somali version of the Amharic title *al-Jaraad*, the Governor of a Muslim province tributary to Abyssinia, dating from the

[1] R. Basset, op. cit. (translation) fasc. 1, p. 10. See also Trimingham, 1952, p. 84.

mediaeval period. These various titles are now all more or less synonomous; although amongst the Daarood, something still remains of a former hierarchy of lineage leaders in which the lowest rank was that of *Islaan*,[1] followed in increasing authority by *Ugaas*, *Garaad*, and *Boqor*. Traditionally, the head of the Majeerteen 'Ismaan Maḥamuud lineage, bore the title *Boqor*, with nominal jurisdiction, not only over all the Majeerteen, but also over all the clans of the Harti division of the Daarood clan-family.

Although the Sultan is a symbol for the unity of the clan, the office is not indispensable. Not every clan can boast a Sultan and the same apparently applied also in the past. In the north, the 'Iise have one (called *Ugaas*) who receives a salary from both the Ethiopian and French governments and who usually lives at DireDawa in Ethiopia. Although various political restrictions make it difficult or impossible for him to move freely amongst his people, he is generally acknowledged by all the 'Iise of French, and British Somaliland, and of Ethiopia. The Gadabuursi had formerly a dynasty of Sultans (*Ugaas*) but disputes between claimants for the title, exacerbated by the division of the clan between Ethiopian and British administration, led to its lapse. A recent attempt in the British Protectorate to resuscitate it failed; members of the clan could not reach agreement on a candidate.

Amongst the Isaaq, the Habar Awal have one Sultan, who is of the Sa'ad Muuse sub-clan and a stipendiary of the Administration. The 'Iise Muuse sub-clan have on various occasions tried to appoint their own Sultan to express their autonomy and sense of independence from the Sa'ad Muuse but have so far not established a permanent title. Both the Arab and 'Iidagalle clans have Sultans paid by the Protectorate government. The Habar Yuunis have none, although there is a pretender to the title with a small following. The Habar Tol Ja'lo have recently created the position, but their Sultan, who belongs to the Jibriil Abokor Muuse segment of the clan, is not recognized by all the Habar Tol Ja'lo and does not receive a salary from the Administration. The Ḍulbahante have two Sultans (*Garaads*), one for each of the two large segments into which the clan is divided. The *Garaad* of the Maḥamuud Garaad, is recognized by the Government and receives a stipend. *Garaad* Jaama' of the Faaraḥ Garaad has only recently been recognized, having successfully maintained his prestige by opposing the Administration. Finally in the Protectorate, the *Garaad* of the Warsangeli, the most celebrated and strongest of

[1] Amongst the Isaaq and in the north-west of Somaliland, *islaan* is not a title but means simply oldman or elder, sometimes in a derogatory sense.

northern Sultans, is recognized by the Administration and receives a salary.

Although only a *primus inter pares*, the clan-head is a symbol for and focus of the agnatic solidarity of his clan. While a clan is divided by contract (*ḥeer*) into dia-paying groups it has at the same time a distinctive sense of unity transcending its divisions, and a sense of solidarity which varies with the situation. It is the territorial exclusiveness of the clan, and the fact that it periodically unites as a corporate political unit, which its Sultan represents. To some extent ritually, and a least nominally politically, a clan-head is responsible for the prosperity and well-being of his people and their stock. Within his own lineage he enjoys greater respect than amongst other lineages of his clan. When, however, the various lineages of a clan unite in opposition to an external threat, the Sultan's unique position places him ideally at the front of his clan elders. With their support, he represents his clan in external relations, as for example when deputations of different clans parley with each other in an attempt to settle a dispute. And within his clan, he should concern himself with the general welfare of his people. Indeed, amongst his clansmen, a Sultan is ideally an arbitrator and peacemaker concerned with the maintenance of clan solidarity. It is in this role particularly, that local traditions and early accounts[1] depict the Sultan as mediating between rival lineages of his clan. These ideal characteristics are epitomized in the proverb 'Three things bring the downfall of Sultans; biased judgement (in the settlement of disputes), dry-handedness (meaness), and indecision' (*Saddeḥ b'aa boqornimo kaa qaadda: gar wee'san, iyo ga'an guḍan, iyo guddoon jili'san*).

These functions are still to some extent exercised today, and indeed encouraged by the Administrations, but few Sultans have the influence with which their predecessors are credited. To some extent traditional accounts are no doubt exaggerated, as is suggested by the trenchant phrases in which Burton describes the Somali clan-head's lack of effective authority.[2] In the early days of colonization, the tenuous position of the clan-head was not at first properly appreciated, and half-hearted attempts were made to make the institution the foundation of a system of indirect rule. The Italians appear to have gone farther in this direction than

[1] See e.g. Guillain, 1856, vol. ii; L. Robecchi-Bricchetti, *Somalia e Benadir*, Milan, 1899; Burton, 1856; and later Cerulli, 1919.

[2] Burton, op. cit., vol. i, p. 122, p. 167; vol. ii, p. 142; etc.

the British partly, perhaps, because some of the leaders with whom they had to treat enjoyed more power than is generally characteristic of the office. During the insurrection led by Sayyid Maḥammad 'Abdille Ḥassan, the British Administration also flirted with this policy in seeking to restore order and to fight the Dervish leader through Sultans of outstanding ability such as *Garaad* Maḥamuud 'Ali Shirre of the Warsangeli. But no firm system of indirect rule through clan-heads was ever established. Today, with the appointment of elders as Akils and Local Authorities, the institution has lost some of its lustre, and the increasing recognition of the dia-paying group as the basic jural and political unit seems to have weakened the integrity of the clan, and with it the office of Sultan. But only in exceptional cases to which I refer presently was the institution ever one of real authority.

Generally then in northern Somaliland the office of clan-head has little intrinsic power attached to it. Where a Sultan is the popular choice of his people he naturally, however, enjoys a certain prestige because of his unique position. But there is no formal court other than the *ad hoc* councils in which the Sultan often presides. A Sultan has no emissaries or soldiers to enable him to enforce his rulings, and he lives no more lavishly than many another well-to-do clansman. In spite, moreover, of his role as arbitrator, by no means all disputes within a clan are brought to him for settlement. It is now-a-days usually only in extreme cases and where there is considerable administrative pressure to reach a settlement, or where it is incumbent upon all the segments of a clan to unite for their self-preservation, that the Sultan figures as a mediator.

Because of his privileged position and the nominal respect paid to him, he is sometimes offered gifts of tribute (*abaalgud, sado*) and shown other gestures of respect. Sometimes, as on his installation, he may be given a girl in marriage by his people without any payment of bride-wealth. In return, a Sultan is expected to show hospitality. Generosity and liberality earn him praise and fame, often even outside his own clan. In speaking of their Sultans, Somali tend to emphazise the dignity of the office, the weightiness of their words, and the authority of their rulings and decisions. But these are tributes of respect rather than statements of fact. Merely by holding office, a Sultan enjoys little more influence and power than another Akil or elder. It is only through the possession of those qualities which give any Somali elder a following that a Sultan can exert effective leadership. Today, the office is little more than an empty title, and it is the holder's personality which primarily decides his influence.

I have used the title 'Sultan' because this is how Somali generally describe their clan-heads, and because, although they have little or none of the power and pomp of the Sultans of Arabian classical literature, Somali like to think of their Sultans as approximating in some degree to this ideal. The closest approach to centralized Muslim government was achieved in the petty sultanates of the Muslim state of Adal, which flourished precariously between the tenth and sixteenth centuries, virtually disappearing after the reversal of Imaam Aḥmad Granhe's conquests in Ethiopia. Yet it is fairly clear that the Sultans of Zeila' and Adal never exercised continuous jurisdiction over their Somali followers. As has been said the history of Adal shows that, founded by Arabian settlers, the state's existence was constantly threatened by its egalitarian Somali population. At best, possessing only a slight degree of centralized goverment and inherently unstable, Adal existed precariously on the fringes of nomadism, in which it was from time to time submerged, and ultimately perished utterly.[1]

Echoes of a slightly more developed institution than that typical today occur in the traditions of the Gadabuursi and 'Iise. When a new *Ugaas* was appointed amongst the Gadabuursi, a hundred elders, representative of all the lineages of the clan, assembled to form a parliament to promulgate new *ḥeer* agreements, and to decide what legislation they wished to retain from the reign of the previous *Ugaas*. The compensation rates for delicts committed within the clan were revised if necessary, and a corpus of Gadabuursi law, as it were, placed on the statutes for the duration of the new *Ugaas's* rule. This was called 'the law of the Sultan and the 100 men' (*ḥeerka boqorka iyo boqolka nin*). From the 100 elders, twenty-four were selected as a permanent advisory council for the *Ugaas* (the *shirka boqorka*). This council formed a central legal court (*guddi*) to which all disputes which could not otherwise be settled should be taken. The *Ugaas* and his court toured the country, moving amongst the various segments of the clan settling disputes, and receiving gifts of tribute and hospitality. There is said to have been no standing army or specialized functionaries to enforce the decisions of the Sultan's court other than the Midgaans attached to the royal lineage who acted as emissaries. The 'Iise had traditionally a similar arrangement with a permanent court of forty-four men attached to their *Ugaas*. But in both these cases the Sultans were leaders on the

[1] See Trimingham, op. cit. pp. 96–7.

egalitarian Somali pattern, settlers of disputes and arbitrators vaguely responsible for the prosperity and fortune of their clans, not heads of a Muslim state.

Amongst the Daarood, however, a more centralized system on the Islamic pattern appears to have existed from time to time in the past. The Majeerteen are the first-born clan (*'urad*) of the Harti division of the Daarood clan-family. Their Sultan, of the 'Ismaan Maḥamuud lineage with the title *Boqor*, had formerly nominal jurisdiction over all the Daarood clans descended from Harti. But with the dispersal of the Harti clans, and their growth in strength and independence, the paramouncy of the 'Ismaan Maḥamuud lineage outside the Majeerteen lapsed. The Ḍulbahante and Warsangeli for example, both descended from Harti, today do not acknowledge the supremacy of the Majeerteen. There is often friction between the Ḍulbahante and Majeerteen particularly, and recently when peace had been concluded between the Ḍulbahante and Habar Tol Ja'lo, fighting broke out between the former and the Majeerteen. Thus the jurisdiction of the office has become confined to the Majeerteen clan alone, and here its authority has greatly diminished since colonization. The last leader to invest his office with any power seems to have been the celebrated *Boqor* 'Ismaan, whom Guillain (circa 1850) describes as coming to the coast twice yearly to collect tribute from his subjects. This was the Sultan who signed treaties with the Italian State in 1889 and 1901.[1] Prior to this, about 1870, the Majeerteen Sultanate was divided by a quarrel between 'Ismaan, and his kinsman Yuusuf 'Ali Kenadiid,[2] the latter becoming Sultan of Obbia.

The Majeerteen Sultan possessed more power than was typical of a Somali clan-head. He laid claim to a tax on the harvest of aromatic trees, and to pearl fishing along the coast. He had prior rights to the looting of any ship wrecked on the coast: he exercised rights over the control of pasturage and woodland, and he imposed a land tax and stock tax. In addition he possessed a small standing army which he sent to carry out his instructions and collect his state revenue.[3] What he collected, often only with difficulty, as a state-tax, was in fact the obligatory Muslim alms (*seko*)[4] which Somali normally pay privately to the poor and to sheikhs and *wadaads* (often their own poor kinsmen). The appropriation of the *seko* by a centralized government is foreign to Somali thought today, and contrary to their egalitarian ideals. It is of interest, however, to note that a clan meeting of the Ḍulbahante at Las Anod in December 1957, which discussed matters

[1] Cerulli, 1919. p. 17.

[2] See Robecchi-Bricchetti, 1899, pp. 200 ff; A. Hamilton, *Somaliland*, London, 1911, p. 186.

[3] Guillain, 1865, vol. ii, pp. 443 ff; Cerulli, 1919, pp. 46–9

[4] See *Encyclopaedia of Islam*, vol. iv, article '*zakat*', pp. 1202–05.

of general Ḍulbahante interest including the maintenance of peace, education and closer relations with Government, proposed the establishment of a clan betterment fund, contributions to which were to be received by *Garaad* Jaama'.

Vestiges of a similar degree of centralized administration on the pattern of a Muslim Sultanante, survive today in the Protectorate amongst the Warsangeli.[1] Prior to 1920, the *Garaad* had at his command a small standing army with which, with British support, he fought Sayyid Maḥammad 'Abdille Ḥassan's forces. But the *Garaad's* powers are dwindling under modern administration.

Sultanates such as these, generally only arose on the coast or through commanding an important trade route, and were largely dependent on the possession and control of a port or other exploitable economic resources. They were in direct trade and diffuse political relations with Arabia, received occasional Arab immigrants, and were the centres from which Islam expanded with trade into the interior. They had to fight to maintain their positions of supremacy against the periodic incursions of raiding parties of nomads, and their authority was never great. Surrounding nomadic groups only acknowledged them when they had to, or when an external challenge welded them briefly together. In the mediaeval period, the threat was the expansionist policy of Christian Abyssinia, and the stimulus, the immigration of Arab proselytizers and the messianic fervour of early Islam. And all these petty centres of weak government, intrinsically foreign to the egalitarian character of Somali nomadic life, depended for their success upon able leadership. They were founded, built up, and held together by men of outstanding character, and when successive Sultans did not possess these characteristics, whatever their economic resources, they lapsed into the anarchy of Somali pastoral democracy.

V

Once established, the office of clan-head is in principle hereditary in the lineage of its foundation. Succession is normally by primogeniture, although the office may be tied to a particular uterine group and the Sultan required to be born of a woman of a particular clan. Thus, for example, the Warsangeli *Garaad* is preferably the son of a woman of the Habar Yuunis Muuse 'Arre. The Ḍulbahante Faaraḥ Garaad in turn, favour a man born of a Habar Yuunis or

[1] Cf. Burton, op. cit. vol. ii, p. 141.

Ogaadeen mother, and the Majeerteen, the son of a woman of the Dir clan. The eldest son with the requisite uterine qualifications inherits the title unless he is patently unfit for office or unacceptable to the majority of his clan.

The lineage in which the title is vested is neither necessarily the genealogically senior (*'urad*) lineage nor the 'long branch' (*laanḍeer*) segment. Different clans adopt different principles in tying the position to a particular lineage. Neither of the two Ḍulbahante *Gaaraads* is of the 'long branch' segment of his lineage. The title of *Ugaas* for the 'Iise clan belongs to the Wardiiq segment, which is politically the weakest of the six primary segments of the clan, and one of the three not agnatically descended from the clan eponym.[1] 'Iise say specifically that the title is bestowed on this lineage because it is 'lucky' and enjoys blessing and moreover because it is numerically weakest. A Sultan is always supposed to be endowed with blessing rather than necessarily being strong in arms. It is significant, however, that in the case of the Warsangeli whose *Garaad* has unusual influence, the title descends in the numerically dominant segment of the clan.

VI

The weak ritual implications of the title of clan-head have been mentioned. There is some connexion between the office and the prosperity of a clan. This is not highly formalized, nor of much importance, but it is reflected in the ceremonial installation (*waa la boqrayaa*) of a new Sultan. This to Somali is the most lavish and most colourful ceremony of public life. It is always held in the rainy seasons, preferably in the spring when there is abundance and as many clansmen as possible can congregate in one place. The ritual attending the ceremony is scant and to some extent varies from clan to clan. An essential feature, however, which is always present, is the public acknowledgement of the newly appointed Sultan when fresh green leaves are placed upon his head. This is usually initiated by a person who, for one reason or another (sometimes he is of the *'urad* lineage), is considered lucky. The annointing with leaves is called *'aleemasaar*[2] and refers to the ideal expectation that the Sultan's reign will be blessed with abundance and prosperity. Elders and *wadaads* greet the Sultan offering him presents and gifts, and shake his hand.[3] Dances and

[1] See above, p. 191.

[2] Literally, 'putting on leaves'.

[3] In shaking hands with a Sultan it is customary to cover one's hand, as a sign of respect.

cavalry displays are performed in his honour. With these and other gestures he is acclaimed. The particular significance of the *'aleemasaar* ceremony is that it is an acclamation; it represents a mutual promise (*ballan*) of loyalty. When the horsemen display their skill, and bring their galloping beasts to a halt before their clan-head, they greet him with cries of praise. Feasting and dancing follow, lasting as long as local conditions of plenty permit. The poor are fed, women ululate, and men of religion pray for the prosperity of the Sultan and his people. Finally sacrifices are made to secure the blessing of the Prophet and of God on the appointment.

Ideally, the installation is held at the place where traditionally the first Sultan of the hereditary title was acclaimed. Thus the 'Iise crown their heads at Zeila'; the Gadabuursi traditionally celebrate the accession of their *Ugaas* in the Harawe Valley; and the Warsangeli at Ragad, a flat, richly covered plain to the south of Las Koreh. But it is not always possible to hold the ceremony in the traditional site since the luxuriant conditions necessary for the gathering of so large a number of clansmen may be absent and resort may have to be had to some more favoured place. The accession is always associated in Somali minds with conditions of abundance and plenty (*bashbash iyo barwaaqo*); not merely because it is only under such conditions that a great number of people can assemble in one place for some time, but also because the installation should take place in favourable conditions. The ceremony should be held near water, because it is desired that the Sultan should be 'near water' so that his reign may be bountiful.

The pastoral Somali have a few large ceremonies and little ritual. For its interest, therefore, I reproduce here a summary of a very full account of the traditional Gadabuursi installation ceremony given me by Sheikh 'Abdaraḥmaan Sheikh Nuur, the present Government Kadi of Borama.[1] Clansmen gather for the ceremony in a well-wooded and watered place. There is singing and dancing, then stock are slaughtered for feasting and sacrifice. The stars are carefully watched to determine a propitious time, and the future *Ugaas* is chosen by divination. Candidates must be sons or brothers of the former *Ugaas* and the issue of a woman who has only been married once. She should not be a woman who has been divorced or a

[1] Sheikh 'Abdaraḥmaan is the inventor of the Gadabuursi Somali script (see Lewis, *B.S.O.A.S.*, 1958, xxi/1, pp. 134–156) and an authority on Gadabuursi custom and history on which he has written in Arabic.

widow. Early on a Monday morning a man of the Reer Nuur, (the *laanḍeer* of the Gadabuursi) plucks a flower or leaf and throws it upon the *Ugaas*. Everyone else then follows his example. The man who starts the *'aleemasaar* acclamation must be a man rich in livestock, with four wives, and many sons. Men of the Mahad Muuse lineage then bring four vessels of milk. One contains camels' milk, one cows' milk, one sheeps' milk, and the last goats' milk. These are offered to the *Ugaas* who selects one and drinks a little from it. If he drinks the camels' milk, camels will be blessed and prosper, if he drinks, the goats' milk, goats will prosper, and so on. After this, a large four-year-old ram is slaughtered in front of him. His hair is cut by a man of the Gadabuursi[1] and he casts off his old clothes and dons new clothes as *Ugaas*. A man of the Reer Yuunis puts a white turban round his head, and his old clothes are carried off by men of the Jibra'iin, a small, slightly despised lineage.

The *Ugaas* then mounts his best horse and rides to a well called Bugay, near Geris, towards the coast. The well contains deliciously fresh water. Above the well are white pebbles and on these he sits. He is washed by a brother or other close kinsman as he sits on top of the stones. Then he returns to the assembled people and is again acclaimed and crowned with leaves. Dancing and feasting recommence. The *Ugaas* makes a speech in which he blesses his people and asks God to grant peace, abundant milk, and rain—all symbols of peace and prosperity (*nabad iyo 'aano*). If rain falls after this, people will know that his reign will be prosperous. That the ceremony is customarily performed during the *karan* rainy season makes this all the more likely. The *Ugaas* is given a new house with entirely new effects and furnishings and a bride is sought for him. She must be of good family, and the child of a woman who has had only one husband. Her bride-wealth is paid by all the Gadabuursi collectively, as they thus ensure for themselves successors to the title. Rifles or other fire-arms are not included in the bride-wealth. Everything connected with the accession must be peaceful and propitious.

This brief account is of the traditional installation ceremonies among the Gadabuursi. I cannot say to what extent it would be followed today were the Gadabuursi to agree upon a candidate for the office of *Ugaas*. I believe however, that many of the details recorded here would be dispensed with. This would accord with the diminished lustre of the position and agree with the fact that in other clans a Sultan is no longer what the Gadabuursi describe theirs to have been in the past. The symbolism of the ceremonies requires little comment. The installation must be held at a propitious time and the candidate must be born of a woman free from the taint of divorce.

[1] Hair-cutting which is regarded as a menial task, is normally performed by Midgaans.

He should be acclaimed on a Monday (at the beginning of a new week) and the man who first acknowledges him as *Ugaas* must conform to Somali conceptions of prosperity.

All these requirements reflect the view that a Sultan should be endowed with blessing (*baraka*) bestowed upon him by God. On assuming office, the new *Ugaas* has to shed his old personality by having his hair cut and by donning new clothes. The ride to the well near the coast where he is washed and placed on top of a pile of white stones emphasises again the ideal that he should be associated with prosperity; hence rain should fall on his appointment. He is also brought into contact with the three staples of the nomad's resources, the milk of sheep, goats and camels. All this stresses the dependence of the people on their livestock and the delicate balance which exists between famine and plenty. Finally, the importance of peace in a hostile and belligerent society is strongly brought out.

VII

Somali, as has been observed make a formal distinction between secular and religious activities in terms of *wadaad*, man of religion and *waranleh*, warrior. In contrast to the position in many other Muslim societies where sheikhs have temporal as well as religious authority, in northern Somaliland sheikhs are by definition excluded from full participation in political life.[1] *Wadaads* and sheikhs are not leaders in lineage politics. In Somaliland they have in principle religious jurisdiction only. This distinction was clearly expressed on one of my first formal meetings with the elders and *Garaads* of the Ḍulbahante and their sheikhs. The sheikhs stood in a separate group and it was explained to me that they were the spiritual, but not the temporal leaders of the clan. Political leadership I was told and soon came to realize, lay in the hands of the clan elders and *Garaads*.

The distinction between the two spheres of action is to some extent blurred. Some elders who are political leaders are also sufficiently versed in the Quran and other books of Muslim learning to be called, and sometimes to act as *wadaads*. Prominent sheikhs, again, are often profitably engaged in trade and

[1] See e.g. *Encyclopaedia of Islam*, vol. iv, article 'shaikh', p. 275; R. B. Serjeant, *The Saiyids of Ḥaḍramawt*, S.O.A.S. London, 1957; A. Jaussen, *Coutumes des Arabes au pays de Moab*, Paris, 1908; H. A. Macmichael, *A History of the Arabs in the Sudan*, Cambridge, 1922; R. Montagne, *La civilisation du désert*, Paris, 1947, E. E. Evans-Pritchard, *The Sanusi of Cyrenaica*, Oxford, 1949; J. Caro Baroja, *Estudios Saharianos*, Madrid, 1955.

are frequently large stock-owners or in the north-west, farmers. But ideally, because of their position as holymen, sheikhs and *wadaads* take no direct part in fighting and bloodshed. Their prestige as religious leaders depends upon their conforming to the precepts of Islam, to a higher degree than is required of ordinary men. For them, all stolen or looted property are unclean in a religious sense (*ḥaaraam*) and no sheikh or *wadaad* should eat stolen meat.

The position of *wadaad*, which carries the title *Aw* prefixed to a man's name (as for example Aw Jaama 'Ḥassan), is acquired through devotion to religion and training in the Shariah, the Quran, and in the traditions of the Prophet. In practice, a man with only a smattering of Arabic, some knowledge of prayers, and the ability to read portions of the Quran is regarded as a *wadaad*. Many *wadaads*, however, display considerable learning and it is not uncommon to meet a humble *wadaad* in the interior with a library of over a dozen Muslim works with all of which he is familiar. The title 'sheikh' is reserved for men who are usually literate in Arabic, and who have a more thorough knowledge of the Shariah and religious works. Many Somali sheikhs have travelled widely in other Muslim countries where they have studied in centres of Islamic learning renowned throughout the Muslim world. Some, particularly in association with the Dervish Orders to be mentioned presently, have contributed to a flourishing local religious literature.[1] In Somaliland, the traditional centres of Muslim scholarship are Harar, Zeila', and Mogadishu. More recently, in the north some of the centres of the Sufi Orders, such as Qolonqol in the Ogaden, have assumed prominence.

The duties of sheikhs and *wadaads* are closely circumscribed; they attend to the religious life of their lineage-group. Where there is a mosque, even if it is only of mud and wattle or thatch, and a sufficient congregation, they direct the Friday prayers. They lead all religious feasts and activities, and the periodic celebrations in honour of a Sufi saint, or lineage or clan ancestor. Children who wish to learn the Quran, the Shariah, and the works of the saints, even if they do not wish to devote their lives wholely to religion, come under their instruction. Perhaps out of every ten men one has had formal religious instruction at some time—often only for a few months, or irregularly during the course of his life.

[1] For a description of some of these Somali works see, Cerulli, 1923, particularly pp. 22–5; Lewis, 1958 (a) pp. 135–143.

The pupils begin by learning by rote from wooden tablets and soon acquire some familiarity with Arabic and the Quran. Most local centres have at least one Quranic school, often attached to a mosque or tomb of a saint, where boys gather for religious instruction. Many a sheikh or *wadaad* devotes almost all his time to teaching children, and living chiefly upon the fees which he charges. Often a lamb or the equivalent in cash is paid for every section of the Quran[1] which a pupil masters, and when he has finished the course, a young camel is usually asked for by the teacher. Scattered throughout northern Somaliland there are hundreds of these elementary schools where the rudiments of Muslim education are acquired. In addition the local centres of the Dervish Orders provide higher instruction, particularly in the elements of Islamic mysticism (Sufism). Other teachers again, are itinerant, and travel about the country with their Sufi novices living largely on charity, and performing sacrifices and ceremonies for their hosts when asked to do so.

In the interior, a sheikh or *wadaad* living with his kinsmen, performs all those duties fulfilled by Government Kadis in the towns. They solemnize marriage, advise on the interpretation of the Shariah in divorce, and to a limited extent in inheritance, and they assess compensation for injuries. As has been seen, although they are firmly attached to Islam, the Somali pastoralists interpret the Shariah in the light of their segmentary lineage principles and those aspects of the Shariah which conflict with these principles are ignored. Far from weakening the authority of the religious law, the foreign Administrations have, if anything, strengthened it in the jurisdiction which they allow to official Kadis. For the latter, with the weight of Government support behind them, are in a position to apply the Shariah more widely than *wadaads* can in the interior.

As well as acting as unofficial kadis, sheikhs sell amulets[2] and prophylactic potions, bless the sick by prayer and sacrifice, and similarly treat diseases of livestock. Various procedures are followed but all involve the use of passages from the Quran for their sacred properties.

In proportion to a sheikh's charismatic power his person is sacred. It is considered both shameful and dangerous to steal

[1] Somali divide the Quran into thirty sections (*juus*) which do not correspond exactly to the division into *suras*. Girls are normally excluded from this formal religious instruction.

[2] I was constantly plagued by sheikhs and *wadaads* for paper on which verses of the Quran were to be written for sale as amulets and cures.

property belonging to a sheikh and even in lineage and clan hostilities these ideals are to some extent respected. Thus when the Habar Tol Ja'lo and Ḍulbahante clans were making peace, settling their outstanding blood-debts, and returning looted stock, camels raided from the herds of one of the most important and influential sheikhs of the Ḍulbahante, were returned with greater alacrity than livestock belonging to other members of his clan. Instances are also cited, particularly by sheikhs, of the misfortunes which have befallen those who have stolen their property, and sometimes a sheikh is employed to curse the footprints of a thief since this is believed to bring sickness and misfortune until the stolen article is returned.

Sheikhs and *wadaads* are given gifts rather than payments for the services which they fulfill. When any public religious ceremony is being performed, they collect contributions (*siyaaro*)[1] with which to purchase the necessary tea, sugar, incense, and beasts for sacrifice. They are treated hospitably and given gifts when they read the Quran and recite religious poetry in praise of the Prophet and saints at a funeral service, or feast of remembrance (*ḥus*) or sacrifice in honour of a deceased kinsman or lineage ancestor. Thus those sheikhs or *wadaads* who own few livestock can virtually live on charity from their religious works.

It is believed to be meritorious to show kindness to a poor sheikh or *wadaad* (as indeed to any poor person). Such offerings please God and bring an automatic reward, if not in this life, certainly in heaven, and Somali are very generous in this respect. Many sheikhs and *wadaads* enjoy additional respect for the powers of their blessing when they are themselves considered to be saints (*weli*, pl. *awliyo*), or are descended from a famous saint, or even if they are merely the custodians of a saint's shrine.

Sheikhs and *wadaads* perform all these functions and are indispensable in possessing knowledge of the appropriate ritual approach to the Prophet and to God. Men and women reach God in prayer through the mercy of the Prophet and the grace of local saints, but unless they are learned in religion and Arabic they are unable to have direct access to the holy books in which God is revealed. Thus the presence of a sheikh or *wadaad* is necessary for the success of any sacrifice whether its aim is to avert misfortune or sickness, to secure blessing and prosperity, or to influence the elements, as for example in bringing rain.

[1] Cf. Ar. *ziyaara*. These are voluntary offerings (*sadaqo*) not to be confused with the obligatory *seko*, see above, p. 208.

But the most important structural role of *wadaads* is in mediating between hostile lineages. We have already seen how, in lineage councils, their primary duty is to secure the blessing of God and the Prophet. Delegations sent by one group to invite another to negotiate peace, or to collect blood-debts, often include *wadaads* and affines or matrilateral kinsmen. Affines, and matrilaterally related men, are particularly suitable for this purpose because of their dual kinship ties. *Wadaads*, because they are not not warriors (*waranleh*) and owe allegiance to the ideals of Muslim brotherhood as opposed to the sectional values of clanship, are theoretically ideal mediators. Today, as in the case of prominent elders and Sultans, they are encouraged to play this role by the Administrations.

Many sheikhs and *wadaads* take their duties as peace-makers seriously. But they do not themselves settle disputes, or judge between disputants, for this is the work of elders in council, and of informal courts of arbitration. Their task is to incline rival parties to make peace. The terms of settlement are for the groups concerned to decide and the rights and wrongs of an issue judged by a panel of arbitrators. Through appeal to the brotherhood of Muslims enemies can be exhorted and enjoined to stop fighting, but other than binding the disputants by putting them on oath, sheikhs have generally no ritual sanctions at their disposal to enforce a peaceful conclusion. Oaths of peace, moreover, may be overridden by the need to maintain access to pasture and water by force of arms.

VIII

Wadaads mediate between man and man, and between man and God. Ideally they stand for the pan-Somali values of Islam where all Muslims are brothers in religion (*'ikhwaan*) irrespective of their lineage and dia-paying group allegiance. Fighting within the Muslim community is in principle sinful, and in terms of these values, Somali condemn what they practise. The conflict between the ideal of the brotherhood of the faithful is at its most acute in the lives of *wadaads*, who by definition are to some extent torn in both directions. Thus nationalist politicians and religious idealists meet on common ground in opposing the dia-paying group system, which, as the epitome of *ḥeer* and clanship, they regard as the fundamental obstacle to the promotion of national and Muslim solidarity. Yet, although many sheikhs tacitly, and a few openly, condemn the extension of responsibility for wrongs by clanship and contract, their own security is tied to membership of dia-paying groups. A very few sheikhs, violently opposed to the traditional Somali system of group solidarity which they take to be a serious shortcoming in the local practice of Islam, claim to have made vows pledging themselves not to share in the *ḥeer* agreements of their kinsmen. By refusing, even tactitly, to participate in blood-feuds, they have put themselves outside society. But naturally their number in northern Somaliland is very small. Even in the self-contained and relatively autonomous cultivating religious settlements such as that at Sheikh,[1] blood-wealth is paid not according to the strict interpretation of the Shariah where by the Shafi'ite doctrine the culprit alone should bear the burden of compensation in deliberate murder, but by dia-paying group. Most Somali are aware that here their practice parts company with the Shariah, but only a few wholeheartedly condemn it.

Thus, although men of religion stand for the transcendental and common values of Islam, as opposed to the sectional interests of their dia-paying groups, it is extremely difficult for them to dissociate themselves from their lineage and contractural ties. The external component of pan-Somali Islam is in practice diversified through attachment to the various Dervish Orders which the Somali follow. All Somali (with the exception of a few officials and members of the new élite and political parties) belong nominally to an Order, although few are formal initiates. A distinction is in fact made between a sheikh who has authority to administer the rites of admission to an Order (a *sheikh al-tariiqa*) and a sheikh who has the title of sheikh for his learning (*sheikh al-'ilmi*) independently of his position in a *tariiqa*. But most sheikhs and *wadaads* like other clansmen are àttached to a *tariiqa*.

IX

Sufism, the revitalizing force which arose in Islam between the ninth and tenth centuries, reaching in its classical form its aesthetic and theological climax in the twelfth and thirteenth centuries, is well-developed in Somaliland. As is well-known, the adherents of Sufism belong to the congregations or communities (in many Muslim countries *zaawiya*, in Somaliland, *jamaa'a*) of the various Orders

[1] See above, Chapter IV.

(sg. *tariiqa*, 'The Way')[1] into which the movement is divided according to the doctrines and services (in Somali *dikri*; Ar. *dhikr*) ordained by the founders of the Orders. *Tariiqa* means 'path', in the sense of the 'Way of God', to be followed in the quest for grace. The aim of the *tariiqa* is illumination in a mystical sense, and eventually absorption in God (gnosis). It is not necessary here to go further into the theosophic beliefs concerning the various 'stations' or 'states' which mark the progress of the believer in his quest for illumination and identification with God, because these are not widely known in Somali Sufism, and not important in the lives of the majority of the adherents of the various Somali Orders.[2]

I have referred elsewhere to the dual character of the Somali cult of saints. The majority of Somali saints are the ancestors of lineage groups, and most of the remainder the founders or past leaders of the Dervish Orders. For his godliness and virtue the founder of an Order is held to be nearer to God or even to have achieved gnosis and to exemplify in his teaching and life the 'True Path' which it behoves the zealous to follow. The founder is a guide who through his particular qualities of piety and devotion, and by his special virtue including the grace bestowed upon him by God, leads his disciples towards God. And although they emphazise that they all aim at the attainment of the same ends, the leaders of the different *tariiqas* each believe and teach that their particular Order is the 'true' path of devotion. The blessing of the founder of each Order passes to those who follow in his path and dedicate their lives to his example. In practice this end is believed to be achieved through adherence to the specific discipline and ritual practices enjoined by the founder and by the celebration of his mystical works. The crucial position of the founder is indicated in the doctrine of the Aḥmadiya Order which holds that 'Sayyid Aḥmad (the founder) is in the door of the Prophet, and the Prophet is in the door of God.' If men's prayers are to be answered through the mediation of the Prophet, a powerful advocate is needed. It is this intercessory role which the founders of the Orders fulfill.

The principal *tariiqas* in Somaliland are the Qaadiriya and Aḥmadiya. The first is the earliest and best-known *tariiqa* in Islam, founded by Sayyid 'Abdul Qaadir al-Jiilaani who died at Baghdad in 1166 A.D., and who is renowned throughout the Muslim world for his blessing and miraculous works. The introduction of the Order

[1] Ar. *ṭariiqa*.
[2] For further information on Somali Sufism see Cerulli, 1923; Lewis, 1955–56.

(known locally in northern Somaliland after its main proselytizer as Seyla'iya) is generally attributed to Sheikh 'Abdarahmaan Seyla'i who died at Qolonqol in the Ogaden in 1883. There is also a southern branch known as Uwaysiya, after Sheikh Uways Maḥammad al-Baraawi (of the Digil Tunni clan) who introduced it into southern Somalia, and who died at Biyoley in 1909.

The Aḥmadiya which is a modern reformist movement, was founded by Sayyid Aḥmad ibn Idriis al-Faasi (1760–1837) at Mecca in Arabia. Subsequent branches of the Order were brought to Somaliland by followers of Sayyid Aḥmad's successors and there are now two movements in northern Somaliland. The Saaliḥiya, founded by Sayyid Maḥammad Saaliḥ (a pupil of Sayyid Aḥmad's), and brought to the north in the eighteen-nineties by Sheikh Ismaa'iil Sheikh Isaaq (Ḍulbahante, died 1935), has the larger following. To it belonged Sheikh Maḥammad 'Abdille Ḥassan, whose anomalous role as at once a religious and political leader I shall discuss presently. The Order has also a considerable following in southern Somalia. The Dandaraawiya, the other and much smaller branch of the Aḥmadiya in northern Somaliland, was introduced by the founder himself, Sayyid Maḥammad al-Dandaraawi about 1885.

The Qaadiriya, the oldest established Order, is strong in the centre and west of northern Somaliland with Dandaraawiya supporters forming a small enclave, particularly round Hahe and Sheikh, the two cultivating centres of the Dandaraawiya Order. The Saaliḥiya number most of their followers in the east.

Tariiqa affiliation cuts across clan and lineage boundaries. The Gadabuursi, the 'Iise, and most of the Isaaq follow the Qaadiriya, as do most of the Ogaadeen clan (Daarood). Some of the Habar Yuunis as for example the Muuse 'Arre, Muuse Isamaa'iil, and 'Eli Si'iid, however, support the Saaliḥiya. The Habar Awal, Aadan 'Iise, and some of the Maḥammad 'Iise, follow the Dandaraawiya as do a few of the Habar Yuunis particularly the Muuse 'Abdalle. The bulk of northern Saaliḥiya support comes from the Warsangeli, the majority of the Ḍulbahante (both Daarood), and most of the Habar Tol Ja'lo. Although particular lineages tend traditionally to follow a particular *tariiqa* in consequence of its early introduction amongst them, Somali emphasize that *tariiqa* affiliation is a matter of personal choice. A man need not follow the *tariiqa* of his father or kinsmen.

All the Orders have a weakly hierarchical internal organization. The local heads who have been deputed by higher authorities to administer the rites of admission to the Order are known as 'sheikhs of *tariiqa*'. Sometimes the Arabic title *khaliifa* is used, but not commonly and is more characteristically reserved for the leaders at the headquarters from which the Orders originate. The Aḥmadiya generally, including both the Saaliḥiya and Dandaraawiya, look to Mecca, although the Dandaraawiya have their centre in southern Egypt. To these centres outside Somaliland local donations are from time to time sent.

The Qaadiriya, on the other hand is much more firmly rooted locally, widely separated both in time and space from Baghdad where it originated. Its members have much less contact with other adherents outside Somaliland, and successive generations of local sheikhs of *tariiqa* have appointed their local successors to pass on the Order. The local heads of the Saaliḥiya, however, are usually appointed, or at least confirmed in their appointments, by the heads of the Order in Mecca. For the Orders as a whole there are in fact few regional heads and there is considerable rivalry, particularly amongst the Qaadiriya, between different leaders. Indeed the Saaliḥiya taunt their rivals, saying that every Qaadiriya sheikh is a 'sheikh of *tariiqa*'.

In each of the Orders there are a few *wadaads* and local sheikhs who have been fully initiated into the rites by the regional sheikhs of *tariiqa*. There are also a small number of novices (sg. *muriid*) who have joined the *tariiqa* and are under instruction in its mysteries. But the vast mass of adherents are not initiates and simply profess allegiance to the Order followed by the *wadaads* and sheikhs of their lineage. In a few places in northern Somaliland the Orders have established autonomous religious settlements of 'brethren' such as that described in Chapter IV.[1] But settlements of this kind are more common in the more favourable climatic conditions of southern Somaliland.

The *tariiqas* followed in Somaliland are highly orthodox. All are Sunni following the Shafi'ite school of Muslim Law. But it should be noted that although the more learned sheikhs refer to their orders as Sufi, this word is popularly construed as a term of abuse. It is reserved in common speech for the fanatics, often with very little learning, who at religious ceremonies, shout and let off fireworks, dance hysterically, and commit other excesses. Somali often declare that those who behave in such a way have been rendered mad by religious ecstacy.

Doctrinal and ritual differences are greatest between the Qaadiriya and Aḥmadiya (including the Saaliḥiya and Dandaraawiya). Basically, these differences stem from rivalry over the respective powers of intercession of the founders Sayyid 'Abdul Qaadir and Sayyid Aḥmad. Through its founder each *tariiqa* has its separate doctrine and its own ritual. Each has a distinctive liturgy (collected in hagiologies) and different prayer-tasks (sg. *wirdi*). The Aḥmadiya

[1] See above, pp. 95-100.

are generally more puritanical; smoking and the chewing of the stimulant leaves of *qaat* (Catha Edulis) are forbidden; women as well as men are expected to be devout, and to observe the proprieties in dress (as for example in wearing the veil). The Qaadiriya on the other hand not only approve the use of *qaat* but even chew it in their religious ceremonies, and many also smoke. Their public rites are also generally flamboyant, in contrast to the more restrained practices of the Aḥmadiya. The two Orders differ also in habits of dress. The rosary with which the Aḥmadiya recite their devotions has a tassle with ten beads on the end of it, a feature which the Qaadiriya rosary lacks. Again in conformity with their more local character, the Qaadiriya often go bare-headed, with their hair worn long and oiled with ghee in the traditional Somali fashion. The Aḥmadiya favour the wearing of the turban tied in such a way that an end hangs out, as they say, in imitation of the Prophet. Finally the Aḥmadiya hold their weekly Sufistic ceremonies (*dikri*, literally 'remembrance') on Sunday and Wednesday evenings, while the Qaadiriya hold theirs on Tuesdays and Thursdays. These are some of the external features which distinguish the Orders and which derive, as I have said, from deeper conflicts over the spiritual status of their founders.

Despite these distinctions, however, the *tariiqas* are not mutually exclusive, and a person may be an adherent of both the Qaadiriya and Aḥmadiya at the same time. Yet there is often tension between them. This leads sometimes even to actual clashes between members of the Orders, particularly when both are active in the same region. And in some outbreaks of fighting between the Orders sheikhs and *wadaads* have been involved. Thus during the rebellion led by Sheikh Maḥammad 'Abdille Ḥassan, there was great bitterness between his followers of the Saaliḥiya, and the Qaadiriya, who opposed his rule and sided with the colonial governments. Accusations of irreligious behaviour were made by each, each condemned the other in preaching and poetry, and their rivalry culminated in the assassination by a party of Maḥammad 'Abdille's forces of Sheikh Uways, one of the chief Qaadiriya leaders. Conflict between the two *tariiqas* dates in fact from the time when the Aḥmadiya first made its appearance in Somaliland and found the Qaadiriya already established.

At the moment, in northern Somaliland there is a reverse movement with the Qaadiriya attempting to infiltrate from the Ogaden into districts where the Saaliḥiya is generally followed. Competition has become acute in the Haud and there have been several incidents. In Ainabo township in 1955 for example, there was a clash between adherents of the two Orders. The Qaadiriya were holding a religious procession (*shellaad*), chanting hymns (*qasiidas*) in praise of Sayyid 'Abdul Qaadir. Trouble began when their procession halted outside the Saaliḥiya mosque (each Order usually has a separate mosque in towns); and a fight soon developed in which the police intervened to arrest thirteen people who were subsequently charged with breach of the peace. At the trial it became clear that this was only one of several minor incidents between the two Orders caused by the infiltration of the Qaadiriya into the region. Of the ten Qaadiriya accused, six were Ḍulbahante, two Habar Tol Ja'lo, one a *shariif* from the Ogaden and one a *wadaad* of the Sheikhaash lineage of *wadaads*,[1] also from the Ogaden. Of the Saaliḥiya all three accused were Tol Ja'lo. This demonstrates how common *tariiqa* affiliation may temporarily unite people even of opposed clans (here the Habar Tol Ja'lo and Ḍulbahante).

X

Although *tariiqa* affiliation thus unites men of different and often opposed lineage-groups, in opposition to members of other *tariiqas*, such religious solidarity is always ultimately subordinated to lineage ties. Common *tariiqa* allegiance cannot withstand, in a situation of lineage conflict, the demands of rival agnatic interest. As its mystical charter, each *tariiqa* carefully cherishes its blessed 'chain'—the list of successive heads of the Order through whom illumination is traced. This 'chain of blessing' (*silsilad al-baraka*)[2] as has been mentioned is opposed by sheikhs to their clan and lineage genealogies. But it is the latter which ultimately control the actions of *wadaad* and 'warrior' (*waranleh*) alike. Indeed the pervasive character of clanship and contract is forcibly illustrated by the way in which many religious groups are organized in lineages.

There are in Somaliland a considerable number of religious clans and lineages whose members are all nominally *wadaads*. These are in effect local Dervish Orders, following the precepts and teaching of their saintly ancestor through whose blessing they practise as *wadaads*. Their lineage eponym is celebrated as a Sufi saint and their lineage genealogy is at once the 'chain of blessing' and the mainspring of political solidarity. It might be held that by these criteria all Somali lineages and clans are in effect Dervish Orders. But the members of the religious sections in question are all regarded as *wadaads*, while in 'warrior' clans and lineages only those learned in religion are so classed. A further and important point of distinction is that an ancestor of

[1] See below, p. 224.

[2] Also called *silsilad al-tariiqa* or *silsilad al-maqaam*.

a warrior lineage is normally regarded as a saint only in the context of sacrifice, whereas the ancestors of religious lineages are considered more specifically as the founders of a strict path of devotion, and as sources of charisma in a wider sense.

Such priestly lineages are generally called *Reer Aw*[1], or simply *wadaaddo*, (the plural of *wadaad*). Although they are in effect Dervish Orders themselves, their members generally also profess allegiance to one of the main *tariiqas*. They are all nominally 'men of God', possessed of blessing by definition, rather than necessarily learned in the Shariah. But while they usually contain a higher proportion of practising *wadaads* and sheikhs than other 'warrior' lineages and clans, not all their members make religion their profession. From time to time they are of course, involved in lineage friction and here their charismatic qualities afford them a measure of protection against wanton attack. For as in the case of a sheikh or *wadaad* of a 'warrior' lineage, it is dangerous to molest their property.

Religious lineages are of two types; one group consists of those of Somali descent which belong to the various Somali clan-families. The other priestly lineages trace descent outside the field of Somali clanship directly to Arabia. In the first category are the Ḥer and Gaadsan (both of the Dir clan-family) and the Wayteen and Abba Yuunis (both Daarood). These are scattered amongst the Ogaadeen clan. In the same category are the Reer Fiqi Shinni of Hawiye descent living with the Ḍulbahante in the east of the British Protectorate. Typical of the second group are the Sheikhaash (or Sheikhaal) who are very numerous and widely distributed in Somaliland. The largest segment, itself widely dispersed, is the Reer Fiqi 'Umar, of whom the Reer Sheikh Aw Qutub[2] are an important branch in the Ogaden. The Reer Fiqi 'Umar as a whole trace descent from Khaliif Abuu Bakr aṣ-Ṣaddiiq, the first of the orthodox Caliphs elected to succeed the Prophet in 632 A.D. In a similar position are lineages of *wadaads* bearing the title '*shariif*' (pl. *ashraaf*) through their descent from Ḥassan 'Ali Abuu Ṭaalib (son of 'Ali, the Prophet's cousin and son-in-law) and thus claiming kinship with the aristocracy of Islam. These are widely scattered throughout Somaliland; large groups live in southern Somalia, and to a lesser extent in the Ogaden, but in British Somaliland, there are only a few isolated families.

Apart from the charismatic qualities ascribed to them, all

[1] Literally the people who are *aw; aw* being the title prefixed to the name of a *wadaad* or sheikh.

[2] The eponym's shrine at Sheikh in British Somaliland (the village is named after him) is an important place of pilgrimage not only for his own descendants, but also for many other Somali clansmen. The title '*qutub*' bestowed upon him is the mystical 'pole'—an exhalted state of Sufistic illumination.

these groups have the same structure and institutions as other 'warrior' Somali lineage-groups. They are based on clanship and organized into dia-paying groups, and most in northern Somaliland live as nomadic pastoralists. But while they are sometimes directly implicated in clan strife their reputation for 'blessing' makes them ideal mediators.

I have mentioned these religious lineages to show again how pervasive the Somali clan and contractual system is. In northern Somaliland just as few *tariiqas* have succeeded in establishing autonomous religious communities, these groups have assumed the characteristic form of 'warrior' clans and lineages. It is only within the general structure of Somali clanship in terms of the distinction between 'warriors' (*waranleh*) and men of religion (*wadaad*) that to a certain degree they stand in a class apart. And because in their constitution they combine clanship and contract with religious unity they have greater corporate solidarity than a religious Order not so organized.

XI

Religious leadership in 'warrior' clans is given to sheikhs and *wadaads*, but they are usually excluded from authority in clan politics. Yet there are occasional exceptions. I have already mentioned that through their learning some elders on occasion act as *wadaads* although they are primarily political leaders. Conversely sheikhs possessed in large measure of those general qualities which make for leadership in Somaliland sometimes exercise secular power. This is particularly the case in relation to the colonial administrations[1] where Islam and local Muslim practice are opposed by religious leaders to Western influence. Here the issues concerned are less those of particular lineages than, in principle at least, of the people as a whole. Thus on occasion *wadaads* have been able to head rebellious movements protesting against the introduction of administrative measures which had been interpreted as contrary to Islam. Thus, the main opposition to the introduction of secular western education for instance, came from religious leaders who accused the Administrations of seeking to undermine Islam.

But in the recent history of the Somali the outstanding example

[1] This applies to some extent even in Somalia under Somali government and administration, where the Somali government stands for progressive western democracy and many *wadaads* for the traditional practice of Islam.

of a sheikh who was at once a political and religious leader was Sheikh Maḥammad 'Abdille Ḥassan (Ogaadeen, Bah Geri). From 1900 to 1920, when he died of natural causes, the sheikh, led with conspicuous success the rebellion against the British, Italian, and Ethiopian governments, which earned him the nickname of 'The Mad Mullah'. He was a man of great learning, having studied religion in many Muslim centres outside Somaliland, and combined in unusual measure all those qualities of panache and skill in the management of human frailties which Somali most admire. Today he is still a legendary figure known familiarly as 'Ina 'Abdille Ḥassan',[1] and as perhaps the greatest of Somali poets. Much of his verse turned on religious themes and many of his poems have found a permanent place in the Somali poetic heritage.

As a follower of Sayyid Maḥammad Saaliḥ, from whom he had received the *tariiqa* at Mecca, he preached the cause of the Saaliḥiya with messianic zeal. He insisted on strict adherence to the Shariah and condemned smoking and the chewing of *qaat*. He denounced theft, adultery, and those who failed to pray regularly and to follow the Shariah closely. He preached that women should be properly clad and advocated the wearing of the veil. He held that it was unlawful for men even to talk to, or to enter the houses of women other than their own wives.

As his influence grew through his unique personal powers, he became increasingly in demand as a mediator in lineage disputes, and the fame of his piety spread widely. In 1899 he came in contact with Christian missionaries in British Somaliland, and turned violently against the Administration, denouncing all those Somali who acquiesced to Christian proselytization as traitors to Islam.

His insurrection had much of the character of the Mahdiate in the Sudan, but Somali insist that he never himself claimed the title 'Mahdi' which historians have given him.[2] Instead, he assumed the title of 'Sayyid', referring to the Somali genealogies which record descent from Quraysh. He began his campaign as a fervid preacher of the Saaliḥiya, thereby earning the hatred of

[1] *Ina* means 'son of' cf. Ar.*ibn*. By a characteristic inversion, famous men in Somaliland are often referred to in this way as the sons of insignificant and little known fathers.

[2] For a brief biography see *Encyclopaedia of Islam*, vol. iii, p. 667–68, and the less objective accounts of D. Jardine, *The Mad Mullah of Somaliland*, London, 1923, and F. S. Caroselli, *Ferro e Fuoco in Somalia*, Rome, 1931.

the established Qaadiriya, but it is generally accepted that he ended his career as a tyrannical opponent of all who refused to accept his rule.

Some of his earliest and closest adherents, deserted him in the later stages of his career when he was accused of violating the Shariah. A letter bearing the signature of Sayyid Maḥammad Saaliḥ, and condemning his activities, was received by Maḥammad 'Abdille in 1909,[1] but there is some doubt as to its authenticity. With his personal charisma and religious fame, he applied all the traditional devices of Somali politics to build up the strong following with which he successfully weathered the long series of major campaigns against him. He employed cavalry with great dexterity in guerilla attacks on the more cumbersome armies of his adversaries. British forces sustained heavy losses on many occasions; much money was spent to little purpose and much gallantry displayed and many awards for bravery made. Only in 1920 when aeroplanes bombed his fort at Taleh, was the rebellion decisively crushed.

His followers were known as *Daraawiish*, which is the name used by Saaliḥiya for their adherents, and wore white robes and turbans. They were organized loosely into striking forces with a minimum of administration and kept under strict discipline by the Sayyid himself and his immediate lieutenants. No rigid hierarchy was established, although the Sayyid selected men he could trust as leaders under him; the loyalty of his followers depended always directly on his own extraordinary qualities as a leader. Within his company he enforced the strict practice of the Shariah and defaulters were savagely punished. In cases of assault within his community he is said himself to have paid compensation to the offended party. Looted property was distributed in part amongst his followers and in part accrued to a central fund which he himself controlled. Thus amongst his followers, who came from many different clans, lineages, and dia-paying groups, he strove to replace clan and contractual allegiance by devotion to himself. Externally he made full use of kinship ties to summon support and applied his influence as a mediator to further his cause. Where he was not sufficiently strong to demand allegiance and failed to succeed by persuasion, he forged affinal links by marrying women of the groups concerned. In his lifetime he contracted over twelve marriages.

The Sheikh's *jihaad* shows how although pastoral Somali society is constitutionally opposed to the bestowal of power in

[1] For a translation of this letter see Jardine, 1923, pp. 184–85.

such degree on one person, particularly on a sheikh, there is always the possibility that under suitable conditions a man of religion of outstanding personality can marshal widespread public support and assume political leadership.

XII

Having discussed the powers and fields of action of elders, Akils, Sultans, and *wadaads*, I turn now to an examination of the constitution and function of the informal courts (sg. *guddi*) mentioned in the previous chapter.

Where a dispute occurs between individuals of the same dia-paying group, or in the case of the western cultivators even between members of adjacent settlements sharing a common water-hole, it is generally taken before an open council of the elders concerned. This *shir* acts as a court (*guddi*) deciding guilt and awarding judgement; but appeal may lie from it to a neutral panel of arbitrators composed of un-related elders of proven skill in mediation and judgement. Whether the elders of a group themselves decide the issue or whether they allow mediation by arbitrators, the decision taken, if they accept it, is enforced by them. Examples of cases decided in this way will be given presently. Within his dia-paying group (and amongst the cultivators to a lesser extent within his local community) a man is bound by clanship and contract 'like rope' to accept the rulings of his elders, and direct punitive sanctions are available to ensure that justice is effected.

Where, however, parties of different dia-paying groups have recourse to a panel of arbitrators the court has no direct sanctions with which it can enforce its rulings. This will become clear from the description of *guddi* procedure which follows. Indeed whether or not litigants of rival dia-paying groups accept the decision of the arbitrators whom they summon to judge between them, depends very much on the structural context. If their kinsmen wish to reach a peaceful settlement, either through fear of war or pressure from the Administration, and if they consider that the judges' decision is a reasonable one, they will see that it is executed. If necessary, pressure will be put upon the parties directly concerned to force them to accept the award. But the panel of arbitrators, in itself, has no punitive sanctions with which it can coerce litigants into accepting its judgements.

Members are appointed to such an *ad hoc* court on account of their knowledge of customary procedure (*ḥeer*, in general), and their reputation as wise judges (*ḥeerbeegti*).[1] Famous arbitrators are widely in demand and tour the country hearing cases amongst different lineages. It will be recalled that this was one of the important functions attributed to Sultans in the past but which is less in evidence today. There is no formal position of magistrate as such; elders well-known for the wisdom of their awards are simply called as need arises to sit on a court. Proceedings are usually initiated by the plaintiff (*muddi'i*) often under pressure from his close kinsmen, and with the consent of the defendant (*mudda'alay*). The very fact that a joint approach is made is indicative of a desire to settle a dispute. Moreover, elders chosen to arbitrate must be acceptable to both parties. Various objections are customarily allowed as tending to bias the conduct of a case. Thus, except when the parties are both close kinsmen and the affair is being settled within a dia-paying group, kinship ties to either party are regarded as prejudicial to a fair judgement.[2]

Arbitrating panels vary in size. Often four or five elders are considered sufficient. But where dia-paying group elders hear a case themselves concerning members of their own group many men may take part as judges. Between dia-paying groups, the court's size tends often to vary with the gravity of the case and the structural distance of the parties to the dispute. The more important the issue, and the greater the structural distance between the plaintiff and defendant, the larger is likely to be the court which hears the case.

Once a group of elders has been appointed to act as a court of arbitration a 'recorder' (*doodqaad*) is appointed to repeat loudly each important point made by the speakers during the hearing. Where the court has a large audience, the proceedings are thus broadcast to all those in attendance. The case for the plaintiff is presented in the form of pleadings. The plaintiff may speak directly himself, or he may appoint a representative whom he considers more skilled in oratory to speak on his behalf.[3] The court usually sits under a shady tree or in any other suitable spot.

[1] Lit. 'those who are expert in *ḥeer*'.

[2] A judgement given where there is a relationship between the arbitrators and the litigants is known as *garsokeeye*.

[3] This is known as *igmo*, delegation, deputation.

The plaintiff, or his representative, appears before the judges and after identifying himself states his case. When the plaintiff has finished his statement, he withdraws to consult with a kinsman[1] who has come to support him. He then returns to the court and is asked if he has completed his case (*ma daabad baa*) or if he has anything further to add. He begins his concluding address with the phrase: 'In the name of God, the Compassionate, the Merciful' and gives a rapid summary of his case. He then signifies that he has reached a conclusion (*daabad*) and the defendant is called. If the latter still disputes the plaintiff's allegations he replies to them denying and refuting them where he can. When he has finished his statement he consults his advisers and then returns to summarize his refutation of the plaintiff's case. Both parties are then dismissed and the arbitrators deliberate in private.

In the hearing of statements made by the plaintiff and defendant described above neither party is cross-questioned and the panel of arbitrators bases its understanding of the essential point or points at issue directly upon the submissions made to it. The court recorder may be asked by the arbitrators if they have omitted any important point raised by either party. When they are satisfied that they understand the crux of the dispute and can proceed to determine which party is in the right the court recorder is sent to the plaintiff and defendant to collect the panel's fee for adjudication.

The arbitrating elders then proceed to test the statements of the litigants by asking them to produce witnesses.[2] These are not cross-questioned but merely asked to say 'what they know' and the success or failure of the plaintiff's case depends in the first instance upon the support of his witnesses. Three witnesses are normally required and if all add their testimony to the plaintiff's, judgement is given in his favour. If, however, only two witnesses corroborate his charges against the defendant, he is himself required to swear a 'triple oath' (*Wallaahi iyo Billaahi iyo Tallaahi*) to the rightness of his case.[3] This is taken as conclusive proof of his

[1] This is called *hojis*.

[2] The defendant can object to the plaintiff's witnesses as he can to the choice of arbitrators on the grounds of kinship connexion or other ties likely to prejudice them in the plaintiff's favour.

[3] Where a witness supports the statement of his party he is said to have 'opened' on his behalf, and where a witness fails to support him he is said to have 'broken'. The oath taken by a litigant when one of his witnesses fails him is known as 'splint' (*lugqabta*) and refers to the fact that this procedure is regarded as a subsidiary support.

allegations. Should, however, only one witness support the plaintiff then those of the defendant are summoned and the same procedure repeated on his side. The corroboration of three witnesses decides the case in favour of the defendant and if only two support him he in turn is required to swear a triple oath which is taken as proof of his innocence. Where a charge of homicide is involved or of other grievous injury the Shafi'ite *qasaama* procedure may be applied where the triple oath is replaced by a stronger testimony of fifty oaths. Sometimes, since it is often regarded as even more binding, the divorce oath has to be taken. By this if a party is subsequently found to have given false testimony his marriage or marriages are automatically nullified.

It is to be noted that in this procedure the onus is first put upon the plaintiff to prove his case but passed to the defendant to refute if the plaintiff's witnesses fail him. Thus the failure of the plaintiff to establish his case is not considered sufficient proof of the defendant's innocence. Having decided what the crux of the case is, judgement is awarded for or against the plaintiff solely on the statements under oath of the witnesses of the parties—or if the witnesses fail on the swearing of the principals. No other juridical techniques are employed to test the veracity of statements or to obtain evidence.

The panel of assessors has, as I have said, no coercive powers which it can apply to enforce its findings for it is only an arbitrating body. Thus when the court fee (*hagarbay*) has been collected from the litigants, and before their witnesses are called, the panel addresses a homily to the plaintiff and defendant explaining its competence and emphasizing the wisdom and experience of its members. Appeal is made to the good sense of the disputants as reasonable men familiar with Somali principles of equity and fair-play. They are reminded also that by summoning the *guddi* they have given evidence of readiness to accept its decision and they are requested to submit in good faith to its judgement and to entertain no feelings of ill-will towards the assessors who administer judgement impartially.

Either party may contest judgement and give notice of intention to appeal (*gawdis*). Different clans have different standards of reasonableness in the number of appeals allowed before a dispute is regarded as insoluble by arbitration. Given a reasonable decision, reasonable that is to public opinion, structural pressures determine whether an award will be accepted or disputed.

Failure to settle produces a state of tension between lineages and leads ultimately to fighting and to administrative intervention.

XIII

A Somali adage states that 'to dispute the judgement of a court is to dispute with God' (*gardiid waa Allaah diid*) and again, it is said that 'the man who breaks customary rulings is the enemy of all', but these are statements which only hold in the context of strong solidarity. In practice, it is only when the parties are willing to settle their differences, or are constrained to do so by their kinsmen, that the awards of arbitrators are effective. Disputes between close-kinsmen of the same dia-paying group are usually quickly settled. Fighting between individual members of a dia-paying group when several other members are present, leads to prompt and concerted action. The disputants are separated; if necessary they are seized by young men on the instructions of the elders, and brought for trial before a dia-paying group council. When compensation has been determined according to the group's contract or a fine imposed it must be paid, or at least promised, or punitive action will be taken by the group as a whole. A recalcitrant member of a dia-paying group is bound to a tree and several of his best sheep or a coveted camel slaughtered before him until he agrees to the judgement of his elders. The slaughtered stock are eaten by the elders. This procedure is called by the Gadabuursi[1] *buḍ iyo laan*, 'with cudgel and stave.'

Coercion is often necessary to secure compliance with the decisions taken by the elders of a dia-paying group or larger lineage. But it is only exercised where there is a strong sense of political solidarity. I have already pointed out in the previous chapter how dissentions over the settlement of compensation often lead to the fission of dia-paying groups where the groups concerned lack stability. A Ḍulbahante clansman was assaulted by another man of his lineage. The case was taken before a panel of ten elders of his primary lineage-group and damages valued at thirty-three-and-a-third camels were awarded against the culprit. When the latter refused to pay the compensation, he was forced by his close agnates to meet half the amount while the remainder was settled by his dia-paying kinsmen. Thus, although dia-paying group contracts lay down the damages for various categories of injury and insult it is often only when

[1] The phrase *buḍ iyo siddeetan* 'cudgel and eighty (youths)' is also used by the Gadabuursi.

pressure is brought to bear upon the culprit by his elders that the terms of a treaty are honoured.

The sanction of killing animals from a man's herds and flocks until he agrees to follow the decisions of his elders is usually called *yakays*.[1] It is, as I have said, applied in all cases where a man refuses to accept the rulings of his kinsmen and elders whether judgement has been awarded by them directly or whether they have decided to honour the award of an impartial court of arbitration. But most characteristically amongst the pastoralists, this sanction is applied in the context of fighting. When a man is summoned to join a raiding party and refuses without adequate excuse, he is liable to *yakays*. Similarly, if a woman allows a man to sleep with her when he has been posted on sentry duty she may be punished. Where a woman is at fault, a particularly fine mat may be seized from her hut and burnt. Deserters from battle are similarly treated, and if, during an action, a group of men go off to raid on their own account without the permission of their leader they are liable to be punished unless they share what booty they capture with the main party.

XIV

To complete the discussion which was begun in Chapter IV of the effects of the adoption of agriculture, of the change from a wholely pastoral to a part cultivating economy, it is now necessary to consider how the structural range within which legal sanctions are effective is modified by these new economic conditions. Apart from its part in our analysis, this has a wider relevance in relation to the general study of changes in social and political structure attendant upon the transition from a pastoral to an agrarian economy. Here it is important to re-emphasize that in northern Somaliland this transition, which is only partial, is recent and only of some fifty years' standing.

The cultivating communities of north-western Somaliland have a wider field of common interests than the nomadic pastoralists. For, although they have not replaced dia-paying group solidarity, ties through permanent settlement to locality give rise to corpor-

[1] The verb is '*yaki*'; he will be punished' is *waa la yakaynayaa*. The Arabic expressions *khasiraad* (a fine) and *karbaash* (corporal punishment) are also used in this context. According to Mr. Imaam Maḥammad, the verb *hagarbi* is used similarly, in the east of the Protectorate. *Yaki* is apparently of Galla origin. Another expression is *ganaaḥ* (from the Arabic *janaaḥ*).

ate interests outside dia-paying group affiliation. Consequently, while amongst the nomads sanctioned behaviour is a feature of dia-paying group solidarity only, amongst the cultivators it extends to some extent outside dia-paying groups. Common interests based on local contiguity to some degree cut across dia-group allegiance and create a wider field of behaviour sanctioned by local public opinion rather than merely by lineage vengeance. The local interests of the members of adjacent settlements, who are not necessarily all of the same dia-paying group, centre in the maintenance of the communal water-points necessary to the husbandry of cattle. When the ponds are dug out or strengthened from time to time, or in the dry season fenced in to prevent their use by unauthorized strangers, collective labour is employed. Here the cooperation of all the able-bodied men of those settlements which use them is required. A day is appointed for the work (often a Friday) and the men of the local settlements are summoned. People who fail to assist without reasonable cause are fined. At Odejiid in 1957 the customary fine for a day's absence from work without adequate excuse was five rupees (7 Shs. 50 cents). If a defaulter fails to pay the penalty imposed, the local elders send strong young men to seize some of his sheep or goats. These are kept until the fine is paid. If the fine remains unpaid, a sheep or goat is slaughtered and eaten by all those who have been working on the pond. Similarly men who fail to contribute to the common pool of food which the labourers share at mid-day are liable to punishment.

In such collective work the rôle of sheikhs and *wadaads* is not to participate with their own hands, but as usual, to bless the proceedings. Other than their elders, the workers have no formal leaders and the *wadaads* standby exhorting the men to greater efforts with blessings such as 'Health and Strength' (*'aafimaad hela*).

Disputes over the boundaries of fields and over access to the water-points, particularly in the dry seasons when water is scarce are common. These are normally settled by local elders and very rarely give rise to feuds between lineages except where the structural distance in agnation between the parties is very great. For all the people of the settlements sharing a common pond are concerned to maintain local peace. Breaches of the peace are judged and punished by the local elders even when the persons responsible do not belong to the same dia-paying group. The following example shows how a typical dispute (in this case over access to a local water-hole) is settled.

The dispute occurred while I was at Odejiid, in the winter months of 1956 after the local pond had been fenced in to prevent strangers molesting the little water available.[1] Two young men from different settlements were on guard at the entrance to the fence round the pond. A herd of cattle belonging to a brother of one of the sentries, whose settlement was several miles distant, arrived for watering. Permission had already been given by the elders for the stock to have access to the water. But the second man who was on watch refused to allow the cattle to enter the gate. This led to a quarrel between the two guards and the second struck the first across the face and knocked him down. Men from the adjacent settlements at once rushed to the pond and drove the two men apart. The sentry who had been assaulted flew into a rage and withdrew to his hut where he seized a cudgel and a knife. Armed with these weapons he returned to the pond to take his revenge. He was stopped at the gate, however, by the elders who were still arguing with his assailant. Close-kinsmen led him off and tried to calm him. No further incidents occurred that day, and the following morning about forty elders gathered in council outside the settlement in which the man who had been assaulted lived. Proceedings were opened by the local sheikh who asked God's blessing and prayed that peace might be restored between the disputants. The elders then discussed the case. It was decided that the youth who had struck the first blow and who had refused to allow the cattle to water should pay a fine (*yakays*) of fifteen shillings to the local elders. The other who had seized weapons and sought to aggravate the dispute after the elders had intervened was fined seven shillings and fifty cents (five rupees). The disputants who attended the proceedings, were enjoined to forget their quarrel and to make it up. They were warned that if they did not to so they would be further punished. After these decisions had been taken and the two culprits had agreed to abide by their elders' decision they were blessed by the sheikh, and the elders dispersed.

In this case both parties belonged to the same dia-paying group, but the dispute was quickly settled by the local elders not only because it represented an attack on lineage solidarity but more important in this instance because it threatened the peace of all the members of the settlements using a common water-point.

The settlement of the following case is of interest because, while

[1] The pond in question is that shared by settlements III to VII in the map on page 111, above.

demonstrating the same principles of local solidarity, it concerns the relations between a man and his co-wives. A quarrel broke out between a well-known elder at Odejiid and his son by his first wife. The elder had a sore back and asked his first wife if she had any ghee for him to drink as medicine. She said she had not. Her husband then asked if she would kill a sheep for him from her flock. She tartly refused and advised him to go and buy one. The husband lost his temper and asked the woman's son—who was looking after the uterine estate—to give him some ghee. The youth said that he would see what could be done. The mother then came to her husband and declared that none of her ghee would be given to him and that he would have to buy a sheep. She upbraided him for neglecting her in favour of his new wife. 'You don't want us, you don't want our stock,' she shouted angrily. She then launched into a long tirade against her husband complaining of his neglect and unfair treatment. The elder seized a stick and began to beat her. Her son, who was about twenty years old, lost his temper in turn but wisely ran away. Close-kinsmen of the husband took hold of him and tried to prevent him striking his wife. Eventually the couple were separated and the man returned to work in his field.

In the evening when he came back to his new wife's hut his anger flared up again. He took a long knife and went to the pen of his first wife. There he killed a large four-year old sheep. He also threatened to kill others but his kinsmen came and prevented him from doing any further damage. His arms were bound with rope as he struggled violently and he was led back to the hut of his young wife. After sitting quietly there for two hours he promised to cause no further trouble and was released.

The following morning was spent by the local elders of the settlements at Odejiid in considering what all felt to be a most serious breach of the peace. Several men, who happened to be visiting for various reasons not connected with the case, joined in the discussion. Pending a formal hearing, the culprit was warned by the elders not to interfere further with the flock allocated to his senior wife and to treat his wives equally. He spent most of the day sitting in the house of his junior wife where I visited him. He complained of the pain in his back which he acknowledged wryly his actions of the night before had not helped to cure. He was indeed extremely sorry for himself and chastened by the action of the elders. The wife with whom he had quarrelled was sitting in her hut with her sister and mother who were comforting her, and all three were engaged in cutting up the meat of the slaughtered sheep preparatory to cooking it. The son had gone out to the pond where he was sulking and refused to meet his father.

In the evening, the elders assembled a *guddi* and summoned the culprit and his son. About twenty men were present including the local sheikh and several *wadaads*. One of the oldest men in the region. of the locally dominant Jibriil Abokor segment, opened the meeting with a prayer and made a speech on the evils of enmity between father and son and the necessity to treat co-wives equally as demanded by the Shariah. He was a witty speaker and quoted several proverbs which produced a friendly atmosphere in the gathering. The next to speak was the local sheikh. Other elders followed and after the matter had been considered at some length the two disputants were summoned. The father was advised to separate the houses of his two wives which at the time of the dispute were in the same settlement. It was hoped that this would ease the tension between the women. He was also told to treat his wives fairly and warned that if he failed to do so he might be fined. He promised to pay heed to these instructions. His son in turn was cautioned to respect and obey him and both were urged to shake hands and to forget their quarrel.

The proceedings throughout were fairly informal, no formal statement of a case against the elder or his son was made nor did either dispute that they had acted wrongly. All assumed that the events had taken place as I have recorded them and no witnesses were called. The elders in fact did little more than admonish the elder and his son and most of those present condemned their actions. It was clear that the primary concern of all was to reconcile the two men and the two wives. The cultivators attach considerable importance to marriage as a stable relationship and go to great lengths to heal a breach between husband and wife. I have already shown that this view of the binding character of marriage is reflected in the lower incidence of divorce amongst the cultivators in comparison with the situation among the nomadic pastoralists.[1]

The cultivators, as has been observed, are less belligerent than the pastoralists. They value peace highly and consider it essential that every effort should be made to settle a dispute locally without resort either to the Government or to arms. In disputes over the definition of land for cultivation between the cultivators and their pastoral neighbours, or between the two main cultivating groups—the Jibriil Abokor and Gadabuursi—recourse is sometimes had to fighting, but much less frequently than in the nomadic society. Such indeed is the sense of local solidarity, independently of dia-paying group affiliation, and the feeling that disputes should be settled by local elders without the assistance of the Government, that a person who takes a case to the Administration without first consulting his elders is liable to punishment

[1] See above, p. 138.

(*yakays*). An interesting example occurred among the Gadabuursi. In the collection of blood-wealth among the agricultural Gadabuursi it is customary to allow a group which has sustained injury and which is receiving compensation to abuse the property of the killers. In the case in question this rule was violated. When representatives of the aggrieved dia-paying group came to collect their compensation and destroyed some sorghum in a field belonging to a kinsman of the murderer, the farmer reported their action to the police. Several men were arrested and the kinsmen of the deceased protested strongly to the killer's group. Their representations were accepted and the farmer who had informed the police was punished.

XV

Settlement creates a wider field of collective interest than exists amongst the pastoral nomads. Members of fixed local communities practising mixed farming have to cooperate in a wider range of activities than is required of the pastoralists. In his daily work in the fields and in his use of a common water hole for his stock a farmer needs the regular assistance of his neighbours, who are not necessarily always members of his dia-paying group. Failure to participate in corporate local activities and actions prejudicial to the general peace are thus subject to penal sanctions. Because there is a wider range of collective solidarity, there is correspondingly a more comprehensive range of delicts. To some extent the rule of law and relative order characteristic of internal dia-paying group solidarity is extended to embrace all the members of a local community who share a common water-hole and who help each other in the work of cultivation. Elders thus have in these circumstances a more extensive field of jurisdiction and greater coercive powers.

Decisions taken by the local elders may be disputed, but in his resistance to them the cultivator is subject to more compelling sanctions than is the pastoral nomad. If the latter quarrels with the kinsmen of his dia-paying group, he can leave them to drive his flocks and herds elsewhere and join another dia-paying group. Admittedly in the case of individuals rather than small groups this extreme course of action is seldom resorted to. But if a farmer is expelled from his local group he cannot take his land with him, and his rights in it may lapse. Thus the prospect of expulsion from a farming community is an economic sanction of compelling force in an area where arable land is scarce and costly.

Although in the agricultural settlements of north-western Somaliland elders thus have greater authority than in the temporary encampments of nomadic hamlets, no new political offices have developed. The formal political structure of both the cultivators and pastoralists is similar save in respect of the wider jurisdiction of elders in the farming areas. In contrast to the situation in southern Somalia where amongst the sedentary Digil and Rahanwiin, agriculture and ethnic and clan admixture have led to the formation of a more hierarchically structured political system, the northern cultivators have preserved the political institutions of their pastoral kinsmen modifying them only in respect of the limited solidarity which springs from vicinage.[1]

The spread of order and the greater emphasis given to the control of disputes through the judicial functions of elders without recourse to feud, has encouraged the Protectorate Administration to set up a Rural District Council for the Sa'ad Muuse farming areas centred on Gebile, Arapsiyo, and Tug Wajale, with headquarters at Gebile. A similar Rural Local Government Council for the Gadabuursi was opened at Borama in 1957. Among the pastoralists, such local councils have been established only in major townships and their jurisdiction is limited to them. The Gebile and Borama Rural Councils, have the power to collect trade-licence fees, zariba dues,[2] slaughter fees, and responsibility for sanitation, public markets, and elementary Islamic education. They have moreover, some jurisdiction in the control of cultivation and grazing areas. I mention the establishment of these councils because they reflect the more stable constitution of the cultivating communities. This is evinced in the wider range of cooperation, in the growing, if still minimal, sentiments of attachment to locality as such, in the more comprehensive judicial powers of elders, and also apparently in the greater stability of conjugal relations. My figures at least indicate that the Jibriil Abokor cultivators have a lower divorce rate than the pastoralists which is in keeping with the importance which they attach to stable marriage.

As was pointed out in Chapter IV, the situation in the few sedentary agricultural religious communities is similar. Here local contiguity based on ties to land is supplemented by a closer

[1] On the hierarchical political system of the Digil and Rahanwiin, see Colucci, 1924 passim; Lewis, 1955, pp. 92–5, 119–121; Lewis, 1957, 37–41.

[2] This is a form of octroi for livestock and grain brought to market in specified townships.

adherence in practice to the ideals of Muslim brotherhood than is achieved in the nomadic environment. The *tariiqa* communities have a more formalized political structure. Except in matters relating to serious physical injury or homicide, which are still governed by dia-paying group affiliation, the elders of a *tariiqa* community control the conduct of its members. To some extent, more certainly than amongst the pastoral nomads, the sheikh of a settlement has political authority.

These considerations indicate how settlement and cultivation modify the characteristic legal and political institutions of the pastoralists. Amongst the agriculturalists it becomes possible to speak of criminal law where the jural and political unit extends beyond the dia-paying group. In the nomadic environment co-operation, bound rigidly by contract and clanship, relates mainly to hostility under ecological conditions which foster fierce competition for sparse resources. It is characteristic of the pastoralists that they should regard punishment (*yakays*)[1] as primarily a military sanction applied in the context of lineage strife. For them, social cohesion is generally thought of and is in fact usually manifest in relation to the threat of war and feud. For apart from unity in war, there are few occasions when camel-husbandry requires extensive co-operation. There is co-operation amongst kinsmen of the same dia-paying group in the watering of camels from deep wells in the dry season and economic assistance for kinsmen who have become impoverished, but it is diffuse. The members of pastoral dia-paying groups are not in daily contact, and lack that tight web of day-to-day social relations centring in the use of a common water-hole characteristic of Somali land husbandry. Amongst the nomads, men honour their contractual bonds with their kinsmen when they unite to fight to defend rights of access to grazing and water, or to obtain the restitution of stolen property, or to exact compensation for other injuries which they have sustained. This characteristic of northern Somali society is modified in the agricultural environment by the influence of local contiguity.

XVI

These tendencies towards change amongst those who have re-

[1] It is of interest to note that both amongst the cultivators and the pastoral nomads, livestock seized as a punishment are regarded as unclean and forbidden (*ḥaaraam*) in a religious sense and are not eaten by sheikhs or *wadaads*. With stock taken by raiding parties they are regarded as stolen property.

cently adopted cultivation in the north-west do not, however, alter the fact that what is generally characteristic of the northern Somali political system is its striking lack of formal political offices. Even the office of clan-head is generally little more than a nominal title corresponding to the degree of social and territorial exclusiveness which the clan more than other orders of grouping possesses. At the other extreme, at the level of the dia-paying group, the basic jural and political unit of association, the Local Authorities and Akils appointed by the Administrations exercise representative powers only. Within these units and at every level of association policy is determined by the majority decisions of all the adult men of the group concerned meeting in *ad hoc* councils. This lack of stable and formally defined political offices thus seems consistent with the extreme fluidity of political groupings.

Religious authority which though sometimes organized hierarchically through official positions in the Sufi Religious Orders is hardly more precisely defined. Ideally it is sharply distinguished from political authority in terms of the general division which Somali draw between 'warriors' and 'men of God' (*wadaads*). Although the distinction is sometimes blurred in practice, ideally men of religion do not exercise political authority in a secular sense; their primary function is to mediate between warriors and between warriors and God. In situations, however, where Somali view an external threat as an attack on their autonomy as Muslims religious leaders of great charisma can assume positions of politico-religious power. Such political authority tends, by its very nature, to be transient and to last only as long as the external threat persists with a certain intensity. More characteristically, religious charisma bestows spiritual power which does not lead to the assumption of political authority. Indeed Somali see the spiritual or mystical power which men of God possess as a natural complement to their lack of political authority and ideal divorcement from secular loyalties and fighting. In the next chapter which examines the general implications of the rule of force in some detail it will be seen that this division between the different kinds of power which warriors and *wadaads* possess is one aspect of a general distinction which Somali make between the secular power of the politically strong and the spiritual power of the weak.

8

Force and Feud

THE northern Somali are essentially a warlike people who readily engage in battle or raiding to redress wrongs and injuries, to release pent-up enmities, to acquire or maintain honour, and to gain access to natural resources or to conserve their rights over them. The aim of aggression is not so much to subjugate enemies completely as to establish political ascendency. Somali wars are thus not properly wars of conquest, except in the limited sense of often giving the victors temporary grazing or watering rights in a particular region. While livestock are seized as booty and many raids made solely to loot camels, captives are rarely taken in battle since Somali have little use for them and do not seek to humiliate their adversaries in this fashion.[1]

In a society such as this, where fighting potential very largely determines political status, feud and war[2] are instruments of power politics; they are the chief means by which the relations between groups are regulated. For ultimately, even under modern administration, the rights of groups are effectively protected only by force. In the form of collective vengeance, self-help is cannalized by lineage affiliation and given structural definition through the complementary principles of clanship and contract. With some exception only among the cultivators, outside and over and above dia-paying groups no impartial power except the Administration exists to control relations between lineages. In these circumstances, the ease with which individuals and groups resort to violence within the Muslim community and contrary to the principles of Islam has to be viewed in the ecological context of acute competition for sparse resources, and in the abrogation of individual responsibility through group loyalties.

[1] Women however are sometimes abducted.

[2] Since all Somali recognize the payment of compensation for injuries all disputes at every level of segmentation can be composed. It is not therefore useful to make a rigorous sociological distinction between war and feud; and I use these terms here in much the same sense speaking rather of war, however, when hostilities are general and involve large groups.

It seems also likely that in the past lineages were in a position to fight each other to a stand-still whereas the presence of the Administrations now prevents this yet at the same time hinders the full release of tension by limiting the opportunities for its dissipation.

Where the orbits of movement of lineages overlap, interpenetration being greater normally with lineages of the same clan than between clans, there is competition for access to common resources. Particularly in the dry seasons, when water and pasture are both scarce, ecological pressures are marked and rivalry between groups within the same sphere of movement intense. Disputes often arise directly over the use of water and to a lesser extent over grazing, as in the incident at Galgal mentioned in a previous chapter.[1] But even when hostility does not spring immediately from rivalry over common resources, ecological pressures influence the pattern of relations between groups. Dependence upon common pasturage and water creates underlying currents of hostility, and when pressure is acute, these are readily touched off even by quite trivial incidents. Thus amongst the Dulbahante the wooden watering trough has become a proverbial symbol of fighting in the dry seasons, although disputes have many other immediate causes.

The more lineages are competitive within the same pastures, the greater the likelihood of tension between them and the smaller the chances of speedy and peaceful settlement. Thus quarrels between individuals which result in loss of life or property or both, are often quickly followed by retaliation where there is little thought of negotiation. Within a clan bitter feuds develop and persist, often for many years and sometimes generations, erupting spasmodically as later incidents occur, and being temporarily forgotten only in the context of wider hostilities.

This, for example, is the situation between the 'Ali Geri and Barkad primary lineages of the Ḍulbahante, who for years have been at feud and were only reconciled when to protect their common grazing and watering rights all the Ḍulbahante joined forces against the Habar Tol Ja'lo. Thus it is inherent in the segmentary lineage system that dissensions and friction between lineages should be forgotten when their common interests are threatened by external hostility. In these circumstances dia-paying groups unite as primary lineage-groups and primary lineage-

[1] See above, p. 46.

groups join together as clans. Here the clan is normally the upper limit of political solidarity, and cleavages between clans are necessarily greater than those between their constituent segments. This is also in keeping with the territorial exclusiveness of the clan, limited though this is. And it seems probable that prior to the establishment of colonial administration, the clan had greater distinctiveness as a fighting unit within which it was often essential to compose differences and stifle enmity.

Thus dia-paying groups of different clans are more ready to seek retaliation than closely linked lineages, even when the latter are in keen competition for the same natural resources. At the same time, whether or not the aggressors are themselves prepared to pay compensation depends on the structural distance between the adversaries, on their relative strengths, and on the force of administrative intervention. The nature of the wrong also influences the course of events. A minor issue such as stock-theft is less likely to create serious tension than a graver injury such as homicide, or the abduction of a woman. But between dia-paying groups and lineages of every order of segmentation the ultimate sanctions which underlie negotiation are today still those of force and feud.

Inevitably Government intervention eventually halts fighting between groups and causes compensation to be paid, but this is little deterrent to continued bloodshed. For although the standard rate of blood-wealth represents a considerable amount of capital[1] the spread of responsibility by contract means that those directly implicated often bear little liability. Indeed, the larger groups are and the wider the range of contractual obligations recognized, the less those who shed blood are generally required to pay. Equally, the murderer's contribution to the compensation offered by his lineage tends to decrease as the structural distance between the groups increases. This means that the obligation to pay blood-wealth for a killing is not necessarily a very strong sanction, especially where the groups concerned are large and structurally remote. Moreover, when a lineage has lost one of its members the prospect of receiving a hundred camels hardly outweighs the gain to name and honour which is brought by retaliation. Particularly where groups are large, the profit from accepting compensation is slight compared with the satisfaction obtained by revenge.

[1] Over three hundred pounds.

II

Unsettled disputes leave bitterness which may be increased by ecological competition and to some extent moderated by structural proximity. Somali, as has already been seen, go to enormous lengths in tracing corporate responsibility. A lineage is answerable for all the external actions of its members, and even after his death the kinsmen of the person responsible for a wrong are still held liable for its settlement. Typical of this is the following case. A state of hostility tending towards feud developed in a certain lineage when a man died having been injured twenty-eight years previously. He had in his youth been struck on the head by another boy of his own lineage, but his recovery had never been officially certified by a panel of elders. Complaining of pains in his head and trading on his old injury, he had shortly before his death visited his assailant's kin and been treated hospitably by them. Immediately upon his death, secure in the knowledge that a complete cure had never been acknowledged, the kinsmen of the deceased demanded compensation from the kin of his boyhood assailant, although the latter had died sixteen years previously.

But even when compensation has been offered and accepted for a serious injury or homicide, rancour and enmity tend to persist. This is true even when the parties are closely related. At Odejiid, two sons of brothers were working in a field together. One took up a cudgel to kill a rodent but the other accidentally caught his arm deflecting the blow upon himself and received an injury from which he subsequently died. Both men belonged to the same *jiffo*-paying group and compensation valued at thirty-six camels was gathered by the group and given to the children of the deceased. Those elders who made this settlement took none of the compensation. Thus the matter appeared to be successfully composed and forgotten. But three years later, when I was at Odejiid, this accidental death was being represented as deliberate murder by the deceased's brother, and tension was mounting between the immediate kin of the two cousins. It will be remembered that whether an injury is deliberate or accidental influences its settlement to a greater extent between people of the same dia-paying or *jiffo*-paying group than it does between dia-paying groups. But as this case illustrates although dia-paying solidarity inclines disputants to make peace and often even forces them to do so, it does not necessarily lead to the complete dispersal of hostility and resentment.

Where between dia-paying groups blood has been spilt enmity is all the more likely to persist after full compensation has been paid. Here latent hostility is readily aroused by further acts of aggression and frequently stimulated by ecological competition. When conflict thus develops from the reopening of an old, and rankling wound, past wrongs and hatreds spring quickly to mind and readily find fresh scope for expression. In fanning the flames of anger extempore poems (particularly *geeraar* and *gabay*)[1] composed in indignation at a wrong suffered play an important rôle. Many incidents testify to the power of evocative verse in stimulating and spreading the desire for revenge. But poetry is also effective, though to a lesser degree, in dissipating enmity and in prompting peaceful conciliation.

Thus the payment of compensation while in principle parrying the threat of immediate retaliation does not necessarily bring lasting peace. All dia-paying groups are essentially fighting units so constituted as to provide for the security of their individual members if need be by resort to arms; and only vengeance fully satisfies honour. Here the following account is typical. A man of one dia-paying group killed another of a different dia-paying group but of the same primary lineage. Compensation was agreed to and was gradually paid. But just before it had been completely paid-up the brother of the deceased took vengeance. The first murderer who was known to his enemies could not be found and vengeance was taken on a kinsman who happened to be the son of a famous poet. This precipitate action caused great indignation and was considered an outrage by the members of other segments of the primary lineage concerned and by many others of the clan. The Administration acted promptly, seizing camels from the killers, and allowed the wronged group to choose 200 of these. To this large amount of compensation the close kinsmen of the culprit contributed thirty-three-and-a-third camels as *jiffo*.

From what has been said it will be gathered that in the relations between lineages which regularly meet in their grazing movements there is a perpetual cycle of aggression and concilia-

[1] On Somali folk-literature and poetry, see J. W. C. Kirk, *A Grammar of the Somali Language*, Cambridge, 1905, pp. 170 ff; M. Maino, *La Lingua Somala*, Alessandria, 1954, pp. 44 ff.; M. Laurence, *A Tree for Poverty*, Nairobi, 1954, p. 5 ff; and B. W. Andrzejewski, *Ḥikmad Soomaali*, Oxford, 1956. An excellent example of a *geeraar* composed to inspire vengeance is translated in Kirk, op. cit., p. 172.

tion. Settlements reached with the transfer of compensation are rarely if ever final solutions and in the prevailing struggle for survival there is a vicious circle of dispute, negotiation, conciliation or feud, and further dissension. What a recent writer has called the 'omnipresence of struggle'[1] is marked in northern Somaliland and always near the surface of social relations.

III

To give the reader some conception of the regular swing between war and settlement in this highly competitive and egalitarian society and to indicate the role played by the administrative authorities, I recount briefly some of the main events in the struggle between the Ḍulbahante and Habar Tol Ja'lo clans in the Protectorate over the period from 1951 to 1957.

Relations between the clans have long alternated between hostility and uneasy truce but about 1951 had become particularly strained. Both clans were then pressing heavily on the same grazing resources in the same general area of movement. Conflict was especially strong in the Ain region between Burao, Las Anod, and Erigavo Districts, claimed by the Ḍulbahante. It is difficult to establish the validity of this claim since, while the area may many years ago have been used only by the Ḍulbahante, the Habar Tol Ja'lo have for long grazed their stock in it. Thus as has been pointed out the name *Reer 'Aymeed* which formerly denoted those Ḍulbahante lineages which customarily moved in the Ain region has tended to be replaced by *Reer Oodeed* in conformity with a general movement, stimulated by Habar Tol Ja'lo pressure, of the Ḍulbahante into the southern scrublands of the northern Haud. In any event by 1951, some segments of the Maḥammad and Muuse Abokor lineages of the Habar Tol Ja'lo were penetrating as far south as Do'omo and Merganweyn in the Haud.

In these circumstances Ḍulbahante elders asked the Habar Tol Ja'lo to withdraw northwards but they refused claiming that they required access to the contested pastures if their herds and flocks were to survive.

Both 1951 and 1952 were troubled years in which there were many bitter battles between the clans, and after administrative intervention uneasy periods of truce in which compensation was exchanged. It was during this period that the Galgal fight referred to previously occurred. Outstanding was the massed attack at Goldero on the 9th October, 1952, when a force of some 400 Ḍulbahante clansmen,

[1] S. Andrzejewski, *Military Organization and Society*, London, 1954.

many of whom were armed with rifles, attacked Habar Tol Ja'lo clansmen and killed thirteen. The Ḍulbahante lost ten men.[1]

At the beginning of 1952 an 'Unsettled Areas' Ordinance was gazetted[2] to control movement and discourage encitement to further strife and the Ain region was declared an unsettled area. A peace committee was formed which included amongst other dignitaries the Chief Kadi of the Protectorate (of the Habar Awal clan), rifles were confiscated by the Government and a collective fine of 35,000 shillings (£1,750) imposed on the *Reer Oodeed.*[3] In the two-year period over eighty people had lost their lives in Las Anod district alone. But in spite of administrative pressure the feud continued into 1954 unresolved.

Both the Habar Tol Ja'lo Maḥammad Abokor and Muuse Abokor and the Ḍulbahante were required to execute a bond to the value of 35,000 shillings each, pledging themselves not to engage in further strife. During 1954 relations between the clans remained fairly quiet, but trouble flared up again in 1955 when the Ḍulbahante found themselves fighting on two fronts. In the Ain region, groups of the Habar Tol Ja'lo Maḥammad and Muuse Abokor were pressing on the *Reer Oodeed.* Further to the east, the Habar Tol Ja'lo, Maḥammad Abokor, Aḥmad Faaraḥ, and the Muuse Abokor, Reer Baho, and Reer 'Iidle from Erigavo District, were driving down the axis Yagore-Las Adar-Wudwud in search of grazing and threatening the Ḍulbahante *Reer Nugaaleed.* Little attempt was made by the Habar Tol Ja'lo to seek permission from the Ḍulbahante for access to pastures which the latter traditionally regarded as within their range of movement. In the early part of the year a series of minor engagements occurred on both fronts. And as the water-holes dried

[1] The northern Somali have little formal military organization and armies of this size are uncommon. A military expedition or raiding party is called *'ol* which also means a state of war between groups. There are a considerable number of words for 'war', 'feud', and 'battle' etc. common amongst which are *dagaal, dirir,* and *ḥaraabe.* Somali do not make any rigorous distinction between 'war' between large groups structurally distant, and 'feud' between small closely related lineages. A large force such as that at Goldero is called *guuto,* or *gaas.* A raiding party of cavalry is known as *guluf.* The leader of a company (*amaanduule,* or *abbaanduule*; from *duul* to fly or attack) is appointed for his military accomplishments on an *ad hoc* basis. His is not a permanent position and at different times different men are chosen by the same group to fulfil the role. The leader is entitled to a larger share in any captured booty than that allotted to ordinary members of the party. Those armed with rifles are also allowed a correspondingly larger share in the distribution of loot than those armed only with spears. The martial sanctions invoked to ensure some measure of cohesion and loyalty in a raiding force—for Somali expeditions are not very highly organized—have been discussed in a previous chapter (p. 233).

[2] The Special Districts Ordinance No. 5 of 1953, empowers the Governor to apply emergency provisions in a specified region to maintain effective law and order.

[3] This is now being used to build a school for the *Reer Oodeed.*

up, and the dry season advanced, tension between the clans became acute. As a result the eastern Habar Tol Ja'lo swung eastwards massing round the wells between Las Anod and Las Adar in the hills. Here they began obstructing Ḍulbahante watering parties and the eastern Ḍulbahante moved generally southwards and east of the Las Anod-Wudwud road.[1]

In the Ain region the Maḥammad Abokor and Ḍulbahante *Reer Oodeed* were similarly competing for the use of the same wells and friction between them was increasing. On the 27th of October the District Commissioner Las Anod, completed the hearing of an enquiry into previous unrest in the region. He recommended to the Governor that the Habar Tol Ja'lo 'Umar, Maḥammad Abokor, Reer Yuunis, Reer 'Iidle, Boho, 'Ali Faaraḥ, and 'Ali Barre, and the Ḍulbahante Jaama' Siyaad Reer Warsamme, Reer Khayr, Reer 'Aafi, and the Barkad and Hawiye Fiqi Shinne should be required to execute a bond to keep the peace.[2]

But on November 6th a man of the Reer Aadan Hagar was shot at Shahada (Bohotle) by nine men of the Maḥammad Abokor. After the killing, all the Habar Tol Ja'lo in the vicinity rushed to the local Rural Constabulary post to seek sanctuary. A Ḍulbahante riot which broke out in the village was quelled by the Constabulary, but a man of the Habar Tol Ja'lo Aḥmad Faaraḥ was later found strangled. The elders of both sides later met to discuss these murders. The *Reer Oodeed* asked the Habar Tol Ja'lo to leave their country but the latter refused. Ḍulbahante elders again requested the Habar Tol Ja'lo to withdraw from their pastures and were again refused. In the end the meeting broke up in disorder. Battle was joined at Ina Dan Dan near Muse Godeyr on the 8th of November and both sides lost four men. Police detachments arrived to find a truck unloading reinforcements but they managed to restore order.

On the following day, two more deaths were reported at Balleh Qudah, to the south of Wudwud. One of those killed was a man of the Habar Yuunis Sa'ad Yuunis who were fighting with the Habar Ja'lo against the Ḍulbahante, and the other a man of the Maḥammad Abokor. On November the 10th, a party of Habar Ja'lo Reer Yuusuf armed with rifles, was seen in the Muse Godeyr region by a patrol of Illalos and one man was shot while making off with a rifle. On the same day, a patrol of the Somaliland Scouts (the local military force) who were also policing the area, intercepted a large band of armed men and dispersed them.

There were no incidents on the following day, but on the 12th

[1] The spatial distribution of these various places is shown in the maps pp. 48-54.

[2] The genealogical positions of the Ḍulbahante lineages concerned in this account are shown in the genealogy at the end of the book. For the structural relationships of the Habar Tol Ja'lo segments see the genealogy in Hunt, 1951, pp. 138-9.

some 200 Ḍulbahante riflemen were encountered by a combined Rural Constabulary (Illalo) and police patrol and were dispersed after several arrests had been made. The following night, Jaama' Siyaad and Barkad forces raided Maḥammad Abokor Reer Yuunis and 'Ali Barre hamlets killing two men of the Reer Yuunis and looting their camels. But at dawn the next morning, Reer Yuunis and 'Ali Barre parties pursuing the retreating Ḍulbahante raiders attacked them to the south-west of Wudwud, and killed three men of the Barkad and one of the Turyar (a small despised lineage living with the Ḍulbahante, but not of Ḍulbahante origin). Both groups were then routed by a concerted attack from Government forces.

The next day, a man of the Maḥammad Abokor was killed, two girls wounded, and twenty camels seized from the Habar Ja'lo Sambuur and 'Umar. Administrative forces found that tracks led to Barkad and Jaama' Siyaad encampments. On the 16th, there were no further incidents. And two days later, the Ḍulbahante Hayaag, Khaalid, 'Ali Geri, Wa'ays Aadan, Faaraḥ Hagar, Aadan Hagar, and Yaḥye and the Habar Ja'lo Maḥammad Abokor, Ḥassan 'Abdille, Abokor 'Abdille, Barre 'Abdille, Yuusuf, Aadan Madoobe, Reer Yuusuf, Reer Dood, and Reer Aftiḍeere were all required to sign a bond to refrain from further violence.

This was the position in the Ain region with Government forces, Illalos and police actively patrolling the area to prevent further incidents. In the meantime in the Las Anod region, the Ḍulbahante *Reer Nugaaleed* lineages were struggling with the eastern Habar Tol Ja'lo. On November 15th Ḍulbahante clansmen looted camels of the Maḥammad Abokor in the vicinity of Hargeger. They were pursued, and in the ensuing engagement two men of the Ḍulbahante were killed and two of the Habar Ja'lo. In reprisal, the Maḥammad Abokor attacked two parties of the Naalleeye Aḥmad, Reer Jibriil while on the move, and killed two men and looted all their stock. A force of police and Rural Constabulary was sent out to investigate. On the following day (November 16th) a major battle broke out at Deria Guban in the same region. Government forces arrived to find the fighting over and five men of the Ḍulbahante and four of the Maḥammad Abokor dead. The whole area was now being patrolled by Government forces, and on the 20th of the same month the District Commissioner Las Anod reported that the situation was serious. Reinforcements were sent to restore and maintain order.

Both sides were now under strong pressure to make peace. In December elders of the *Reer Oodeed* and Maḥammad Abokor met at Muse Godeyr and agreed that:

(1) All wells in the area of dispute belonged to the Ḍulbahante with the exception of those at Horafudi and Galgal.

(2) Elders of both sides collect and return to their owners all looted stock and arrange for the payment of compensation for those killed in the battle at Ina Dan Dan.
(3) The Maḥammad Abokor should not bring Habar Ja'lo traders to the area of the wells.
(4) Grazing should be shared equally between both sides.
(5) All trouble-makers of both clans be given up to the Government to prevent their fomenting further strife.
(6) All stock stolen after this agreement should be repaid twice over.

Despite this treaty, sporadic outbreaks of fighting continued. On the 4th January, Ḍulbahante hamlets some ten miles to the north-west of Las Anod were attacked at night and after several shots had been exchanged the raiders were driven off taking with them five burden camels. Later police arrested eleven men of the Habar Ja'lo and recovered four of the camels. About the same time, a party of Habar Tol Ja'lo attacked Ḍulbahante watering at Las Adar and speared to death two youths of the 'Ali Geri and Naalleeye Aḥmad. They were driven off by a Government patrol with which they exchanged shots losing two of their number.

Later in the same month with the situation still tense, both Las Anod and Erigavo Districts were declared 'unsettled areas'. Movement within the regions was strictly controlled and entry forbidden to persons who were not normally resident in them. To prevent the marshalling of forces, the circulation of motor vehicles was prohibited except with the permission of the District Commissioner. Any Local Authority joining a meeting to send out clan forces or in any way inciting clan violence was rendered liable to a fine of 7,500 shillings or up to three years' imprisonment.

These measures severely curtailed the possibilities of further strife and paved the way for a general cessation of hostilities. Throughout the remaining months of the year and indeed until the spring of 1957, peace negotiations continued with the outstanding killings between the clans being settled by payment of compensation. The peace councils were attended by representatives of the Government, by sheikhs and Kadis assessing damages, and on occasion by prominent religious leaders. At a *shir* held at Hudin in January, 1957, the Government Kadi of Ainabo assessed thirty compensations for wounds during a few days. At an earlier period in the negotiations, it had been resolved that where claims for homicide on either side cancelled out, *jiffos* should be paid internally by the lineage of the deceased to his next of kin within a few months. It was also decided that in future killings between the clans compensation should be paid at the rate of 150 camels for a man and seventy-eight for a woman. Both sides were now tired of the struggle and each was anxious to reach a definitive settlement. By March, 1957, peace seemed to have been generally established and most of the claims for compensation agreed to had been honoured. By this time the Ḍulbahante had turned to fight with the Majeerteen of northern Somalia.

IV

I have outlined the history of the Ḍulbahante-Habar Tol Ja'lo war to give some idea of the course taken when the enmities between clans are aggravated by common ecological pressures. While the Habar Tol Ja'lo of Erigavo District were thus occupied with the Ḍulbahante, other lineages based on Burao were fighting with the Habar Yuunis of that District. But Habar Yuunis lineages of Erigavo such as the Sa'ad Yuunis were fighting alongside the Habar Tol Ja'lo against the Ḍulbahante. Here they were united as Isaaq against the Ḍulbahante as Daarood. Such, however, was the depth of enmity between the Habar Yuunis and Habar Tol Ja'lo in Burao District that despite their membership of different clan-families the Habar Yuunis there displayed a spirit of comradeship with the Ḍulbahante.

It is always extremely difficult to discover even the immediate causes of a Somali feud; especially when, after the event, many rival accounts are given. Debts in blood lying between groups may sometimes be allowed to remain outstanding without any immediate reprisal being made, and they may even seem to the observer to have been forgotten. Such circumstances, however, are particularly conducive to the production of prolonged and bitter hostilities when an incident occurs months, and sometimes even years, later.

Thus it was apparently a gross disequilibrium in killings between the Habar Tol Ja'lo and Habar Yuunis[1] from fights some fourteen years previously which provided a setting conducive to the development of strife between the clans in 1955. The first incident occurred early in the year when parties of both clans were grazing in strength and close proximity in the region of Domberelly in the Ethiopian Haud. A quarrel over camel-herding led to the wounding of a youth of the Habar Yuunis, Reer 'Abdi Ḥirsi, by a man of the Habar Ja'lo, Reer Daahir. Immediate retaliation followed resulting in the death of a man of the Habar Ja'lo Reer Daahir. As soon as the victim was known to have died, the Habar Yuunis, 'Abdi Ḥirsi, who were responsible proferred compensation and this was accepted. But

[1] The segmentation of the Habar Yuunis clan is shown in Hunt, 1951, pp. 135-7.

when the blood-wealth came to be handed over there were difficulties and a close kinsman of the murdered man killed another man of the Habar Yuunis, this time of the Reer Wayd. This victim was apparently mistaken for a member of the Reer 'Abdi Ḥirsi. The murder took place in the village of Domberelly itself and led at once to extensive fighting between those of the two clans who were encamped in the region. Within forty-eight hours thirteen Habar Yuunis and twenty-six Habar Ja'lo had lost their lives. This result left the Habar Tol Ja'lo spoiling for revenge.

Fighting continued in various areas, becoming serious towards the end of 1955, and was not settled until the middle of the following year. In December of 1955 collective fines of 150,000 shillings (£7,500) were imposed on the segments of the Habar Yuunis and Habar Ja'lo concerned. Peace talks began the same month at Burao but further incidents occurred. The riot which broke out in the town of Burao in February, 1956, and which began as a dispute over the watering of a camel has already been mentioned in a previous chapter.

By June, following the murder of a man of the Habar Ja'lo Reer Daahir, six elders of the Habar Yuunis, Muuse Ismaa'iil, had been deported to Zeila' for six months. On the 11th of June after months of discussion, thirty-three elders of each side signed a peace-treaty stipulating that for the next three years blood-wealth payable between them should be doubled and livestock looted repaid at twice its value by the family of the thief. It was agreed, moreover, that every effort should be made to bring criminals to justice and to facilitate the collection of evidence. Where a conviction for homicide was obtained by the Crown the compensation payable was to vary with the severity of the sentence imposed. If a sentence of death was passed, the murderer's kinsmen should only pay a *jiffo* of thirty-three camels to the family of the victim. But if a prison sentence of ten years was obtained, 100 camels should in addition be paid as blood-wit.

Over the period of hostilities from early in 1955 to the middle of 1956 over four hundred convictions for offences connected with the strife between the clans were obtained by the Crown.

V

Where there are contributory factors such as competition for the same resources, what begins as a dispute between individuals of different clans and spreads in the dia-paying groups immediately concerned, eventually culminates in generalized clan enmity. The growth of concern on each side does not necessarily proceed at the same rate. The Habar Yuunis were united against the Habar Ja'lo before the latter had committed themselves to supporting the segment of their clan immediately involved in friction with the Habar Yuunis. In addition accidental acts of aggression help to further the extension of hostilities along the lines of clanship. For where two segments of different clans are fighting people of a segment as yet not involved may be killed in error. This happens often and furthers the spread of solidarity on both sides. As hostility increases in range involving an ever widening circle of kinsmen until the whole clan is implicated, the members of each of the opposed groups increasingly view each other as undifferentiated wholes. If for example, a man of one segment of one clan is killed by a segment of another, once enmity is general it is largely irrelevant whether retaliation is directed at the segment immediately responsible or simply at any other lineage which happens to present a convenient target.

Enmity spreads beyond the centres of conflict colouring the relations between all members of the opposed clans wherever they are. Even amongst employees and officials in Government service social relations show marked signs of strain. The sense of clanship is so strong that men naturally identify their interests with those of their kinsmen who are actively engaged in war even when they are themselves concerned to maintain the peace. For those with nationalistic aspirations and for sheikhs by definition neutral, the struggle to remain aloof is fraught with difficulties. Mixed contingents of Government forces quelling a fight between their clansmen tend to resolve the conflict between their loyalty to their kinsmen and to the Government by directing their attacks at those clansmen who are of the opposed lineage. It is indeed a remarkable testimony to their discipline that in situations of hostility as acute as that between the Habar Ja'lo and Ḍulbahante described they do not fight amongst themselves.

A striking instance of the extension of enmity occurred during the struggle between the Habar Ja'lo and Ḍulbahante in 1956. This was an attempted homicide between Habar Ja'lo and Ḍulbahante immigrants in England amongst the Somali community in Cardiff. A twenty-four-year-old Ḍulbahante seaman shot a man of the Habar Tol Ja'lo in the back in Bute Street on the 8th of February. The victim, who recovered, is a well-known figure in the Somali community in Britian and one of the founding members of the Somali Brethren Society, an organization opposed to clanship and concerned with the welfare of Somali immigrants in England. At his trial, the accused alleged that he was being victimized and was stated to have delusions that an organization had been formed to intimidate him. A Medical Officer gave evidence to the effect that he suffered from paranoiac schizophrenia. In passing sentence of five years imprisonment the judge advised the accused that he would receive medical treatment. In spite, however, of the medical evidence the case was regarded in Somaliland as simply another manifestation of Ḍulbahante and Habar Tol Ja'lo hostility. What was significant, was that a man of the Ḍulbahante had tried to kill a man of the Habar Tol Ja'lo.

VI

The supremacy of force (*ḥoog*) and the power conferred by strength have been constant themes in this book. It has been seen that the acquisition and tenure of rights in general depend ultimately upon the ability to defend them, if necessary by fighting against possible aggression. Rights to pasture and water, and to a lesser degree to arable land for cultivation, have been seen to depend upon the force with which those enjoying them can meet the threat of dispossession by a hostile power. It was by war as much by negotiation that the Habar Tol Ja'lo staked their claim to pasture and water their livestock in territory which traditionally the Ḍulbahante regarded as theirs. And in the widest sense the pastoralist's general security rests upon the fighting strength of his dia-paying group and of the lineages and clan to which he belongs. It is this necessity to be able both to retaliate and to pay compensation for injury which sets limits to the minimum size of dia-paying groups.

It is necessary for small groups to seek political security by attachment to stronger lineages. It has been shown how groups which are too small to discharge their blood debts independently, and too weak to afford to neglect them, have either to flee before the threat of reprisal or to seek alliance with stronger groups. For these reasons, small dispersed groups such as the Akisho and Dir are often driven to acquire the protected status of *magan*. Generally within the lineage system, according to the context of hostility, uterine ties are recognized or postulated to remove the natural inequalities in man-power which historical development produces. Weak groups may even be driven to join *gaashaanbuur* coalitions outside the strict bounds of clanship, and in a few cases, to seek full genealogical absorption. The criterion of effective political viability is always in the end fighting potential. Although Somali under modern administration quote the adage 'the weak have found the European as their protector' (*ninki faralahaa frenji baa loo helay*) it is the proverb 'either be a mountain or attach yourself to one' (*buur ahaw ama buur kutiirsanaw*) which reflects the reality of political relations.

I have indicated that fighting strength tends to decide whether or not compensation will be paid for an injury and also the alacrity with which it is handed over. To some extent it also influences the valuation of the amount of damages. Just as to some degree the amount of compensation paid for homicide varies with the personal status of the person killed, so to some extent, even under modern administration, it varies with the political status of the parties concerned. These various factors are illustrated in the following murder case between dia-paying groups of different primary lineages. Two men of the different groups quarreled over precedence in watering at a well. A man of the first (A) was killed by his opponent and camels were seized by the Government from the second and stronger group (B). 100 were given to the bereaved lineage. A few days later, the brother of the deceased not satisfied with the settlement and spurred on by the desire for revenge, shot a man of lineage B. Lineage B elders promptly went in strength to the elders of A and demanded retribution, which the latter agreed to, proferring 200 camels, a rifle, and a girl who was a close relation of the man of A whom lineage B had previously killed. She was actually a sister of the dead man's father. 100 camels with the rifle and the girl were taken by the brother of the lineage B elder killed, and the remaining 100 were shared amongst other members of the group. Lineage B whose numerical strength is several times that of the A, were entitled to claim higher damages than the statutory amount since the killing was in revenge for a death which they had already settled. But the generosity of A and the speed with which they paid damages were generally attributed to their fear of reprisal from a stronger lineage.

VII

The threat of physical force is the dominant sanction in the relations between groups and individuals. Between dia-paying groups this assumes the form of feud and war, and within the dia-paying group is applied through the coercive powers of elders. But there are certain situations in which issues arise that cannot be composed by an appeal to force, and where retaliation by force of arms is inappropriate or even impossible.[1] It is here that tension tends to be channelled through mystical procedures.

Where a father kills his son, or a son his father, vengeance is impossible and compensation cannot be paid, for as Somali put it 'Who would pay and who receive damages?' It has been pointed out that homicide within the Muslim community is in principle sinful and that in war and feud Somali practise what in Islam they condemn. It is particularly between close agnates that the taint of a religious wrong attaches to murder and parricide is viewed with abhorrence although no specific ritual measures are applied to cleanse the culprit. Yet to a man who kills his father a permanent stigma attaches. Parricide, Somali regard indeed as an indication of illegitimacy. I have heard of very few cases. One instance which I did encounter shows how the culprit is regarded and how malevolent powers tend to be imputed to him. A man quarrelled with his father over bridewealth which his father refused to give him, advising him to go and work if he wished to have enough wealth to marry with. The son shot his father. No compensation could be paid since the killer as son of the deceased would have been one of the principal recipients of compensation. Kinsmen concluded that the murderer was a bastard and he was dubbed 'Parricide' (*aabbe diley*). Wherever he went he met with an unfriendly reception and his evil reputation clung to him. Since his act was contrary to all accepted standards of behaviour between father and son he came to be suspected of possessing evil powers, and even perhaps of being a witch. These suspicions received support when the woman he had married after killing his father died within ten days. The consensus of opinion was that she had been cursed. Some twenty years after the murder the stigma 'Parricide' still dogged the man who was virtually a social outcast.

Sometimes the perpetrators of such acts which strike at the very basis of Somali life (*tol*) are surrendered to the Government. Thus on one occasion elders of the Habar Tol Ja'lo, Reer Daahir, brought to the local District Commissioner a man whom they accused of killing his own brother and whom they described as a danger to the community.

There are other circumstances in which what are in effect mystical modes of aggression come into play, and since in comparison with other African societies a striking feature of Somali society is the unimportance of witchcraft and sorcery these call for some consideration. Indeed the relatively small part played

[1] In writing this section I am particularly grateful to a short but stimulating discussion with Professor Max Marwick. See his papers, 'The Social Context of Cewa Witch Beliefs', *Africa*, xxii, 2, pp. 120–35; 3, pp. 215–33.

by sorcery (Somali *fal*,[1] Arabic *siḥir*) is all the more marked in that beneficial magic in its positive aspects has considerable importance.

Magic is utilized to preserve health, to treat sickness and restore virility, and to avert and remedy misfortune and bad luck. Most magical processes depend for their efficacy upon direct or indirect association with Muslim religious practice. Amulets and charms apply the blessing (*baraka*) of the Quran and the miraculous powers of saints—and to a lesser extent of sheikhs—through their more immediate relationship with the Prophet and with God, the ultimate source of all power. Such techniques are, as it were, secondary procedures intimately connected with the primary religious acts of prayer and sacrifice. There is also a considerable body of astrological lore and divination (*faal*; contrast *fal*, above) centring partly in the Somali lunar calendar and partly in Arabic astrology, medicine, and magic.[2] Arabic astrological treatises such as the *kitaab al-Raḥma*, by Jelaal al-Diin 'Abd al-Raḥmaan al-Suyuutii (Cairo, 1938) are very popular in Somaliland and regularly used by many *wadaads* in their treatment of illness. The rosary (*tusbaḥ*) of the Dervish Orders is also popularly used in divination.

Compared with these applications to secure beneficial effects whose attainment is upheld by public opinion, the use of magic as a means of harming a person, or in retaliation for a wrong suffered, is very rare. It might well be held that where, when there is hostility between people, the resort to force is the standard procedure there is little room for magical retribution. This interpretation seems consistent with the contexts in which resort is had to malevolent magic or sorcery, since they are, as I have said, situations in which fighting cannot take place, or where what might be called the mystical power of the defenceless is the only counter to the threat of superior force.

Although the subject cannot be gone into fully here, it is necessary first to say something of Somali ideas of causation. The ultimate focus of causation is God (*Allaah*), conceived of as a largely impersonal power before whom man is impotent and helpless. Sickness and ill-health, good and ill-fortune, all exist with His consent and are ultimately in His control to withold or bestow.

[1] The verb *fal* means to do, to have in mind, perhaps also to scheme, and to put a spell on someone.

[2] For *faal* beliefs in Morocco, see E. Westermarck, *Ritual and Belief in Morocco*, London, 1926, vol. ii, Chapter XII.

Although magico-religious procedures are applied in the treatment of disease in man and beast, illness is very rarely ascribed to magical causes. Nor is it necessarily a direct and specific reflection of the wrath of God. Awards and punishments do not automatically fall due in this life but may be received after death. Man is in any case held to be by nature sinful so that God's disfavour is regarded rather as a constant condition than as an immediate punishment for some transgression. It is indeed because man is known to be far removed from the ideals of religion in his normal behaviour that saints are valued as intercessors. I was often told specifically that because saints have exhibited in their lives special virtue they can the more effectively approach God through the Prophet to seek favours where others less favoured would be likely to fail.

Misfortune does not thus automatically result in feelings of guilt over the commission of a moral or religious wrong. But because God is all-powerful, petitions are made to him to remove the cause of complaint, and resort is had to magical procedures whose efficacy depends upon their foundation in Islam. Only rarely is a particular disaster or misfortune taken as a specific indication of God's displeasure and then usually not by those most concerned. Thus a man of the Habar Awal western cultivators, who passed for being a *wadaad*, once told me that the barren conditions and lack of rain which the nomadic clans of the east suffer was a divine punishment for their continual strife. But the latter tend to view their constant fighting rather as a consequence of the arid conditions in which they struggle to live.

Neither divine retribution nor sorcery provides a regular idiom of immediate causation, and witchcraft exists only in few special contexts. Because they are by definition, though not always in practice, excluded from overt fighting, *wadaads* are sometimes credited with employing magic to uphold their Muslim ideals and also to protect their persons and property. Many tales tell how outstanding sheikhs apply mystical sanctions to punish men who transgress against the Shariah. This use of magic is of course approved as is its employment to protect the property of a *wadaad* against wanton attack. Similarly it is considered perfectly legitimate that a sheikh should be called upon to curse the footprints of an unknown thief who cannot be reached other than by these recondite means. Sheikhs are also credited with taking advantage of their charisma to further their own ends and to defeat rivals, but this is generally regarded as contrary to the principles of Islam.

Thus, one interpretation of the long-drawn-out illness of a former and distinguished Chief Government Kadi in the Protectorate who was receiving treatment for tuberculosis, was that a curse (*habaar*) had been laid upon him by rivals for his position. The Kadi consulted sheikhs expert in the treatment of sorcery (*siḥir*) and eventually recovered. Another less charitable explanation of his illness was that he had sinned against religion and was being punished by one of his ancestors, a famous saint in northern Somaliland. For, as was stated earlier, generally *wadaads* and sheikhs are expected to adhere much more strictly to the precepts of Islam than are 'warriors'; although exceptions are sometimes made on the assumption that a sheikh, with great powers of charisma and devotion to God, may have a special pattern of conduct revealed to him even when this conflicts to some extent with the accepted precepts of the Shariah.

While the blessing of a *wadaad* is respected and his curse feared, the occasions when *wadaads* are believed to resort to sorcery except in legitimately protecting their property are rare. Yet there is a spirit-possession disease known as *wadaaddo* (plural of *wadaad*) particularly prevalent in the north-east of Somaliland. The disease is sometimes diagnosed in people suffering from tuberculosis or pneumonia and the general symptoms are coughing, sneezing, and vomiting with occasional lapses into unconsciousness. This ailment is treated by *wadaads*, particularly those who have previously suffered from it, who adjure the spirit to quit the patient by reading potent verses of the Quran and bathing him with perfume. Perfume in Somaliland has a ritual significance and is associated with religious celebrations. Frequently on Fridays when men are holding a religious ceremony perfume is poured liberally over the hands of those taking part. *Wadaaddo*-spirit possession is not usually attributed to the malicious intent of any particular living sheikh or *wadaad* whom one might have wronged. It is a disease caused by the malevolent *wadaad*-spirits which, like devils (*jinns*), are held sometimes to strike a person without cause. These *wadaads* of the spirit world were, it is believed, formerly the familiars of *Boqor* 'Ismaan, Sultan of the Majeerteen 'Ismaan Maḥamuud; and when he died are said to have been released to trouble people. The disease appears to have spread westwards only within the last fifteen years or so and is not very common. That these spirits should attack people is attributed to the belief that at the death of *Boqor* 'Ismaan his descendants refused to care for his attendant spirits and sent them away.

Wadaaddo-spirits are generally regarded as *jinns*, devils, malignant forces of evil. While everyone knows that there is scriptural warrant for the existence of *jinns*, and many believe that they come out at night to trouble man, many of the most conservative Somali do not believe in *wadaaddo*-spirits and regard the whole thing as a superstition of the gullible. This scepticism is even more pronounced in the case of a similar spirit-possession illness called *saar* which afflicts women rather than men. I mention this disease because to some extent it appears to act as a sanction for the good treatment of a wife by her husband. It is certainly considered by men as a foible of women, and is generally dismissed by them as 'women's nonsense'. Married women too, concede that it is a complaint which afflicts them usually when they have a grievance against their husbands. But as far as women are concerned it is nevertheless a serious affliction.

Saar-spirit possession is extremely common in Ethiopia where it appears to have originated and amounts almost to a spirit-cult.[1] One explanation which I was given for the introduction of the disease into Somaliland, where, in one form it is known as Abyssinian *saar* (*saar Ḥabaashi*), was that the Ethiopians had sent it in retaliation for the many past acts of aggression of Somali against them. In Somaliland there is a fairly well-developed ritual of exorcism conducted mainly by women who have previously suffered from the disease who are considered to have 'authority' over the spirit. Such a woman is called *alaqa*. The exorcism of the spirit—which may not be permanent—and the treatment of the disease are usually conducted by these women who charge very considerable fees. The *saar* spirit is held to like all good things; all luxuries, perfumes, fine clothes, dates, coffee etc., and livestock are sometimes also killed so that blood may be given to appease the spirit. While the *alaqa* takes the majority of these as her reward the patient has also to be given presents, these being given in the name of the spirit possessing her.

Men tend to regard the complaint as a means whereby wives susceptible to the malicious insinuations of old women (who are considered to be ill-disposed) obtain luxuries from their hus-

[1] See Cerulli, *Encyclopaedia of Islam*, vol. iv, p. 1217; Cerulli, 1923, pp. 178–81; Leiris, 1934 (a), (b); Lewis, 1956; Leiris, 1958. Other sources on the spread of the *saar* cult outside the Horn of Africa are cited in Lewis, 1956, p. 147.

bands. One man even suggested that a woman might purposely seek to waste her husband's substance in the treatment of the disease to prevent his having sufficient wealth to marry another wife. It is important to note, however, that I never encountered or even heard of *saar* possession being directly attributed to jealousy between co-wives. Friction between a man's several wives, which is proverbial, is resolved by other means. But to some degree *saar* possession seems to provide a woman with a grievance against her husband with a means of expression for her hostility without recourse to open quarrelling. Yet in the end the instances with which I am familiar show that husbands tend to tire of what they regard as little more than malingering and may seek divorce. Further discussion of *saar* would be outside the scope of this chapter, indeed of this book, and I merely record here that *saar* possession is generally looked at askance by the majority of sheikhs and *wadaads*, the consensus of opinion being that it is unorthodox. In fact cathartic *saar* dances have been banned by public agitation in many districts, both in northern Somaliland and Somalia.

The two preceding types of spirit affliction are subsumed under a more general category of possession known as *gelid* (entering).[1] Here the spirit of a particular person with a specific grievance troubles the individual against whom the grievance lies. Most cases of which I have knowledge are concerned with frustrated or unrequited love between men and women. A man may be visited by the spirit of a girl who loves him or whom he promised to marry but did not. Under treatment in which passages from the Quran are read and the spirit charged to leave the patient by a *wadaad*, the spirit calls out 'I am a girl named Khadiija (say) and I loved this man. He said he would marry me but he did not.' The spirit is cajoled and threatened with the power of God to quit the patient. The context of possession here is consistent with Somali convention in which it is shameful for any open reference to be made to the existence of love or even affection between a man and woman. If a man is guilty of breach of promise when a marriage has been arranged between the respective families he and his lineage may be held responsible for payment of compensation for insult (*ḥaal*), but the woman herself has no direct personal redress. And where a private understanding exists between a man and woman it would be virtually impossible for the matter

[1] From the verb *gal*, to enter, *geli* to insert.

to be discussed openly and assessed by a court of elders. Love, in northern Somaliland is covert, not overt, and men are ashamed of acting in any way which might suggest that they were strongly attached emotionally to, or dependent upon a woman.

Possession by a malicious spirit, referred to as a *gelid*, may also result from an injury committed against or an insult levelled at a beggar, particularly an old woman. Here the sin is one of omission rather than commission. It is not regarded as a wrong which could be avenged by corporate action: it lies outside the scope of recognized delicts. But to refuse alms and kindness to the unprotected and helpless is unwise for two reasons. Those who are poor and defenceless are considered to enjoy the special protection of God. Consequently acts of kindness to them are rewarded and acts of aggression punished. Old women whose husbands are dead, and who have few kinsmen are credited with a general grievance against society and are considered capable of ill-wishing. They are in fact the closest approach in Somali philosophy to the general concept of a witch. The power of casting a spell upon someone who refuses alms is generally described as *gabrro*[1] and the poor are said to possess the evil-eye (*'awri*) which is associated with covetousness. This belief is even extended to creatures considered helpless such as cats. A man who keeps a cat in his house will jokingly refer to it as 'poor and helpless' (*misqiin*) and imply that by caring for it and being kind to it he will be rewarded. Thus to the impoverished, and in a sense underprivileged, mystical power is attributed. Those of poor circumstances and few kinsmen are at once despised and pitied and in their helplessness they are protected by God.

It is again consistent with this interpretation that of the generally scorned *sab* bondsmen the Yibir who are the least numerous, and weakest, and who stand furthest outside Somali society, should be regarded as endowed with the greatest magical powers. Although like the Tumaals and Midgaans they are attached as bondsmen to Somali lineages and protected by their patrons. Yibirs live largely by the gifts they are given as soothsayers and magicians and move about the country practising these arts. Wherever there is a wedding or a child is born, they gather to bless the couple or child and to collect alms which are regarded as theirs by right. These customary gifts made to them in return for their blessing are known as *samanyo* and thus distinguished

[1] Called in the north-east of Somaliland *qumayo*.

from the obilgatory Muslim alms to the poor (*seko*), or voluntary gifts of charity (*sadaqo*) to others. *Samanyo* is theirs by right and if it is withheld the Yibir's curse is feared. Although I have never heard misfortune directly attributed to a Yibir's malevolence, Somali are always uncomfortable in their presence and seek to be rid of them as quickly as possible. They are generally also represented as not being very scrupulous in the practice of Islam and are sometimes derided as 'corpse-eaters' because they are regarded as scroungers, capable of eating even unclean meat.

Somali believe contact with them to be not merely degrading, but also actively defiling. With their small numbers it is often said that no one has seen a Yibir's grave, and they are popularly thought to vanish in a wind when they die.

These beliefs and the obligatory character of the *samanyo* gift are referred by Somali to a tradition according to which the Yibirs descend from a certain Maḥammad Ḥaniif (derogatively called by Somali *Bu'ur Ba'ayr*) who ruled northern Somaliland before the introduction of Islam. About this time, Sheikh Aw Barkhadle, whose shrine some twenty miles to the north-east of Hargeisa is an important place of pilgrimage, came to Somaliland from Arabia and began to teach Islam and Arabic.[1] Maḥammad Ḥaniif, the Yibir ancestor, is represented as having engaged in many evil practices contrary to Islam, including the *ius primae noctis* and eventually a struggle developed between the two leaders. Aw Barkhadle challenged Maḥammad Ḥaniif to use his magical powers to pass through a mountain which he twice accomplished safely. As he was repeating his trick for the third time, however, Aw Barkhadle invoked the superior power of God (*Allaah*) to imprison the Yibir magician and ancestor in the mountain. Thus Islam triumphed and pre-Islamic power was vanquished. It is said that Maḥammad Haniif's descendants were then asked whether they wished to recive the compensation owing to them for the death of their father in a lump sum, or whether they wished it to be a debt owing in perpetuity to all Yibirs. They chose the latter and this is the explanation which is offered of the *samanyo* alms paid to Yibirs by Somali. Although the Yibirs are thought of as possessing magical powers from the devil rather than from God, it is consistent with their insecure position on the fringes

[1] This famous saint of *ashraaf* descent is generally regarded as having come to northern Somaliland in the thirteenth century. Amongst other blessings attributed to him is the creation of a Somali nomenclature for the Arabic vowels thus advancing the teaching of Arabic. The sheikh's system is still that used today in countless Quranic schools throughout Somaliland. His proper name is Sheikh Yuusuf bin Aḥmad al-Kawneen although he is popularly known as Aw Barkhadle ('the blessed one'). For further information see Lewis, 1958 (a), p. 135.

of Somali society that they should be viewed as endowed with magical influence. Because of their slight numerical strength and subservient status Yibirs could not oppose Somali by force of arms and hope to succeed.

The tensions in the contexts discussed here concern individuals rather than groups,[1] and it is in these circumstances that resort is had to supernatural procedures. The situations are those in which enmity and competition cannot be resolved by other means. But between corporate groups, resort is had to feud and physical force. Thus where fighting is inappropriate, or overt hostility impossible, supernatural modes of aggression and of retribution assume prominence. This coincides also with a duality in Somali notions of power. Somali as we have seen at least in theory, sharply distinguish between the secular power of warriors and the spiritual authority of *wadaads*. Those who have power in one sphere have little need of it in the other. At the same time, where secular power is weak, spiritual power is strong. Thus the weak and those who for other reasons cannot have direct recourse to arms are protected by supernatural sanctions. Somali seek strength in everything, and where it is not found in physical force it is sought in the supernatural sphere.

[1] Cf. E. E. Evans-Pritchard, *Witchcraft, Oracles, and Magic among the Azande*, Oxford, 1937, p. 104.

9

Nationalism and Party Politics

I

THIS account of the contemporary structure of northern Somali politics would be incomplete without some discussion of the new political movements to which allusion has been made in earlier chapters. Before concluding with a brief examination of the theoretical implications of the Somali system therefore, I discuss some of the main trends in recent political developments. For the historian and sociologist their significance lies in the close structural similarities which they display to the all-pervasive traditional system. For Somali party politics reveal very clearly the interplay of traditional lineage loyalties. Indeed, one of the main effects of the establishment of legislative bodies (in 1956 in Somalia; and in 1957 in French and British Somaliland) has been to provide a new medium for the expression of these traditional political forces. Nationalism and the new movements, have not superseded or replaced the traditional organization of society; they have merely supplemented it and extended its scope.

To understand their structure it is necessary to go beyond the immediate geographical and cultural limits which we have so far observed. It is essential to deal not only with the northern pastoralists, but also with the cultivating Digil and Rahanwiin tribes of the south. For these southern communities play an important part in the modern political scene in Somalia. In their case the traditional barrier to the extension of national patriotism stems largely from the territorially based local interests which distinguish their political system from that of the northern pastoralists. For in southern Somalia, as has been observed, local contiguity to a considerable extent replaces the lineage and contractual attachments of the nomads. Since, however, the Digil and Rahanwiin make up only a minority of the entire Somali population it is chiefly the northern pastoral mode of life and political assumptions which challenge all attempts to create an effective national patriotism embracing all the Somali communities and welding them together as one nation.

Here the clash of interests is not so much between traditional chiefs and a new élite, for although there is something of this among the Sab of southern Somalia who have a more hierachical political system, in the north there are no strong traditional holders of authority to challenge the ambitions of new leaders. The real struggle is between the elusive goal of nationhood and the day-to-day reality of sectional interests in lineage politics. For these traditional loyalties are part of the pastoral heritage and endure with it.

Because of the apparent poverty of the Somalilands in readily exploitable economic resources, European colonization has not wrought the far-reaching or radical economic changes which might have revolutionized the traditional system. There has been no general agrarian or industrial revolution to completely alter the traditional and little diversified class structure. Such economic developments as there have been, have been on a small scale with a correspondingly slight attraction of foreign capital. In the more fertile regions of southern Somalia, however, some economic influence of importance is exerted by the larger agricultural combines such as the *Società Agricola Italo-Somala*; and further progress is heralded in the foreign aid recently promised by the United Nations and other sources. But at the moment the total labour force is small; and in the British Protectorate the only substantial employer of labour is the Administration. In Somalia over seventy per cent of the population are estimated to live as pastoral nomads, of whom less than thirty per cent practise some cultivation; and of the remainder under twenty per cent are fully engaged in agriculture, leaving some ten per cent active in commerce, fishing, and other forms of enterprise.[2] In the more arid conditions of the British Protectorate, at least eighty per cent of the inhabitants are classified as pastoral nomads.[3]

In Somalia, about thirty per cent of the population are recorded as living in towns, the majority being resident in municipalities, of which there were forty-seven in 1957. In the British

[1] For a recent analysis of Somalia's economy see M. Karp, *The Economics of Trusteeship in Somalia*, Boston, 1960.

[2] See *Rapport . . . Somalie, 1957*, 1958, p. 138.

[3] See *Report of the Commission of Enquiry into Unofficial Representation on the Legislative Council*, Somaliland Government, 1958, p. 4.

Protectorate perhaps a tenth of the population resides in towns. French Somaliland presents a very different picture; almost half the territory's mixed Somali, 'Afar, and immigrant Arab population is concentrated in the highly commercialized port and capital of Jibuti.

Most Somali towns are small, and in northern Somaliland those of importance today are all of recent formation. Galkayu, capital of the Mijertein Province of northern Somalia, has less than 8,000 permanent inhabitants; and Hargeisa and Jibuti, the capitals of British and French Somaliland, contain only about 30,000 persons. Only in the south are there larger urban centres and these are generally much older and more cosmopolitan in character than their northern equivalents.[1] Thus Mogadishu, capital of Somalia, has nearly 90,000 inhabitants, and the port of Merca of equal antiquity, some 50,000. Only in these southern centres is there traditionally a greater occupational stratification than that characteristic generally in Somaliland. Here guilds of craftsmen[2] have undoubtedly contributed to the growth and extension of new political associations and attitudes.

In the north, on the other hand, while the figures quoted above might suggest a higher degree of urbanization than one would expect, this is not symptomatic of 'detribalization'. For northern towns, as has been explained in an earlier chapter, are market centres, part and parcel of the nomadic economy, and traditionally the headquarters of pastoral politics. Today, however, while continuing to be the main foci of pastoral politics they are also the chief centres of social change. And it appears that it is largely the greater security which settlement affords the town-dweller which has fostered the growth of new sentiments and values opposed to the traditional pastoral principles of social cohesion.

Yet although the north has seen no far-reaching economic changes, the proportion of Somali who now engage directly in trade and commerce has increased, and an activity which was once largely monopolized by immigrant Arabian and Indian merchants is now no longer so. In addition, although it has brought few permanent settlers, colonization has naturally developed commerce and stimulated the domestic economy as well as the export trade. But in the absence of any large, perman-

[1] See above, p. 18.

[2] See P. Barile, *Colonizzazione fascista nella Somalia Meridionale*, Rome, 1935, p. 59.

ently domiciled, foreign community,[1] the middle-class of new men, which is rapidly growing up largely in response to modern education, is overwhelmingly absorbed in the Government service. The problem of finding adequately trained Somali staff to replace expatriate officials is acute, particularly in French Somaliland and the British Protectorate. And while education is more widely based in Somalia, here too, difficulties arise and are increased by the pace of replacement of expatriate Italian staff by Somali in the civil service.[2] It is, of course in Somalia, the former Italian colony and foothold for the conquest of Ethiopia, that the influence of an immigrant European community has been felt most strongly. But this is now dwindling, and in 1957 numbered less than 4,400 of whom the majority are Government servants.

Leaving aside these mainly economic considerations, it seems that one of the principal results of colonial rule has been to stimulate the growth of Somali sentiments of unity as Muslims opposed to rule by those whom they class indiscriminately as infidels. Thus Somali nationalist aims tend always to be associated with the ideal of Muslim solidarity opposed to Christian government. This aspect of Christian influence in inspiring nationalist aspirations is particularly strong in what Somali regard as the imperialist policies of the Ethiopian Government.

Moreover, from their position on the sea-board of Ethiopia, Somali have always been in touch with the outside world and are now being gradually drawn into the web of Middle Eastern politics. Since the earliest days of colonization it has been customary for numbers of Somali to travel widely abroad, mainly as seamen and often as stokers, and many have thus visited most of the world's ports and established small immigrant Somali communities such as those in Cardiff, London, and Marseilles. When these men return home to resume the pastoral life they also bring back new aspirations and new ideas. Men of religion also, as has been mentioned, frequently travel widely abroad in search of learning; and the annual pilgrimage to Mecca maintains regular contact with events in the Arabian Peninsula where in

[1] There were nearly 40,000 Arab, Indian, Pakistani, Eritrean, Abyssinian, and other immigrants domiciled in Somalia in 1956. In French Somaliland there are about 6,000 Arab immigrants, and in the British Protectorate only a few hundred Arabs and Indians.

[2] On the higher educational facilities available in Somalia see below, p. 283.

Aden there is a resident Somali community of some size.[1] These external influences were intensified in the last world war when Somali fought as far afield as Burma; and in Somaliland itself the East Africa campaign with its disruptive effects, and the eventual placing of British, Italian, and Ethiopian Somali territories under a common administration from 1941-49, if it did not directly create, certainly helped to foster the concept of a united Somali federation which to a greater or lesser degree dominates the programmes of all the nationalist parties today.

These and other channels of contact are today widened and strengthened through the influence of the press and radio, both from Western and United Arab Republic sources. Programmes in Arabic and Somali from Cairo are widely listened to, the British Broadcasting Corporation now offers a Somali transmission, and local stations in French and British Somaliland and Somalia join with the local presses in disseminating foreign as well as local news. In Mogadishu both the radio and press are now directly under Somali control, and in the British Protectorate, as well as the popular official fortnightly *War Somali Sidihi* (now *The Somaliland News*, published weekly)[2] there are two recently launched independent newspapers published in Arabic. In addition, there is the important factor of extending educational facilities, with opportunities for study abroad in England, Italy, Egypt, India, the United States, and other countries.

It is evident that the forces directly and indeed explicitly conducive to modern political development and to the growth of national patriotism should be most advanced in Somalia under United Nations trusteeship and Italian administration with a ten years' mandate to full independence (1950–60). At the present time, the policies of ever-accelerating encouragement and preparation for self-government in Somalia, and to a lesser extent in the British Protectorate, are among the most potent factors in the stimulation of new political aspirations. Recent developments in French colonial policy, especially through the effects of the *loi-cadre*, are beginning to exert a similar effect.

These in brief are some of the major influences which have impinged upon the traditional structure of Somali society and which, while not radically changing it, are contributing much to the growth of party politics. From these stimuli increasing

[1] The Somali population in the Colony of Aden numbered 10,600 in 1955.

[2] Since March, 1961 called the 'Somali News' and published at Mogadishu.

demands for political autonomy and for fuller participation in the administrative and other services of government arise in all the Somali territories. And while the pastoral order persists, a new, and widening field of activity is now open to traditional lineage rivalries.

II

I propose to discuss in detail the structure of party politics and nationalism only in the British Protectorate and Somalia. French Somaliland has been left out of account partly because I do not know sufficient of recent developments there to deal adequately with them, and partly also because the situation is complicated by the relations between the rival Somali and 'Afar (Danakil) communities, full consideration of which would be outside the scope of this book.[1] I have also excluded discussion of the position of the Somali communities in Harar Province of Ethiopia and in the Northern Province of Kenya. For in both Ethiopia and Kenya, Somali form only a small fraction of the total population and can hardly expect to obtain a controlling interest in Government. But since Ethiopia's first national elections, held towards the end of 1957, there is now Somali representation in the Chamber of Deputies. This is also true of the Kenya legislature where there is now a special Somali representative for the Northern Province.[2]

Of the new political movements in general, it can at once be said that they represent less new principles of social and political unity than novel forms for the expression of traditional interests. This applies equally to the strongly nationalist parties, where pan-Somali nationalism is not so much a complete surrender to a national patriotism transcending lineage loyalties as merely a realignment of lineage and tribal interests at a new level. This can be seen in a preliminary way from the following classification of parties[3] according to their aims and composition.

The first group contains those parties and associations which are simply the modern political organ of a particular clan or lineage, and which, whatever lip-service they may pay to the

[1] For the sake of completeness, however, I include a summary account of the present position in the Côte in Appendix I.

[2] For information on the situation in Harar Province and Kenya, see my *Modern Political Movements in Somaliland*, 1958.

[3] The word 'party' is used here in a wide sense to denote groups and associations at different stages of political development. Most, but not all the 'parties' shown in the table have contested elections.

Types of Party

I. Lineage Parties	
Mahlia Party	Formerly in the British Protectorate
Marreḥaan Union	Somalia (disappeared in 1958)
II. National Parties	
Somaliland National League	British Protectorate
National United Front	British Protectorate
Somali Youth League	British Protectorate, Somalia
Liberal Party (Incorporating the Somali Democratic Party)	Somalia
Greater Somalia League	Somalia.
III. Regional (and tribal) Parties	
Afgoi-Audegle Party	Somalia (no longer in existence)
Banaadir Youth Union	Somalia
Ḥizbiya Digil-Mirifle (Independent Constitutional Party)	Somalia
Shidle Party	Somalia (no longer in existence)
Bajuni Fiqarini	Somalia

ideal of Somali unity, are basically committed to the furtherance of their own sectional interests. Secondly, there are those parties which are entirely opposed to the traditional dividing kinship and contractual ties and to any distinctions within the Somali nation. Their goal is national solidarity, and, eventually, the creation of a great Somali federation of the various territories. It is these parties especially which emphasize the cultural and religious identity and proud sense of exclusiveness of the Somali as a people. The lineage parties have also a firm Muslim basis; but their appeal to religious solidarity is secondary to their common lineage interests and phrased more narrowly in terms of their founding ancestor whom they regard as a Muslim saint. I have already referred to this dual aspect of Somali Islam, where men venerate both lineage ancestors as saints and saints who stand outside the lineage structure and represent the transcendental in Islam.

A good example of this type of modern political organization is provided by the short-lived Hawiye Youth League. This group was formed shortly before the first Assembly elections in Somalia in 1956. Its formation followed a squabble, based partly on individual personalities and partly on lineage affiliation, within the Somali Youth League which at that time was largely dominated by Daarood influence. The founder of the splinter group who belonged to the Hawiye clan-family adopted the name 'Hawiye Youth League' and sought general Hawiye support by organizing a memorial service (*siyaaro*) in honour of the eponym Hawiye. After its failure to win a seat in the elections, however, the group changed its name to the 'Liberal Party of Young Somali' and modified its tactics to appeal to members of all clans and clan families. It has now amalgamated with the Somali Democratic Party,[1] another nationalist organization which gained one seat in the 1956 Somalia Assembly elections, and which is itself a coalition of various elements. One of the more important of these is another basically Hawiye group, the former African Somali Union, which was founded in 1952. Despite its name, this association was in origin primarily an organ for the expression of Hawiye opinion. The majority of its adherents were drawn from that clan-family but it was later reinforced by dissident Daarood followers of the Somali Youth League. By the time of the 1956 Assembly elections it had joined with the nationalist Somali Democratic Party, and the latter as has been said, has since fused with the Liberal Party. I discuss other examples of lineage movements later.

Finally there are those regionally, or tribally based parties, which reflect common regional values and occur only in southern Somalia. These are the southern analogues of the northern pastoral lineage parties, and their limitation to the mainly cultivating regions of southern Somalia reflects the traditional dichotomy in economy and political structure between the two regions. The most important of these is the Independent Constitutional Party which represents the Digil and Mirifle tribes of southern Somalia as a whole and which is at present the main opposition in the Somalia Legislative Assembly. I discuss this party more fully below and mention here two smaller tribal movements, the Shidle and Bajuni parties. The first of these which is no longer in existence, many of its former adherents having joined the Somali Youth League, represented the negroid Shidle cultivating

[1] On this party see further below, p. 288.

peoples of the Shebelle River.[1] The Bajuni Fiqarini which is still active represents the Bantu Bajuni peoples of the southern coast of Somalia.

I shall not discuss in detail here the organization and aims of all the political organizations but generally limit my analysis to those which are most important in the British Protectorate and Somalia. Certain features are shared by almost all the parties. Usually only a small minority of leaders, occupied in the central party administration, are full-time professional politicians in the modern sense. The initiative naturally comes from these men who for the most part belong to the new educated élite. The bulk of active support, especially in the nationalist organizations, derives from the younger educated élite and from traders permanently or semi-permanently domiciled in towns. It will be recalled that it is from those who live in towns that much of the agitation for the abolition of the traditional system of dia-paying responsibility comes. But the small size of the newly educated élite creates a difficult problem since so many are absorbed into government service and thereby excluded from taking an active part in party politics. Here the Government of Somalia allows greater latitude to its employees than does the British Protectorate Administration. In Somalia, a government servant may obtain leave of absence to contest a seat in a constituency outside the District in which he is stationed. If he is successful he is granted extended leave, and when he loses his seat allowed to return to his former position.[2]

But all the parties, whether nationalist or otherwise, ultimately depend upon their more passive adherents and supporters and these are very largely canvassed on the basis of lineage and tribal ties. Regional branches are established in local areas to maintain contact with the central committees and to increase party affiliation. The headquarters organization of the Somali Youth League at Mogadishu includes a President, Deputy-President, Secretary, Treasurer, Comptroller, and some fourteen other members of committee. Regional branch offices exist in most districts of Somalia and the British Protectorate. These have a similar committee organization to that of the party headquarters. The

[1] On the Shidle, see Lewis, 1955, p. 41; and on the Bajuni, V. L. Grottanelli, *Pescatori dell' Oceano Indiano*, Rome, 1955.

[2] For an interesting discussion of this problem see, *Report of the Commission of Enquiry into Unofficial Representation on the Legislative Council*, Somaliland Government, 1958, pp. 16–19.

Somaliland National League, which is limited to the British Protectorate, has its centre at Hargeisa and branches in most districts.

All the parties levy membership fees, and small monthly or annual subscriptions, and they are often assisted by donations from supporters, sometimes from outside Somaliland (as for example from the Somali community in Aden). The Somali Youth League (S.Y.L.) and the Somaliland National League (S.N.L.) both issue badges to their members, the insignia of the latter bearing the inscription 'Be united in the name of God'. Coloured uniforms and banners are also favoured, especially in public demonstrations and political campaigns.[1]

The local branches hold regular meetings, often every week, at which party officials give addresses on the party's aims, and discussions and debates are held on matters of current interest and policy. These are largely social occasions and a prominent feature, at least among the nationalist organizations, is the singing of patriotic songs and slogans which are cast usually in the form of the traditional *gabay* poem. In marked contrast with the north, among the Digil and Rahanwiin women also attend meetings and entertainments and dancing are a regular feature. At one S.Y.L. evening meeting which I attended amongst the Rahanwiin, men and women danced together to the refrain: 'We are Somali, what hope is there for the person who resists the cry "Somali" '?

These regular gatherings recall the religious meetings of the Dervish Orders. To the visitor familiar with the informal character of most pastoral secular assemblies the formality of their proceedings is striking. For the parties seek to inculcate a respect for discipline and for the dignity of their officers. When the local leaders enter a meeting all those present stand up as a mark of respect. Young members are appointed to act as stewards responsible for the orderly conduct of the proceedings. These features of party organization, a degree of hierarchical administration, respect for elected office-bearers, the use of badges and on public occasions of uniforms and banners, and the regular collection of monetary contributions—find parallels in the traditional structure of society only in the religious *tariiqas*, with which at least

[1] The S.Y.L. uniform consists of white trousers and a white shirt, crossed diagonally from shoulder to hip by a red and blue bandolier bearing the slogan 'S.Y.L.' The S.N.L. sash is green and carries their own motto. See illustration viiia.

the nationalist parties also share the aim of furthering Somali unity.

Despite these parallels, however, and the fact that in many instances prominent religious leaders have lent their support to the new political organizations, the majority of political leaders are out of sympathy with the traditional *tariiqa* movements. Here criticism is directed at the alleged abuses of certain sheikhs in collecting extortionate donations from a 'gullible' populace in the name of a saintly ancestor, of whose blessed properties many of the new élite are sceptical. Objection is also made to the strife between the Orders despite their professed identity of purpose, and to the dividing influence which, contrary to their ideals, they exercise in society.[1] Yet, nevertheless, the formal analogy between the old religions organizations and the new secular movements has importance since until recently the *tariiqas* have provided the only channel for promoting the unity of Somali as Muslims, irrespective of their own sectional lineage loyalties.[2] This is recognized by Somali and the religious rebellion against the Christian colonial powers led by Sheikh Maḥammad 'Abdille is now regarded by some as an early expression of Somali nationalism.

III

In the Protectorate, recent political developments tend to confirm the strength of lineage loyalties. But largely through the lack of any extensive political awareness in the modern sense, clear-cut political organizations based on clanship are only beginning to make their appearance. This is not to say, however, that there are no movements of a party type for there are already three nationalist organizations functioning in the Protectorate. The oldest of these is the Somaliland National League which has been in existence under various titles since as early as 1935. The League draws much of its support from the Isaaq clans and also includes some Dir (Gadabuursi, and 'Iise) adherents and some Daarood (Ḍulbahante, and Warsangeli) followers. In keeping with the other Somali nationalist movements, the S.N.L. is strongly Muslim in outlook and aims, and maintains contact

[1] See above, Chapter VII.

[2] In some cases religious leaders have been active in the formation of the new nationalist movements. See Appendix II where an outline of factors of significance in the formation of the S.Y.L. is given.

with the Egyptian Government. Its original policy was to co-operate with the British Government, or with any other body concerned to improve the welfare of the Somali people; but of recent years it has become increasingly extremist. At the moment it represents in the Protectorate the most intensely nationalist pan-Somali movement.

The Somali Youth League, the most important party in the Somalilands as a whole and with headquarters in Somalia is at the present time more moderate in its nationalist aims. In British Somaliland its leaders are generally less experienced than their colleagues in Somalia and its following is not as strong as that of the S.N.L. Much of its support comes from the Ḍulbahante and Warsangeli, but it is also active and counts adherents among the Isaaq and Gadabuursi.[1]

Until recently less of a political party than a convention, is the much more widely based National United Front. The leaders of this organization have generally taken the lead in publicizing Somali demands for self-government outside the Protectorate. The circumstances of the movement's formation are significant for it arose to marshal public opinion against the transfer to Ethiopian administration of the Haud and Reserved Areas (now known as the 'Scheduled Territories') in 1955. It will be recalled that although Britain had recognized Ethiopian claims to the region (of some 25,000 square miles) by a treaty of 1897, it was only in November, 1954, that the territory was completely surrendered to Ethiopian administrative control and incorporated in Harar Province. As I have pointed out,[2] Somali have never recognized the 1897 treaty, and when the territory was actually handed over there was widespread public resentment in the Protectorate. Indeed it was still a very live issue when I was in Somaliland in 1957. There was much public agitation and several demonstrations[3] at the time and out of these the National

[1] It is necessary to emphasize that the above and much of the following was written in 1959: developments subsequent to that date are indicated in summary form in the Preface (p. viii). I discuss the S.Y.L. more fully below.

[2] See above, p. 19.

[3] A delegation consisting of Sultan 'Abdillaahi ('Iidagalle), Sultan 'Abdaraḥiim (Habar Awal), Mr. Dube 'Ali Maḥammad (Habar Tol Ja'lo) and led by Mr Michael Mariano (Habar Tol Ja'lo) visited England in February, 1955, to interview the Colonial Secretary and to arouse British public opinion and support against the transfer. The delegation received considerable publicity in the British Press. See *The Times*, 5, 8, 14, 15 and 23rd Feb. 1955; the *Manchester Guardian*, 23rd Feb. 1955. A second delegation consisting of Mr Mariano of the N.U.F. and Sultan

United Front arose. Somali hostility towards Ethiopia has received further encouragement from such actions as the Emperor's speech on Somali-Ethiopian relations at Qabradare in 1956, when he proclaimed that the future of the Somali people lay with Ethiopia, and suggested that eventually there should be a federation similar to that at present in existence between Ethiopia and Eritrea.[1]

These external threats have helped to further the cause of the Protectorate nationalist organizations and particularly of the N.U.F. which was originally merely an *ad hoc* alliance of the S.N.L. and S.Y.L. and people of neither party. Associated with its aims for the return of the Scheduled Territories, was its campaign for the independence of the Protectorate within the British Commonwealth. When feelings against Ethiopia were most bitter the movement received widespread support, but when it failed to obtain the return of the disputed region to British Administration, much S.Y.L. and S.N.L. backing was lost. Now, although its leaders are amongst the ablest in the Protectorate, it tends to lack any constant following. Its vitality lay in its flexibility of organization, for while the S.N.L. and S.Y.L. are mutually exclusive, until recently it was open to members of either party. It has received impressive monetary support from all sections of the Protectorate community and also from the Somali settlement in Aden. And in keeping with the movement's mediatory character, it has on occasion successfully intervened in clan disputes. Its leaders are amongst the most outspoken in the Protectorate in their condemnation of dia-paying group

Biḥi (Ogaadeen) a refugee from Ethiopia, visited England in September, 1956, to discuss the position again with the Colonial Secretary before proceeding to New York, where it was intended to petition the United Nations Assembly and to seek their intervention to place the Somali case before the International Court. The delegation's visit to the United States aborted and the dispute has still not been placed before the International Court. The difficulties which British Protected Somali have experienced in their movements to and from the area in question, despite the efforts of the British Liason Officer at Jigjiga, have led to repeated representations by the British Government and to Anglo-Ethiopian conferences on the working of the Agreement of November, 1954. Both sides have alleged infringements of the terms of the Agreement and in April, 1956, an unsuccessful attempt was made by the British Government to regain the administration of the region through a mission to the Ethiopian Government led by Mr Dodds-Parker, then Joint Parliamentary Under Secretary for Foreign Affairs.

[1] The Emperor in his speech insisted on the racial and cultural unity of the Somali as a branch of the 'Great Ethiopian family', a turn of phrase which met with little approval in Somaliland.

solidarity and lineage fighting. And in their approach to the solution of this problem they are among the most realistic.

There is little need here to reaffirm the strength of lineage and contractual loyalties in the Protectorate for these have been a constant theme in earlier chapters. It has further been shown how these rivalries tend to be projected into the sphere of administration, especially where Somali are directly concerned in government. Thus, while the establishment of local government councils may eventually foster the growth of nonlineage loyalties, at the moment their proceedings tend to reflect kinship and contractual solidarity.

To some extent the continuing importance of traditional political principles is concealed in the nationalist organizations mentioned. It was clearly apparent, however, in the Mahlia movement, a short-lived society formed between 1952 and 1954 to further the interests of the 'Iise Muuse sub-clan of the Habar Awal. This is the segment which attempted to establish its own independent Sultan.[1]

The strength of clan loyalties and weakness of party political allegiances were strikingly shown in 1957 when a legislative council[2] was opened in the Protectorate. This body at its inception included fifteen members: the Governor as President, and three ex-officio members (the Chief Secretary, Attorney-General, and the Financial Secretary); five official members (the heads of Departments); and six unofficial members nominated by the Governor. For the unofficial seats sixteen nominations were called for and sought in the Protectorate Advisory Council. But the members of this body failed to reach agreement and the discussion of suitable candidates overflowed into a series of hotly debated meetings in Hargeisa in which the leaders of the National United Front played a prominent part. They sought to

[1] See above, p. 197.

[2] Prior to the establishment of the Legislative Council, the only formal central organ for the expression of Somali opinion has been the Advisory Council which, established in 1946, has in principle met annually. This body which consists of forty-eight 'elected and selected' members representative of all Districts and sections of the community has no executive or legislative power. It continues to meet and is nevertheless a very important channel for the expression of public opinion. Most of its members are selected from nominations made at clan and lineage-group *shirs* in the Districts with the assistance of District Commissioners who try to ensure that a reasonably representative body of delegates is sent from each District. An increasingly difficult problem has been to provide for the representation of the new élite and to include adequate representation of religious interests from the leaders of the Dervish Orders.

maintain the principle that candidates should represent the three parties (S.N.L., S.Y.L., and N.U.F.), and be selected by merit and capability irrespective of lineage affiliation. In the end, however, as was to be expected, twenty-four candidates representative of the main clans and lineages in the six Administrative Districts of the Protectorate were proposed, very much on the same basis of representation as in the Advisory Council. Such party solidarity as existed was completely over-ruled by lineage demands.

There is undoubtedly, however, an increasing modern political awareness in the Protectorate. Reference has already been made to the small but growing body of opinion which is opposed to the traditional system of dia-paying solidarity. This progressive desire to break with the traditional has been publicly voiced through such bodies as the Protectorate Advisory Council, and in 1957 in the Legislative Council a motion was tabled calling for consideration of the abolition of 'Somali tribal *Ḥeer*'. After some debate[1] the Government agreed to conduct a public enquiry which is now (1959) proceeding through the District Administration.

At the same time, in 1957 and 1958 several clan meetings, such as that of the Ḍulbahante mentioned above,[2] were being held to establish what are in effect clan betterment societies and associations. Clans and lineages are thus showing themselves to be aware of the need to provide for their interests in the new political field and at the same time to strive for general peace and national unity. These new movements are of the same kind as the earlier Habar Awal Mahlia society mentioned above.[3] With the introduction of elected representation in March 1959, there is now fuller scope for such activity.

Demands for elected Somali representation were made as soon as the Protectorate Legislative Council opened in 1957, and following the report of a commission of inquiry,[4] the legislature was

[1] See *War Somali Sidihi*, No. 128, 30th November, 1957, pp. 3–5.

[2] See above, p. 208.

[3] See above, p. 279.

[4] *Report of the Commission of Enquiry into Unofficial Representation on the Legislative Council*, Somaliland Protectorate Government, 1958. The five members of this commission, two of whom were Somali, while being forced to recognize the unanimous wish of those who made submissions that elections should be divorced from 'tribalism', agreed that it was essential to have a sufficient number of unofficial seats to allow an even representation of the main Protectorate clans. The report suggested that the six Administrative Districts should be used as constituencies and

reconstituted to provide for this early in 1959. The new council consisted of the Governor as President, twelve elected members, two nominated unofficial members, and fifteen official members. The Executive Council remained unchanged in composition comprising the Governor, three *ex-officio* members (the Chief Secretary, the Attorney-General, and the Financial Secretary), and two official members who were heads of Departments; but unofficial elected members were to be consulted from time to time by the Council. Elections were held in March 1959 by secret ballot in a limited number of urban or semi-urban constituencies and by acclamation in the remaining rural constituencies.[1] Despite some effort on the part of the N.U.F. especially and to a lesser extent of the S.Y.L. to campaign on a party basis and to seek the return of candidates on a party ticket, candidates were in fact nominated and elected according to their personal qualities and lineage backing irrespective of any party affiliation or programme. Thus for example in Burao, the Habar Tol Ja'lo clan put forward two candidates, one for the town seat and one for one of the two rural constituency seats, and both were returned unopposed (no candidate was nominated in the other rural constituency). Mr Michael Mariano, Vice-President of the N.U.F., stood for election in the rural constituency of Erigavo West where he was returned unopposed by his own clansmen of the Habar Tol Ja'lo.[2] This is typical of the way in which the elections were contested and won by lineage affiliation and

that each District should be allocated two seats since in most the population 'falls into two main groups fairly evenly divided'. The Report further states: 'In making our recommendations that there should be a minimum of two unofficial elected members to represent each of the six Districts, we have been influenced by what we regard as the most important factor of all, namely the absolute necessity of maintaining a balance between the tribes of the Protectorate'. See *Report* pp. 11–14.

[1] The first class of electoral districts comprised the townships of Hargeisa and Burao and the whole of Berbera District. The second class included both the rural and urban areas of the remaining Districts and the rural areas of Hargeisa and Burao Districts. Hargeisa District was allocated two seats; Burao District two; Erigavo two; Las Anod two; and Borama-Zeila' District two. Voters in the first category of constituencies were required to possess limited property qualifications ranging from owning a dwelling in the constituency to possessing ten camels, ten head of cattle or 100 sheep and goats. Their names had to be registered on electoral rolls before the elections. In the other constituencies this was not necessary and no property qualifications were stipulated. All voters had to be twenty-one years of age, and only men had the vote.

[2] The S.N.L. boycotted the elections since their demands for an immediate unofficial majority had not been acceded to.

members returned as the individual representatives of clans and lineages rather than as representatives of the N.U.F. or S.Y.L.[1]

While still in 1959 lagging behind the aspirations of the most progressive Somali, the pace of advancement has rapidly increased in recent years. Ministerial government with an elected unofficial majority in the legislature had been promised by 1960. The replacement of expatriate by Somali staff was also being accelerated. Of a total of just over 200 officers in the Protectorate Government in 1957, about thirty were Somali. In 1958, sixty-five Somali students (some of them at British Universities) were training outside Somaliland for entry to the civil service. And at the end of the same year there were several Somali Assistant Superintendents of police, two District Officers in charge of Districts, and a number of Somali Assistant District Commissioners and District Assistants.

These developments are altering the traditional position of Government as an alien arbiter in lineage affairs. The Administration is increasingly becoming a consortium of rival lineage and clan interests which people regard in terms of the number of kinsmen they can count in its ranks. Thus as 'Somalization' proceeds the more the civil service as well as the Legislative Council is drawn into the all-pervasive nexus of lineage politics. Even several years ago before Somali held senior ranks, certain Departments were often associated with a particular clan or lineage through the success of early employees in finding positions for their kinsmen. The Agricultural Department for instance, had at one time the reputation of being a largely Ḍulbahante institution despite the fact that the Ḍulbahante are among the least interested of the Protectorate clans in cultivation.

In this connexion the position of the newly installed Somali Administrative Officer or Police Officer deserves mention. The ambiguous position of Local Authorities with allegiance both to the Government and to their dia-paying group has been discussed in Chapter VII.[2] In proportion to his greater authority the District Officer is faced with more intensely opposed loyalties. For kinsmen expect support and assistance from kinsmen, and a Somali District Commissioner is ideally a friend at court. Here kinship may be traced far outside close agnation and the Somali

[1] Of those returned, seven candidates were supporters of the N.U.F.; one of the S.N.L. (despite the S.N.L. boycott); four with no 'party' allegiance. No candidate belonging to the S.Y.L. (as distinct from the N.U.F.) was successful.

[2] See above, p. 201.

official find himself placed in the embarrassing position of appearing to favour the enemies and rivals of his own kinsmen. To counter these difficulties in Somalia, the official policy is apparently to post Somali Provincial and District Commissioners and Police Officers outside their home areas and to move officials fairly frequently from region to region.

IV

Somalia is in most respects the most developed of the Somali territories. The main part of the government of the country is now in Somali hands, although many advisory and technical functions are still performed by expatriate staff. Since July 1956 all Provinces and Districts have been in the charge of Somali Administrative Officers, trained partly locally, and partly overseas in Italy.[1] Political parties have been in existence for a number of years and were mostly already well organized in 1954 when the first national municipal elections were held, and sixteen parties presented candidates. The first elections for the newly opened Legislative Assembly in February 1956, gave a further impetus to party political activity and furnished proof of the success with which modern forms of political activity had been adopted.

With its greater population, more people are politically conscious in the modern sense than at present in the Protectorate. And particularly amongst the new élite, who are also more numerous, there is a strong desire to suppress clan and lineage distinctions and to move away from traditional political loyalties to a wider national patriotism. One aspect of this is the extreme reluctance with which many people in Somalia, particularly party politicians, refer to or even disclose their clan and lineage affiliation. This traditional means of identifying individuals in terms of their group affiliation is becoming unpopular amongst

[1] A School of Politics and Administration was opened in Mogadishu in 1950, providing a three-year diploma course normally followed by a year at a higher institution in Italy. By 1957 this was considered to have fulfilled its purpose in producing a cadre of administrative officials with basic training and became a Technical and Commerical Institute. Meanwhile at a higher educational level a Higher Institute of Law and Economics was opened at Mogadishu in 1954. This Institute offers a two-year Rome University diploma course and in 1960 assumed the status of a University Institute charged with the task of co-ordinating all higher education in Somalia. Between 1952 and 1958 334 students from Somalia had completed further training in Italy.

the new élite who consider it 'backward' and ill-mannered to discuss these things openly. And, whereas in other Somali territories few people give the response 'Somali' when asked their lineage or clan, in southern Somalia, especially in towns, this is now quite common. Again, while the traditional polite greeting for a stranger is to address him as 'clansman' (*ina' adeer*), the usage now increasingly favoured in southern Somalia is to call him 'brother' (*walaal*). In the traditional pastoral system the term 'brother' is not generally applied outside the nuclear or polygynous family except amongst the initiates of a religious Order (*tariiqa*).[1] These various conventions are all consistent with the ardent nationalist aspirations and desire to conquer traditional loyalties which are so evident in Somalia.

Despite these manifestations, however, and despite the self-conscious efforts which are being made in Somalia to weaken the strength of traditional ties and to encourage the growth of wider and less parochial allegiances, contract and clanship (and in the south tribalism) continue to rule the lives of the majority. Party politics reflect traditional group interests, but here on a wider base than in the Protectorate. For the effective lineage interests now represented on a national basis are mainly those of the clan-families. Party politics in Somalia are dominated by the conflicting demands of the Daarood, Hawiye, Digil, and Rahanwiin, and to a lesser extent of the smaller and less compact Dir clan-families. This represents an expansion of political action, an enlargement of the politically significant group, since in the traditional sphere the clan-families are generally too vast, too unwieldly, and too widely scattered to act as effective political units.

In terms of the segmentary structure of Somali society this means that an extended and to some extent novel sense of allegiance is developing between clans widely separated but of the same clan-family. To some extent the centrifugal antagonisms within and amongst clans of the same clan-family are being subordinated to centripetal common interests at the level of the clan-family. Thus in a national struggle for political power through the new channels of municipal councils and the Legislative Assembly, and through an increasingly dominant control in the executive functions of government, men from widely scattered clans of the same clan-family see themselves as

[1] The word used in this sense, however, is the Arabic '*ikhwaan*, brethren, see above, p. 100.

allies against those of other clan-families in a way which previously had little significance.[1]

But the cleavages between clan-families are not the only relevant ones in party politics. The economic, linguistic, cultural and genealogical schism between the Digil and Rahanwiin clan-families as Sab, and the rest, including the Daarood, as Samaale, is also strongly expressed. Indeed the Digil-Mirifle tribal party (now called the Independent Constitutional Party)[2] represents the unity of the various Digil and Rahanwiin tribes and their traditional opposition to the other Samaale peoples of Somalia.

All these cleavages are evident in the structure and activities of the parties, and some have already been referred to.[3] They can be seen clearly in the changing composition and character of the Somali Youth League, the present government party. This organization, although it has a longer history as an informal body,[4] was formally constituted in 1943 when the future of the ex-Italian colony of Somalia was under discussion. Then, as now, the League advocated the amalgamation of the Somali territories (especially of French, British, Ethiopian, and ex-Italian Somaliland) into one independent state.[5]

The campaign for a 'Greater Somalia' and for a United Nations trusteeship mandate of ten years to independence was intensified in the later years of the British Military Administration. In 1946 the British Foreign Minister (then Mr Ernest Bevin) had proposed that Somalia should be joined with the British Protectorate and the Ogaden Province of Ethiopia to form a Greater Somalia under British Trusteeship. A Commission of Investigation (representing Britain, France, the United States, and Russia) visited Somalia at the beginning of 1948 to determine the wishes of the population on their future status and the S.Y.L. forcibly argued their case for a trusteeship to be administered by the Four Powers and not for a return of Italian rule.

[1] I do not of course mean by this that in any absolute sense enmities and divisions within clan-families are forgotten, but merely that in a situation of rivalry with other clan-families they are temporarily concealed. Clearly the more opposition and hostility there is in party politics at the level of the clan-family, the less there is likely to be within a clan-family in traditional politics.

[2] The *Ḥisbiya Dastuur Mustaqiil.*

[3] See above, pp. 271-76.

[4] For fuller details of the circumstances of the League's formation, see Appendix II.

[5] This aim is represented in the national flag of Somalia by the five-pointed Somali star (the fifth point represents the Northern Province of Kenya), which is also the central emblem in the country's new coat of arms.

Despite the fact that opposition to the S.Y.L. programme on the part of the Digil and Rahanwiin led to a riot in Mogadishu in which fourteen Somali and fifty-one Italians lost their lives, the Commission rightly recognized that the S.Y.L. represented the wishes of the majority and so reported to the Four Powers.[1] But the Bevin plan for unification under British administration did not gain international acceptance. And although there was strong resistance in some quarters in Somalia to a return of Italian authority, Italy was appointed in November 1949, as administering power under United Nations Trusteeship and the country given a ten years' mandate to self-government.

The League has thus been from its inception a pan-Somali organization striving to break-down all traditional resistance to a national patriotism. In 1956 it was estimated to have a composition of Daarood fifty per cent; Hawiye thirty per cent; Digil-Mirifle ten per cent; and others ten per cent; and it has until recently tended to be identified particularly with Daarood interests. In the 1956 elections[2] for the legislature it obtained 43 of the available sixty seats, and the Digil Mirifle party (Ḥ.D.M.) gained the largest number (thirteen) of the remainder. The official electoral results are shown in the following table.[3]

[1] See F. E. Stafford, 'The ex-Italian colonies', *International Affairs*, vol. XXV No. 1, January, 1949, pp. 47–55. Italian settlers and government officials were able to exploit the difference between the S.Y.L. and the Digil and Rahanwiin in favour of an expression of pro-Italian feeling, supporting the return of Italian rule. They were involved in the disturbances and are even alleged to have been amongst the principal instigators. For an account which displays a strong anti-Italian bias see E. S. Pankhurst, *Ex-Italian Somaliland*, London, 1951, pp. 222–59.

[2] Voting was then confined to the masculine population, and candidates for election were required to be literate in Italian and Arabic, to be over thirty years of age, and to have been resident at least one year in Somalia. In the municipalities voters were required to be registered on the municipal electoral lists. In the interior, where in accordance with Somali custom every sane male over 21 years of age could vote, voting took place through *ad hoc shirs* at which representatives were appointed to carry collective votes to the recorders. It is alleged and generally recognized that a considerable amount of bribery and purchasing of votes took place. A total of 613 *shirs* were held for the designation of electoral representatives. The sixty Somali seats in the Assembly were allocated to electoral districts on the basis of 14,302 votes per seat. There were seventy seats in all, ten of which were reserved for the ethnic minorities, Italian, Arabian, Indian, and Pakistani.

[3] A total of 614,909 votes were recorded as valid; the S.Y.L. polling 333,820 (54·3%) and the Ḥ.D.M. 159,967 (26%). These figures and the table are reproduced from *Le Prime Elezioni Politiche in Somalia*, A.F.I.S. Mogadishu, 1957. The texts of all legislation relating to the elections will be found in this book and a full account of the results without, however, any indication of the lineage affiliation of the candidates returned.

Allocation of seats to electoral colleges		Seats gained by parties			
		S.Y.L.	Ḥ.D.M.	S.D.P.	Marreḥaan Union
Bosaso	1	1			
Candala-Alula	1	1			
Sol	2	1		1	
Nogal-Darer	4	4			
Galkayu	3	3			
Duse Mareb	2	2			
Obbia*	1	1			
El Bur	3	2		1	
Belet Weyn*	3	3			
Bulo Burti*	5	5			
Baidoa	4	2	2		
Bur Hacaba	5		5		
Bardera	1	1			
Lugh Ferrandi	1				1
Oddur	3		3		
Dinsor*	1		1		
Mogadishu	1	1			
Afgoi-Dafet	2		1	1	
Merca	2	2			
Brava	2	1	1		
Villabruzzi-Balad	3	3			
Itala*	2	2			
Kismayu	2	2			
Margherita-Gelib	3	3			
Afmadu*	3	3			
TOTALS	60	43	13	3	1

* These are electoral districts in which only one list of candidates was presented and no elections were necessary.

Notwithstanding the League's apparent Daarood bias, however, when a Council of Ministers was set-up under the leadership of 'Abdillaahi 'Iise (Hawiye) as Prime Minister, the Hawiye held a majority, for of the five remaining Ministers two were Hawiye, two Daarood, and one Dir.[1] Before discussing the efforts

[1] For the allocation of portfolios, see Lewis, *Modern Political Movements in Somaliland*, 1958, p. 352.

of the Hawiye to consolidate their hold in the League in 1957 and 1958 while some Daarood wavered or withdrew their support, it is necessary to point out that even in 1956 the S.Y.L. did not have an absolute monopoly of the Daarood vote. Quite apart from the weaker and less popular Somali Democratic Party (with in 1956 a composition estimated at, Daarood fifty per cent; Hawiye forty per cent; and others ten per cent) which contested fifteen electoral districts, as widely distributed as those contested by the S.Y.L., but gained only three seats, the Marreḥaan Daarood of the Upper Juba region, based on Lugh Ferrandi, gave most of their support to their own clan party, the Marreḥaan Union and won their local seat.[1] This party was a small splinter group of the Daarood of that region with little appeal to members of the Marreḥaan clan in other areas. By 1958 it had disappeared. But its existence in 1956 serves to show that even then there were clear-cut clan movements as well as other national parties such as the Somali Democratic Party which prevented the S.Y.L. from having the support of all Daarood voters.

Since their assumption of power in 1956 both northern and southern Daarood adherents have from time to time shown a tendency to waver in their allegiance if not actually to withdraw from the League. At various times and on a variety of pretexts, the powerful Majeerteen clan of northern Somalia have sought to dissociate themselves from the party. One issue here has been objection to the remoteness of the capital, Mogadishu, some 500 miles to their south. But a more important cause for discontent among some Daarood adherents of the League has been the moderate policies of 'Abdillaahi 'Iise's government. For these policies have hitherto been directed less to the immediate fulfilment of the nationalist ideal of a 'Greater Somalia' than to the achievement of the economic and social security and prosperity of Somalia.[2] And while the government has pursued, so far without much success, another vital question, the clarification and settlement of the frontier with Ethiopia,[3] this has not silenced all Daarood dissatisfaction.

[1] The Marreḥaan Union member, however, consistently voted with the S.Y.L. in the 1956–58 sessions of the Assembly.

[2] The Prime Minister's statement of his government's programme made before the Somalia Assembly on the 26th September, 1956, is reported in full in the Italian Trusteeship Report to the United Nations for that year (*Rapport . .. Somalie. 1956*, published in 1957, pp. 119–32.

[3] The frontier with Ethiopia has never been defined, Following a convention of May, 1908, an Italo-Ethiopian Commission was appointed in 1910 to determine

Since 1958, Daarood dissenters in the S.Y.L., and others with similar views, have become open to the advances of a new party, the Greater Somalia League, with uncompromising nationalist aims and strongly pro-Egyptian tendencies. But before discussing this movement it is necessary to enlarge briefly on the character of pro-Egyptian sympathies in Somalia generally. In general, the external facet of the nationalist call to Somali to unite as Muslims is a feeling of comradeship with the Muslim world at large, and particularly with the United Arab Republic, as a symbol of Muslim unity and independence. The influence of the Egyptian Radio has been commented upon, and Somalia has a larger number of overt Egyptian propagandists than any other Somali territory. With Egypt there are strong contacts, especially in education since many Somali students go there to study, and a number of expatriate Egyptians teach in Somalia. In 1958 there were some eighty-five such teachers as compared with about forty-five in 1957. There is also an active Egyptian consular establishment in Mogadishu. The results of these and other Egyptian influences were seen in the 1956–7 Suez crisis when, at the time of the Anglo-French invasion of Egypt, a few Somali volunteered for service with their co-religionists. But despite such evidence of at least nominal Egyptian support Somali have at various times protested at Egyptian interference in the internal affairs of their country.[1]

This briefly is the climate of fluctuating pro-Egyptian sympathies to which the founder of the new Greater Somalia League returned after a stay of several years in Egypt. Ḥaaji Maḥammad Ḥusseen belongs to the Reer Ḥamar community of Mogadishu, a group of ancient Arab stock and one which standing outside Somali clanship has played an important part in party politics from their infancy.[2] Ḥaaji Maḥammad, a past President of the S.Y.L. had gone for study to Egypt[3], greatly enhancing his repu-

the principles of allocation of Somali clans and lineage-groups to Ethiopian and Italian jurisdiction. But the commission was only able to establish a boundary over a stretch of eighty kilometres between the wells of Rabodi and Dolo on the Juba River. Since coming under United Nations Trusteeship the question has on several occasions been brought before the General Assembly of the United Nations. A Resolution of December, 1955, urged that the Ethiopian and Italian Governments should continue negotiations to determine the frontier. But in 1957 despite repeated meetings the boundary still remained unsettled. In 1958 an Italo-Ethiopian arbitrating tribunal was established. In 1960 the dispute was still unresolved.

[1] See e.g. *Corriere della Somalia*, 4th January, 1957.

[2] See Appendix II.

[3] Ḥaaji Maḥammad had gone to Egypt in 1950 when the British Military Administration was replaced by the Italian Trusteeship Government. For the Reer Ḥamar people of Mogadishu, see Lewis, 1957, p. 12.

tation in Somalia, at least in some quarters, by his attacks over Radio Cairo against the Colonial Powers in the Somalilands, his violent criticism of 'Abdillaahi 'Iise's policies, and of the Trusteeship Administration. With this popularity he was re-elected to the presidency of the S.Y.L. in July 1957. But after his return to Somalia his continued attacks on the Somali Youth League government led to a contrary reaction. By a narrow majority in April 1958, he was expelled by the Central Committee from his position in the League, and faced with this defeat began immediately to form his own party, the Greater Somalia League, canvassing for support amongst the extremist elements of the S.Y.L. By the end of 1958 he seemed to have achieved a measure of success for in the October municipal elections his party won thirty-six seats although they polled only nine per cent. The S.Y.L. retained their lead with 416 seats polling thirty-seven per cent, and the Digil-Mirifle party if anything strengthened its position polling thirty-six per cent and winning 175 seats. The results for those parties which obtained seats are tabulated below.[1]

Party	Seats Gained
Somali Youth League	416
Digil-Mirifle Party	175
Greater Somalia League	36
Banaadir Youth Union	6
Liberal Party (incorporating the Somali Democratic Party)	27
Others	3
Total	663

The reaction of the S.Y.L. Government to the attempts made by the Greater Somalia League to force an open breach between their Daarood and Hawiye adherents was to intensify political campaigning and to seek new supporters amongst the Digil and Rahanwiin. Their success was shown in the elections for the re-

[1] In these elections women for the first time enjoyed the right to vote and seem to have taken full advantage of it. The age qualification for voters was lowered from the previous national elections to eighteen years of age. In eighteen out of forty-five constituencies the Somali Youth League was returned unopposed.

constituted Assembly in March 1959, when they swept the polls gaining eighty-three of the available ninety seats.[1] The Greater Somalia league did not participate fully; the party's leaders were in prison following rioting in Mogadishu on the 25th of February when the District Commissioner was stabbed and several others injured.[2] Ḥaaji Maḥammad Ḥusseen, the party's leader, had already spent a short time in prison in December of the previous year charged with incitement to rebellion. Of the remaining seven seats two were won by the Liberal Party and five by the members of the Digil-Mirifle Party to whose relations with the S.Y.L. we must now turn.

To understand the activities of the two parties it is necessary to go back to the cleavage in the traditional structure of Somali society between the Digil and Rahanwiin as 'Sab' on the one hand, and the other clan-families as 'Samaale' on the other. This division, it will be recalled, represents the cultural isolation of the Digil and Rahanwiin tribes as cultivating people of mixed Somali and partly negroid origin in a country dominated by the pastoralists who are traditionally a conquering aristocracy. Despite the fact that in 1956 Digil and Rahanwiin support contributed to some ten per cent of the strength of the S.Y.L. by far the bulk of Digil and Rahanwiin tribesmen are adherents of their own tribal party, the Independent Constitutional Party, known formerly by the more direct title Ḥizbiya Digil-Mirifle. This party was formed in 1947, during the British Military Administration of Somalia, largely to oppose the activities of the Somali Youth League (although a few Digil and Rahanwiin were involved in the formation of the League). In 1956 its strength was estimated to comprise Digil and Rahanwiin, ninety per cent;

[1] By a law No. 26 of 12th December, 1958, the membership of the Assembly was increased to ninety. The law introduced many innovations in electoral procedure. In contrast to the previous Assembly elections, the whole country was made into one electoral college, the ninety seats being distributed amongst thirty districts. In each electoral district seats were allocated to each list of candidates in proportion to the number of votes obtained following the method of the natural quotient and of the highest remainders. Each electoral list presented in an electoral district required to contain the names of a number of candidates not less than twice the number of seats allocated to the district and not more than three times that number. Suffrage was universal, all Somali citizens over eighteen years of age enjoying the right to vote by direct and secret ballot. The previous procedure of indirect voting through *shirs* in the rural areas outside municipalities was abolished.

[2] See *Report of the United Nations Advisory Council for the Trust Territory of Somaliland under Italian Administration* (1st April 1958 to 31st March 1959), document T 1444, 1959, pp. 24–31.

Reer Baraawa five per cent; and the other southern tribes five per cent.

As will be seen from the table on page 287, the party's interests are almost entirely confined to its own tribal districts in the arable regions between the Juba and Shebelle Rivers: Baidoa, Bur Hacaba, Oddur, Dinsor, etc., and to the coastal town of Brava where it is supported by many of the ancient city population, the Reer Baraawa.[1] Since the 1956 Assembly elections when it won thirteen seats, the party has generally opposed the S.Y.L. government, especially on matters of internal policy.

This projection of a traditional schism in the Somali nation has found many opportunities for expression. When the new S.Y.L. government announced its moderately progressive policy the Digil-Mirifle Party objected that it contained 'nothing new'. Equally, following the traditional hostility between the Sab and Samaale, the party has alleged discrimination against its tribesmen in appointments to the government service.[2] It continues to campaign strongly for the partition of Somalia and creation in the south of a separate Digil-Mirifle state. Moreover, when in reply to the Ethiopian Emperor's imperialist speech at Qabradare[3] the S.Y.L. Premier made it clear that his country had no wish to be subject to Ethiopian rule and further popular expressions of anti-Ethiopian feeling followed,[4] the Ḥ.D.M. displayed open friendship with Ethiopia. Their hostility to the S.Y.L. even led them to address petitions to the British Administration of the Northern Province of Kenya, seeking the transfer of the Digil and Rahanwiin area to British control. This of course is in direct contrast to the aims of the S.Y.L. nationalists to secure the amalgamation of the Northern Province of Kenya with Somalia. These

[1] On this ancient city population see Lewis, 1955, p. 42; 1957, p. 13.

[2] There are in fact far more Daarood and Hawiye in the public service than Rahanwiin. But this is not a new phenomenon. It is simply largely that more people of pastoral origin (Daarood and Hawiye) have sought employment in such branches of the public service as the police and district administration than Digil or Rahanwiin who have apparently generally found adequate employment in their traditional cultivating economy. In 1956 the proportions by ethnic group and clan-family in the public service were estimated at Daarood thirty-five per cent; Hawiye twenty-eight per cent; Digil and Rahanwiin fifteen per cent; Reer Baraawa five per cent; Reer Ḥamar five per cent; and others including Arabians, twelve per cent. These figures are to be compared with the proportions in the population—Daarood eighteen per cent; Hawiye thirty-eight per cent; Digil and Rahanwiin twenty-nine per cent (based on the 1953 population estimate).

[3] See above, p. 278.

[4] See e.g. the article in *Somalia d'Oggi*, (Mogadishu), Anno 2, No. 1, January, 1956, p. 4 ff.

are some of the more striking public demonstrations of the projection into party politics of the traditional cleavage between the Sab and Samaale. Not surprisingly, in social relations also, a degree of strain is evident between Sab and Samaale members of the Assembly, despite all protestations to the contrary and despite the nationalist ideal of the equality of all Somali irrespective of clan or tribal origin.

It would be entirely wrong, however, to regard the schism between the 'Sab' and 'Samaale' as an insuperable obstacle to co-operation between the two communities; it is merely one of the main lines of division in Somali society. Digil and Rahanwiin were among the founding members of the Somali Youth League and some support for the League has always come from the Sab. And as has been observed above, at the time of the elections for the Somalia Assembly in March 1959, when the S.Y.L. were faced with the threat of Daarood defections to the newly-formed Greater Somalia League, they naturally turned to look for support amongst the Digil and Rahanwiin. Several leaders of the Independent Constitutional Party joined the S.Y.L. bringing with them considerable Digil and Rahanwiin support; and five members of the new government formed by 'Abdillaahi 'Iise in June 1959 were Digil and Rahanwiin.

Before discussing the membership of the 1959 S.Y.L. government further, I turn to a cabinet crisis which occurred after the elections but before the formation of the new government. This concerned the proscription of the Greater Somalia League and Banaadir Youth Union following their part in the disorders which accompanied the March Assembly elections. Allegedly in response to Egyptian representations, the Minister of the Interior revoked the S.Y.L. cabinet decision to ban the two parties and ordered the reopening of their headquarters. This immediately led to a crisis in which the Minister resigned, his portfolio being temporarily taken over by the Prime Minister. A few days later, the other Daarood member of the cabinet tendered his resignation as a gesture of clan-family solidarity. His resignation was not, however, accepted and he remained in office. Nevertheless the cabinet had lost an influential Daarood member. The new cabinet formed in June 1959 contained five Daarood members, five Hawiye, and the five Digil and Rahanwiin already mentioned. This represented a considerable expansion of the government to a total of fifteen Ministers and Under-Secretaries. This even balance between the rival clan-families, however, did not appear to have recaptured much Daarood support and was indeed attacked as representing a return to 'tribal' interests.

V

This brief analysis of party politics in British Somaliland and Somalia is, I hope, sufficient to show how in a general way traditional political principles are carried forward into the new sphere.[1] It will be evident, particularly in Somalia where modern tendencies are most advanced, that in party politics a precarious balance is struck between conflicting traditional group interests. Thus the segmentary pastoral system where one group of lineages unites in opposition to another continues within the structure of party politics. It would be strange if this were not so, since although modern organs of government have been adopted and modern forms of political expression, the traditional structure of society has not radically altered.

The most significant development is the assumption of party-political solidarity by the clan-family. This extension of effective political allegiance is very clearly seen in Somalia where the competing interest-groups are clan-families rather than smaller units, and at a higher level of division, the 'Sab' opposed to the 'Samaale'. This at the same time implies a wider unity in the traditional political structure where today the smaller units are apparently losing something of their autonomy in favour of more extended loyalties. And this may be amongst the factors which are responsible for the decreased incidence of clan-fighting in Somalia at the present time.[2] Dangerous though it is to make predictions, it would seem likely that the projected union of the Protectorate with Somalia, if accomplished, would lead to a similar extension of loyalties in the Protectorate. And the placing of the two territories under a single government would increase the contacts between widely separated clans of the same clan-family, and alter the balance of lineage power in each country with concomitant effects in party politics.

[1] Dr A. Castagno has made a much fuller study of modern party politics in the Somalilands than I was able to undertake. When his results are published they should throw much light on the structure of contemporary party politics.

[2] An important contributary factor here is the zeal and energy displayed by Somali administrative officers. Despite the conflict which often exists between a Somali official's duty and his lineage affiliation, Somali at least are not subject to the same pressure of political criticism which their Italian predecessors experienced.

I have concentrated upon the divisions in Somali society because it is only through them that the Somali political structure can be understood as a dynamic system. It is equally only possible to understand the present party political structure in terms of the alignments and realignments of traditional interest groups.

To stress the importance of traditional political allegiances is, of course, not to say that all modern political behaviour is merely a matter of these interests alone. As has been indicated, in the towns, and especially in those of the south, economic, educational, and other developments have produced new political factors which in some situations are more or less independent of traditional interests. The leaders of the new élite are sometimes able to ignore their traditional political ties or to subordinate them to wider national interests. Equally they may deliberately exploit them to promote their own personal fortunes or those of their party. In Somaliland, as elsewhere, party politicians use every means at their command to achieve their objectives.

This of course is not to criticize the achievements of the nationalist leaders in their efforts to overcome and suppress their traditional divisions or their endeavours to subordinate lineage to national interests. Particularly when viewed in relation to the traditional social order, recent progress in both Somalia and the Protectorate is remarkable. And the government of Somalia has shown considerable resilience in maintaining its position despite its serious internal conflicts; and with a well-organized local administration and police force has dealt promptly and effectively with disorders such as those of February 1959. Today there is undoubtedly in both Somalia and British Somaliland a growing national awareness, despite the persistence of particularistic group interests. Other modernist trends are evident in a tendency amongst some Somali to discount their proud traditions of Arabian origin, to minimise their conflicts with Ethiopia, and above all to see themselves as Africans faced with similar problems to those of other nascent African nations. At the same time, moreover, party politics clearly provide some outlet for traditional lineage rivalry; and the endemic competition between and amongst lineages is increasingly deflected into a wider struggle not merely for legislative control, but also to secure the maximum possible share in new economic developments, in social services, in education, and in progress in general.

10

Conclusion

I

This analysis of the structure of northern Somali politics has been written primarily as a contribution to Somali Studies. But certain features of the Somali system differ so markedly from the general characteristics of segmentary lineage political systems that they merit further discussion. In these concluding pages, therefore, I summarise what seem to be the more important points of distinction between the principles of government in Somali society and in other segmentary lineage systems which have been described.

The concept of a political constitution based on a segmentary lineage system derives principally from Evans-Pritchard's analysis of the Nuer of the Sudan and has since been elaborated from studies of societies so organized in many different parts of the world. Recently the subject has been further advanced by discussion of the theoretical significance of lineage systems in a general classification of types of political structure.[1] Here a significant point of discussion has been the relationship between ties to lineage and to local community. Most writers have emphasised the importance of local patriotism—what Maine called

[1] In addition to the works of Evans-Pritchard and Fortes which have already been cited and their collation, *African Political Systems*, Oxford, 1940, the following are of particular relevance.

D. Forde, 'Fission and Accretion in the Patrilineal Clans of a Semi-Bantu Community in Southern Nigeria' *Journal of the Royal Anthropological Institute*, 68, 1938, pp. 311–38; P. Mayer, *The Lineage Principle in Gusii Society*, International African Institute memorandum XXIV, Oxford, 1949; M. Gluckman, in J. C. Mitchell and J. A. Barnes, *The Lamba Village*, Communications from the School of African Studies, No. 24, Cape Town, 1950; L. Bohannan, 'A Genealogical Charter', *Africa*, XXII, 1952, pp. 301–15; A. Southall, *Lineage Formation among the Luo*, I.A.I. Memorandum XXVI, Oxford, 1952, and *Alur Society*, Cambridge, 1956; M. Fortes, 'The structure of Unilineal Descent Groups', *American Anthropologist*, LV, 1953, pp. 17–41; J. A. Barnes, *Politics in a Changing Society*, O.U.P., London, 1954; M. G. Smith, 'On Segmentary lineage Systems,' *J.R.A.I.*, 86, 1956, pp. 39–81; I. Schapera, *Government and Politics in Tribal Societies*, London, 1956; R. Firth, 'A Note on Descent Groups in Polynesia', *Man*, 1957, pp. 4–8; M. Fried, 'The Classification of Corporate Unilineal Descent Groups', *J.R.A.I.* 87, 1957, pp. 1–31; E. E. Bacon, *Obock. A Study of Social Structure in Eurasia*, New York, 1958; and J. Middleton and D. Tait (eds.) *Tribes Without Rulers*, London, 1958.

'local contiguity' and found little evidence of in early society[1]—as a fundamental principle of political unity. This has been shown to play a dominant part in the organization of politics in all those lineage societies which have so far been described and even in societies whose climatic and ecological conditions impose a nomadic, or near nomadic, pattern of life.[2] It is true for example, for the semi-nomadic Beduin of Cyrenaica[3] as much for the transhumant Nuer of the Sudan; but the extent to which permanent attachments and rights to land as pasturage are involved in the political relations of the more truly nomadic Arab peoples of other areas is still not very clear.[4]

While local contiguity thus plays a dominant part in the political constitution of most lineage societies it seems likely that some at least of those pastoral peoples who range as widely in their grazing movements as the northern Somali must share the lack of strict ties to locality which we have stressed in earlier chapters. For it is this feature which, springing from the particular adjustment of the northern Somali nomads to their environment, first distinguishes their segmentary political system from that of more sedentary peoples. While often at the level of the clan there is some correspondence between land and lineage, at other levels of segmentation local contiguity plays a small part in Somali political allegiance. Their patriotism is the patriotism of clanship and contract and generally devoid of fixed territorial associations. Only amongst those of nomadic origins who in the north-west of Somaliland have adopted agriculture fairly recently are lineages more widely localized. It is for these reasons that in this account I have eschewed the term 'tribe', taking it to denote a group defined primarily by local contiguity.

II

If in general the northern Somali pastoralists have transitory and

[1] *Ancient Law*, World's Classics edition, 1954, p. 109. Maine, of course, stressed the importance of kinship in blood rather than of local contiguity in primitive society, a view which is critically examined in Schapera, 1956.

[2] See e.g. Middleton and Tait, op. cit., p. 5; *African Political Systems*, p. 10; and Schapera, op. cit.

[3] See e.g. E. E. Evans-Pritchard, *The Sanusi of Cyrenaica*, Oxford, 1949, pp. 55–7.

[4] For two recent works which bring together some of the literature on the Arab nomads from an anthropological point of view see Bacon, op. cit., and L. Cabot Briggs, *The Living Races of the Sahara Desert*, Massachusetts, 1958.

shifting land relations, their lineage structure, however diversified, remains constant and is a general principle of political association. Except in contract (*ḥeer*) there is no other single channel along which political relations are organized. This gives clanship as an organizing principle of political association a primacy which it does not appear to possess in other segmentary lineage societies where there are stable territorial units. Since, moreover, except among the north-western cultivators, lineages do not possess fixed land rights and have no ritual or religious attachment to locality, political ascendancy is not defined in these terms.[1] In northern Somaliland the chief criterion of political status is strength; and one lineage is dominant in relation to others mainly from its numerical superiority and fighting potential.

With the weight Somali attach to force as the ultimate arbiter in their political relations, lineages which from the genealogical position of their founding ancestors are formally equivalent, are only in fact equivalent when they possess parity of strength. The political evaluation of relative strength which I have referred to as the 'size factor' may thus alter the genealogically defined pattern of relations between groups. But the defining criterion of a conventional lineage system is that political relations are cast in a genealogical idiom and that genealogies represent the actual balance of power between groups. Thus as Middleton and Tait state '. . . co-ordinate segments which have come into existence as a result of segmentation are regarded as complementary and as formally equal, even if in actuality they are not so in population, wealth or in other ways.'[2] This means that where force is the fundamental means of regulating disputes, groups whose genealogical positions do not correspond to their actual political positions have to seek alliance with others. And since genealogies should thus provide an exact representation of the existing political order they may have to be manipulated. This process of genealogical adjustment seems to be general in segmentary lineage societies of this type.[3]

[1] Contrast the basis of dominance among the Nuer, *The Nuer*, pp. 211–3.

[2] Middleton and Tait, op. cit. p. 7.

[3] See e.g. L. Bohannan, op. cit. p. 309; G. Mayer, op. cit., p. 33: Southall op. cit. p. 32, however, shows that the Luo often gloss over discrepancies between the strict genealogical positions of groups and their actual power without necessarily adjusting their genealogies. Here divergencies from the genealogical paradigm are seen as the difference between ideal and practice.

Somali, however, do not see the problem in this light for clanship is not the sole idiom in which their political relations are cast. Agnation alone does not determine the limits of political and jural responsibility. It is here, particularly, that contract enters as a principle defining the extent of the political community at any point in time. And it is contract, working generally, but not always, within the framework of agnation and with or without the added justification of uterine connexion, which regularizes genealogical discrepancies. Thus where genealogies do not conform to the actual balance of power between the groups which they represent the northern Somali pastoralists rely on contract; and genealogical fictions are generally rare.

Contract, I have argued, is by extension the basis of customary practice in general, and Somali political and legal relationships represent a marriage of lineage status and contract. It would thus not be true to say of the Somali, as Professor Gluckman has said of the Lozi,[1] that their law is exclusively the law of status; for in any given situation contract determines the range within which genealogically founded relationships are regarded as legally and politically binding. Equally, the political and jural status of individuals, defined at birth by their membership of determinate lineages, may be altered by contracts of their own making. In this sense Somali contract might be regarded as a form of the Social Contract of the political philosophers.[2] And although it is perhaps misleading to consider these features of Somali society in the light of Maine's famous formula for the 'movement of the progressive societies'[3] from Status to Contract since his use of contract was so much wider and his context of discussion primarily ancient Greece and Rome, it is perhaps worth noting that there is no evidence to suggest that Somali *ḥeer* is in a

[1] M. Gluckman, *The Judicial Process among the Barotse of Northern Rhodesia*, Manchester University Press, 1955, p. 28.

[2] For a conveniently accessible discussion of contractual theories, see J. W. Gough, *The Social Contract*, Oxford, 1957.

[3] Maine's view of the slight importance of contract in early society was of course not shared by French sociologists of the school of Durkheim. Mauss and Davy, for example, constantly argued for the presence of contracts, covenants, and conventions, especially those of a religious character, and in terms of them sought to explain the development of institutions such as gift exchange. See e.g. G. Davy, *La Foi Jurée*, Paris, 1922; M. Mauss, *Sociologie et Anthropologie*, Paris, 1950. Georges Davy regarded status and contract as originally inextricably intertwined. What Maine viewed as an evolution—or revolution—from one extreme to the other, Davy saw as a gradual process of segregation—not as the complete replacement of one by the other.

historical sense a development away from lineage status. Indeed in their rebellion against the constraining forces of tradition and movement towards an increased degree of individual responsibility it is above all contract (*ḥeer*) which modern Somali politicians most bitterly attack.

But the most important aspect of contract is the manner in which it supplements clanship, and also controls and modifies it, concentrating the diffuse ties of agnates at a particular level of segmentation in a given situation. Compared to other segmentary lineage societies where ties to locality supply one of the main strands in the web of government, it seems that in the Somali system where local contiguity is weak contract replaces it as a political principle of fundamental importance. It would be rash to make predictions; but it would seem reasonable to seek parallels in other, at present little known, nomadic societies with a segmentary lineage structure, with a similar system of shifting land relationships, and with an equally strong military bias.[1]

III

A further characteristic of significance is the wide range through which clanship (supplemented by contract) is effective in mobilizing large political communities, however transitory their unity. Descent in Somaliland is traced through a greater number of generations and over a wider span than is usual in other segmentary lineage societies where the largest effective political units are usually smaller.[2] At the same time, the number of points of possible unity and division is multiplied; for the four main points of segmentation which we have distinguished represent merely the principal axes about which corporate relations re-

[1] The closest analogy which I have so far discovered are the contractually defined *'asaba* blood-compensation paying groups among the nomads of the Spanish Sahara. See Julio Caro Baroja, *Estudios Saharianos*, Madrid, 1955, pp. 17–22.

[2] Thus the average maximal political units of the Nuer, Dinka, Lugbara, Konkomba and Amba for instance, are all considerably smaller than the average northern Somali clan. See Middleton and Tait, op. cit. At the same time in these and other segmentary lineage societies which have been described the maximal genealogical span is smaller. The longest genealogy among the Tiv, Lugbara, Amba, Konkomba, Dinka, and Mandari is reported to contain few more than a dozen generations; and Professor Gluckman (in the preface to W. Watson *Tribal Cohesion in a Money Economy*, Manchester Univ. Press, 1958) points out that this is also the average for the Nuer, Beduin of Cyrenaica, Tallensi, Ashanti, Barotse, Zulu and for the Polynesian Tikopia.

volve. This multiplicity of segmentation and the fact that at every level of fragmentation within the clan-family lineages may act as segmentary corporations[1] appears to be in keeping with the minimal development of distinct political offices. For it is difficult to see how such a diffuse and mobile pattern of groupings could be combined with a rigid political and administrative organisation embodying stable offices of government.

Apart from the specialized but not strongly developed office of clan Sultan, an office which is in any case not indispensable to clan unity, all adult men are elders and, with the exception traditionally of dependent *sab* bondsmen, all have an equal voice in the informal councils which control group relations. Thus at different levels of grouping the elders concerned are empowered by contractual treaty to control and direct the policies of their kinsmen. This means little more than that within any political community affairs are controlled by the will of the majority. Their contracts detail common responsibilities and norms of conduct and lay down penalties and damages sanctioning them. But as a means of enforcing contractually defined obligations, coercion is most characteristically regarded, and in practice is applied mainly in relation to hostilities.

Somali constantly stress the constraining force of their lineage and contractual duties, but men normally enjoy a high degree of freedom in their personal activities. In the sphere of social relations the threat of attack is the principal check to the individual in his quest for water and pasture for his livestock. And it is largely in the necessity to be able to meet force with force that Somali see the primary purpose of their contractual and kin alliances. Co-operation however, is not of course only limited to time of war. Agnates, especially those who are contractually bound, assist each other in the arduous task of watering camels from deep wells, and help each other in time of scarcity and want, and in many other ways which are not essentially political nor directly related to the threat of aggression. But, nevertheless, it is his unity with his kinsmen against aggression, and his collective responsibility with them in feud and war, which dominates the way in which the pastoralist values the support of his kin. Given that vast reaches of northern Somaliland are extremely difficult to police effectively, that competition in their arid environment

[1] For an interesting discussion of the corporate character of lineages as 'Corporations Aggregate' in Maine's terminology, see Smith, loc. cit. pp. 60–70.

is acute and strife perpetual, and that rights are ultimately upheld effectively only by force, it is as an agency of collective security that the Somali system of corporate solidarity operates.

IV

If this functional reasoning is accepted it can readily be seen how towns modify the traditional pattern of northern Somali pastoralism. Towns are traditionally the centres of the pastoral system and the majority of clansmen who live in them maintain effective economic and political ties with their kinsmen in the pastures. But at the same time, towns are more readily susceptible to the rule of law under modern administration than the interior; and this, with the development of at least rudimentary social services, betokens a diminished need for the support of kinsmen. Moreover in them new economic activities are developing, however slowly, and new lines of association between individuals. And these factors, with the reaction to modern influences in education, the example of Arab and African nationalism elsewhere, and the more developed urban practice of Islam, have stimulated movements which aim at the abolition of the kin and contractual cleavages which traditionally divide society.

Yet because of the persistence of the traditional economic and political structure, the new and essentially urban political and nationalist movements conform in large measure to the segmentary bias of society. The main channels of connexion between individuals remain those of the pastoral system and people's interests and aspirations largely continue to follow these traditional lines. Thus modern party political forms have been most successfully adopted, but they have, of necessity, been accommodated to the indigenous pastoral pattern. Moreover, the introduction of party politics and of representative government has, if anything, widened the sphere of action of traditional political principles. Nationalism itself has provided a new stage on which, in the same rôles but new costumes, traditional segmentary lineage interests are played out.

APPENDIX

SOME FACTORS CONNECTED WITH THE FORMATION OF THE SOMALI YOUTH LEAGUE

In Somalia the earliest attempts to form a society explicitly concerned to further Somali interests and to seek fuller participation in government appear to date back to the period between 1937 and 1940. At this time, the initiators were a handful of individuals mainly of the Rahanwiin and Digil tribes with one man of tne Hawiye. All were employees of the Italian Government.

When British forces occupied Somalia in February, 1941, and a British Military Administration was set up, it was at once faced with the problem of revivifying the economy and social life of the country. For with the severance of relations with Italy, the various para-statal organizations which had monopolized trade and commerce under the fascist regime largely collapsed. The new government encouraged local business and trade, no longer protecting monoplistic practices. And individuals whether Arab, Italian, or Somali, who had capital began to engage actively in commerce on their own account.

Moreover, by removing the restrictions of the old regime on social and political activities, encouragement was given to the formation of associations and societies among the 9,000 strong Italian community in Mogadishu as well as among the population at large. In the period 1941–43 various Italian societies formed, covering all shades of political opinion. Somali sometimes attended their meetings and occasionally joined those of the Italian Communist Club where the principle of the equality of all races was stressed and also the advances in economic and social progress reported to be being achieved under the communist regime in the Soviet Union.

At the same time, and particularly after the battle of El-Alamein, the British Political Officer in Mogadishu held weekly meetings for Somali. At these he spoke on international affairs ,outlining the progress of the war and emphasizing the successes of the Allies at the expense of the Axis Powers. In keeping with the climate of feeling at the time, he explained how the British, Russian, and American Allies were liberating the world from Nazi tyranny, and how, once the war was won, all races and peoples would enjoy freedom. Such statements with those of the communists helped to quicken Somali nationalist aspirations. They reinforced the aspirations of progressive Somali and helped to develop the intense consciousness of cultural identity and exclusiveness which is characteristic of Somali and which to some extent found expression through Islam in the rebellion led by Sheikh Maḥammad 'Abdille Ḥassan in the period 1900–1920. Amongst those who were influenced by these stimuli and who played a crucial part in what was later to become the Somali Youth League was Yaasiin Ḥaaji 'Ismaan Shirmarke of the Daarood Majeerteen. Others who were also attracted were certain leaders of the Somali Dervish Orders, opposed in principle to the dividing bonds of clanship and inspired by ideals for the unity of all Somali as Muslims.

The British Military Administration naturally favoured aspirations which were opposed to the traditional dividing forces in Somali society and which were on the side of progress. With the assistance of the British Political Officer at Mogadishu, the new trends were marshalled together and moved towards the formation of a youth club. The Somali Youth Club, as the society which resulted was then called, was formally constituted on the 15th May, 1943, a date which turned out to be of wider significance since it marked the final defeat of German and Italian forces in Africa.

At its foundation in 1943, the Club had thirteen founding members. Four were Daarood (the most important being Yaasiin Ḥaaji 'Ismaan, who died shortly after); three were Rahanwiin and Digil; three Reer Ḥamar; and one Isaaq. Thus while people of the Rahanwiin and Digil cultivating tribes and of the ancient city population of Mogadishu (the Reer Ḥamar) played an important part, the nomadic clans (chiefly the Daarood) were also strongly represented. At the time the club did not have a clearly defined nationalistic programme, although the desire to triumph over traditional schisms and to move towards self-government was strong. Nor did the movement arouse widespread interest in Somalia generally. In the years immediately following, however, as concern over the future status of Somalia grew, the club began to spread its wings and to marshal wider support. By 1948 when the Four Power Commission visited the territory to discover Somali wishes for their future, the club had changed its title to the Somali Youth League and was well organized as a political group. In the early days of the club its members had sometimes encountered the hostility of the police, who were largely Somali of the Daarood clan-family, through their refusal to declare their lineage membership when questioned. But towards the close of the British Military Administration, the party, as it then was, had gained a firm following amongst the police which contributed much to its expansion in the country at large.

In 1959, the Central Committee of the League had the following composition: twelve Hawiye; four Daarood; one Rahanwiin; and two Reer Ḥamar.

BIBLIOGRAPHY[1]

SHEIKH AḤMAD BIN ḤUSSEEN BIN MAḤAMMAD 1945 — *Manaaqib as-Sheikh Ismaa'iil bin Ibraahiim al-Jabarti*, Muṣṭafa al-Baabii al-Ḥalabii Press, Cairo.

'ALI SHEIKH MAḤAMMAD 1954 — 'The origin of the Isaaq peoples' *The Somaliland Journal*, vol. i, no. 1, pp. 22–6, Hargeisa (British Somaliland).

AMMINISTRAZIONE FIDUCIARIA ITALIANA DELLA SOMALIA 1958 — *Economic Requirements of the Territory of Somalia on the expiration of the Trusteeship Mandate*, Rome.

AMMINISTRAZIONE FIDUCIARIA ITALIANA DELLA SOMALIA 1957 — *Le Prime Elezioni Politiche in Somalia*, Mogadishu.

AMMINISTRAZIONE FIDUCIARIA ITALIANA DELLA SOMALIA 1957 — *Rapport du Gouvernement Italien à l' Assemblée générale des Nations Unies sur l'administration de tutelle de la Somalie, 1956*. Rome.

AMMINISTRAZIONE FIDUCIARIA ITALIANA DELLA SOMALIA 1958 — *Rapport du Gouvernement Italien à l' Assemblée générale des Nations Unies sur l'administration de tutelle de la Somalie, 1957*. Rome.

Il Corriere della Somalia (journal) Mogadishu.

ANDERSON, J. W. D. 1954 — *Islamic Law in Africa*, London.

ANDRZEJEWSKI, B. W. AND GALAAL, M. H. I. 1956 — *Ḥikmad Soomaali*, Oxford.

SHARIIF 'AYDARUUS SHARIIF 'ALI 1955 — *Bughyat al-amaal fii taariikh as-Soomaal*, Mogadishu.

BARILE, P. 1935 — *Colonizzazione fascista nella Somalia meridionale*, Rome.

BELL, C. R. V. 1953 — *The Somali Language*, London.

BURTON, R. F. 1894 — *First Footsteps in Eastern Africa*, Memorial Edition, two vols. London.

[1] For a fuller bibliography of works on the Somali published prior to 1955 see Lewis, 1955, pp. 177–89. The titles of other works referred to in the text, but not dealing directly with the Somali, are cited fully where they occur and are not included here.

CAHIERS DE L'AFRIQUE ET L'ASIE, V. 1959 — *Mer Rouge, Afrique Orientale*, Paris.

CAROSELLI, F. S. 1931 — *Ferro e Fuoco in Somalia*, Rome.

CASTAGNO, A. A. 1959 — 'Somalia' *International Conciliation*, No. 522, New York.

CERULLI, E. 1919 — 'Il diritto consuetudinario della Somalia Italiana settentrionale', *Bolletino della Società Africana d'Italia*, Anno xxxviii, Naples.

CERULLI, E. 1923 — 'Note sul movimento Musulmano nella Somalia' *Rivista degli Studi Orientali*, 10, pp. 1–36, Rome.

CERULLI, E. 1929 — 'La Somalia nelle cronache etiopiche', *Africa Italiana*, II, pp. 262–5, Rome.

CERULLI, E. 1931 — 'Tradizioni storiche e monumenti della Migiurtinia', *Africa Italiana*, IV, pp. 153–169.

CERULLI, E. 1936 — *Studi Etiopici I. La lingua e la storia di Harar*, Rome.

CERULLI, E. 1957 — *Somalia, Scritti vari editi ed inediti I*, Rome.

CERULLI, E. 1936 — 'Maḳdis͟hū' *Encyclopaedia of Islam*, vol. iii, pp. 165–6, Leiden.

CERULLI, E. 1936 — 'Muḥammad B. 'Abd Allāh Ḥassān Al-Mahdī'; *Encyclopaedia of Islam*, vol. iii, pp. 667–8, Leiden.

CIAMARRA, G. 1911 — 'La struttura giuridica della Somalia' in *Relazione sulla Somalia Italiana, Camera dei Deputati*, doc. xxxviii, Rome.

COLUCCI, M. 1924 — *Principi di diritto consuetudinario della Somalia Italiana meridionale*, Florence.

CRUTTENDEN, C. J. 1849 — 'Memoir of the Western or Idoor tribes inhabiting the Somali coast of North-East Africa', *Journal of the Royal Geographical Society*, xix, pp. 49–76.

CURLE, A. T. 1937 — 'The ruined towns of Somaliland', *Antiquity*, vol. xi, pp. 315–327.

DESCHAMPS, H. 1948 — *L'Union française, Côte des Somalis. Réunion, Inde*, Paris.

DRAKE-BROCKMAN, R. E. 1912 — *British Somaliland*, London.

DRYSDALE, J. G. S. 1955 'Some Aspects of Somali rural society today' *The Somaliland Journal*, vol. 1, no. 2, Hargeisa (British Somaliland).

FERRANDI, U. 1903 *Lugh. Emporio commerciale sul Giuba*, Rome.

GILLILAND, H. B. 1952 'The vegetation of eastern British Somaliland', *Journal of Ecology*, vol. 40, No. 1, pp. 91–124.

GOLDSMITH, K. L. G. and LEWIS, I. M. 1958 'A Preliminary Investigation of the Blood Groups of the 'Sab' Bondsmen of Northern Somaliland', *Man*, vol. lviii, pp. 188–190.

GROTTANELLI, V. L. 1955 *Pescatori dell' Oceano Indiano*, Rome.

GUIDI, I. 1889 'Le canzioni ge'ez-amarina in onore di Re Abissino', *Rendiconti del Reale Accademia dei Lincei*, V, Rome.

GUILLAIN, C. 1856 *Documents sur l'histoire, la géographie et le commerce de l'Afrique Orientale*, 3 vols, Paris.

HAMILTON, A. 1911 *Somaliland*, London.

HUNT, J. A. 1951 *A General Survey of the Somaliland Protectorate, 1944–1950*, London.

HUNTINGFORD, G. W. B. 1955 *The Galla of Ethiopia, the Kingdoms of Kaffa and Janjero. Ethnographic Survey of Africa. North Eastern Africa, Part II*; London.

SHEIKH ḤUSSEEN BIN AḤMAD DARWIISH 1955 *Amjaad*, Aden.

JARDINE, D. 1923 *The Mad Mullah of Somaliland*, London.

KARP, M. 1960 *The Economics of Trusteeship in Somalia*, Boston.

KIRK, J. W. C. 1905 *A Grammar of the Somali Language*, Cambridge.

LAURENCE, M. 1954 *A Tree for Poverty: Somali Poetry and Prose*, Nairobi.

LEIRIS, M. 1934a 'Le culte des Zars à Gondar', *Aethiopia*, iv, pp. 96–136.

LEIRIS, M. 1934b *L'Afrique Fantôme*, Paris.

LEIRIS, M. 1958 *La Possession et ses aspects théâtraux chez les Éthiopiens de Gondar*, Paris.

LEWIS, I. M. 1955 — *Peoples of the Horn of Africa. Somali, Afar, and Saho. Ethnographic Survey of Africa. North Eastern Africa, Part I*, London.

LEWIS, I. M. 1955/6 — 'Sufism in Somaliland: A Study in Tribal Islam', *Bulletin of the School of Oriental and African Studies*, xvii/3, pp. 581–602; xviii/1, pp. 146–160.

LEWIS, I. M. 1957 — *The Somali Lineage System and the Total Genealogy* (cyclostyled), Hargeisa (British Somaliland).

LEWIS, I. M. 1958a — 'The Gadabuursi Somali Script', *Bulletin of the School of Oriental and African Studies*, xxi/1, pp. 134–156.

LEWIS, I. M. 1958b — 'Modern Political Movements in Somaliland', *Africa*, xxviii, No. 3, pp. 244–61; No. 4. pp. 344–64. Reprinted as *Modern Political Movements in Somaliland*, International African Institute Memorandum XXX, Oxford.

LEWIS, I. M. 1959a — 'Clanship and Contract in Northern *Africa*, xxix, pp. 274-293.

LEWIS, I. M. 1959b — 'The names of God in Northern Somali', *Bulletin of the School of Oriental and African Studies*, xxii/1, pp. 134–40.

LEWIS, I. M. 1959c — 'The Galla in Northern Somaliland', *Rassegna di Studi Etiopici*, xv, pp. 21–38.

LEWIS, I. M. 1960 — 'Problems in the Development of Modern Leadership and Loyalties in the British Somaliland Protectorate and U.N. Trusteeship Territory of Somalia', *Civilizations*, x, pp. 49–62.

LEWIS, I. M. 1960 — 'The Somali Conquest of the Horn of Africa', *Journal of African History*, No. 2, pp. 213-30.

LEWIS, I. M. 1961a — 'Force and Fission in Northern Somali Lineage Structure' *American Anthropologist*, vol. 63, pp. 94-112.

LEWIS, I. M. 1961b — *Marriage and the Family in Northern Somaliland.*

MAINO, C. 1959 — *La Somalia e L'opera del Duca Degli Abruzzi*, Rome.

MAINO, M. 1953 — *La Lingua Somala, Strumento d'insegnamento professionale*, Allessandria.

MARES, R. C. 1954 — 'Animal husbandry, animal industry, and animal disease in the Somaliland Protectorate—Parts I and II'. *The British Veterinary Journal*, vol. 110, Nos. x and xi.

MATHEW, G. 1953 — 'Recent Discoveries in East African Archaeology', *Antiquity* no. 108, pp. 212–18.

MELLANA, V. 1957 — *Diritto Processuale Islamico Somalo.* Mogadishu.

MORENO, M. M. 1955 — *Il Somalo della Somalia*, Rome.

MORGANTINI, A. M. 1954 — 'Quelques résultats préliminaires de l'enquête sur la population de la Somalie menée en 1953'. *Proceedings of the World Population Conference, 1954*, volume vi, New York.

PANKHURST, E. S. 1951 — *Ex-Italian Somaliland*, London.

PIRONE, M. 1954 — 'Leggende e tradizioni storiche dei Somali Ogaden', *Archivio per L'Antropologia e la Etnologia*, vol. lxxxiv, pp. 119–128.

PIRONE, M. 1954 — 'Le popolazioni dell 'Ogaden', *Archivio per L'Antropologia e la Etnologia*, vol. lxxxiv, pp. 129–143.

PUCCIONI, N. 1937 — *Le popolazioni indigene della Somalia Italiana*, Bologna.

ROBECCHI-BRICCHETTI, L. 1889 — *Somalia e Benadir*, Milan.

SERGI, G. 1897 — *Africa: Antropologia della Stirpa Camitica*, Turin.

SHIHAAB AD-DIIN, ed. and trs. Basset R. 1897–1909 — *Futuuḥ al-Ḥabasha*, Paris.

SOMALILAND GOVERNMENT — *War Somali Sidihi* (now *The Somaliland News*), published weekly, Hargeisa.

SOMALILAND GOVERNMENT 1956 — *Colonial Reports: Somaliland Protectorate, 1954–55*, London.

SOMALILAND GOVERNMENT 1958 — *Report of the Commission of Enquiry into Unofficial Representation on the Legislative Council*, Hargeisa (British Somaliland).

[1] Since March 1961, the *Somali News* published weekly in Mogadishu.

STAFFORD, F. E. 1949 — 'The ex-Italian Colonies', *International Affairs*, xxv, pp. 47–55.

TRIMINGHAM, J. S. 1952 — *Islam in Ethiopia*, Oxford.

WRIGHT, A. C. A. 1943 — 'The interaction of various systems of law and custom in British Somaliland and their relation with social life', *Journal of the East African Natural History Society*, 17, 1–2, pp. 66–102.

ZOLI, C. (ed) 1927 — *Notizie sul territorio di riva destra del Giuba. Oltre-Giuba*, Rome.

REFERENCES PUBLISHED SINCE 1961

ADAM, H. M. AND GESHEKTER, C. 1980 — *The Revolutionary Development of the Somali Language.*

ANDRZEJEWSKI, B. W. 1975 — "The Rise of Written Somali Literature," *African Research and Documentation*, pp. 7–14.

1977 — "Five Years of Written Somali: A Report on Progress and Projects," *Bulletin of African Studies: Notes and News* (supplement to *Africa*).

1978 — "The Modernisation of the Somali Language," *Horn of Africa*, pp. 39–45.

ARONSON, D. R. 1980 — "Kinsmen and Comrades: Towards a Class Analysis of the Somali Pastoral Sector," *Nomadic Peoples.*

ASAD, T. (ed.) 1973 — *Anthropology and the Colonial Encounter.*

BLACKBURN, R. (ed.) 1972 — *Ideology in Social Science: Readings in Critical Social Theory.*

DAHL, G. AND HJORT, A. 1976 — *Having Herds.*

FARAH, NURUDDIN

1970 — *From a Crooked Rib.*

1976 — *A Naked Needle.*

1979 — *Sweet and Sour Milk.*

GALAL, MUUSE — *Hikmad Soommaan* (Somali Wisdom).

GLUCKMAN, M. 1950 — "Kinship and Marriage Among the Lozi of N. Rhodesia and the Zulu of Natal," A. R. Radcliffe-Browne and D. Forde (eds.), *African Systems of Kinship and Marriage.*

GOODY, J. 1978 *The Domestication of the Savage Mind.*

HERSI, A. A. In press *The Arab Factor in Somali History.*

JOHNSON, J. W. 1974 *Heellooy Heelleellooy: The Development of the Genre Heello in Modern Somali Poetry.*

KUPER, A. 1973 *Anthropologists and Anthropology: The British School, 1912–1972.*

LAITIN, D. 1977 *Politics, Language and Thought: The Somali Experience.*

LEWIS, I. M. 1962 *Marriage and the Family in Northern Somaliland* (East African Studies No. 15).

1962 "Lineage Continuity and Modern Commerce in N. Somaliland," in Bohannan and Dalton, *Markets in Africa.*

1964 "Recent Progress in Somali Studies," *Journal of Semitic Studies,* 9, pp. 122–134.

1965 "Problems in the Comparative Study of Unilineal Descent," in Banton (ed.), *The Relevance of Models for Social Anthropology.*

1968 "From Nomadism to Cultivation: The Expansion of Political Solidarity in Southern Somalia" in Douglas and Kaberry (eds.), *Man in Africa.*

1968 Introduction, *History and Social Anthropology,* pp. ix–xxviii.

1969 *Peoples of the Horn of Africa.*

1971 *Ecstatic Religion.*

1973 *The Anthropologist's Muse.*

1958 reprinted 1973 in "Modern Political Movements in Somaliland," *Africa,* pp. 244–261; 344–364; C. Turnbull, *Africa and Change.*

1977 "Confessions of a "Government" Anthropologist," in *Anthropological Forum,* vol. iv., pp. 226–238.

1979 "The Cushitic-Speaking Peoples: A Jigsaw Puzzle for Social Anthropologists," *L'Uomo.*

1980 "Conformity and Contrast in Somali Islam," in *Islam in Tropical Africa.*

1980 *A Modern History of Somalia: Nation and State in the Horn of Africa.*

LOIZOS, P. (ed.)
1977 "Anthropological Research in British Colonies," *Anthropological Forum,* vol. iv, no. 2.

LULING, V.
In press *A Southern Somali Sultanate: The Geledi.*

MAHAMMAD, SAYYID
1974 *Diiwaanka Gabayada Sayid Maxamad Abdulle Xassan* (a collection of the poetry of Sayyid Mahammad). Mogadishu.

MIRREH, ABDI GAILEH
1978 *Die sozialökonomischen Verhältnisse der nomadischen Bevölkerung im Norden der Demokratischen Republik Somalia.*

MOHAMAD, O. O.
1975 *From Written Somali to a Rural Development Campaign.* Mogadishu.

MONOD, T.
1975 *Pastoralism in Tropical Africa.*
1979 *Pastoral Production and Society.*

PETERS, E. L.
1980 "Aspects of Bedouin Bridewealth Among Camel Herders in Cyrenaica," in J. Comaroff, *The Meaning of Marriage Payments.*

SAHLINS, M.
1961 "The Segmentary Lineage: An Organisation of Predatory Expansion," *American Anthropologist,* 63, 322–345.

SALAD, M. K.
1977 *Somalia: A Bibliographical Survey.*

SAMATAR, S. S.
In press *Poetry in Somali Politics: The Case of Sayyid Mahammad 'Abdille Hassan.*

SWIFT, J.
1979 "The Development of Livestock Trading in Nomad Pastoral Economy: The Somali Case," in *Pastoral Production and Society.*

SHEIKH JAAMA UMAR ISE
1976 *Taariikhdii Daraawiishta (History of the Dervishes).* Mogadishu.

INDEX

AFTERWORD

Some reflections on a long engagement in Somali anthropology*

I

This account is frankly autobiographical and often anecdotal. I hope, however, that it will not sound too egotistical or boastful. I hope, also, that while it is primarily a record, as I see it, of a particular anthropologist's involvement in a particular fieldwork situation, it may have wider resonance and so contribute to debate on the moral entanglements of anthropologists and those they study. The work discussed involves both 'theoretical' and 'applied' anthropology, informed in both cases by a spirit of engagement, which I argue is fully compatible with our normal standards of professional objectivity. A further aim, here, is to demonstrate how applied anthropology – for too long treated by self-styled 'theorists' as a disreputable pariah – can itself be applied to elucidate theoretical problems – particularly within an ongoing programme of academic research.

Let me first outline my 'philosophical' position on the scope and role of social anthropology. As I have recorded elsewhere (Lewis, 1973; 1976, pp. 34–35; 1986, p. 8; 1995, pp. 99ff.), I take social anthropology, the study of 'Others', to be an inherently exploitative profession, based as it is (in ethnography) on plagiarising (and analysing) someone else's culture. The anthropologist here seeks, to a certain extent, to become an expert on this alien culture, expert enough, anyhow, to make a career out of it. It is difficult to think of a serious anthropologist without some ethnographic 'property' (perhaps Lévi-Strauss is an exception, although not in his own eyes). This situation is not dissimilar from that in archaeology where, as is well-known,

* An earlier version of this essay was presented at the conference on 'Somalia Reassessed', held at Uppsala University in April 1995 and organised by Bernhard Helander. I am grateful to the participants for helpful comments and also to my friend and senior colleague, Isaac Schapera, who kindly read the revised text with his usual care, suggesting a number of valuable improvements.

there is professional rivalry over 'concessions' to excavate particular sites.

If ethnography, based on first-hand field work, as I assume, constitutes the heart of the social anthropological enterprise, it can, I believe, be viewed as a kind of 'thick journalism', based on intensive description, with the anthropologist cast in the role of scribe. This implies a responsibility which, to be discharged professionally, requires accurate reporting. I personally see no point in 'anthropological' accounts of other societies that fail to produce portraits recognisable to those portrayed as well as to professional colleagues. I thus have little interest in post-modernist accounts, however delicately confectioned, which interpose a swirling veil of interpretative mist between the anthropologist and those he writes about. This is a form of obfuscation which, however appealing to its practitioners, has disappointingly little to contribute to the comparative study of social and cultural institutions that I consider to be the central purpose of our discipline.

The account which follows, traces my ever-increasing personal involvement in Somali issues. It is a record of anthropological engagement – perhaps entrapment describes it better – which, some methodologically puritan colleagues might consider, exceeds the bounds of anthropological 'neutrality'. In my case, as I hope the following discussion shows, I would claim that while I was certainly sympathetic to Somali nationalist aims (and even in a small way helped to further them) this did not interfere with, or detract from my efforts to understand local-level political processes. Rather, this dual interest in external and internal Somali politics, provided a creative tension, and I would have found it personally impossible to ignore the wider nationalist struggle in which the people I was studying were so profoundly engaged. I have always been amazed at the ease with which so many of my contemporaries (and some of their students) have managed to insulate their field studies, and subsequent publications, from consideration of the wider political processes in which, willingly or unwillingly, their 'people' participated. From this perspective, the rhetoric favoured by macro- and meta-Marxists, to explain specific local conditions as a result of unspecific global forces, seems to me something of an excuse for not properly addressing the wider local political context of their fieldwork. Here, as elsewhere, it seems that the deep-seated romantic strain in our subject which encourages such 'desert island disc' anthropology has much to answer for.

I should also emphasise that if, in many of the following episodes, I was strongly motivated by humanitarian considerations, I also sought to derive from each new Somali encounter further insight into Somali society. In fact, I cannot recall any occasion when, however involved in relief or development work, my frequent visits to Somalia did not enrich and expand my knowledge of Somali culture and society. More specifically, as I have emphasised elsewhere (Lewis, 1968, xxi), I am not alone in believing that the study of social change and of crisis situations offers otherwise unobtainable insights into the flexibility and resilience of institutions whose range of tolerance is indeed powerfully tested in such contexts.

II

These general remarks may, I hope, serve to introduce the narrative which follows. Here, in order to highlight the changing flux of political trends over time, and their corresponding reflections in ideology, I follow a mainly chronological sequence.

I started fieldwork in Somalia/Somaliland in 1955 over forty years ago, having just published my first book on Somalia: *Peoples of the Horn of Africa: Somali, Afar and Saho* (London: International African Institute, 1955). This was a library, scissors-and-paste work, based on my Oxford post-graduate B. Litt. thesis (1953), written as part of my pre-fieldwork training in anthropology under the supervision of Franz Steiner and Godfrey Lienhardt, and strongly under the spell of that Institute's flamboyant director, E. E.Evans-Pritchard, who in his rather casual way supervised my doctoral research. My initial, doctoral, field research (1955–1957) was financed by a grant from the British Colonial Social Science Research Council, and because no unattached foreign personnel were permitted to work in British Somaliland, I was affiliated to the refreshingly eccentric Somaliland government service. As a typical product of Evans-Pritchards' training, I was initially very worried about this attachment, since I feared it would curtail my freedom of action. However, as I have explained in part elsewhere (Lewis, 1977; 1994), the truth proved to be very different and, without any compromise to my freedom of action, I was privileged to enjoy many benefits from my relations with the dedicated and frequently unconventional expatriates with whom I had dealings. Most were tolerant of what some found to be my bizarre activities, although a few regarded my research as a self-indulgent, exploitative exercise of little direct benefit to Somalis. (Officially designated 'the Anthropologist', I was the last and lowest category on the civil service list.) The Protectorate administration, it must be understood, was a proud elitist organisation numbering less than 200 expatriates and 25 locally recruited Somali officers. This administration was strongly committed to serving Somali interests, and often at variance with the Foreign Office which saw relations with Ethiopia as of greater importance than Somali concerns. But ultimately, of course, British policy in the Horn of Africa was determined by the Foreign Office and the pro-Somali colonial officials were left to deal with the local consequences.

Before going to Somaliland with my wife[1] in 1955, and while studying Somali grammar with my great friend the legendary Somali linguist B.W. Andrzejewski, I had already become involved in London with visiting delegations of nationalist activists. These Somali politicians were campaigning for the restoration of the Haud grazing area, which had just been surrendered by the British to Ethiopia (see Lewis, 1988, pp. 150–151). This gave me an entrée with some of the nationalist figures in Somaliland but, in the field, I still had to spend day after day trying to explain to disbelieving and potentially volatile nomads in the interior that I was not personally responsible for this betrayal of Somali interests. Not, that I necessarily succeeded in convincing my listeners!

[1] My wife was with me throughout my first period of fieldwork in Somaliland from 1955 to 1957 and, as I discovered on my latest visit in 1992, is still remembered as being a 'very tall person'. We were provided with accommodation in District headquarters by the Protectorate Administration. These served as my base for field trips into the surrounding countryside (the 'bush' as it was known to urban Somalis). Before our first child was born in Hargeisa my wife accompanied me on some of these expeditions. We used a Bedford pick-up truck, with desert tyres, and on the insistence of the administration, travelled with a Somali driver and four 'camp-followers' (unarmed rural ex-policemen) who belonged to different clans. This team, as I have recorded elsewhere, constituted a kind of itinerant anthropological workshop. Following the administrative pattern, with a cook and his assistant, with tents and a forty-four gallon drum of water, this little nomadic unit was largely self-contained (at one point we carried hens with us) and could move over long distances into the grazing settlements of the pastoralists with their herds. The Protectorate administration kindly provided me with the services of a veteran official interpreter who was about to retire. But after three months, his impatience at my repeated questions to different people on the same topic (a clear sign of defective memory), became mutually intolerable and we parted company. This was a great spur to developing some minimal fluency in Somali which, after Andrzejewski's training in basics, at least enabled me to ask the questions I wanted to ask, and to gradually make more and more sense of the answers (Cf. Lewis, 1994, pp. 1–18).

In 1956, in the course of this first spell of fieldwork, I spent a month touring round Somalia, at the time of the transfer of power in internal affairs from the Italian UN Trusteeship Administration to the first Somali government under Abdillahi Ise. (Naively, I was so impressed with the pace of political developments in the south that, when I returned to the Protectorate, I took it upon myself to urge the northern nationalists there to get a move on, even making this point in brief exhortations at political meetings).

As my original fieldwork thus coincided with the formation and development of modern nationalist politics, I had the privilege of studying at first hand the aims, objectives, and manoeuvres of some of the new political leaders. This experience was recorded in my accounts of 'traditional' and modern Somali politics which analysed how the segmentary lineage system was powerfully reflected in party politics, and even in those nationalist organisations which sought to transcend lineage rivalries (Lewis, 1957, 1958, 1961, 1965/88). I was additionally fortunate to be doing fieldwork in this transitional political situation amongst the unruly Somali nomads, under the relative security and comfort of the British *raj*.[2] Nevertheless, on various occasions I experienced at first hand the powerful currents of chauvinist hostility towards foreigners, especially non-Muslims (traditionally classed as 'pagans'), which is so firmly embedded in Somali culture. I was stoned by groups of children on a number of occasions. More frighteningly, when attending a ceremony at a famous Islamic shrine, I was attacked by an excited, perhaps ecstatic, devotee brandishing a huge sword though, fortunately for me, my would-be assailant was restrained, by a more tolerant religious leader and lineage elder. These and other similar experiences were salutary, since they provided direct testimony of grass roots ethnic nationalism, and of the manner in which Islam served as a vehicle for Somali national sentiments.

In these diverse circumstances, linked to different aspects of nationalism old and new, as well as local elders I met a wide range of

[2] My official report (Lewis, 1957) to the local administration and the colonial office, was written in the field in discussion with numerous Somali friends. It was reproduced locally and circulated amongst the small circle of senior expatriate and Somali administrative officers. This produced a series of detailed comments, which were surprisingly laudatory and enthusiastic (the Acting Chief Secretary wrote to me to say that he had read it from start to finish three times). Their remarks included statements regretting that this material had not been available to them ten or fifteen years earlier, when it might have helped to shape policy. This highlights the fact that this piece of 'colonial' research was totally disinterested, and was not initiated or financed with the aim of furthering colonialism.

senior Somali officials and politicians, spanning the spectrum of clans, many of whom subsequently became leading personalities in one way or another, and with most of whom I have maintained contact since. My links with these figures were reinforced by my frequent subsequent field trips and visits to Somalia, and by my writing (and later broadcasting) on Somali nationalism both in books and newspapers.[3]

But of course my enduring relationships were not only with people who were, or became, leading political figures. One of my most fruitful encounters was with Aw Jama Umar Ise, who has become the justly celebrated oral historian of Sayyid Mohammed Abdille Hassan and his poetry (Ise, 1974). When I first met him in Las Anod District in the 1950s, Aw Jama was a typical Somali 'bush' *wadaad*, an itinerant sheikh of a somewhat fundamentalist disposition and extremely suspicious of me and my activities, moving as I did among the Dulbahante nomads, seeking information about their customs and institutions and writing down their genealogies. Like most un-Westernised Somalis whom I met, his initial assumption was that I was a British spy, and I found him somewhat menacing in early encounters I had with him. Some years later I met Sheikh Jama in Mogadishu and discovered that he had become a self-taught oral historian and was busy collecting the poetry of Sayyid Mohammed Abdille Hassan having received encouragement and equipment (a tape-recorder) from the much-respected commander of the Somali police force, General Mohammed Abshir (later imprisoned by his arch rival, President Siyad, and eventually one of the leaders of the Somali Salvation Democratic Front in the North Eastern Regions). Aw Jama explained to me that he had closely observed my ethnographic activities and, deciding that I was harmless, he had concluded that what I was doing was worthwhile, but could be done better by a native Somali speaker with knowledge

[3] I was amazed and flattered to learn from a friend, posted to the British Embassy in Addis Ababa in the 1980s, that a senior Ethiopian official had referred to me as one of the founders of Somali nationalism! It was perhaps not surprising therefore, that when, on behalf of the Anti-Slavery Society in early 1980, I organised a small international conference on nationalism and self-determination in the Horn of Africa, this provoked a vigorous diplomatic campaign by the Ethiopian government. Infuriated that we were trying to bring together centralist (pro-Ethiopian government) and anti-centralist perspectives, the Ethiopian regime was particularly incensed that, as they saw it, we were helping to legitimate the nationalist causes of its separatist opponents (the Eritreans and Somali Ogadenis). When their outraged protests to the French government led to the banning of our meeting in France (where we had intended to hold it), this small, unimportant academic workshop was re-routed to a quiet Oxford college where it took place without incident (see Lewis, 1983).

of the religious background. I had thus inadvertently made a convert and we became friends and colleagues.[4]

III

In 1962 I returned to Somalia for three months to conduct further fieldwork amongst the cultivating Digil and Rahanwiin in the Bay region, examining how their clan organisation differed partly, as I argued, for ecological reasons, from the lineage system of the northern nomads (Lewis, 1969).[5] Two years later, I was back again in the south to carry out a land tenure survey in the same region for FAO – my first piece of applied anthropology. In the course of this three months' visit, I happened to meet, walking in the street in Mogadishu, the then prime minister, Abdirazaq Haji Husseyn. These were the days before Somali leaders felt it necessary to have elaborate security, and when they conducted themselves in the egalitarian pastoralist style: in fact the prime minister and I patronised the same barber. He took me by the hand in the democratic Somali way, and invited me to meet his cabinet. He introduced me to them as 'the fellow who writes about us. We don't always like what he writes – but the important thing is that he *writes about us*!' I also remember about this time, after I had published a sympathetic account of the Somali struggle to secure the independence and unification of the Somalilands, I received a cable from the Secretary to the Somali cabinet, congratulating me on my efforts – with the exhortation 'pray continue'.[6]

As the concept of journalistic reporting became familiar to Somalis in this period, I often found that once I had described my aims and activities to people I was meeting for the first time, I was identified as a 'journalist', a description with which I had no serious quarrel. Other more traditional Somalis referred to me in Somali by the more attractive, generic title 'writer'.

On another occasion in the 1960s, I gave a public lecture at the University Institute in Mogadishu with the rather dry (and no doubt

[4] In this period of my association with the Dulbahante pastoralists, partly through gifts and partly by purchase, I also acquired the nucleus of a small herd of camels. Although I have not seen them myself since the 1960s I receive reports on their well-being from time to time, most recently by cassette in 1995.

[5] Being on a slender budget I was fortunate to be lent a landrover by the police and a tent by the army.

[6] I had already participated in the preparation of some official documents setting out Somali nationalist aims.

pompous) title: 'The peopling of Somalia – the history of tribal and clan migrations'. The chairman was Mohammed Haji Ibrahim Egal, later (1996) President of the Somaliland Republic, then Minister of Education in Somalia. As I proceeded to recount what I thought could be gleaned, from oral and written sources (especially the Italian masters, Cerulli and Colucci) of migration history, the packed audience became more and more excited and restless. The atmosphere became very highly charged. When I had finished Mohammed Haji Ibrahim Egal got up, and having quickly assessed the situation announced that 'As there were no further questions' he would close the meeting. He and I then beat a hasty and rather undignified retreat.

This was at the time of the 'exs' when the English (or Italian) term 'ex-clan' ('ex' for short) had been introduced into Somali nationalist discourse (and standard Somali) to reflect the new political realities where, officially, divisive clans belonged to an earlier, more primitive stage of society. Western-educated Somalis who rejected the term 'clan', now referred to people's 'ex-clans' rather than their 'clans' (cf. Lewis, 1979). In this context, the traditional Somali enquiry, 'What is your clan?' (or *tol* 'lineage')[7] designed to elucidate the political identity of the person questioned, received the proud answer: 'Somali'. Clanism, thus attracted the same opprobrium as tribalism in multi-ethnic states elsewhere. (Interestingly, I cannot recall African nationalists in such contexts elsewhere employing the expression 'ex-tribe').

More generally and fortunately for me, however, I was becoming known in Somalia for broadcasts on the BBC World Service which were sympathetic to the nationalist cause. My original mentor in Somali, and close friend, the linguist, B.W. Andrzejewski, and I cooperated closely and often visited Somalia together. We had become in Somali eyes something of an exotic double act and were not infrequently mistaken for each other. Thus I would meet Somalis who would greet me as 'Andrzejewski' and ask me to give their regards to Lewis and Andrzejewski had many similar experiences. When we were both in town at the same time this sometimes caused confusion. On occasion, Goosh Andrzejewski was reproached for 'not understanding the clan

[7] I do not know exactly when the term was invented, but in the 1980s I was told that the Somali for anthropologist was, appropriately *tol yaqaan*, literally 'he who knows clans and clanship'. This of course was rather a dubious occupational category when people were particularly conscious of their internal lineage divisions and resented any enquiries of foreigners which touched on these politically sensitive identities.

system properly', just as I was criticised for not speaking Somali so fluently and for possessing a much weaker knowledge of Somali proverbs. But, where we were conflated into a single hybrid-Somali-speaking foreign Somali specialist, I benefited enormously from the huge reputation enjoyed by Andrzejewski for his linguistic fluency and deep knowledge of Somali oral culture. With the addiction which Somalis all share, in the interior as much as in towns, to radio broadcasting, I do not think it is an exaggeration to say that by the 1980s, if not before, we had both become household names. Fame of this kind is, perhaps, not often enjoyed by anthropologists or linguists and, while satisfying to the ego, creates responsibilities which may not always be easy to recognise or to discharge adequately.

IV

As a political anthropologist, my relations with the Somali government inevitably became more complex, when the army commander, General Mohammed Siyad Barre, came to power in the 'bloodless coup' of 1969. Although I still had value as a sympathetic observer and publicist of Somali nationalist aims, my accounts of internal politics were often regarded as irritating, to say the least. Since clans had now been officially destroyed (and cremated in public rituals orchestrated by the Russians) so that there were no longer even 'ex-clans' (or, as I tried to joke, 'ex-exs'), someone who wrote about the internal dynamics of Somali politics, as I did, was not very welcome in Siyad's police state. I had of course, above all, to be especially careful lest my behaviour might endanger friends who could risk imprisonment for associating with me. Nevertheless, because of my role as a protagonist of Somali nationalist aims, particularly during the Ogaden war (when I broadcast on the BBC several times a week, for several months), I was reluctantly tolerated by the regime for a time – but only just.

After a two-month study visit to Somalia in 1974 when, as a British Academy Visitor, I was attached to the Somali Academy of Sciences and Culture (modelled loosely on its Soviet equivalent), and drawing also on information collected on previous visits since the 1969 coup, I put together an analysis of General Siyad's power structure. Slightly tongue-in-cheek, I called this 'Kim il-Sung in Somalia'. There were North Korean links and parallels, deliberate and unintended, but the regime really depended primarily on an alliance of three related

(Daarood) clans; the President's own clan, his son-in-law's (head of the National Security Service), and his mother's – the strategically critically significant, Ogaadeen (see Lewis, 1979b; 1994).[8]

There was a striking contrast, of course, between my view of the Somali power structure and the official line of 'Scientific Socialism' (in Somali: *hanti wadaag ilmi ku disan*; literally, wealth-sharing based on wisdom), a locally adapted construct with an Islamic twist, developed by young leftist Somali professionals and strongly oriented towards development. Marx and Lenin were conjoined with Siyad to form an inspiring trinity in which the supremacy of Siyad was strongly emphasised. For this reason, I sometimes referred to Somali scientific socialism as 'scientific Siyadism'. An encounter in the 1970s in which I participated between the Marxist French social anthropologist, Claude Meillassoux and the Director of the Somali Institute of Public Administration, illustrated this quite vividly. Meillassoux was strongly critical of Somali socialism, forcefully asserting that Somalis did not understand what Marxism was. The Somali Director, one of those apparatchiks involved in the elaboration of this exotic Somali ideology, became infuriated with Meillassoux and, eventually, silenced him with the pronouncement: 'Look Meillassoux: we don't need Marx, Marx needs us!'. The Somali defeat in the Ogaadeen war demonstrated that this was, alas, an overconfident assessment.

After the traumatic experience of that war, the flood of refugees which it brought in its train, and deserted by the Soviet Union (which had changed sides to support Ethiopia) Siyad desperately sought support from the USA. Scientific socialism, consequently, was soft-pedalled. This had an amusing impact on the publication of a three volume study called *Marxist Governments: a World Survey* (ed. B. Szajkowski, 1981) to which I contributed a chapter on Somalia. In admirably democratic style, this was accorded parity of page length to the Soviet Union. The book was assembled *before* the Ogaadeen war, but was ready to come out *after* that debacle, by which time Somalia's

[8] I showed a draft of this piece to several Somali friends in London. I had hoped to get some feedback and I certainly succeeded. The Somali Ambassador, whom I had known since student days in Oxford, came to see me brandishing a telex from President Siyad, who wanted to know if I intended publication. This seemed to confirm my line of analysis and I explained that I did intend publishing, but discretely in a festschrift in honour of my immediate predecessor at LSE, Isaac Schapera. I later learned from a contact who worked in Siyad's private office that the President had personally annotated a copy of my paper with remarks such as: 'Who does this sh.. think he is?' I felt then that I could not have been too wide of the mark!

super-power partnership had changed dramatically. The publishers proposed to design book jackets for each volume with pictures of the relevant heads of state and approached the Somali embassy in London and spoke to the ambassador, courteously requesting a photograph of General Siyad, for use on a book cover. 'What book?', the ambassador asked. When it was explained to him, there was a pregnant pause. Then the ambassador said: 'If you say we have a Marxist government, we will sue you!'[9]

V

As I hope will be plain, inspired by Evans-Pritchard I have always regarded my research as concerned primarily with seeking to provide an accurate translation of Somali culture and society, within the canons of our western (anthropological) frame of reference. Although inevitably to some extent couched in technical terms, the latter should be generally intelligible to non-specialists. It thus seemed to me natural to become involved in applied anthropology, where the results might benefit the Somali public and, at the same time, where the work itself offered further opportunities for testing the validity of earlier research and analysis, and even of extending it. In the 1960s, I started with the FAO, trying to elucidate the social structure of the Digil-Mirifle agro-pastoralists of southern Somalia in the context of a land-tenure survey. This enabled me to acquire further, first-hand data on the mixed clan structures of the southern cultivating Somalis which contrasted markedly with the segmentary system of the northern nomads (Lewis, 1969; 1994. Cf. Helander, 1996).

A decade later, having campaigned in England for aid for Somalia during the 1974/5 East African drought crisis, and having helped to publicise Somali aims in the Ogaadeen struggle of 1977 (with frequent broadcasts on the BBC overseas service; and in other ways), I accepted (in 1978) an invitation from USAID to advise on the sociological aspects of a range of rural development projects.[10] In the course

[9] Unfortunately the diverting prospect offered by this warning, of endless debate in an English court of law about the nature of Marxist governance was not realised. The Embassy did not pursue the matter further.

[10] In the wake of the Ogaadeen war and the withdrawal of the Russians, USAID for civilian projects was greatly expanded in Somalia. However, the Americans were unwilling to provide the equivalent military aid requested by Siyad, though later they made some concessions.

of this work, which involved a three months tour in Somalia, I first encountered directly, the concepts of 'social and environmental soundness' as basic requirements of development project planning – along with concern for the 'poorest of the poor', and 'women'. In theory, these criteria sounded impressive. In practice, however, I soon found that such certificates of project soundness were all too casually bestowed, often by poorly qualified 'social scientists'. They were, operationally, little more than an empty cipher, a matter of the new, politically correct, development rhetoric with little basis in reality. Indeed, I came to the conclusion that, essentially, what was at stake here was a legitimisation exercise. These theoretically unexceptionable considerations were ritually invoked to certificate often poorly designed projects. At the same time, the actual procedures of assessment were themselves likely to be flawed since the assessors themselves often turned out to be eventually involved in project implementation. There was little serious, technically qualified, independent scrutiny of projects – and far too many vested interests (cf. Lewis 1995a). In this particular case, I learnt more about the shortcomings of aid practice in project-planning and development than about Somali society, although I did also make some discoveries about how kinship ties had been utilised in drought-relief fishing and agricultural 'cooperatives'. The assessment of social soundness obviously provided an attractive opportunity for anthropologists, but one which, if it was not to be abused, required high standards of professionalism.

Such independent assessment could, indeed, prove useful as I later found in the course of a brief assignment for the British Overseas Development Agency, looking at the likely effects of a tse-tse fly eradication project along the Shebelle and Lower Juba rivers, which enabled me to get an up-to-date understanding of the complexity of tenurial relations in this commercially attractive region. Given the predatory interests of pastoralists in seeking to extend their grazing areas and watering facilities in this fertile region to say nothing of plantation 'developers' (encouraged by the government), it did not require great imagination to see that a likely consequence of tse-tse eradication would be to intensify land-grabbing efforts by those with the strongest political muscle at the expense of the local riverine cultivators. Such findings were not particularly congenial to the authorities.

My next experience in the applied area was essentially of a didactic nature, and perhaps the most satisfying to date, although the eventual outcome was rather modest. In the 1970s, the Swedish research and development agency SAREC, which was generously supporting the Somali National Academy of Science and Culture (a university-linked national research organisation), was requested to establish a training programme in applied anthropology for Somali graduates and suitably qualified civil servants. The head of SOMAC at the time, a formidable woman who had herself studied anthropology, believed this subject was important for effective development planning, and persuaded SAREC to initiate this training programme in cooperation with me at the London School of Economics. This modest programme, using the LSE master's degree in anthropology (taken over one or two years according to the student's background), produced about 10 Somali researchers with this qualification. The majority went back to Somalia and took up research positions at the Academy. A major success, which perhaps alone justified the programme, was Dr Ahmad Yusuf Farah whose highly original anthropological study of the local frankincense industry (Farah 1994) and innovative field studies of local-level Somali peace initiatives (Farah, 1993) are well-known to Somali specialists.

The two, more conventional, development experiences that followed (both ambitious projects) were much less satisfactory. In August 1985, the Deputy High Commissioner of the UNHCR in Geneva approached me to see whether, in the wake of the huge influx of refugees following the Ogaadeen war, I would design a research methodology to elicit qualitative and quantitative demographic data to strengthen management planning techniques for the provision of refugee support programmes in Somalia. With no accurate means of assessing the actual size and demographic composition of the refugee camp populations, the provision of adequate food supplies and health services was becoming increasingly difficult. A simple 'head-count' in late 1981 of camp 'residents' had produced a figure of just under one million (about a quarter of the normal population of Somalia). The data collected were very approximate and generated prolonged controversy between the Somali authorities and the main aid donors. Eventually, a 'planning figure' of 700,000 was grudgingly accepted by both sides as a compromise which, since it satisfied neither party, gave rise to further acrimonious debate. UNHCR headquarters in Geneva were sympathetic to the needs of Somalia, but felt they required scientifically established demographic information to persuade major donors to continue their support and asked me to supply this. Despite the obvious difficulties which such a project would encounter and after consulting quite widely with Somali friends and specialists, I came to the conclusion that I should accept this challenge. I was swayed, I think, particularly by the goodwill which I sensed the UNHCR in Geneva had for the Somali refugees, evident in the readiness with which the UNHCR accepted our idea of the need to distinguish between 'camp-based' and 'camp-resident' populations. There were clearly many *bona fide* refugees who were not always resident, all the time, in a particular camp. An estimate, based on 'camp-based' refugees, would tend to be generous and would have been very favourable to the Somali case.

Drawing on the demographic expertise of colleagues at LSE, and under the aegis of the International African Institute of which I was Honorary Director at the time, I therefore assembled a team of suitably qualified specialists. Our project design combined standard demographic procedures, using a 10 per cent household random sampling technique, with anthropological surveys which would produce in-depth profiles of a carefully selected number of refugee camps. The anthropologists proposed, though mostly non-Somalis, were all Somali-speaking and drawn from a number of different countries. Our aim was not only to provide national and regional totals of refugee camp populations, but also to provide accurate predictive trends: birth and mortality rates; age and sex distribution. This, naturally, was information important for realistic planning.

Following detailed discussions in Geneva in October 1985 between the UNHCR, Somalia's National Refugee Commission delegation, and my colleagues and I from the IAI, it was decided that we should make a preliminary field visit to Somalia under terms of reference which were agreed at the time. This, in effect, a feasibility study, lasted a month and was completed in late November. Our report (Lewis, 1986), in the form of a detailed blueprint for the study which we were ready to implement, was presented in Geneva in January 1986 and accepted by the UNHCR who prepared a draft agreement for the Somali authorities to initiate the study. After prolonged negotiations, it became clear that President Siyad would not sign the agreement. As the Permanent Secretary in the Foreign Ministry, with whom I discussed the problem in Mogadishu, explained, his President was not interested in the benefits our project might secure for the refugee relief programme. General Siyad did not see why he had to have a demographic 're-enumeration' of his country's refugee population when Western donors had not imposed this on Afghanistan. The Somalis, Siyad said, were such staunch allies of the West and so committed to the struggle against communism that reassurances over figures were unnecessary. Siyad's political short-term memory was rather selective.[11]

My final fling in southern Somalia was an abortive attempt in 1987, hard on the heels of the UNHCR fiasco, to mount a study of Somali labour migration to the Gulf States. Again under the aegis of the International African Institute, and this time with USAID funding, our aim was to carry out a systematic sample study of the extent of migrant labour (the so-called 'Somali muscle drain') and its impact on the families of migrants in Somalia where this source of income played a vital role in the national economy. We were particularly interested in the mobilisation of kinship connexions by migrants to find employment in the foreign labour market, and in the transfer of remittance money and goods back to their families in Somalia. Careful documentation and analysis of the use of lineage ties here would further elucidate the economic role of kinship-based trust (cf. Lewis, 1962) and its mobilisation by entrepreneurs in migrant labour in the modern context, a project which we presented as 'applied anthropology', but which I saw as contributing to the theory of lineage organisation. This important sector of the Somali informal economy was again controversial, involving the closely guarded secrets of entrepreneurs at various levels. However, our Somali social anthropologists (trained on the SAREC-LSE programme) were confident that they could carry out this delicate investigation successfully and I think they were right. The matter was, in fact, never put to the test. USAID was unable to provide the local currency needed to pay staff salaries.

VI

As the Somali crisis developed after the downfall of General Siyad in 1991, I became involved with friends and colleagues at the British NGO, ActionAid – which had considerable experience in Somalia – in helping to establish an umbrella organisation (The Inter NGO Committee for Somalia: INCS) in London to monitor the unfolding

[11] Of course, there were many interested parties involved in the refugee aid programme, starting with the President himself, and the rather appropriately titled 'Extraordinary Commissioner for Refugees'. The number of rackets was legion, and Siyad and his henchmen evidently reckoned that they could get away with cocking a snook at their Western patrons at least for the time being. Events proved them right in the short-run. They felt that they could dispense with UNHCR goodwill at a time when they were brazenly looting the refugee camps for army recruits (cf. J.M. Ghalib, 1995, pp. 146–158).

Somali tragedy and to try to coordinate a concerted NGO response. When most organisations had withdrawn from Somalia, the few who were still represented there, or hoped to return, seemed willing to make common cause at least at the level of sharing information and concerted discussion of future operations. The uneasy, inter-agency rivalry was, naturally, evident from the start of our meetings, and as soon as major international intervention got under way, interest in our small cooperative effort began to diminish and it gradually fell into abeyance. I also joined with a group of Somali colleagues in North America, and the Swedish social anthropologist, Bernhard Helander to campaign for international intervention to rescue the victims of war and famine in southern Somalia. Over the months, and eventually years, which followed I became a regular commentator on radio and television, nationally and internationally, frequently making as many as four or five broadcasts a week at times of peak media interest in the unfolding Somali tragedy. In this spirit, I accepted an invitation from the *Sunday Times* newspaper (30 August 1992) to contribute a two page spread, setting out the background to the collapse of the Somali state and the epidemic of internecine killing. I advocated intervention by a single nation military force, preferably in view of their local (Djibouti) experience, the French Foreign Legion. I also recommended the establishment of an interim UN administration to restore essential services, mobilising the support of local clan elders and, working from a local community basis, with priority given to those areas whose traditional leaders had already managed to achieve a reasonable degree of public order. These proposals irritated some Westernised Somalis who read the article and found it embarrassing and derogatory. Actually, however, there was evidence from inside Somalia at this time that a substantial body of opinion would have welcomed such a radical approach, especially if it had been combined with the effective dismantling of the militias of the major warlords – which would perhaps actually have been feasible at this juncture. These reactions were fairly predictable.

To my surprise, my article also attracted the attention of the British Foreign Secretary (Mr Douglas Hurd), who, along with other EEC Ministers, had been persuaded to undertake a brief visit to Mogadishu to obtain a first-hand impression. I was summoned to the Foreign Office for a discussion on the Somali situation. My proposals for intervention assumed an ideally tailored and appropriately motivated and directed international action, willing to risk the lives of international personnel in the effort to overcome the man-made famine in southern Somalia, and to provide sufficient security in the country to permit the Somalis to dispense with the warlords who had wrecked their state. As events were soon to show, however, it was naively optimistic to imagine that the international community could undertake such responsibilities in such an effective manner. What national interests (outside Somali fantasies) could possibly justify such risks?

In the real world events proceeded differently, although initially with some promise. In July 1992 and before my encounter with the British Foreign Minister, I was approached by the newly appointed UN Special Envoy to Somalia, Ambassador Mohammed Sahnoun, and by the Swedish Life and Peace Institute, Uppsala, to suggest how the UN should proceed with its new peace-making efforts in Somalia. The Life and Peace Institute had been given the task by the UN (financed by Sweden as part of its aid to Somalia) of forming a 'reference group' of experts on Somalia. Being relatively unfamiliar with the field, they asked me who they should invite to join the panel, and I suggested a number of specialists from different countries and disciplines.

The first meeting of the group with the participation of Ambassador Sahnoun and other UN officials was held in Uppsala in August 1992. Unfortunately, I was not able to go there myself, having recently returned from the Horn of Africa[12] with 'heart failure'.

However, Mohammed Sahnoun called in on me in London on his way back to East Africa, and impressed me with his grasp of Somali politics and his commitment to improving the situation in Somalia. Thereafter, I kept in close touch with the 'reference group', attending some of the later meetings. Like everyone else with Somali connections, I wanted to try to help. But after Sahnoun resigned over his disagreements with the UN bureaucracy (cf. Sahnoun, 1995), and the Life and Peace Institute became more closely involved with the political wing of UNOSOM, and clearly interested in high profile activity, the role of the 'reference group', in my opinion, largely deteriorated into that of reluctant and sometimes unconscious legitimation. Rather like the Somali faction leaders, our UNOSOM interlocutors told us one thing when they attended 'reference group'

[12] On this last visit to the area I spent the month of March as an academic visitor at the University of Addis Ababa and during that time briefly visited Hargeisa in the north. Having recently broadcast many critical assessments of the exploits of both the Somali warlords, Aydeed and Ali Mahdi, I did not venture to Mogadishu which was still engulfed in conflict.

meetings, and then went off and did something else. Part of the difficulty here, perhaps, lay in the lack of any clear definition about the position of the 'reference group', an issue to which the Life and Peace Institute might have been expected to give more attention.[13]

It also seemed to me that, in common with other well-intentioned external champions of peace, the activities of the Life and Peace Institute were excessively Eurocentric and, particularly initially, did not take sufficient account of the Somali techniques of peace-making which were brought to their attention. Certainly, for all its many good works, the organisation's Horn of Africa unit was not very responsive to constructive criticism of its activities in Somalia which, generally, lacked independent monitoring and assessment. No doubt these criticisms could be made more strongly of a host of NGOs working in Somalia in the last few years, where humanitarian aid has become a major industry.[14] This was particularly true, of course, of the UN and was one of my major criticisms (made also by many other commentators) of UNOSOM (cf. Lewis, 1993a; 1993b; Lewis and Mayall, 1996; Menkhaus, 1995).

VII

Many social scientists have written at length on the theme of knowledge as *power* but have overlooked the fact that, in certain situations, knowledge is a *constraint* and *ignorance* is more powerful. It has to be said also that the local recipients of foreign aid often also prefer that donors should be as ignorant as possible of local conditions. It is then much easier to manipulate well-meaning expatriate aid merchants (cf. Lewis, 1995a). Such ignorance can be presented as a virtue in the form of not knowing local society, and hence appearing 'neutral' and 'objective'.

[13] I am not of course arguing that those who voluntarily give technical advice have the right to see it acted upon. But if the recipient of that advice repeatedly returns for further unpaid counsel from those same advisers, that recipient might reasonably be expected to explain what use he makes of the advice so solicited. But after the departure of Sahnoun our 'think tank' was treated rather casually.

[14] Although I cannot claim direct knowledge of all of them, I have been impressed by their general lack of local (i.e. Somali) knowledge, and their unwillingness to try to remedy this by serious briefing programmes for their expatriate staff. All too often, they appear to prefer to operate largely regardless of, and oblivious to, the possibly unintended effects of their interventions. There is usually some symbolic lip-service paid to the importance of appreciating the local culture but, in general, ignorance seems the preferred mode of operation.

The preference of aid consumers for ignorance on the part of their donors is well-illustrated in my most recent (1995/96) involvement in Somali affairs. At the end of 1994, the European Union office for Somalia in Nairobi approached LSE,, and I was invited to develop a project to explore decentralised forms of government which might be suitable for Somalia. The aim was to make some technical contribution to the on-going Somali debate on political construction and reconstruction. Originally, the term 'constitution' had appeared in the description, but in deference to local sensitivities (and in my view more appropriately) this was replaced by the more general term 'structures'. The request reflected the realisation that Somalia had disintegrated to such an extent that decentralised regional structures were required if any progress was to be made towards political reconstruction. After the failure of previous UN efforts to cajole the warlords and faction leaders into forming a national government, this seemed a more promising approach. It appealed particularly to me also, although with some chagrin, since the disintegration (or more accurately, 'segmentation') of Somalia into lineage factions was a depressing endorsement of my on-going analysis of Somali politics (cf. Lewis, 1994). The same segmentary pattern was equally evident in local community organisations among Somali refugees in the countries where they had found political asylum.[15]

With colleagues at LSE, Professor James Mayall (International Relations) and I put together proposals for the study which we discussed with the EU Special Envoy Ambassador Illing. In the course of our negotiations, pressures were exerted by some of the more notorious Somali warlords who objected to the involvement of prominent Somali specialists. These critics in Mogadishu maintained that it was not necessary to include anyone with prior specialist knowledge of Somali society. Indeed, they claimed that objectivity and neutrality required their exclusion. Despite these objections, Illing argued that the study would be pointless if it did not take account of the special characteristics of Somali political culture. So, after making a few cosmetic alterations to our advisory team, we went ahead and produced the review of decentralised forms of government and prepared a 'menu

[15] In contrast, various neo-Marxists who had not carried out any systematic fieldwork, had long claimed that Somali clanship was an atavistic force doomed to oblivion in the modern world. From this ideological rather than factually informed perspective, my analysis was a typical exercise in 'neo-colonialist anthropology'; see A.I. Samatar, 1989, Kapteijns, 1991.

of options', presenting their salient advantages and disadvantages, as requested. Our report (Lewis and Mayall, 1995b), was produced in a full English version, and in an English and Somali summary. We also produced an oral Somali version in cassette form. Our English version (first presented to the public at a workshop at LSE in August 1995, attended by the EU and UNDP representatives and other dignatories) quickly attracted widespread Somali interest and comment from Somali 'intellectuals' throughout the world (not least on the internet).

Criticism from English- and Italian-speaking Somalis was interesting, if often contradictory. Some claimed that our report was biased in favour of one clan group or another (never of course the commentator's own clan). This was claimed by people of every clan. At the same time, following the most tortuously clan-partisan arguments, we were accused of advocating the break-up of the Somali state (which Somalis might be said to have achieved very effectively on their own). Equally, these critics, and others, accused us of sharing, in common with other non-Somali social scientists, the mistaken view that the Somali people represented a single ethnic group which excluded the existence of minority groups in Somalia.

While it is true that Somali nationalist rhetoric projected this undifferentiated image of ethnic homogeneity, and this had been widely publicised in popular and journalistic accounts, it was not the picture presented in the serious scholarly literature. The mixture of Somali core homogeneity, regional diversification, and minority ethnic communities is well-documented in the works of the Italian scholars who formed the first generation of students of Somali culture (Colucci, 1924; and the extraordinarily prolific Cerulli: 1918–64). It features again in the next generation of empirically based sociological studies by myself (Lewis, 1961–1996), Abdi Mirreh (1978), V. Luling (1971), Said S. Samatar (1982, and with Laitin, 1987), and Bernhard Helander (1996 etc.). Cultural distinctions naturally also feature strongly in the work of the Italian team of linguistic specialists on Somali, headed by Annarita Puglielli in Rome.

The point for Somali political sociology is that in this segmentary society, with its attached (or unattached) ethnic minorities, the divisions may be suppressed or accentuated according to context and interest. As I and others have sought to demonstrate over the years, this pattern of multiple political identity is part of the logic of the segmentary system and is responsible for the debilitating fragility of Somali nationalism which has not succeeded in moving from the 'mechanical' to the 'organic' mode of solidarity (in Durkheim's terminology). In the 1950s, 60s and 70s, when nationalist rhetoric was strong, the accent was on homogeneity: in the wake of the collapse of the Somali state, the accent has been powerfully on differentiation.

Both these contradictory themes were expressed in the reactions, as recorded above, which our European Union report elicited from some westernised Somalis. It should be noted, however, such is the overwhelming power of the Somali oral tradition, that literacy in these European languages (and impressive oral mastery) does not necessarily include nuanced ease in reading academic texts. But, given the Somali addiction to radio and widespread use of radio cassettes (rather than written letters) in comunication, we expect that the oral version will reach a wider cross-section of the non-English speaking Somali public in Somalia. There are many difficulties in adapting the written version for oral use in a form that is compatible with traditional Somali assumptions and values, and it would be rash to claim that these have been satisfactorily surmounted. Nevertheless, notwithstanding these qualifications, it would be interesting to see how the reaction of Somali speakers, who are not literate in English or Italian, compares with that of those who have these linguistic skills and have responded to the written version.

Non-literate Somalis, of course, constitute the majority of the population, and are the people to whom non-Somali speaking foreigners in the aid and diplomatic communities have no direct access. Their views are filtered (and modified) by the Anglophone and Italophone 'intellectuals' who act as their mouth-pieces in such inter-cultural dialogues. This is one reason, of course, why non-Somali speaking foreigners who work with Somalis may acquire rather distorted views of what the majority of the Somali public actually thinks and wants.[16]

Finally, it seemed appropriate that this initiative from the literate West, designed to stimulate Somali debate on future forms of government, should be presented to this traditionally profoundly un- (rather than merely de-) centralised society in its own oral medium.

[16] One idealistic young aid worker I met in the course of this EU project, thought it might be wrong to refer to Somali 'clans' as this might give them legitimacy. This is a point of view that might seem patronising to clan elders, although not to those Westernised Somalis who, because of the negative loading they give to it, resent the emphasis placed on clans by some foreign commentators. Few of the latter, it need hardly be said, have the understanding of the political significance of clanship possessed by ordinary Somali elders who do not despise this ancestral heritage.

Somalis, who understandably recall with nostalgia and pride their former nation-state, and many of the foreigners concerned in one way or another with Somali futures, often do not seem to realise the enormity of this political aspiration. It is very difficult to establish and maintain order in an uncentralised segmentary society, especially when the majority of a traditionally bellicose people are armed with modern weapons. Here military technology powerfully reinforces traditional 'anarchic' tendencies in Somali society, empowering individuals and the representative segmentary units to which they belong, while discouraging the formation of centralised government.

With their erstwhile (if sometimes far from overwhelming) monopoly of force, in these unpromising conditions the colonial powers were only able, with difficulty, to establish and administer state structures encapsulating the Somali people. By the time of independence in 1960, sentiments of (partly reactive) national solidarity were strongly evident and fuelled, as well as fed upon the Pan-Somali struggle for independence in the neighbouring Somali territories. In the ten years of civilian government in Somalia, elections and competition for material resources in urban contexts and in the national context greatly expanded the arenas of rivalry between clans and their segments, bringing into sharp conflict groups which had previously never interacted, and hardly even knew of each other's existence.

Although clanship (*tol*) has always been an ideological force and resource (cf. Lewis, 1994), its manipulation by unscrupulous urban-based politicians and entrepreneurs has vastly increased over this period. The resulting reactive clan cauldron was already threatening to boil over when the army commander, General Mohamed Siyad Barre seized power in 1969. In the following years, as Pan-Somali aspirations were gradually dampened, and as modern weapons began to circulate widely in a population already deeply disturbed by Siyad's divide-and-rule politics, his own position became increasingly parlous. His final overthrow in 1990 in which hordes of nomadic warriors from the interior (mainly Habar Ghedir) played such a prominent part, recalls Ibn Khaldun's famous theory of oscillating dynastic change.

In the present (1998) context, the universal distribution of automatic weapons reinforces all these divisive trends. The extraordinary resilience and pliancy of Somali lineage ties over such a long period, and in an environment which today includes a vast network of commercial relations, could hardly be more tellingly demonstrated. These ambivalent reflections on the theme of Somali clanship are prompted by our EU study, which has thus inadvertently contributed to my on-going programme of research and documentation on Somali society.

I. M. Lewis

REFERENCES

Ahmed, A. J. (ed.) 1994. *The Invention of Somalia*. New Jersey: Red Sea Press.

Cassanelli, L. V. 1982. *The Shaping of Somali Society: reconstructing the history of a pastoral people 1600–1900*. Philadelphia: University of Pennsylvania Press.

— and Besteman, C. (eds) 1996. *The Struggle for Land in Southern Somalia: the war behind the war*. Boulder: Westview Press.

Colucci, M. 1924. *Principi di diritto consuetudinario della Somalia Italiana Meridionale*. Florence: Societa Editrice 'La Voce'.

DeLancey, Mark W. *et al.* (compilers) 1998. *Somalia*. World Bibliographical Series, vol. 92. Oxford: Clio Press.

Djama, M. 1995. *L'Espace, le lieu, les cadres du changement social en pays nord-Somali. La plaine du Hawd (1884–1990)*. Paris: Ecole des hautes études en sciences sociales, thèse de doctorat.

— 1997. 'Trajectoire du pouvoir en pays somali', *Cahiers d'études africaines* xxxvii (2). 146, pp. 403–425.

Farah, A. Y. (with I. M. Lewis) 1993. *The Roots of Reconciliation: peace-making endeavours of contemporary lineage elders*. London: ActionAid.

— 1994. *The Milk of the Boswellia Forest: frankincense production among the pastoral Somali*. Uppsala: EPOS.

Ghalib, J. M. 1995. *The Cost of Dictatorship: the Somali experience*. New York: Lilian Barber Press.

Helander, B. 1988. 'The Slaughtered Camel: coping with fictitious descent among the Hubeer of southern Somalia', PhD dissertation, Uppsala University.

—1996a. 'Rahanweyn sociability: a model for other Somalis?' in R. Hayward and I.M. Lewis (eds) *Voice and Power: the culture of language in North-East Africa*. London: School of Oriental and African Studies. pp. 195–204.

— 1996b. 'The Hubeer in the land of plenty: land, labor and vulnerability in a southern Somali clan' in C. Besteman and L. Cassanelli (eds) *The Struggle for Land in Southern Somalia: the war behind the war*. Boulder: Westview Press.

Ise, Aw. J. U. 1974. *Taariikhdii Daraawiishta (History of the Dervishes)*. Mogadishu: Somalia Government.

Iye, A. M. 1995. *Le Verdict de l'arbre: le xeer Issa*. Dubai: International Printing Press.

Kapteijns, L. 1991. 'Women and the Somali Pastoral Tradition: the corporate kinship and capitalist transformation in northern Somalia', Boston: African Studies Centre, Working Papers in African Studies no. 153.

Keenadid, Y. C. 1984. *Ina Cabdille Xasan el la sua attivita letteraria*. Naples: Istituto Universitario Orientale.

Laitin, D. and Samatar, S. S. 1987. *Somalia: nation in search of a state*. Boulder: Westview Press.

Lewis, I. M. 1955. *Peoples of the Horn of Africa: Somali, Afar and Saho*. London: International African Institute. [Revised edition, Haan, 1994]

— 1957. *The Somali Lineage System and the Total Genealogy: a general introduction to basic principles of Somali political institutions*. Hargeisa: Somaliland Government.

— 1958. 'Modern political movements in Somaliland', *Africa*, 28(3): 244–261; 28(4): 344–363.

— 1961. *A Pastoral Democracy: pastoralism and politics among the Northern Somali of the Horn of Africa*. London: Oxford University Press for the International African Institute. [second edition, New York: Homes and Meier 1982]

— 1969. 'From nomadism to cultivation: the expansion of political solidarity in southern Somalia', in M. Douglas and P. Kaberry (eds) *Man in Africa*. London: Tavistock, pp. 59–77.

— 1976. *Social Anthropology in Perspective*. Harmondsworth: Penguin.

— 1979 'Kim il-Sung in Somalia: the end of tribalism?' in P. Cohen and W. Shack (eds) *The Politics in Authority*. London: Oxford University Press, pp.13–44.

— 1981. 'Somali Democratic Republic' in B. Szajkowski (ed.) *Marxist Governments: a world survey*. London: Macmillan.

— (ed.) 1983. *Nationalism and Self-determination in the Horn of Africa*. London: Ithaca Press.

— 1986a. *Religion in Context: cults and charisma*. Cambridge: Cambridge University Press.

— (ed.) 1986b. *Blueprint for a Socio-demographic Survey and Re-enumeration of the Refugee Camp Population in the Somali Democratic Republic*. Geneva: UNHCR.

— 1988 [1965]. *A Modern History of Somalia: nation and state in the Horn of Africa*. Boulder: Westview Press.

— 1993a. 'Making History in Somalia: humanitarian intervention in a stateless society', London: London School of Economics: Centre for Global Grievance, Discussion Paper 6.

— 1993b. 'Misunderstanding the Somali crisis', *Anthropology Today*, 9(4): 1–3.

— 1994. *Blood and Bone: the call of kinship in Somali society*. New Jersey: Red Sea Press.

— 1995a. 'Anthropologists for sale?' in A. Ahmed and C. Shore (eds) *The Future of Anthropology: its relevance to the contemporary worlds*. London: Athlone Press, pp. 94–109.

— 1995b. (with J. Mayall) (ed.) *Decentralised Political Structures for Somalia*. London: London School of Economics for the European Union.

— 1998. *Saints and Somalis: Islam in a clan-based society*. London: Haan and Lawrenceville, N. J.: Red Sea Press.

Luling, V. 1971. 'A Southern Somali Sultanate: the Geledi', unpublished PhD thesis, University of London.

Menkhaus, Ken 1995. *Key Decisions in the Somalia Intervention*. Pew Case Studies in International Affairs. Washington, DC: Georgetown University, Institute for the Study of Diplomacy.

Mirreh, A. G. 1978. *Die Sozialökonomischen Verhältnisse der nomadischen Bevölkerung im Norden der Demokratischen Republik Somalia*. Berlin: Akademie Verlag.

Sahnoun, M. 1994. *Somalia: the missed opportunities*. Washington, DC: United States Institute of Peace.

Samatar, A. I. 1989. *The State and Rural Transformation in Northern Somalia, 1884–1986*. Madison: University of Wisconsin Press.

Samatar, S. S. 1982. *Oral Poetry and Somali Nationalism*. Cambridge: Cambridge University Press.

— (ed.) 1992. *In the Shadow of Conquest: Islam in colonial north-east Africa*. New Jersey: Red Sea Press.

Schraeder, Peter J. (compiler; with the assistance of Erick J. Mann) 199 *Djibouti*. World Bibliographical Series, vol. 118. Oxford: Clio Press.

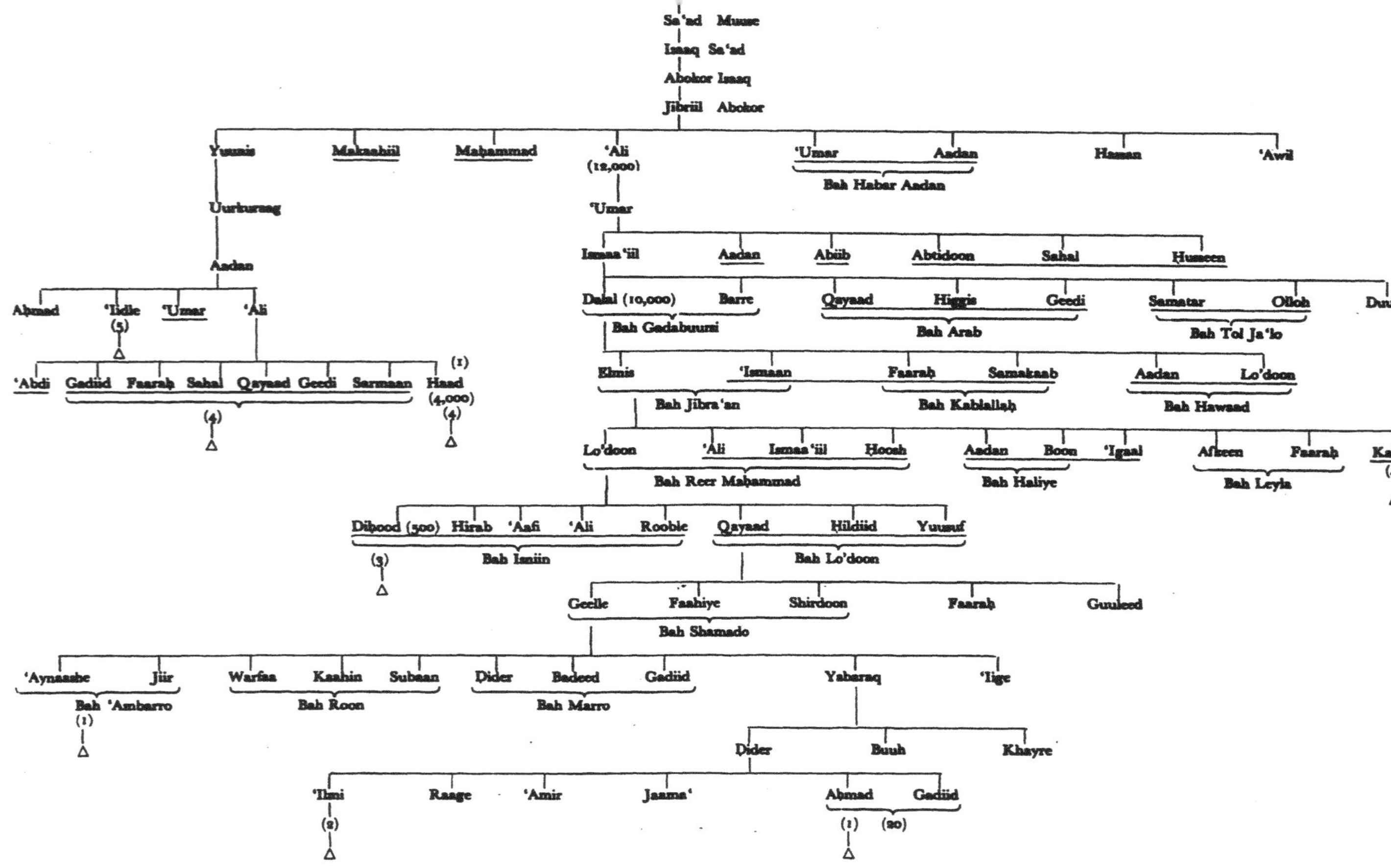

1. The Reer Haad 'Ali comprises two dia-paying groups whose segmentation is shown above (p. 154).
Names underlined denote dia-paying groups, e.g. Kaliil.
Vertical lines ending in a triangle (△) represent the number of generations which a living man counts to a given ancestor.

Genealogy of Dulbahante clan

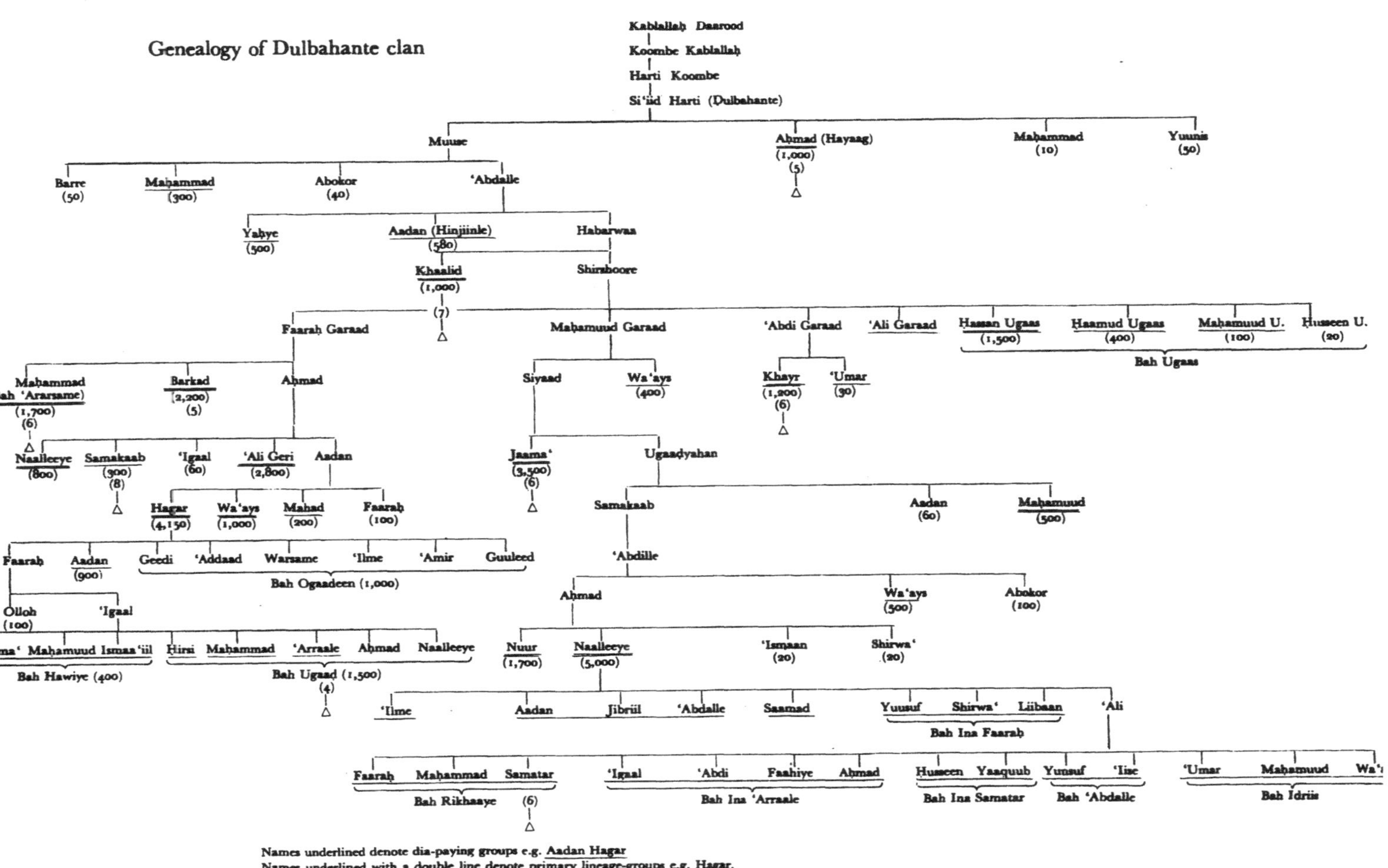

Names underlined denote dia-paying groups e.g. Aadan Hagar
Names underlined with a double line denote primary lineage-groups e.g. Hagar.

www.ingramcontent.com/pod-product-compliance
Ingram Content Group UK Ltd.
Pitfield, Milton Keynes, MK11 3LW, UK
UKHW042314100125
453423UK00001B/11